THE ARCTIC
p 139

GERMANY &
THE ALPINE STATES
pp 76-77

THE LOW
COUNTRIES
pp 68-69

Iceland
p 67

NORTHERN EUROPE
pp 66-67

RUSSIA & KAZAKHSTAN
pp 94-95

EUROPEAN RUSSIA
pp 86-87

THE BRITISH
ISLES
pp 70-71

CENTRAL
EUROPE
pp 80-81

EUROPE
pp 62-89

EASTERN
EUROPE
pp 84-85

ASIA
pp 90-109

FRANCE
pp 72-73

ITALY
pp 78-79

SOUTHEAST
EUROPE
pp 82-83

TURKEY &
THE CAUCASUS
pp 96-97

CENTRAL
ASIA
pp 100-101

EAST
ASIA
pp 104-105

JAPAN &
KOREA
pp 102-103

SPAIN &
PORTUGAL
pp 74-75

Malta
p 88

Cyprus
p 88

THE
MEDITERRANEAN
pp 88-89

Israel
p 99

SOUTHWEST
ASIA
pp 98-99

Ryukyu
Islands
p 105

NORTH AFRICA
pp 122-123

SOUTH
ASIA
pp 106-107

PACIFIC

OCEAN

WEST AFRICA
pp 124-125

EAST
AFRICA
pp 126-127

Andaman
& Nicobar
Islands
p 107

SOUTHEAST
ASIA
pp 108-109

AFRICA
pp 118-129

SOUTHWEST
PACIFIC
pp 136-137

SOUTHERN
AFRICA
pp 128-129

INDIAN

OCEAN

**AUSTRALASIA
& OCEANIA**
pp 130-137

Samoa
p 136

AUSTRALIA
pp 132-133

NEW ZEALAND
pp 134-135

ANTARCTICA
p 138

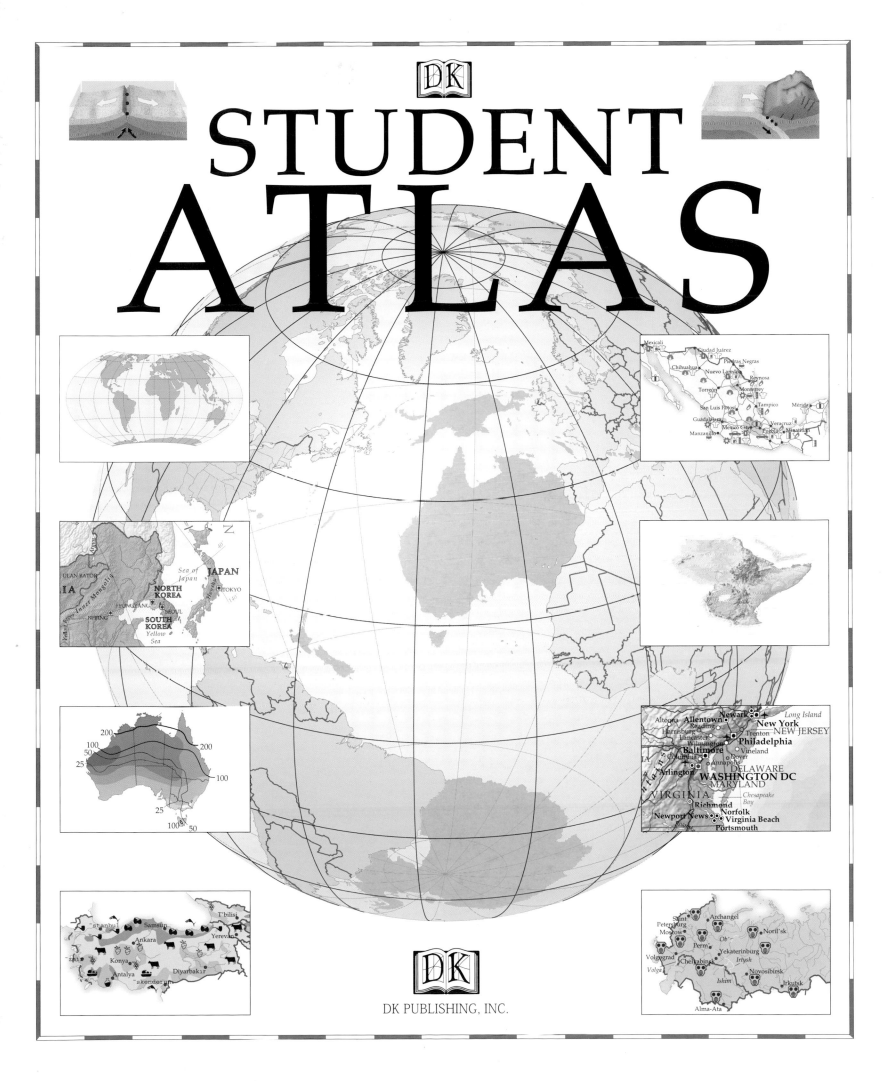

STUDENT ATLAS

DK PUBLISHING, INC.

FAMILY LEARNING

A DORLING KINDERSLEY BOOK

EDUCATIONAL CONSULTANTS
David Lambert, Department of Education, University of London, David R Wright, BA MA

TEACHER REVIEWERS
US: Ramani DeAlwis; UK: Kevin Ball, Pat Barber, Stewart Marson

DORLING KINDERSLEY CARTOGRAPHY

MANAGING EDITOR   MANAGING ART EDITOR
Lisa Thomas   Philip Lord

PROJECT EDITORS   PROJECT DESIGNERS
Debra Clapson, Wim Jenkins, Jill Hamilton (US)   Rhonda Fisher, Karen Gregory

EDITORIAL CONTRIBUTORS   DESIGNERS
Thomas Heath, Kevin McRae, Constance Novis,   Carol Ann Davis, David Douglas Nicola Liddiard
Iris Rossoff (US), Siobhan Ryan

MANAGING CARTOGRAPHER   SENIOR CARTOGRAPHIC EDITOR
David Roberts   Roger Bullen

CARTOGRAPHERS
Pamela Alford, James Anderson, Sarah Baker-Ede, Dale Buckton,
Tony Chambers, Jan Clark, Martin Darlison, Sally Gable, Jeremy Hepworth,
Michael Martin, Simon Mumford, John Plumer, Jane Voss, Peter Winfield

DATABASE MANAGER   DIGITAL MAPS CREATED IN DK CARTOPIA BY
Simon Lewis   Phil Rowles, Rob Stokes

PLACENAMES DATABASE TEAM   EDITORIAL DIRECTION
Natalie Clarkson, Julia Lynch   Andrew Heritage

PICTURE RESEARCH   PRODUCTION
Louise Thomas   David Proffit

First American Edition, 1998
2 4 5 8 10 9 7 5 3 1
Published in the United States by DK Publishing Inc.
95 Madison Avenue, New York, New York, 10016
Visit us on the World Wide Web at http://www.dk.com

Student Atlas.
      p.   cm.
      Summary: Maps, illustrations and text describe various aspects of
   countries of the world including physical features, population,
   standards of living, natural resources, industries, environmental
   issues and climate.
      ISBN 0-7894-2399-5
      1. Children's atlases   [1. Atlases] 1. DK Publishing, Inc.
   G1021 .S78 1998   <G&M>
   912--DC21   97-45730
                          CIP
                          MAPS

Reproduction by Colourscan, Singapore, and The Printed Word, London.
Printed and bound in Great Britain by Butler & Tanner Ltd

ACKNOWLEDGMENTS
The publishers are grateful for permission to reproduce the following photographs:
t=top, b=bottom, a=above, l=left, r=right, c=center

Axiom: J Spaull 74br. **Bridgeman Art Library**: Hereford Cathedral, Trustees of the Hereford Mappa Mundi 8tr.
J Allan Cash: 120cr. **Bruce Coleman Ltd:** C Ott 92cr(below); Dr E Pott 4bc; H Reinhard 19cr; J Murray 130bl; Peter Terry 19crr.
Colourific: Black Star/R Rogers 111br; Frank Herrmann 119bc. **Comstock**: 17tc. **James Davis Travel Photography**: 26cr
(above),27bl, 44tr, 119tr. **Robert Harding Picture Library**: 6tr(below); 21c, 21cr, 22br, 28bl, 30br, 30cr, 31bl, 38tr, 92cr(above);
118bl; A Tovy 120br; Adam Woolfitt 62br; 65br, C Bowman 110tr; Charcrit Boonson 90cr(below); David Lomax 20tr; Franz
Joseph Land 19tr; G Boutin 120cl(below); G Renner 17c, 118cr(above); Gavin Hellier 31tr; Geoff Renner 39cr(above);
H P Merten 23tl; Jane Sweeney 23bl; Louise Murray 93tr; Peter Scholey 91tr; Philip Craven 28cl; Robert Francis 23cr;
Schuster/Keine 62cr(above); Simon Westcott 90br. **Hutchison Library:** A Zvoznikov 19cl; J Nowell 93bl; R Ian Lloyd 10cl.
Image Bank: Carlos Navajas 17bl; M Isy-Schwart 17bc; P Grumann 64cr(below); Steve Proehl 30cr(below); Terje Rakke 17br.
Images Colour Library: 19c, 26br, 62cr(below), 118br. **Impact**: Bruce Stephens 26cr(below); Jeremy Nicholl 121cl(below);
Mark Henley 20bl; Paul O'Driscoll 63cr; Robin Lubbock 118br. **Frank Lane Picture Agency**: D Smith 19bc; W Wisniewsli 17cr.
Magnum: Chris Steele Perking 120tr(below); Ian Berry 64br; Jean Gaumy 65cl. **N.A.S.A**: 9tc. **N.H.P.A**: M Wendler 4cl, 60bl.
Oxford Scientific Films: Konrad Wothe 19tc; L Gould 4tr; Nobert Rosing 28cl. **Panos Pictures**: Alain le Garsheur 93tr;
Alain le Garsmeur 31cl(below); Alberto Arzoz 63tr; Bruce Paton 121bl; Jeremy Hartley 120bl; Maria Luiza M Cavalho
110cl(below); Paul Smith 61cr; Rhodri Jones 111bl; Ron Gilling 119cr; Trygve Bolstad 22bl. **Edward Parker**: 17cr(above).
Pictor International: 4tc, 10bc, 18tr, 20br, 26tr, 26bl, 29bc, 36bc, 38bl, 38br. **Planet Earth Pictures**: J Waters 111bc.
South American Pictures: Robert Francis 92br; Tony Morrison 60cr, 61cl. **Spectrum Colour Library**: 29tr. **Frank Spooner
Pictures**: Gamma/E Baitel 91cl. **Still Pictures**: J Frebet 111cr; R Seitre 90cr(above). **Tony Stone Images:** 17tr, 110cl; A Sacks
28cr; Alan Levenson 92cr; Charles Thatcher 39tr; D Austen 131cr; D Hanson 17cl; Donald Johnson 62bc; Earth Imaging
6tr(above); G Johnson 90bl; H Strand 111tr; Hans Schlapfer 38bc; J Jangoux 19bcr; J Warden 60bc; John Garrett 121br;
L Resnick 121tr; Larry Ulrich 37br; P Chesley 130tr; Paul Chesley 36br; Randy Wells 19br; Robert Frerck 65tr; Tom Walker 36bl;
Tony Craddock 65cr. **Telegraph Colour Library**: 29tr. **Travel Ink**: Colin Marshall 22bc; Ian Booth 27cl. **Trip**: A Kuznetsov 92bc;
H Rogers 90cr; M Barlow 110bl; N Ray 10tr; Robert Belbin 92bl; V Kolpakov 93cr(below); V Sidoropolev 64cr; W Jacobs 130c.
World Pictures: 131tr. **ZEFA Picture Library**: 19bcl, 19cl, 63bc; Bramaz 30bl; Damm 119bc; Heilman 60cr(below); K Siewert
60cl; Kitchen 19bll; Sunak 91cr; Surpress 61tr. **Jacket**: Robert Harding Picture Library: T Gervis front bl; Louise Murray
back tr; G Renner back tl. **Tony Stone Images**: Tony Craddock front bc; Donald Johnson back br.

CONTENTS

LEARNING MAP SKILLS

THE WORLD

THE WORLD ATLAS

NORTH AMERICA

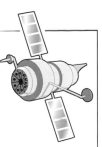

EUROPE

ASIA

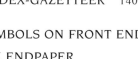

SOUTH AMERICA

AFRICA

AUSTRALASIA & OCEANIA

POLAR REGIONS

KEY TO MAP SYMBOLS ON FRONT ENDPAPER
FLAGS ON BACK ENDPAPER

AMAZING EARTH

Earth is unique among the nine planets that circle the Sun. It is the only one that can support life, because it has enough oxygen in its atmosphere and plentiful water. In fact, seen from space, the Earth looks almost entirely blue. This is because about 70% of its surface is under water, submerged beneath four huge oceans: the Pacific, Atlantic, Indian and Arctic oceans. Land makes up about 30% of the Earth's surface. It is divided into seven landmasses of varying shapes and sizes called continents. These are, from largest to smallest: Asia, Africa, North America, South America, Antarctica, Europe, and Australia.

WATERY WORLD

The Earth's oceans and seas cover more than 142 million sq miles – that is twice the surface of Mars and nine times the surface of the moon.

Beneath the ocean waves lies the biggest and most unexplored landscape on Earth. Here are coral reefs, enormous, open plains, deep canyons, and the longest mountain range on Earth – the Mid-Atlantic Ridge – which stretches almost from pole to pole.

THE SHAPE OF THE EARTH

Photographs taken from space by astronauts in the 1960s, and more recently from orbiting satellites, have proven beyond doubt what humans had worked out long ago – that the Earth is shaped like a ball. But it is not perfectly round. The force of the Earth's rotation makes the world bulge very slightly at the Equator and go a little flat at the North and South Poles. So the Earth is actually a flattened sphere, or a "geoid."

☐ HEIGHTS AND DEPTHS

The Pacific Ocean contains the deepest places on the Earth's surface – the ocean trenches. The very deepest is Challenger Deep in the Mariana Trench which plunges 36,060 ft into the Earth's crust. If Mount Everest, the highest point on land at 29,029 ft, was dropped into the trench, its peak wouldn't even reach the surface of the Pacific.

☐ WATER

Over 97% of the Earth's water is salt water. The total amount of salt in the world's oceans and seas would cover all of Europe to a depth of three miles. Less than 3% of the Earth's water is fresh. Of this, 2.24% is frozen in ice sheets and about 0.6% is stored underground as groundwater. The remainder is in lakes and rivers.

☐ COASTS

The total length of the Earth's coastlines is more than 300,000 miles – that is the equivalent of 12 times around the globe. A high percentage of the world's people live in coastal zones: of the ten most populated cities on Earth, eight are situated on estuaries or the coast.

☐ BIODIVERSITY

Today, almost six hundred million humans, approximately one million animal species, and 355,000 known plant species depend on the air, water, and land of planet Earth.

WET EARTH

Tropical rain forests grow in areas close to the Equator, where it is wet and warm all year round. Although they cover just 7% of the Earth's land, these thick, damp forests form the richest ecosystems on the planet. More plant and animal species are found here than anywhere else on Earth.

DRY EARTH

Deserts are among the most inhospitable places on the planet. Some deserts are scorching hot, others are freezing cold, but they have one thing in common – they are all dry. Very few plant and animal species can survive in these harsh conditions. The world's coldest and driest continent, Antarctica (*left*), is a cold desert.

☐ VANISHING FORESTS

10,000 years ago, thick forests covered about half of the Earth's land surface. Today, 33% of those forests no longer exist, and more than half of what remains has been dramatically altered. During the 20th century, more than 50% of the Earth's rain forests have been felled.

DIFFERENT WORLD VIEWS

Because the Earth is round, we can only see half of it at any one time. This half is called a hemisphere, which means "half a sphere." There are always two hemispheres – the half that you see and the other half that you don't see. Two hemispheres placed together will always make a complete sphere.

NORTH AND SOUTH

Equator 0°

The Equator is an imaginary line drawn around the middle of the Earth, where its circumference is greatest. If we cut along the Equator, the Earth separates into two hemispheres: the Northern and Southern Hemispheres. Most of the Earth's land is the Northern Hemisphere. Europe and North America are the only continents that lie entirely in the northern hemisphere. Australia and Antarctica are the only continents that lie entirely in the southern hemisphere.

The Southern Hemisphere contains three of the Earth's four great oceans: the Pacific, Indian, and Arctic Oceans.

EAST AND WEST

The Earth can also be divided along two other imaginary lines – the Prime Meridian (0°) and 180° – which run opposite each other between the North and South Poles. This creates eastern and western hemispheres. The continents in the eastern hemisphere are traditionally called the Old World, while those in the western hemisphere – the Americas – were named the New World by the Europeans who explored them in the 15th century.

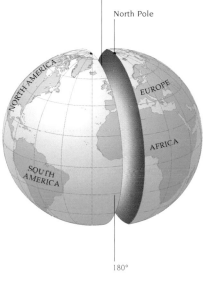

Prime Meridian (0°)

North Pole

180°

PLANET WATER, PLANET LAND

The Earth can also be divided into land and water hemispheres. The land hemisphere shows most of the land on the Earth's surface. The water hemisphere is dominated by the vast Pacific Ocean – from this view, the Earth appears to be almost entirely covered by water.

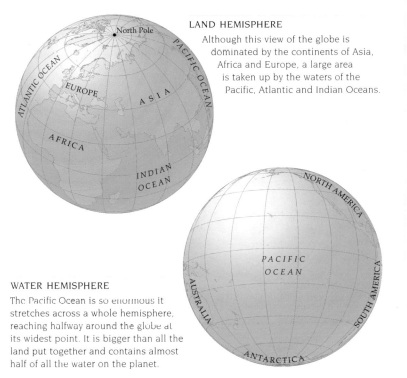

LAND HEMISPHERE

Although this view of the globe is dominated by the continents of Asia, Africa and Europe, a large area is taken up by the waters of the Pacific, Atlantic and Indian Oceans.

WATER HEMISPHERE

The Pacific Ocean is so enormous it stretches across a whole hemisphere, reaching halfway around the globe at its widest point. It is bigger than all the land put together and contains almost half of all the water on the planet.

THE SEASONS

As the Earth orbits the Sun, it is also spinning around an imaginary line called its axis, which joins the North and South Poles. The Earth's axis is not quite at right angles to the Sun, but tilts over at an angle of 23.5°. As a result, each place gradually moves closer to the Sun and then farther away from it again. Summer in the Northern Hemisphere is when the north is closest to the Sun. In winter, the Northern Hemisphere tilts away from the Sun, receiving far less heat and light. In the Southern Hemisphere the seasons are reversed, with summer in December and winter in June.

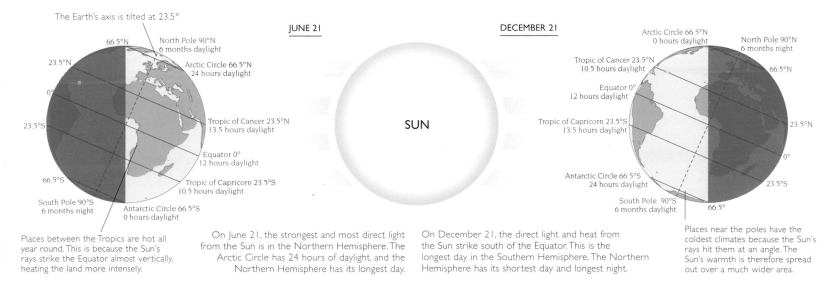

JUNE 21

SUN

DECEMBER 21

The Earth's axis is tilted at 23.5°

North Pole 90°N
6 months daylight

66.5°N

23.5°N

Arctic Circle 66.5°N
24 hours daylight

0°

23.5°S

Tropic of Cancer 23.5°N
13.5 hours daylight

Equator 0°
12 hours daylight

66.5°S

Tropic of Capricorn 23.5°S
10.5 hours daylight

South Pole 90°S
6 months night

Antarctic Circle 66.5°S
0 hours daylight

Arctic Circle 66.5°N
0 hours daylight

North Pole 90°N
6 months night

Tropic of Cancer 23.5°N
10.5 hours daylight

66.5°N

Equator 0°
12 hours daylight

Tropic of Capricorn 23.5°S
13.5 hours daylight

23.5°N

0°

Antarctic Circle 66.5°S
24 hours daylight

South Pole 90°S
6 months daylight

66.5°

23.5°S

Places between the Tropics are hot all year round. This is because the Sun's rays strike the Equator almost vertically, heating the land more intensely.

On June 21, the strongest and most direct light from the Sun is in the Northern Hemisphere. The Arctic Circle has 24 hours of daylight, and the Northern Hemisphere has its longest day.

On December 21, the direct light and heat from the Sun strike south of the Equator. This is the longest day in the Southern Hemisphere. The Northern Hemisphere has its shortest day and longest night.

Places near the poles have the coldest climates because the Sun's rays hit them at an angle. The Sun's warmth is therefore spread out over a much wider area.

MAPPING THE WORLD

The main purpose of a map is to show, or locate, where things are. The only truly accurate map of the whole world is a globe – a round model of the Earth. But a globe is impractical to carry around, so mapmakers (cartographers) produce flat paper maps instead. Changing the globe into a flat map is not simple. Imagine cutting a globe in half and trying to flatten the two hemispheres. They would be stretched in some places, and squashed in others. In fact, it is impossible to make a map of the round Earth on flat paper without some distortion of area, distance, or direction.

MODELS OF THE WORLD

Satellite images can show the whole world as it appears from space. However, this image shows only one half of the world, and is distorted at the edges.

A globe (*right*) is the only way to illustrate the shape of the Earth accurately. A globe also shows the correct positions of the continents and oceans and how large they are in relation to one another.

LATITUDE

We can find out exactly how far north or south, east or west any place is on Earth by drawing two sets of imaginary lines around the world to make a grid. The horizontal lines on the globe below are called lines of latitude. They run from east to west. The most important is the Equator, which is given the value 0°. All other lines of latitude run parallel to the Equator. and are numbered in degrees either north or south of the Equator.

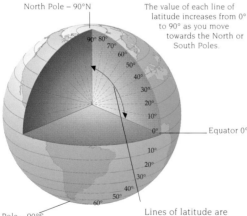

North Pole – 90°N

The value of each line of latitude increases from 0° to 90° as you move towards the North or South Poles.

90° 80°
70°
60°
50°
40°
30°
20°
10°
0° ——— Equator 0°
10°
20°
30°
40°
50°
60°

South Pole – 90°S

Lines of latitude are measured from the center of the Earth. An angle is then measured from here in relation to the Equator.

One degree of latitude is approximately 70 miles.

Lines of latitude divide the world into "slices" of equal thickness on either side of the Equator.

LONGITUDE

The vertical lines on the globe below run from north to south between the poles. They are called lines of longitude. The most important passes through Greenwich, England, and is numbered 0°. It is called the Prime Meridian. All other lines of longitude are numbered in degrees either east or west of the Prime Meridian. The line directly opposite the Prime Meridian is numbered 180°.

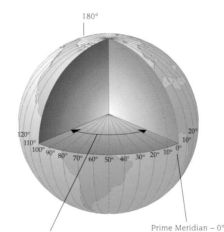

180°

120°
110°
100° 90° 80° 70° 60° 50° 40° 30° 20° 10° 0°
20°
10°

Prime Meridian – 0°

Lines of longitude are also measured from the center of the Earth. This time, the angle is taken in relation to the Prime Meridian.

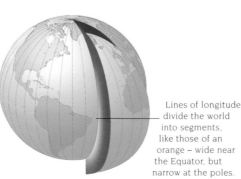

Lines of longitude divide the world into segments, like those of an orange – wide near the Equator, but narrow at the poles.

WHERE ON EARTH?

When lines of latitude and longitude are combined on a globe, or as here, on a flat map, they form a grid. Using this grid, we can locate any place on land, or at sea, by referring to the point where its line of latitude intersects with its line of longitude. Even when a place is not located exactly where the lines cross, you can still find its approximate position.

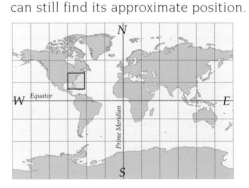

The map above is of the eastern US. It is too small to show all the lines of latitude and longitude, so they are given at intervals of 5°. Miami is located at about 26° north of the Equator and 80° west of the Prime Meridian. We write its location 26°N 80°W.

MAKING A FLAT MAP FROM A GLOBE

Cartographers use a technique called projection to show the Earth's curved surface on a flat map. Many different map projections have been designed. The distortion of one feature – either area, distance, or direction – can be minimized, while other features become more distorted. Cartographers must choose which of these things it is most important to show correctly for each map that they make. Three major families of projections can be used to solve these questions.

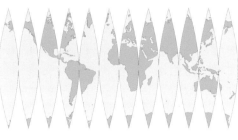

To make a globe, the Earth is divided into segments or "gores'" along lines of longitude.

1 CYLINDRICAL PROJECTIONS

These projections are "cylindrical" because the surface of the globe is transferred onto a surrounding cylinder. This cylinder is then cut from top to bottom and "rolled out" to give a flat map. These maps are very useful for showing the whole world.

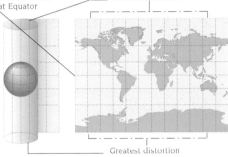

The cylinder touches the globe at the Equator. Here, the scale on the map will be exactly the same as it is on the globe. At the northern and southern edges of the cylinder, which are farthest away from the surface of the globe, the map is most distorted. The Mercator projection (*above*), created in the 16th century, is a good example of a cylindrical projection.

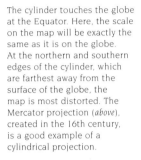

Scale accurate at Equator
Greatest distortion
Greatest distortion

2 AZIMUTHAL PROJECTIONS

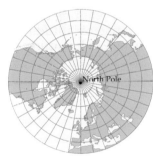

North Pole

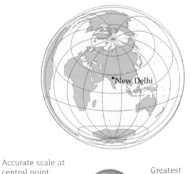

New Delhi

Azimuthal projections put the surface of the globe onto a flat circle. "Azimuthal" means that the direction or "azimuth" of any line coming from the center point of that circle is correct. Azimuthal maps are useful for viewing hemispheres, continents, and the polar regions. Mapping any area larger than a hemisphere gives great distortion at the outer edges of the map.

Accurate scale at central point
Greatest distortion

The circle only touches the globe's surface at one central point. The scale is only accurate at this point and becomes less and less accurate the farther away the circle is from the globe. This kind of projection is good for maps centering on a major city or on one of the poles.

3 CONIC PROJECTIONS

Conic projections are best used for smaller areas of the world, such as country maps. The surface of the globe is projected onto a cone that rests on top of it. After cutting from the point to the bottom of the cone, a flat map in the shape of a fan is left behind.

The conic projection touches the globe's surface at one latitude. This is where the scale of the map will be most accurate. The parts of the cone farthest from the globe will be the most distorted and are usually omitted from the map itself.

Greatest distortion
Most accurate scale

PROJECTIONS USED IN THIS ATLAS

The projections that are appropriate for showing maps at a world, continental, or country scale are quite different. The projections for this atlas have been carefully chosen. They are ones that show areas as familiar shapes that are distorted as little as possible.

1 World Maps

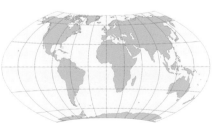

The **Wagner VII** projection is used for our world maps as it shows all the countries at their correct sizes relative to one another.

2 Continents

The **Lambert Azimuthal Equal Area** is used for continental maps. The shape distortion is relatively small and countries retain their correct sizes relative to one another.

3 Countries

The **Lambert Conformal Conic** shows countries with as little distortion as possible. The angles from any point on the map are the same as they would be on the surface of the globe.

HOW MAPS ARE MADE

New technologies have revolutionized mapmaking. Computers and information from satellites have replaced drawing boards and drafting pens, and the process of creating new maps is now far easier. But mapmaking is still a skilled and often time-consuming process. Information about the world must be gathered, sorted, and checked. The cartographer must make decisions about the function of the map and what information to select in order to make it as clear as possible.

THE MAPPA MUNDI

Maps have been made for thousands of years. The 13th-century Mappa Mundi, meaning "known world" shows the Mediterranean Sea and the Don and Nile rivers. Asia is at the top, with Europe on the left, and Africa to the right. The oceans are shown as a ring surrounding the land. The map reflects a number of biblical stories.

HISTORICAL MAP MAKING

For centuries, maps were drawn by hand. Very early maps were no more than a pictorial representation of what the surface of the ground looked like. Where there were hills, pictures were drawn to represent them. Later maps were drawn using information gathered by survey teams. They would carefully mark out and calculate the height of the land, the positions of towns, and other geographical features. As knowledge and techniques improved, maps became more accurate.

This detailed hand-drawn map of the southern coast of Spain was made in about 1750. The mountains are illustrated as small hills and the labels have been hand lettered.

NEW TECHNIQUES

Today, cartographers have access to far more data about the Earth than in the past. Satellites collect and process information about its surface. This is called remote-sensed data. Further information may be drafted in the traditional way. Locations can be verified by GPS (Global Positioning Systems) linked to satellites. Computers are now widely used to combine different kinds of map information. Any computerized map is produced using a GIS (Geographical Information System).

Computers make it easier to change map information and styles quickly. This map of the southern coast of Spain, made in 1997 has been made using digital terrain modeling (see below) and traditional cartography.

MODERN MAPMAKING

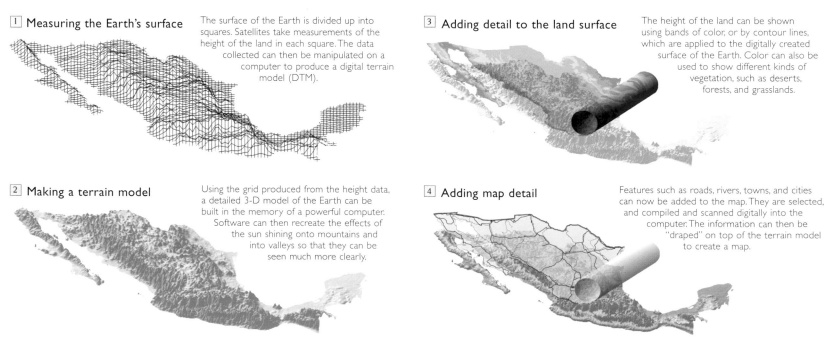

1 Measuring the Earth's surface

The surface of the Earth is divided up into squares. Satellites take measurements of the height of the land in each square. The data collected can then be manipulated on a computer to produce a digital terrain model (DTM).

3 Adding detail to the land surface

The height of the land can be shown using bands of color, or by contour lines, which are applied to the digitally created surface of the Earth. Color can also be used to show different kinds of vegetation, such as deserts, forests, and grasslands.

2 Making a terrain model

Using the grid produced from the height data, a detailed 3-D model of the Earth can be built in the memory of a powerful computer. Software can then recreate the effects of the sun shining onto mountains and into valleys so that they can be seen much more clearly.

4 Adding map detail

Features such as roads, rivers, towns, and cities can now be added to the map. They are selected, and compiled and scanned digitally into the computer. The information can then be "draped" on top of the terrain model to create a map.

SHOWING INFORMATION ON A MAP

A map is a selective diagram of a place. It is the cartographer's job to decide what kind of information to show on a map. They can choose to highlight certain kinds of features – such as roads, rivers, and land height. They can also show other features such as sea depth, place names, and borders that would be impossible to see either on the ground or from a photograph. The information that can be shown on a map is influenced by a number of factors, most notably by its scale.

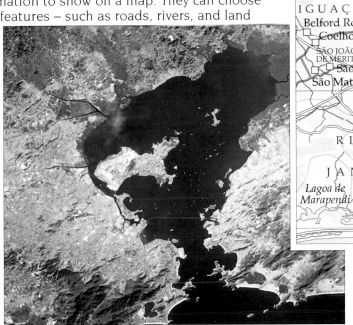

This is a satellite photograph of the harbor area of Rio de Janeiro in Brazil. Although you can see the bay and where most of the housing is, it is impossible to see roads or get any sense of the position of places relative to one another.

This is a map of the same area as you can see in the photograph. Much of the detail has been greatly simplified. Towns are named and marked; contours indicate the height of the land; and roads, railroads and borders between districts have been added.

SCALE

To make a map of an area it needs to be greatly reduced in size. This is known as drawing to scale. The scale of the map shows us by how much the area has been reduced. The smaller the scale, the greater the area of land that can be shown on the map. There will be far less detail and the map will not be as accurate. The maps below show the different kinds of information that can be shown on maps of varying scales.

WAYS TO SHOW SCALE

When using a map to work out what areas or distances are in reality, we need to refer to the scale of that particular map. Map scales can be shown in several ways.

1 **Representative fraction**
One unit on the map would be equal to 1,000,0000 units on the ground.

1:1,000,000

2 **Linear scale**
The line is marked off in units which represent the real distances of the map, given in both miles and kilometers.

SCALE BAR

0 km   10   20

0 miles   10   20

3 **Statement of scale**
It means that 1 inch on the map represents 1 mile on the ground.

1 inch represents 1 mile

LONDON 1:21,000,000

This small-scale map shows the position of London in relation to Europe. Very little detail can be seen at this scale – only the names of countries and the largest towns.

LONDON 1:5,500,000

At a scale of 1 to 5,500,000 you can see the major road network in the southeast of the UK. Many towns are named and you can see the difference in size and status.

LONDON 1:900,000

This map is at a much larger scale. You can see the major roads that lead out from London and the names of many suburbs, places of interest, and airports.

LONDON 1:12,500

This is a street map of central London. The streets are named, as are places of interest, train and subway stations. The scale is large enough to show plenty of detail.

READING MAPS

Maps use a unique visual language to convey a great deal of detailed information in a relatively simple form. Different features are marked out using special symbols and styles of print. These symbols are explained in the key to the map and you should always read a map alongside its key or legend. This page explains how to look for different features on the map and how to unravel the different layers of information that you can find on it.

PHYSICAL FEATURES

All the regional and country maps in this atlas are based on a model of the Earth's surface. The computer-generated relief gives an accurate picture of the surface of the land. Colors are used to show the relative heights of the land; green is for low-lying land, and yellows, browns, and grays are for higher land. Water features like streams, rivers, and lakes are also shown.

1 WATER FEATURES

On this map extract, the blue lines show a number of rivers, including the Salween and the Irrawaddy. The Irrawaddy forms a huge delta, splitting into many streams as it reaches the sea.

2 RELIEF

These mountains are in the north of Southeast Asia. The underlying relief on the map and the colored bands help you to see the height of the land.

HUMAN FEATURES

Maps also reveal a great deal about the human geography of an area. In addition to showing the location of towns and roads, different symbols can tell you more about the size of towns and the importance of a road. Borders between countries or regions can only be seen on a map.

3 BORDERS

Borders on the map are marked by a thick purple line. The boundary between Laos and Vietnam is in sparsely populated mountainous terrain, with the border generally running along a mountain range.

KEY TO MAP SYMBOLS

BOUNDARIES

————	Full international border
- - - -	Disputed border

COMMUNICATION FEATURES

————	Major road
————	Minor road
————	Railroad
✈	International airport

DRAINAGE FEATURES

————	Major river
————	Minor river
◯	Lake
▢	Wetland

LANDSCAPE FEATURES

△	Mountain

POPULATED PLACES

◦	Less than 50,000
○	50,000–100,000
◉	100,000–500,000
▣	Greater than 500,000
●	Capital city

NAMES

MYANMAR	Country
PARACEL ISLANDS (disputed by China, Taiwan, & Vietnam)	Dependent territory
JAKARTA	Capital city
Sarawak	Cultural region
Chin Hills	Landscape feature
Puncak Jaya 16,535ft	Mountain/pass
Red River	River/lake
Java Sea	Sea feature

LAND HEIGHT / SEA DEPTH

LAND HEIGHT	SEA DEPTH
Above 13,120ft	0–820ft
6,560–13,120ft	820–1,640ft
3,280–6,560ft	1,640–3,280ft
1,640–3,280ft	3280–6,560ft
820–1,640ft	6,560–9,840ft
330–820ft	9,840–13,120ft
0–330ft	Below 13,120ft

CITIES AND TOWNS

▣	Over 500,000 people
◉	100,000–500,000
○	50,000–100,000
◦	Less than 50,000

4 SETTLEMENTS

The symbol for a settlement can tell you its position, population, and political status. Most towns are shown by a circle or a square. These represent the size of their population. Where the dot for a town is colored red, this shows that it is a capital city such as Kuala Lumpur in Malaysia.

FINDING PLACES

Alphanumeric grid references

All the maps in this book are indexed using their alphanumeric grid reference – for example, G4. To find a place you must first look up its page number and then its grid reference. Read the letters and numbers off the bottom and side of the grid. Using rulers held at right angles to one another you will find the point where the lines meet. The place will be located within this square.

Latitude and longitude references

The lines of latitude and longitude are known as graticules. They are shown on the map as thin blue lines with the value of their latitude or longitude given as a blue number at the edge of the map.

5 ROADS AND RAILROADS

a The major road and railroad links between Hue and Nha Trang hug the Vietnamese coast. A string of coastal towns is often connected by road and rail in this manner.

Chiang Mai, in northern b Thailand, is linked to the capital Bangkok to the south by railroad and road. At Chiang Mai, the mountains are too high for the railroad to continue, and only roads go north into Myanmar.

USING THE ATLAS

This Atlas has been designed to develop map-reading skills and to introduce readers to a wide range of different maps. It also provides a wealth of detailed geographic information about the world today. The Atlas is divided into four sections: **Learning Map Skills**; **The World About Us**, covering global geographic patterns; the **World Atlas**, dealing with the world's regions and an **Index-Gazetteer**.

LEARNING MAP SKILLS

Maps show the Earth – which is three-dimensional – in just two dimensions. This section shows how maps are made; how different kinds of information are shown on maps; how to choose what to put on a map and the best way to show it. It also explains how to read the maps in this Atlas.

THE WORLD ABOUT US

These pages contain a series of world maps that show important themes, such as physical features, climate, life zones, population, and the world economy, on a global scale. They give a worldwide picture of concepts that are explored in more detail later in the book.

Text introduces themes and concepts in each spread.

Introduction to projections: different projections and how they work.

Choosing the best projections: the map projections used in this book.

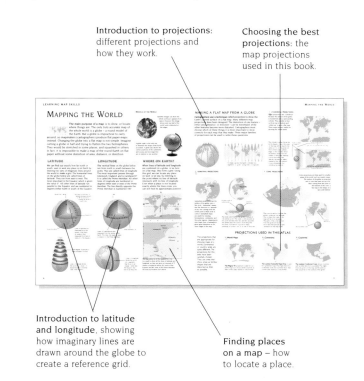

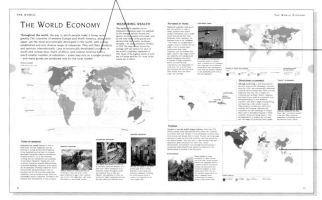

Photographs illustrate examples of places or topics shown on the main map.

World maps show geographic patterns on a global scale.

Introduction to latitude and longitude, showing how imaginary lines are drawn around the globe to create a reference grid.

Finding places on a map – how to locate a place.

CONTINENTAL MAPS

A cross section through the continent shows the relative height of certain features.

A detailed physical map of the continent shows major natural geographic features, including mountains, lakes and rivers.

Photographs and locator maps illustrate the main geographic regions and show you where they are.

The political map of the continent shows country boundaries and country names.

The industry map shows the main industrial towns and cities and the main industries in each continent. It also shows the wealth of each country, relative to the rest of the world.

CONTINENTAL GEOGRAPHY PAGES

Humans have colonized and changed all the continents except Antarctica. These pages show the factors which have affected this process: climate, the availability of resources such as coal, oil and minerals, and varying patterns of land use. Mineral resources are directly linked to many industries, and most agriculture is governed both by the quality of the land and the climate.

The climate map shows the main types of climate across the continent and where the hottest and coldest, wettest and driest places are.

CONTINENTAL PAGES

These pages show the physical shape of each continent and the impact that humans have made on the natural landscape – building towns and roads and creating borders between countries. They show where natural features such as mountain ranges and rivers have created physical boundaries, and where humans have created their own political boundaries between states.

The mineral resources map shows where the most important reserves of minerals, including coal and precious metals, are found.

The land use map shows different types of land and the main kinds of farming that take place in each area.

REGIONAL MAPS

The main part of the Atlas contains detailed maps of countries and regions. Each of these is accompanied by a series of small thematic maps, models, and charts, which give information about the climate, where people live, how they use the land, the different kinds of industry, and important environmental issues.

TERRAIN MODEL

A computer-generated landscape model shows what the land really looks like. There are no roads or towns to mask the physical geography of the country or region. Mountain ranges, plains, and river basins can be easily seen.

COLORED THUMB TAGS

Each section has its own color code.

Learning Map Skills

The World About Us

Europe

Asia

North America

South America

Africa

Australasia and Oceania

Antarctica and the Arctic

CLIMATE MAPS

These maps show the temperature and rainfall patterns in January and July. Colored bands indicate temperatures: blue for low temperatures, orange for high ones. Rainfall is represented by black lines with a number giving the average amount of rain. These are called isohyets.

Isohyets show the rainfall patterns in inches per year. The areas between the lines are either over or under the figures shown on the ishohyets.

JANUARY

Here the rainfall is between 2 and 4 inches per year.

The hottest areas are colored orange.

JULY

LOCATOR GLOBE

This shows the location of the country or region both within its continent and in relation to the rest of the world.

EUROPE

MAP GRID

Each main map has a grid. Using the grid will help you to find a place on the map. Grid references are expressed as letters (running from left to right across the frame), and numbers (running from the top to the bottom of the frame), for example, A 4, G 6. Everything on the map is referenced in the **Index-Gazetteer** at the back of the book.

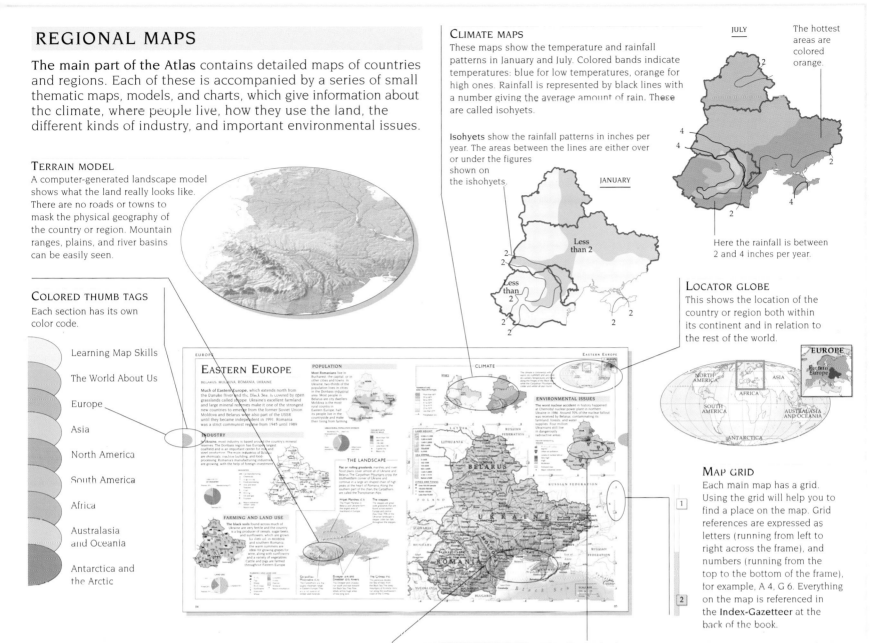

REGIONAL MAPS

The main map on each regional page shows the main topographical features of the area: the height of the land, the major roads, the rivers, and lakes. It also shows the main cities and towns in the region – represented by different symbols.

LAND HEIGHT

6,560–13,120ft
3,280–6,560ft
1,640–3,280ft
820–1,640ft
330–820ft
0–330ft

SEA DEPTH

0–160ft
160–330ft
330–820ft
820–1,640ft
1,640–3,280ft
3,280–6,560ft

CITIES AND TOWNS
◉ Over 500,000 people
● 100,000–500,000
○ 50,000–100,000
○ Less than 50,000

Railroad

Longitude line

Latitude line   Road

Minor town

Major city

River

Mountains

Compass rose used to indicate the orientation of each regional map.

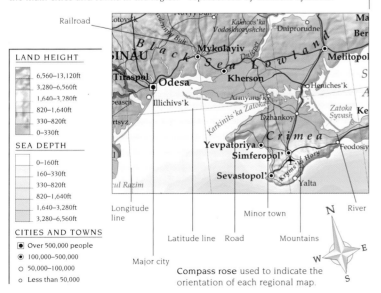

THEMATIC MAPS

These small maps show various aspects of the geography of the country or region. The environment maps cover topics such as the effects of pollution. Industry, land use, and population maps locate the major industries, types of agriculture, and the distribution of population.

Diagrams are used to show the geographic information on the map statistically..

Bucharest 2.5%   Kiev 3.2%
Dnipropetrovs'k 1.3%

Rural population 36%

Other towns and cities 57%

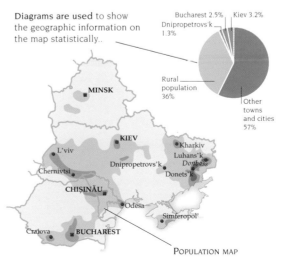

POPULATION MAP

INDUSTRY MAP

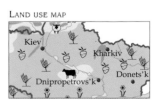

LAND USE MAP

Kiev   Kharkiv

Dnipropetrovs'k   Donets'k

ENVIRONMENT MAP

THE PHYSICAL WORLD

This map shows the main physical features of the world: the mountain ranges, the great rivers and lakes, deserts, grassland plains, seas, and oceans. No human settlements are named on this map – only the physical or landscape features.

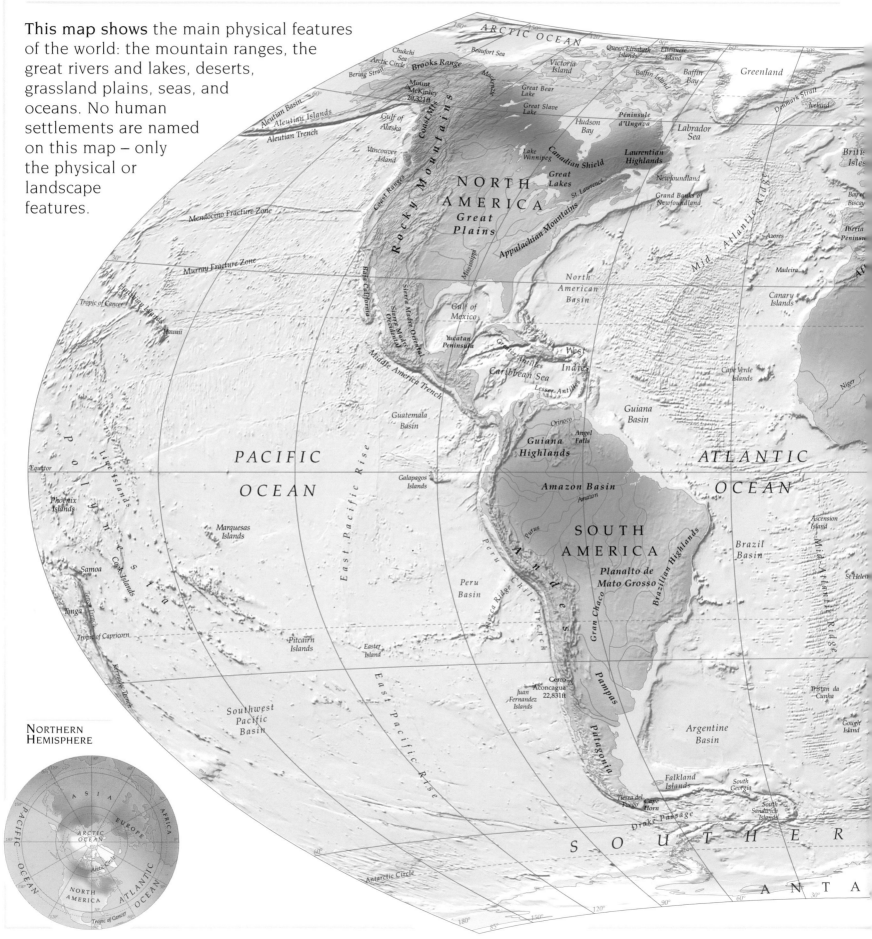

ARCTIC OCEAN

Chukchi Sea
Arctic Circle
Brooks Range
Bering Strait
Mount McKinley 20,321ft
Aleutian Basin
Aleutian Islands
Aleutian Trench
Gulf of Alaska
Vancouver Island
Coast Ranges

Beaufort Sea
Mackenzie
Victoria Island
Great Bear Lake
Great Slave Lake
Hudson Bay
Lake Winnipeg
Canadian Shield
Great Lakes
St. Lawrence

Queen Elizabeth Islands
Ellesmere Island
Baffin Island
Baffin Bay
Péninsule d'Ungava
Laurentian Highlands
Newfoundland
Grand Banks of Newfoundland
Labrador Sea

Greenland
Denmark Strait
Iceland
British Isles
Bay of Biscay

NORTH AMERICA
Great Plains

Mendocino Fracture Zone
Murray Fracture Zone
Tropic of Cancer
Hawaiian Islands
Hawaii

Rocky Mountains
Sierra Nevada
Sierra Madre Oriental
Sierra Madre Occidental
Baja California
Appalachian Mountains
Mississippi
Gulf of Mexico
Yucatan Peninsula

North American Basin
Mid - Atlantic Ridge
Azores
Madeira
Canary Islands
Iberia Peninsula
Niger

Middle America Trench
Guatemala Basin
Greater Antilles
West Indies
Caribbean Sea
Lesser Antilles
Orinoco
Angel Falls
Guiana Highlands
Guiana Basin
Cape Verde Islands

PACIFIC OCEAN

Equator
Galapagos Islands
Amazon Basin
Amazon

ATLANTIC OCEAN

Phoenix Islands
Line Islands
Marquesas Islands
East Pacific Rise

Purus
SOUTH AMERICA
Planalto de Mato Grosso
Brazilian Highlands
Brazil Basin

Ascension Island

Samoa
Cook Islands
Tonga
Tonga Trench
Kermadec Trench

Peru Basin
Peru-Chile Trench
Nazca Ridge
Andes
Gran Chaco

St Helena
Mid-Atlantic Ridge

Tropic of Capricorn
Pitcairn Islands
Easter Island
Peru-Chile Trench

Pampas
Patagonia
Argentine Basin

Tristan da Cunha
Gough Island

Southwest Pacific Basin
East Pacific Rise

Cerro Aconcagua 22,831ft
Juan Fernandez Islands

Falkland Islands
South Georgia
South Sandwich Islands

Tierra del Fuego
Cape Horn
Drake Passage
SOUTHERN

ANTA

ASIA
EUROPE
AFRICA
PACIFIC OCEAN
ARCTIC OCEAN
Arctic Circle
ATLANTIC OCEAN
NORTH AMERICA
Tropic of Cancer

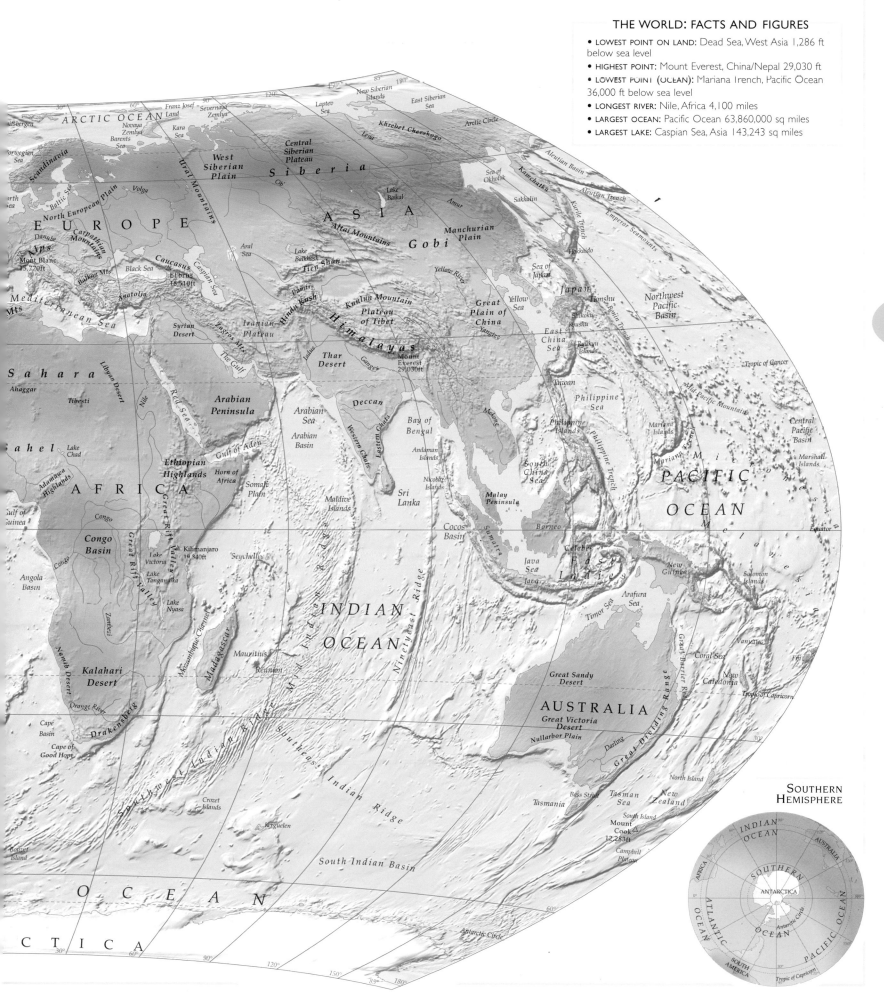

THE WORLD: FACTS AND FIGURES

- **LOWEST POINT ON LAND**: Dead Sea, West Asia 1,286 ft below sea level
- **HIGHEST POINT**: Mount Everest, China/Nepal 29,030 ft
- **LOWEST POINT (OCEAN)**: Mariana Trench, Pacific Ocean 36,000 ft below sea level
- **LONGEST RIVER**: Nile, Africa 4,100 miles
- **LARGEST OCEAN**: Pacific Ocean 63,860,000 sq miles
- **LARGEST LAKE**: Caspian Sea, Asia 143,243 sq miles

ARCTIC OCEAN
Svalbard
Franz Josef Land
Novaya Zemlya
Severnaya Zemlya
New Siberian Islands
East Siberian Sea
Laptev Sea
Kara Sea
Barents Sea
Arctic Circle
Khrebet Cherskogo
Norwegian Sea
Scandinavia
North European Plain
Baltic Sea
Ural Mountains
West Siberian Plain
Central Siberian Plateau
Siberia
Lena
Ob
Amur
Sea of Okhotsk
Kamchatka
Aleutian Basin
Kuril Trench
Aleutian Trench
Emperor Seamounts
EUROPE
Danube
Volga
Carpathian Mountains
Alps
Mont Blanc 15,770ft
Balkan Mts
Black Sea
Caucasus
El'brus 18,510ft
Caspian Sea
Aral Sea
Lake Balkhash
Tien Shan
Altai Mountains
ASIA
Gobi
Manchurian Plain
Lake Baikal
Sakhalin
Hokkaido
Northwest Pacific Basin
Mediterranean Sea
Anatolia
Mts
Sahara
Ahaggar
Tibesti
Libyan Desert
Syrian Desert
Zagros Mts
Iranian Plateau
The Gulf
Pamirs
Hindu Kush
Kunlun Mountain
Plateau of Tibet
Himalayas
Indus
Thar Desert
Ganges
Mount Everest 29,030ft
Great Plain of China
Yangtze
Yellow River
Yellow Sea
East China Sea
Japan
Honshu
Shikoku
Kyushu
Ryukyu Islands
Sea of Japan
Taiwan
Tropic of Cancer
Mid Pacific Mountains
Bonin Trench
Sahel
Lake Chad
Adamawa Highlands
Nile
Red Sea
Arabian Peninsula
Gulf of Aden
Ethiopian Highlands
Horn of Africa
Somali Plain
AFRICA
Arabian Sea
Arabian Basin
Deccan
Western Ghats
Eastern Ghats
Bay of Bengal
Maldive Islands
Andaman Islands
Sri Lanka
Nicobar Islands
Malay Peninsula
South China Sea
Mekong
Philippine Islands
Philippine Sea
Mariana Islands
Mariana Trench
Central Pacific Basin
Marshall Islands
PACIFIC OCEAN
Micronesia
Melanesia
Gulf of Guinea
Congo
Congo Basin
Congo
Great Rift Valley
Lake Victoria
Kilimanjaro 19,340ft
Lake Tanganyika
Lake Nyasa
Seychelles
Cocos Basin
Borneo
Celebes
East Indies
Java Sea
Java
Sumatra
New Guinea
Solomon Islands
Angola Basin
Zambezi
Madagascar
Mozambique Channel
Mauritius
Réunion
Mid Indian Ridge
Ninetyeast Ridge
INDIAN OCEAN
Arafura Sea
Timor Sea
Vanuatu
Coral Sea
Great Barrier Reef
New Caledonia
Fiji
Kalahari Desert
Namib Desert
Orange River
Drakensberg
Cape Basin
Cape of Good Hope
Southwest Indian Ridge
Southeast Indian Ridge
Crozet Islands
Kerguelen
Great Sandy Desert
Great Victoria Desert
AUSTRALIA
Nullarbor Plain
Darling
Great Dividing Range
Tropic of Capricorn
Bouvet Island
South Indian Basin
Tasmania
Bass Strait
Tasman Sea
North Island
New Zealand
South Island
Mount Cook 12,283ft
Campbell Plateau
OCEAN
ANTARCTICA
Antarctic Circle

SOUTHERN HEMISPHERE

INDIAN OCEAN
AUSTRALIA
AFRICA
SOUTHERN OCEAN
ANTARCTICA
ATLANTIC OCEAN
PACIFIC OCEAN
SOUTH AMERICA
Antarctic Circle
Tropic of Capricorn

THE EARTH'S STRUCTURE

The shape and position of the Earth's oceans and continents make a familiar pattern. This is just the latest in a series of forms that the Earth has taken in the hundreds of millions of years since its creation. Massive forces inside the Earth cause the continents and oceans to move apart and together again, forming larger landmasses and then breaking them apart – a process known as plate tectonics. The movement is very slow – but over millions of years, the changes can be enormous.

DYNAMIC EARTH

The heart of the Earth is a solid core of iron surrounded by several layers of very hot – sometimes liquid – rock. The crust is relatively thin and is made up of a series of "plates" that fit closely together. Movement of the molten rock deep within the mantle of the Earth causes the plates to move, creating changes in the surface features of the Earth.

THE EARTH'S PLATES

Continental plate

Oceanic plate

Plate boundary or margin

Continental and oceanic plates are tectonic plates – made from crustal rock on which continents or oceans float

INSIDE THE EARTH

Rocky crust

Inner core – made of iron

Outer core – liquid iron and nickel

Mantle – made from solid and molten rock

TECTONIC PLATES, VOLCANOES AND EARTHQUAKES

▲ Volcanic zone

Earthquake zone on land

⇨ Direction of plate movement

ᴠᴠᴠᴠᴠ Rift valley

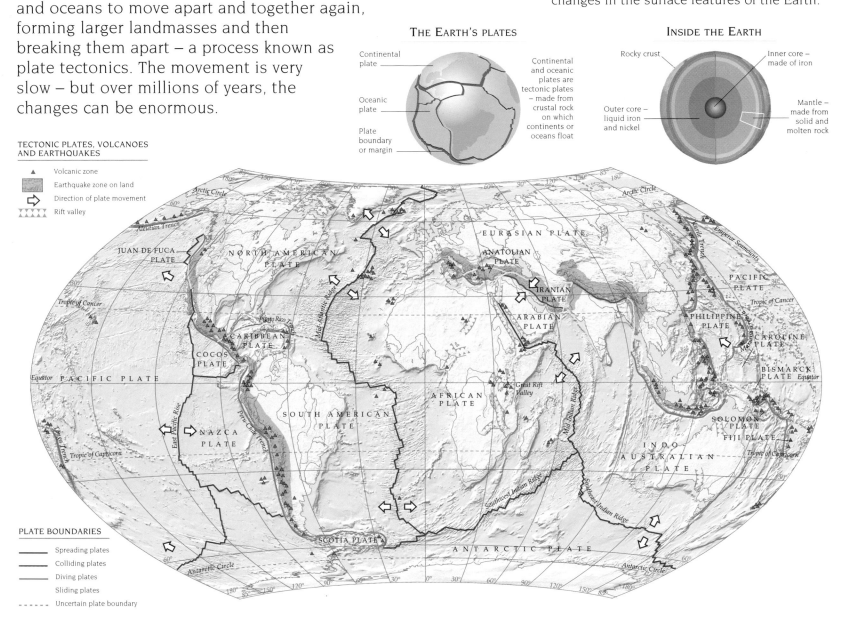

PLATE BOUNDARIES

—— Spreading plates

—— Colliding plates

—— Diving plates

—— Sliding plates

- - - - Uncertain plate boundary

PLATE BOUNDARIES

The point where two plates meet is known as a plate boundary. As the Earth's plates move together or apart or slide alongside one another, the great forces that result cause great changes in the landscape. Mountains can be created, earthquakes occur, and there may be frequent volcanic eruptions.

SPREADING PLATES

Earthquake zone

Ocean floor

Magma pushed upward

Solid mantle

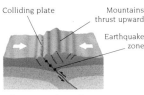

As plates move apart, magma rises through the outer mantle. When it cools, it forms new crust. The Mid-Atlantic Ridge is caused by spreading plates.

COLLIDING PLATES

Colliding plate

Mountains thrust upward

Earthquake zone

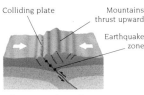

When two plates bearing landmasses collide with one another, the land is crumpled upward into high mountain peaks such as the Alps and the Himalayas.

DIVING PLATES

Earthquake zone

Mountains

Ocean plate

Continental plate

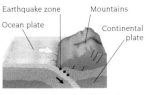

When an ocean-bearing plate collides with a continental plate it is forced downward under the other plate and into the mantle. Volcanoes occur along these boundaries.

SLIDING PLATES

Earthquake zone

Fault line

Plate

Plate

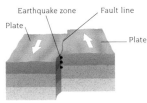

As two plates slide past each other, great friction is set up along the fault line that lies between them. This can lead to powerful earthquakes.

SHAPING THE LANDSCAPE

The Earth's surface is made from solid rock or water. The land is constantly reshaped by external forces. Water flowing as rivers or in the oceans erodes and deposits material to create valleys and lakes and to shape coastlines. When water is built up and compressed into solid sheets of ice, it can erode more deeply, creating deeper, wider valleys. Wind also has a powerful effect: stripping away vegetation and transporting rock particles vast distances.

RIVERS

Most rivers have their sources in mountain areas. They flow fast through the mountains, eroding deep V-shaped valleys. As they reach flatter areas they begin to meander in great loops, both eroding and then depositing rock particles as they slow down.

GLACIERS

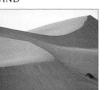

In cold areas, close to the poles or on mountaintops, snow is built up into rivers of ice called glaciers. They move slowly, eroding deep U-shaped valleys. When the glacier melts, ridges of eroded rock called moraines are left at the sides and end of the glacier.

SEA ACTION

The oceans change the landscape in two major ways. They batter cliffs, causing rock to break away and the land to retreat, and they carry eroded material along the coast, to make beaches and sandbars.

WIND

Wind can erode and break down rock into smaller boulders and stones and eventually into sand. Desert sand dunes are shaped by the force of the wind and vary from ripples to hills 650 ft high.

LANDSLIDES

Heavy rain can loosen soil and rock beneath the surface of slopes. As this moves, the top layers slip, forming heaps of rubble at the base of the slope.

THE WORLD'S OCEANS

Just over two-thirds of the Earth's surface is covered by water and more than 98% of this water is contained in the oceans. Movements within the Earth shape the ocean floor in the same way they do the land surface, creating mountain ranges, trenches, and plateaus, and changing the shape and size of the oceans. The difference between an ocean and a sea is simply its size; oceans are much bigger.

POLAR OCEANS

The Southern and Arctic Oceans contain large icebergs that have broken away from the ice shelf.

INDIAN OCEAN

The Indian Ocean covers about 20% of the world's surface. Ocean swells, starting deep in the Southern Ocean, often cause flooding in Sri Lanka and the Maldives.

PACIFIC OCEAN

The Pacific is the largest and deepest ocean in the world. It contains an arc of volcanic islands, including Japan, Indonesia, and New Guinea, known as the "Ring of Fire."

ATLANTIC OCEAN

The Atlantic Ocean was formed about 180 million years ago. The land that now forms Europe and Africa pulled apart from the Americas to create an ocean 1,900 miles wide.

CLIMATE AND LIFE ZONES

This map shows the different climates found around the world. Climates are particular combinations of temperature and humidity. Climates are affected by latitude, the height of the land, winds, and ocean currents. Climates can change, but not overnight. Weather is local and consists of short-term events such as thunderstorms, hurricanes, and blizzards.

Hurricanes are violent cyclonic windstorms, driven by heat energy gathered from tropical seas. The Caribbean islands and the east coast of the US are particularly prone to hurricanes.

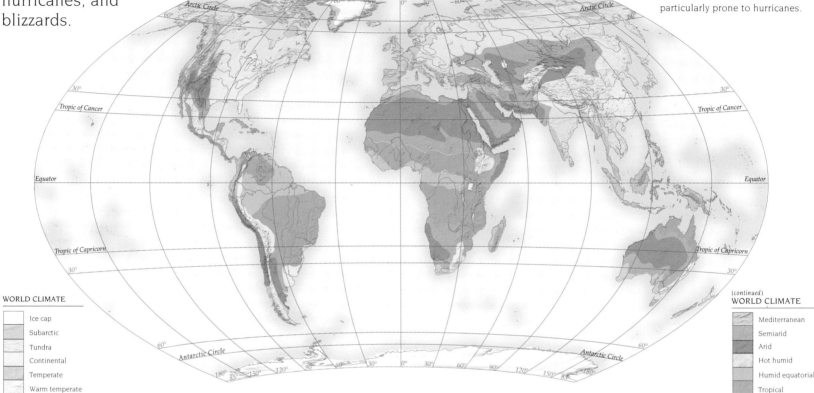

WORLD CLIMATE

- Ice cap
- Subarctic
- Tundra
- Continental
- Temperate
- Warm temperate

(continued) WORLD CLIMATE

- Mediterranean
- Semiarid
- Arid
- Hot humid
- Humid equatorial
- Tropical

WINDS

All over the Earth there are a series of large-scale wind patterns called prevailing winds that have a direct effect on weather and climate. The direction of the wind depends on global air pressure. Winds travel from areas of high pressure to areas of low pressure. The westerlies, polar easterlies, and northeast and southeast trade winds are all prevailing winds. The Equator is known for its light winds – referred to as the Doldrums. Changes in the direction of the prevailing winds can have a serious impact on the weather all over the planet.

WINDS

- Cool wind
- Warm wind

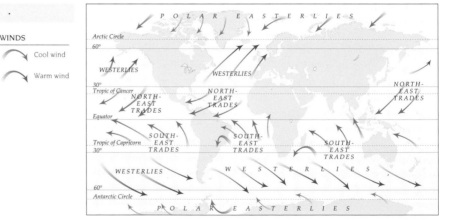

OCEAN CURRENTS

Ocean currents help distribute heat around the Earth and have a great influence on climate. Convection currents circulate massive amounts of warm and cold water around the oceans. Warm water is moved away from the tropics to higher latitudes and cold water is moved toward the tropics.

OCEAN CURRENTS AND SURFACE TEMPERATURES

- Cold currents
- Warm currents
- El Niño

- 68 – 86°F
- 50 – 68°F
- 32 – 50°F
- Seawater 28° – 32°F
- Sea ice (average) below 28°F

LIFE ZONES

The map below shows the Earth divided into different biomes – also called biogeographical regions. The combination of climate, the type of landscape, and the plants and animals that live there are used to classify a region. Similar biomes are found in very different places around the world.

POLAR REGIONS

The North and South Poles are permanently covered by ice. Only a few plants and animals can live here.

TUNDRA

Tundra is flat, cold, and dry, with few trees. Plants such as mosses and lichens grow close to the ground.

DESERTS
Very little rain falls in desert areas, whether they are hot deserts such as the Sahara or cold deserts like the Gobi.

CONIFEROUS FORESTS
Tall coniferous trees such as pine and spruce, with spines or needles instead of leaves, grow in the far north of Scandinavia, Canada, and the Russian Federation.

BROADLEAF FORESTS
Broadleaf or deciduous forests once covered temperate regions over most of the Northern Hemisphere. They contain trees of many varieties – all of which shed their leaves every year.

TEMPERATE RAIN FORESTS
Evergreen, broadleaved trees need a warmer, wetter climate than deciduous trees. They are known as temperate rain forests.

MEDITERRANEAN
Close to the shores of the Mediterranean Sea, the vegetation consists mainly of herbs, shrubs, and drought-resistant trees.

BIOME TYPES

- Mountains
- Polar regions
- Tundra
- Tropical rain forests
- Dry woodlands
- Savanna
- Temperate grasslands

(continued)
BIOME TYPES

- Mediterranean
- Coniferous forests
- Temperate rain forests
- Broadleaf forests
- Cold deserts
- Hot deserts
- Wetlands

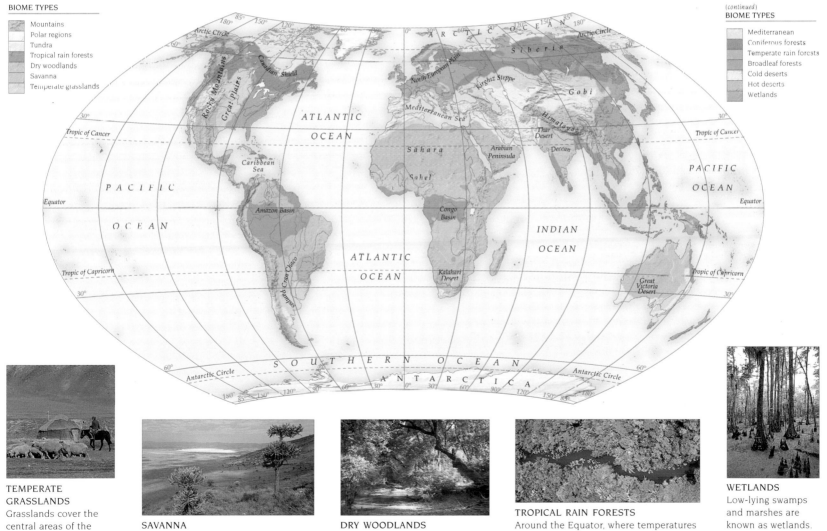

TEMPERATE GRASSLANDS
Grasslands cover the central areas of the continents. They are known in the middle latitudes as prairies, steppe, and pampas.

SAVANNA
The savanna consists of woodland interspersed with grassland. These regions lie between the tropical rain forest and hot desert regions.

DRY WOODLANDS
Dry woodlands are found at the edge of grasslands. They contain small trees and shrubs adapted to dry conditions.

TROPICAL RAIN FORESTS
Around the Equator, where temperatures are high and there is plenty of rain, tropical rain forests flourish. Trees grow continuously and are tall with huge, broad leaves.

WETLANDS
Low-lying swamps and marshes are known as wetlands. They are often home to a rich variety of animal, plant, and bird species.

WORLD POPULATION

Favelas – or shanty towns – have grown up many South American cities because of overcrowding.

There are now nearly six billion people on Earth. The population has increased to more than three times that of 1900. Before that date, the number of people increased slowly because people were born and died at similar rates. With improved living conditions, better medical care, and more efficient food production, more people survived to adulthood, and the population began to grow much faster. If growth continues at the present rate, the world's population is likely to reach 8.5 billion by the year 2020.

POPULATION STRUCTURES

Measuring the numbers of old and young people gives the age structure of a country or continent. If there are large numbers of young people and a high birthrate, the population is said to be youthful – as is the case in many African, Asian, and South American countries. If the birthrate is low but many people survive into old age, the population distribution is said to be aging – this is true of much of Europe, Japan, Canada, and the US. Extreme events like wars can distort the population, leading to a loss of population in certain age groups.

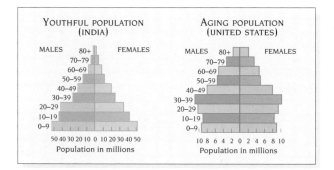

YOUTHFUL POPULATION (INDIA)	AGING POPULATION (UNITED STATES)
MALES 80+ FEMALES	MALES 80+ FEMALES
70–79	70–79
60–69	60–69
50–59	50–59
40–49	40–49
30–39	30–39
20–29	20–29
10–19	10–19
0–9	0–9
50 40 30 20 10 0 10 20 30 40 50	10 8 6 4 2 0 2 4 6 8 10
Population in millions	Population in millions

POPULATION DENSITY

The main map (*center*) and the map below both show population density – the number of people who live in a given area. The map below shows the average population density per country. You can see that European countries and parts of Asia are very densely populated. The large map shows where people actually live. While the average population density in Brazil and Egypt is quite low, the coasts of Brazil and the areas close to the Nile River in Egypt are very densely populated.

DENSE POPULATION

Huge crowds near the Haora Bridge in Calcutta, India – one of the world's most densely populated cities.

POPULATION DENSITY

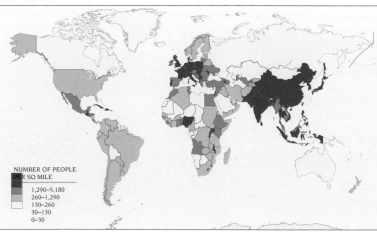

NUMBER OF PEOPLE
PER SQ MILE

- 1,290–5,180
- 260–1,290
- 130–260
- 30–130
- 0–30

SPARSE POPULATION

The cold north of Canada has one of the lowest population densities in the world. Some people live in extreme isolation, separated from others by lakes and forests.

85° 180° 150° 120° 90° 60° 30°
Arctic Circle
60°
30°
Tropic of Cancer
Equator
Tropic of Capricorn
30°
60°
Antarctic Circle
180° 85° 150° 120° 90° 60° 30°

URBAN GROWTH

The 20th century has seen a huge increase in the number of people living in urban areas. This has led to more large cities and the development of some "super cities" such as Mexico City and Tokyo, each with more than 20 million people. In 1900, only about 10% of the population lived in cities. Now it is closer to 50% and soon the figure may be nearer two in three people. Some continents are far more "urbanized" than others: in South America nearly 80% of people live in cities, whereas in Africa the figure is only about 30%.

LEVELS OF URBANIZATION

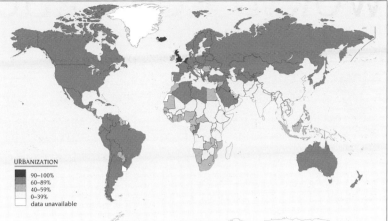

URBANIZATION
- 90–100%
- 60–89%
- 40–59%
- 0–39%
- data unavailable

POPULATION GROWTH

The rate of population growth varies dramatically between the continents. Europe has a large population but it is increasing slowly. Africa is still sparsely populated, but in some countries such as Kenya, the population is growing very rapidly, increasing pressure on the land. China and India have the world's largest populations. Both countries now have laws designed to curb the birthrate.

CONTROLLING GROWTH

In 1980, fewer than 25% of women in less-developed countries used birth control. Education programs and more widely available contraceptives are thought to have doubled this figure. But many families still have no access to contraception.

AN AGING POPULATION

In some countries, a low birthrate and an increasingly long-lived elderly population have greatly increased the ratio of old people to younger people, putting a strain on health and social services. For example, in Japan, most people can now expect to live to at least 80 years of age.

POPULATION DENSITY
(People per sq mile)
- Below 3
- 3–13
- 13–29
- 30–51
- 52–130
- 131–260
- 261–520
- Above 520

BIRTHRATE

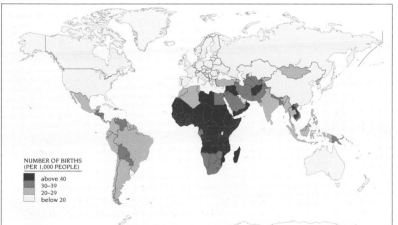

NUMBER OF BIRTHS (PER 1,000 PEOPLE)
- above 40
- 30–39
- 20–29
- below 20

LIFE EXPECTANCY

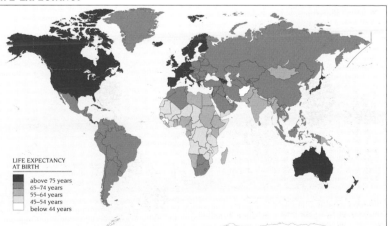

LIFE EXPECTANCY AT BIRTH
- above 75 years
- 65–74 years
- 55–64 years
- 45–54 years
- below 44 years

THE WORLD ECONOMY

Throughout the world, the way in which people make a living varies greatly. The countries of western Europe and North America, along with Japan, are the most economically developed in the world, with a long-established and very diverse range of industries. They sell their products and services internationally. Less economically developed countries in south and central Asia, much of Africa, and Central America have a much smaller number of industries – some may rely on a single product – and many goods are produced only for the local market.

MEASURING WEALTH

The wealth of a country can be measured in several ways: for example, by the average annual income per person; by the volume of its trade; and by the total value of the goods and services that the country produces annually – its Gross Domestic Product or GDP. The map below shows the average GDP per person for each of the world's countries, expressed in $US. Most of the highest levels of GDP are in Europe and the US; most of the lowest are in Africa.

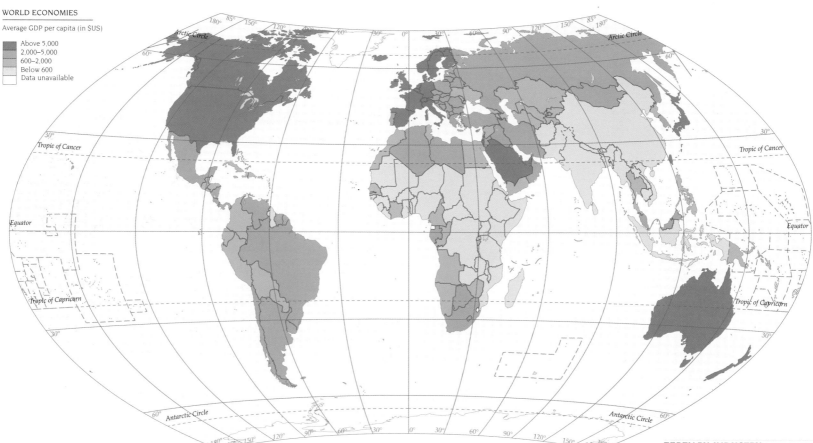

WORLD ECONOMIES

Average GDP per capita (in $US)

- Above 5,000
- 2,000–5,000
- 600–2,000
- Below 600
- Data unavailable

TYPES OF INDUSTRY

Industries are usually defined in one of three ways. Primary industries such as farming or mining involve the production of raw materials such as food or minerals. Secondary industries make or manufacture finished products out of raw materials: clothing and car manufacture are examples of secondary industries. People who work in tertiary industries provide different kinds of services. Banking, insurance, and tourism are all examples of tertiary industries. Some economically advanced nations such as Germany and the US now have quaternary industries, such as biotechnology which are knowledge-creation industries, devoted to the research and development of new products.

PRIMARY INDUSTRY

Tobacco leaves are picked and laid out for drying in Cuba, one of the world's great producers of cigars. Many countries rely on one or two high-value "cash crops" like tobacco to earn foreign currency.

SECONDARY INDUSTRY

This skilled Thai weaver is producing an intricately patterned silk fabric on a hand loom. Fabric manufacture is an important industry throughout South and Southeast Asia. In India and Pakistan, vast quantities of cotton are produced in highly mechanized factories, but many fabrics are still hand woven.

TERTIARY INDUSTRY

The City of London is one of the world's great finance centers. Branches of many banks and insurance companies, including the world-famous Lloyds of London, are clustered into the City's "square mile."

PATTERNS OF TRADE

Almost all countries trade goods with one another in order to obtain products they cannot produce themselves, and to make money from goods they have produced. Some countries – for example those in the Caribbean – rely mainly on a single export, usually a food or mineral, and can suffer a loss of income when world prices drop. Other countries, such as Germany and Japan, export a vast range of both raw materials and manufactured goods throughout the world. A number of huge companies, known as multinational corporations, are responsible for more than 70% of world trade, with divisions all over the world. They include firms like Exxon, Coca Cola, and IBM

CONTAINER SHIPS

Many products are transported around the world on container ships. Containers are of a standard size so that they can be efficiently transported to their destinations. Some ships are specially designed to carry perishable goods such as fruit and vegetables.

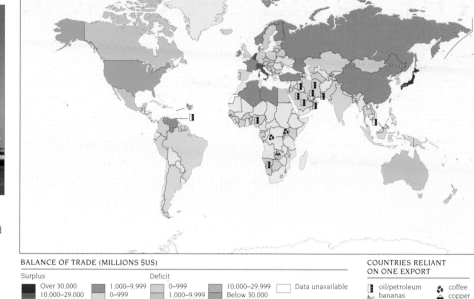

BALANCE OF TRADE (MILLIONS $US)

Surplus			Deficit		
Over 30,000	1,000–9,999	0–999	10,000–29,999	Data unavailable	
10,000–29,000	0–999	1,000–9,999	Below 30,000		

COUNTRIES RELIANT ON ONE EXPORT

- oil/petroleum
- coffee
- bananas
- copper

MEXICO
BRAZIL
SOUTH KOREA
TAIWAN
PHILIPPINES
MALAYSIA
SINGAPORE
INDONESIA

DEVELOPING ECONOMIES

Although world trade is still dominated by the more economically developed countries, since the 1970s, less economically developed countries have increased their share of world trade from less than 10% to nearly 20%. Countries such as Brazil, Mexico, Malaysia, and South Korea, aided by investment from their governments or from wealthier countries, were able to begin manufacturing and exporting a wide variety of goods. These products include cars, electronics, clothing, and footwear. Multinational companies can take advantage of cheaper labor costs to manufacture goods in these countries. Moves are being made to limit the exploitation of workers who are paid very low wages for producing luxury goods.

ASIAN "TIGER" ECONOMIES

The economies of Malaysia, Taiwan, and South Korea boomed in the late 1980s, attracting investment for buildings such as the Petronas Towers (*above*).

TOURISM

Tourism is now the world's largest industry. More than 500 million people travel both abroad and in their own countries as tourists each year. People in more developed countries have more money and leisure time to travel. Tourism can bring large amounts of cash into the local economy, but local people do not always benefit. They may have to take low-paid jobs and experience great intrusions into their lives. Tourist development and pollution may damage the environment – sometimes destroying the very attractions that led to the development of tourism in the first place.

ECOTOURISM

These tourists are being introduced to a giant tortoise, one of the many unique animals found in the Galapagos Islands. A number of places with special animals and ecosystems have introduced programs to teach visitors about them. This not only educates people about the need to safeguard these environments, but brings in money to help protect them.

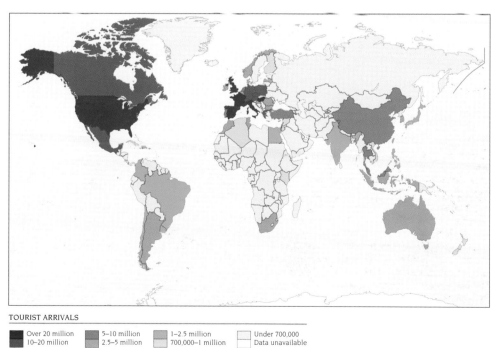

TOURIST ARRIVALS

Over 20 million	5–10 million	1–2.5 million	Under 700,000
10–20 million	2.5–5 million	700,000–1 million	Data unavailable

BORDERS AND BOUNDARIES

There are more countries in the world today than ever before – over 190 – whereas in 1950, there were only 82. Since then, many former European colonies and Soviet states have become independent. The establishment of borders for each of these countries has often been the subject of disagreement.

Military borders
At the end of wars, new borders are often drawn up between the countries – frequently along cease-fire lines. They may remain there for many years. At the end of the Korean War in 1953, North and South Korea were divided close to the 38° line of latitude. This border has remained heavily fortified.

The longest border
The border between the US and Canada is the longest continuous border in the world. It cuts through the center of the Great Lakes. West of the Great Lakes, the border runs along the 49° line of latitude.

Enclaves
If part of a country's territory has become separated from the rest of the country, and is surrounded by foreign territory, it is called an enclave. Kaliningrad is part of the Russian Federation, but is cut off from it by Lithuania and Belarus.

River borders
Over one-sixth of the world's national borders are formed by rivers. Long stretches of the Danube River form natural borders in southeastern Europe.

Mountain borders
Mountain ranges such as the Pyrenees, Alps, and Himalayas form natural borders between many countries. In the Andes, border disputes between Chile and Argentina centered on finding the highest point in the mountain range that divided them.

Straight line borders
The borders of many countries in Africa and other former colonial territories are straight lines. This was the simplest solution for colonial administrators, who often knew little of the country's geography or population.

Lake boundaries
Countries that lie next to lakes usually place their borders in the middle of the lake. Complicated agreements between colonial powers led to the awkward division of Lake Nyasa in Africa.

Territorial disputes
There are still many disputed territories and borders. One of the most serious territorial disputes is between India and Pakistan, over Jammu and Kashmir, which has led to three wars since 1947.

THE ATLAS
OF THE
WORLD

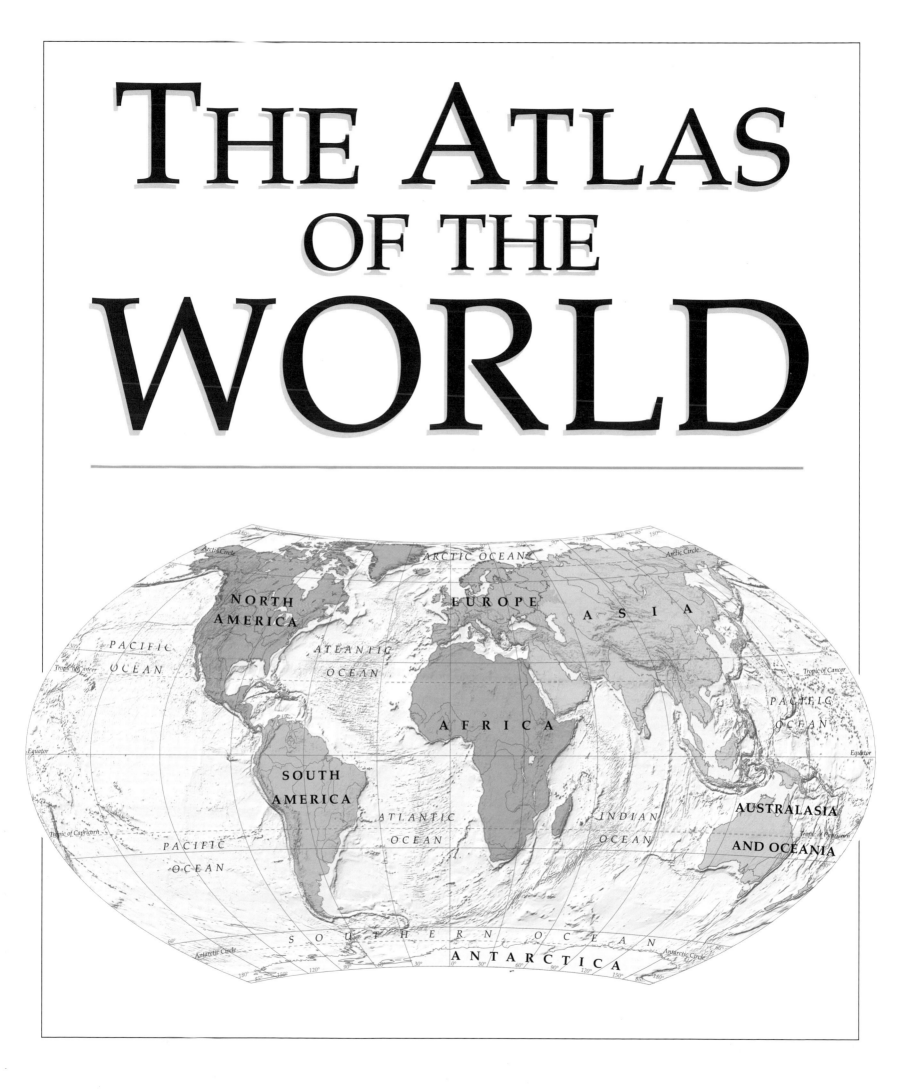

THE NATIONS OF THE WORLD

The world is divided into 192 independent countries and about 60 overseas territories or dependencies. The largest country is the Russian Federation covering 6,592,000 sq miles; the smallest is Vatican City in Rome, with an area of 0.17 sq miles.

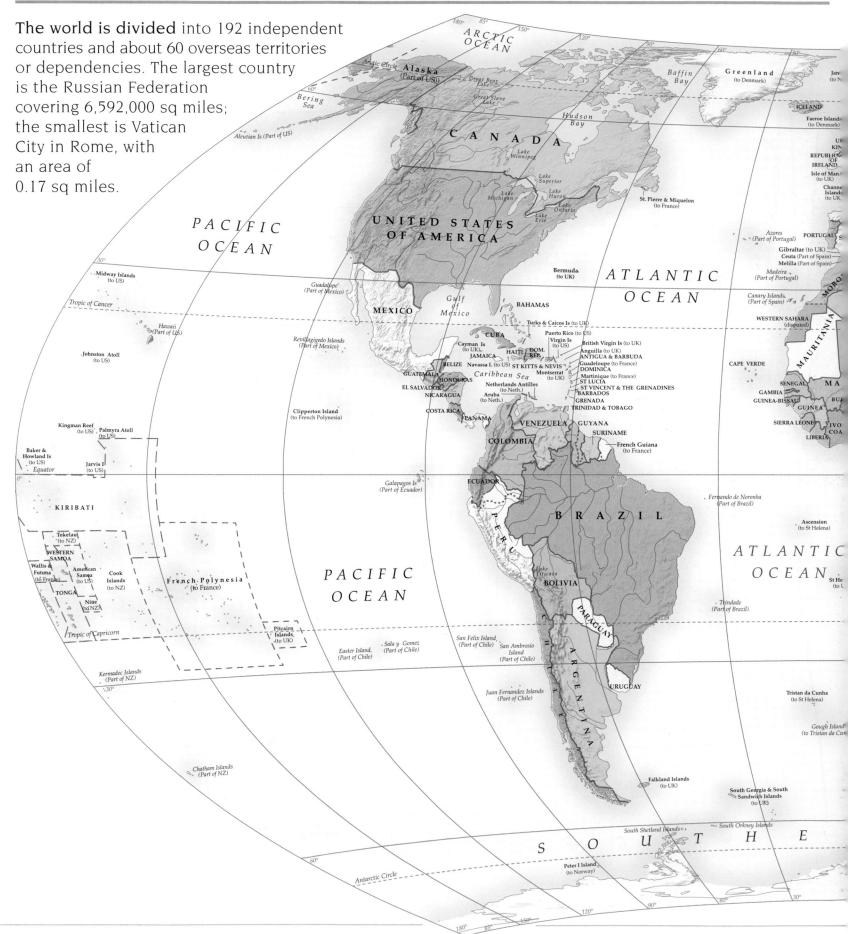

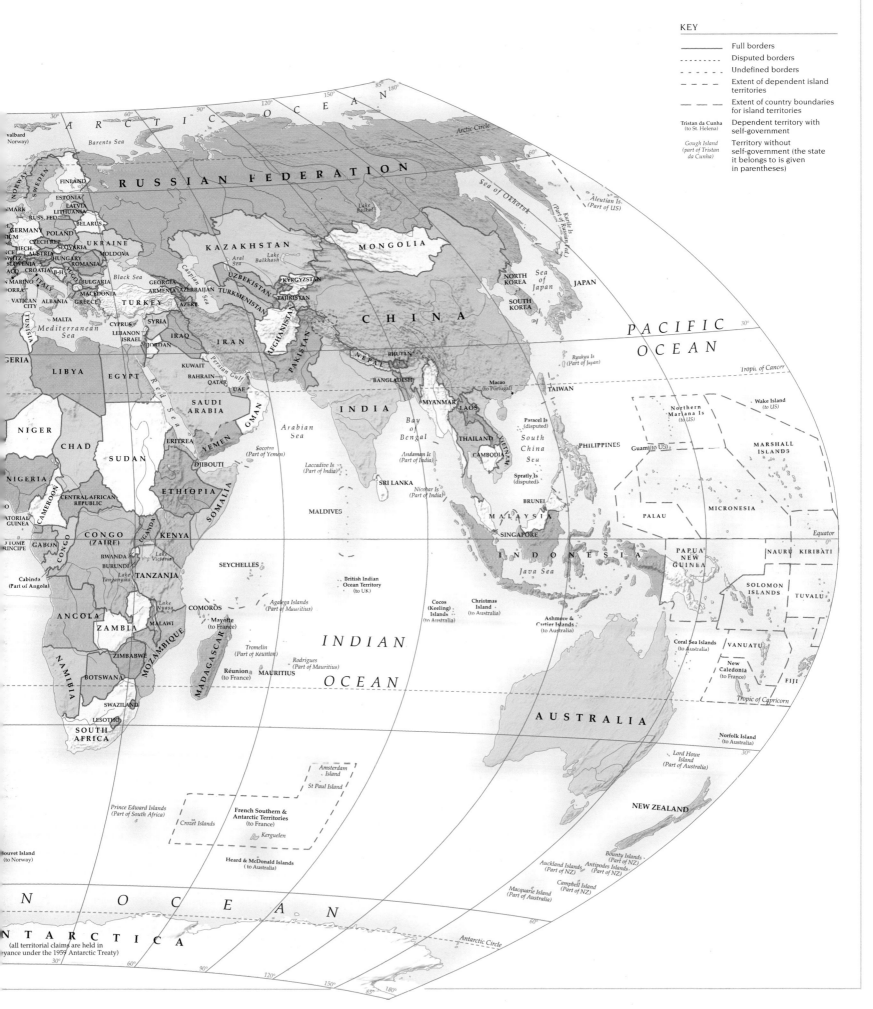

Full borders

Disputed borders

Undefined borders

Extent of dependent island territories

Extent of country boundaries for island territories

Tristan da Cunha (to St. Helena) Dependent territory with self-government

Gough Island (part of Tristan da Cunha) Territory without self-government (the state it belongs to is given in parentheses)

A R C T I C   O C E A N

Svalbard (Norway)

Barents Sea

Arctic Circle

NORWAY

SWEDEN

FINLAND

ESTONIA

LATVIA

LITHUANIA

DENMARK

RUSS. FED.

BELARUS

GERMANY

POLAND

NETHERLANDS

CZECH REP.

SLOVAKIA

UKRAINE

SWITZ. AUSTRIA

SLOVENIA

HUNGARY

MOLDOVA

CROATIA

ROMANIA

B-H

SAN MARINO

ITALY

BULGARIA

ANDORRA

MACEDONIA

VATICAN CITY

ALBANIA GREECE

MALTA

TUNISIA

Mediterranean Sea

CYPRUS

LEBANON

ISRAEL

SYRIA

JORDAN

RUSSIAN   FEDERATION

Sea of Okhotsk

Lake Baikal

Aleutian Is. (Part of US)

Kurile Is (Part of Russian Fed.)

KAZAKHSTAN

Aral Sea

Lake Balkhash

MONGOLIA

Black Sea

GEORGIA

ARMENIA AZERBAIJAN

UZBEKISTAN

KYRGYZSTAN

Caspian Sea

TURKMENISTAN

TAJIKISTAN

AZERB.

TURKEY

NORTH KOREA

Sea of Japan

JAPAN

SOUTH KOREA

CHINA

IRAQ

IRAN

AFGHANISTAN

PACIFIC OCEAN

ALGERIA

LIBYA

EGYPT

KUWAIT

BAHRAIN

QATAR

Red Sea

Persian Gulf

PAKISTAN

UAE

NEPAL

BHUTAN

BANGLADESH

Ryukyu Is (Part of Japan)

Tropic of Cancer

Macao (to Portugal)

TAIWAN

SAUDI ARABIA

OMAN

Arabian Sea

INDIA

MYANMAR

LAOS

Bay of Bengal

Paracel Is (disputed)

Northern Mariana Is (to US)

Wake Island (to US)

NIGER

CHAD

SUDAN

ERITREA

YEMEN

DJIBOUTI

Socotra (Part of Yemen)

THAILAND

VIETNAM

CAMBODIA

South China Sea

PHILIPPINES

Guam (to US)

MARSHALL ISLANDS

Andaman Is (Part of India)

Laccadive Is (Part of India)

Spratly Is (disputed)

NIGERIA

ETHIOPIA

SOMALIA

SRI LANKA

Nicobar Is (Part of India)

MALDIVES

BRUNEI

PALAU

MICRONESIA

CENTRAL AFRICAN REPUBLIC

EQUATORIAL GUINEA

CAMEROON

UGANDA

KENYA

MALAYSIA

SINGAPORE

Equator

SAO TOME & PRINCIPE

GABON

CONGO

CONGO (ZAIRE)

RWANDA

BURUNDI

Lake Victoria

Lake Tanganyika

TANZANIA

SEYCHELLES

British Indian Ocean Territory (to UK)

I N D O N E S I A

Java Sea

PAPUA NEW GUINEA

NAURU KIRIBATI

Cabinda (Part of Angola)

Agalega Islands (Part of Mauritius)

Cocos (Keeling) Islands (to Australia)

Christmas Island (to Australia)

Ashmore & Cartier Islands (to Australia)

SOLOMON ISLANDS

TUVALU

ANGOLA

ZAMBIA

MALAWI

Lake Nyasa

COMOROS

Mayotte (to France)

Coral Sea Islands (to Australia)

VANUATU

ZIMBABWE

MOZAMBIQUE

MADAGASCAR

Tromelin (Part of Réunion)

Rodrigues (Part of Mauritius)

I N D I A N   O C E A N

New Caledonia (to France)

FIJI

NAMIBIA

BOTSWANA

Réunion (to France)

MAURITIUS

A U S T R A L I A

Tropic of Capricorn

SWAZILAND

LESOTHO

SOUTH AFRICA

Norfolk Island (to Australia)

Amsterdam Island

St Paul Island

Lord Howe Island (Part of Australia)

Prince Edward Islands (Part of South Africa)

Crozet Islands

French Southern & Antarctic Territories (to France)

Kerguelen

NEW ZEALAND

Bouvet Island (to Norway)

Heard & McDonald Islands (to Australia)

Bounty Islands (Part of NZ)

Auckland Islands (Part of NZ)

Antipodes Islands (Part of NZ)

Macquarie Island (Part of Australia)

Campbell Island (Part of NZ)

N   O C E A N

A N T A R C T I C A

(all territorial claims are held in abeyance under the 1959 Antarctic Treaty)

Antarctic Circle

CONTINENTAL NORTH AMERICA

North America is the world's third largest continent, stretching from icy Greenland to the tropical Caribbean. The first people came from Asia more than 20,000 years ago. Their descendants spread across the continent, ate fish, meat, and wild and cultivated plants, and developed a wide variety of cultures and languages. About 500 years ago, immigrants from Europe, Africa, and Asia began to arrive in North America, bringing their own languages and cultures to the "New World."

4,600 miles

3,540 miles

CROSS SECTION THROUGH NORTH AMERICA

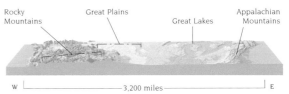

Rocky Mountains | Great Plains | Great Lakes | Appalachian Mountains

W — 3,200 miles — E

The land rises from the Pacific Ocean to the Rocky Mountains. Farther east, the continent flattens into the Great Plains and the freshwater Great Lakes – gouged out by glaciers at the end of the last Ice Age. The Appalachian Mountains are older than the Rockies, and are very worn down.

PHYSICAL NORTH AMERICA

The high peaks of the Rocky Mountains of Canada and the US tower above the lower mountains of the western coasts. These ranges stretch from the icy north of Alaska, south to Mexico and Central America. The heart of the continent is flatter, and much of it is drained by the mighty Mississippi-Missouri river system.

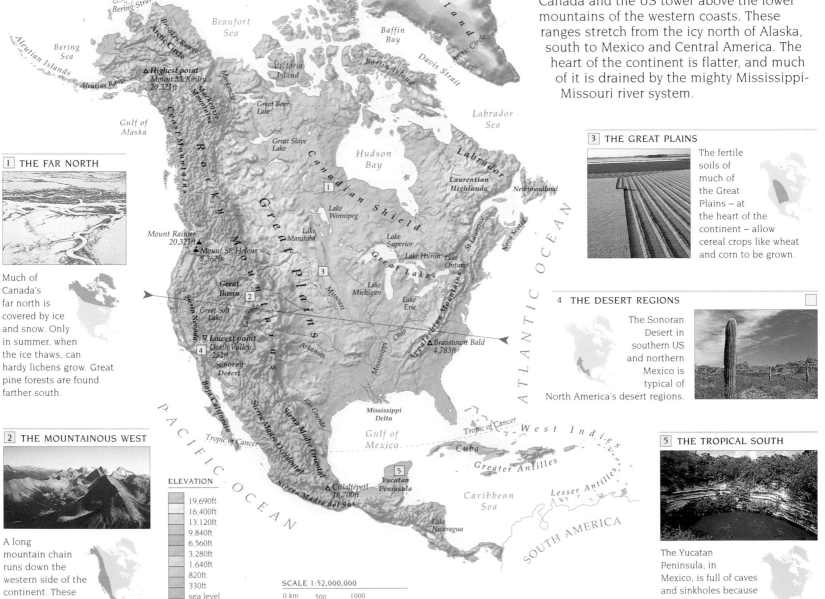

ARCTIC OCEAN

ASIA

Bering Strait

Brooks Range
Arctic Circle

Beaufort Sea

Greenland

Baffin Bay

Arctic Circle

Davis Strait

Aleutian Islands

Bering Sea

Aleutian Range

△ Highest point
Mount McKinley
20,321ft

Mackenzie Mountains

Victoria Island

Baffin Island

Coast Mountains

Mackenzie

Great Bear Lake

Labrador Sea

Gulf of Alaska

Great Slave Lake

Hudson Bay

Laurentian Highlands

Newfoundland

Rocky Mountains

Canadian Shield

Labrador

Great Plains

Lake Winnipeg

Mount Rainier
20,321ft

Lake Manitoba

Lake Superior

Nova Scotia

▲ Mount St. Helens
8,362ft

Lake Huron
Lake Ontario

St. Lawrence

Sierra Nevada

Great Basin

Lake Michigan

Lake Erie

Appalachian Mountains

Great Salt Lake

Missouri

Colorado

▽ Lowest point
Death Valley
-282ft

Ohio

△ Brasstown Bald
4,783ft

ATLANTIC OCEAN

Sonoran Desert

Arkansas

Mississippi

Baja California

Rio Grande

Mississippi Delta

Sierra Madre Occidental

Gulf of Mexico

Tropic of Cancer

West Indies

PACIFIC OCEAN

Tropic of Cancer

Cuba

Greater Antilles

Lesser Antilles

Sierra Madre Oriental

△ Citlaltépetl
18,700ft

Yucatan Peninsula

Caribbean Sea

Sierra Madre del Sur

Lake Nicaragua

SOUTH AMERICA

ELEVATION

19,690ft
16,400ft
13,120ft
9,840ft
6,560ft
3,280ft
1,640ft
820ft
330ft
sea level
below sea level
◄ cross section

SCALE 1:52,000,000

0 km   500   1000

0 miles 250   500   750   1000

1 THE FAR NORTH

Much of Canada's far north is covered by ice and snow. Only in summer, when the ice thaws, can hardy lichens grow. Great pine forests are found farther south.

2 THE MOUNTAINOUS WEST

A long mountain chain runs down the western side of the continent. These mountains are young, and are still being formed.

3 THE GREAT PLAINS

The fertile soils of much of the Great Plains – at the heart of the continent – allow cereal crops like wheat and corn to be grown.

4 THE DESERT REGIONS

The Sonoran Desert in southern US and northern Mexico is typical of North America's desert regions.

5 THE TROPICAL SOUTH

The Yucatan Peninsula, in Mexico, is full of caves and sinkholes because the humid tropical climate accelerates erosion.

POLITICAL NORTH AMERICA

The US, Canada, and Mexico are all federal countries. This means that political power is shared between the national government and the state government. Canada and the US are democracies with a long history of freedom and equal rights. Governments in the countries south of the US have been less stable, often ruled by dictators or harsh regimes. Many people have suffered for their political beliefs. Until about 20 years ago many of the Caribbean islands were ruled by European countries as colonies.

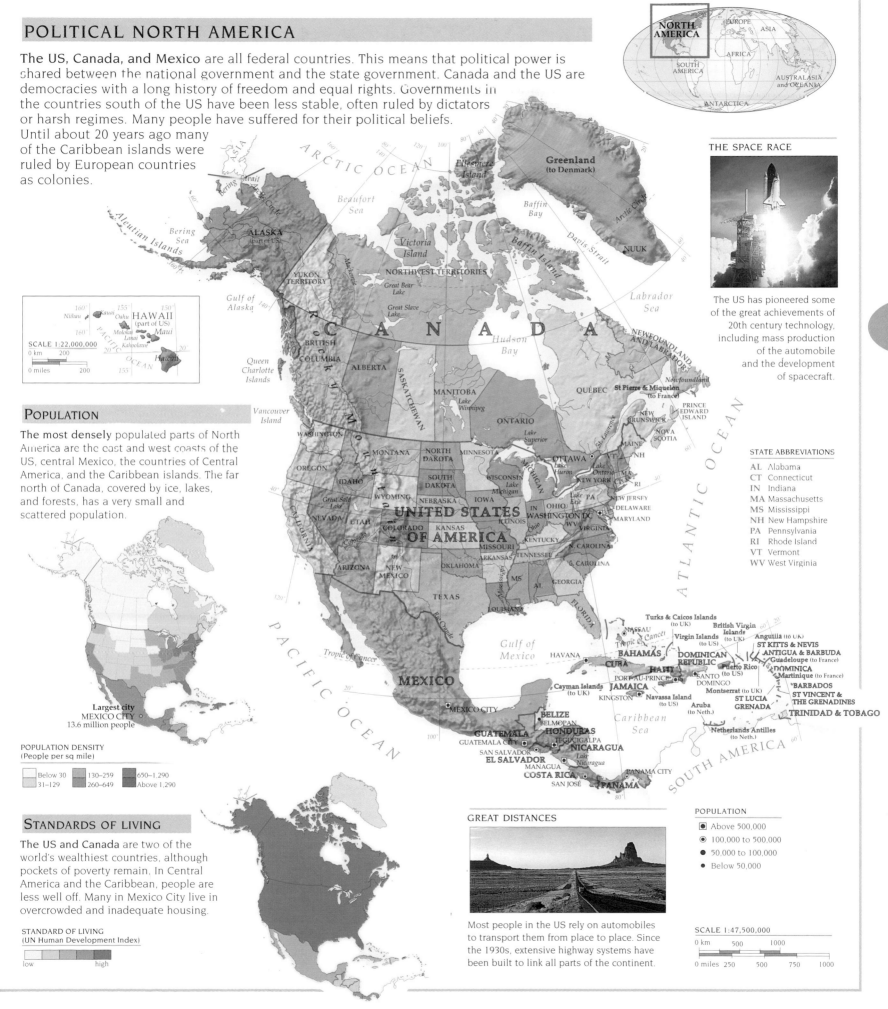

THE SPACE RACE

The US has pioneered some of the great achievements of 20th century technology, including mass production of the automobile and the development of spacecraft.

POPULATION

The most densely populated parts of North America are the east and west coasts of the US, central Mexico, the countries of Central America, and the Caribbean islands. The far north of Canada, covered by ice, lakes, and forests, has a very small and scattered population.

Largest city
MEXICO CITY
13.6 million people

POPULATION DENSITY
(People per sq mile)

Below 30	130–259	650–1,290
31–129	260–649	Above 1,290

STANDARDS OF LIVING

The US and Canada are two of the world's wealthiest countries, although pockets of poverty remain. In Central America and the Caribbean, people are less well off. Many in Mexico City live in overcrowded and inadequate housing.

STANDARD OF LIVING
(UN Human Development Index)

low ▭▭▭▭▭ high

GREAT DISTANCES

Most people in the US rely on automobiles to transport them from place to place. Since the 1930s, extensive highway systems have been built to link all parts of the continent.

STATE ABBREVIATIONS

AL Alabama
CT Connecticut
IN Indiana
MA Massachusetts
MS Mississippi
NH New Hampshire
PA Pennsylvania
RI Rhode Island
VT Vermont
WV West Virginia

POPULATION

◉ Above 500,000
◎ 100,000 to 500,000
● 50,000 to 100,000
• Below 50,000

SCALE 1:47,500,000
0 km   500   1000
0 miles 250   500   750   1000

SCALE 1:22,000,000
0 km   200
0 miles   200

HAWAII (part of US)

29

NORTH AMERICAN GEOGRAPHY

Canada and the US are among the world's wealthiest countries. They have rich natural resources, good farmland, and thriving, varied industries. The range of different industries in Mexico is growing, but other Central American countries and the Caribbean islands rely on one or two important cash crops and tourism for most of their incomes. They have a lower standard of living than the US and Canada.

INDUSTRY

The US and Canada have an extremely wide range of industries, from mining and the processing of farm produce, to heavy and light manufacturing and service industries like banking. A variety of goods are produced, including airplanes, cars, and computers. Oil exports and machine assembly are Mexico's main industries. In Central America and the Caribbean nations, most industry is based on agricultural produce.

MINERAL RESOURCES

North America still has large amounts of mineral resources. Canada has important nickel reserves, Mexico is renowned for its silver, and bauxite – used to make aluminum – is found in Jamaica. Oil and gas are plentiful, particularly in the Arctic northwest by the Beaufort Sea, and farther south by the Gulf of Mexico.

MINERAL RESOURCES
- Bauxite
- Copper
- Iron
- Nickel
- Phosphates
- Uranium
- Silver
- Oil/gas field
- Coal field

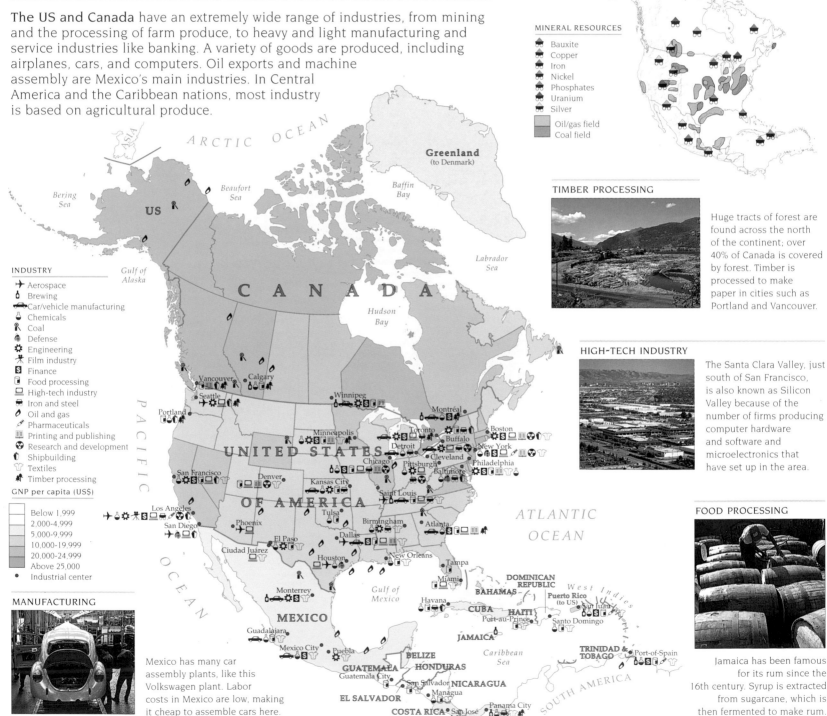

INDUSTRY
- Aerospace
- Brewing
- Car/vehicle manufacturing
- Chemicals
- Coal
- Defense
- Engineering
- Film industry
- Finance
- Food processing
- High-tech industry
- Iron and steel
- Oil and gas
- Pharmaceuticals
- Printing and publishing
- Research and development
- Shipbuilding
- Textiles
- Timber processing

GNP per capita (US$)
- Below 1,999
- 2,000-4,999
- 5,000-9,999
- 10,000-19,999
- 20,000-24,999
- Above 25,000
- • Industrial center

TIMBER PROCESSING

Huge tracts of forest are found across the north of the continent; over 40% of Canada is covered by forest. Timber is processed to make paper in cities such as Portland and Vancouver.

HIGH-TECH INDUSTRY

The Santa Clara Valley, just south of San Francisco, is also known as Silicon Valley because of the number of firms producing computer hardware and software and microelectronics that have set up in the area.

FOOD PROCESSING

Jamaica has been famous for its rum since the 16th century. Syrup is extracted from sugarcane, which is then fermented to make rum.

MANUFACTURING

Mexico has many car assembly plants, like this Volkswagen plant. Labor costs in Mexico are low, making it cheap to assemble cars here.

CLIMATE

Much of northern Canada lies within the Arctic Circle and is permanently covered by ice or the sparse vegetation known as tundra. Southern Canada and much of central US have a continental climate, with hot summers and cold winters. The southern parts of the US, Central America, and the Caribbean have a hot, humid tropical climate. The islands and the eastern and central states of the US often experience hurricane-force winds, waterspouts, and tornadoes.

Coldest place
NORTHICE (Greenland)
Temp. -87°F

Wettest place
HENDERSON LAKE (BC, Canada)
Annual rainfall 262 in

Hottest place
DEATH VALLEY (CA, USA)
Temp. 135°F

Driest place
BATAQUES (Mexico)
Annual rainfall 1.2 in

EXTREME WEATHER EVENTS

Symbols indicate climatic extremes

CLIMATE

- Ice cap
- Tundra
- Subarctic
- Cool continental
- Warm temperate
- Mediterranean
- Semiarid
- Arid
- Humid equatorial
- Tropical
- Hot humid

NORTH AMERICA'S HOTTEST PLACE

Death Valley in California is the hottest and driest place in the US. Strong, dry winds sweep through the valley, constantly reshaping the sand and salt deposits that cover its floor.

LAND USE AND AGRICULTURE

On the Great Plains of Canada and the US, vast quantities of cereal crops, including corn and wheat, grow in the fertile soils. Cattle are also raised on great ranches throughout these regions and on the foothills of the Rocky Mountains. In California, vegetables and fruits are grown with the aid of irrigation. Bananas, coffee, and sugarcane are grown for export in Central America and the Caribbean, while sorghum and corn are grown as subsistence crops.

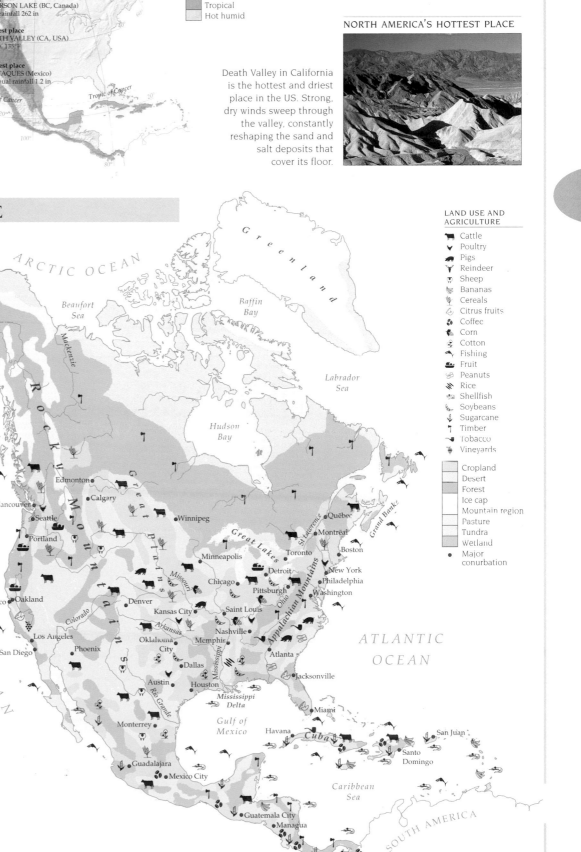

LAND USE AND AGRICULTURE

- Cattle
- Poultry
- Pigs
- Reindeer
- Sheep
- Bananas
- Cereals
- Citrus fruits
- Coffee
- Corn
- Cotton
- Fishing
- Fruit
- Peanuts
- Rice
- Shellfish
- Soybeans
- Sugarcane
- Timber
- Tobacco
- Vineyards

- Cropland
- Desert
- Forest
- Ice cap
- Mountain region
- Pasture
- Tundra
- Wetland
- Major conurbation

BANANA PLANTATION

Banana plantations are common in the Caribbean and Central America. The fruit is grown for local consumption and for export to the US and Europe, where they are valued for their flavor and nutritional qualities.

FISHING

The Grand Banks off the eastern coast of Canada were once home to almost limitless fish stocks. Overfishing has reduced the number of fish to very low levels. Quotas limiting the numbers of fish caught help the numbers to rise.

WESTERN CANADA

ALBERTA, BRITISH COLUMBIA, MANITOBA, NORTHWEST
TERRITORIES, SASKATCHEWAN, YUKON TERRITORY

The first inhabitants of Canada's western provinces
were Native Americans. By the late 1800s, the Canadian
Pacific Railroad was completed and European settlers
moved west, turning most of the prairie into huge grain
farms. North of the prairies lie the vast, empty territories
that have significant Native American populations.
In 1999, part of the Northwest Territories, known as
Nunavut, will become a self-governing Inuit homeland.

FARMING AND LAND USE

More than 20% of the world's wheat is
grown in Canada's prairie provinces:
Manitoba, Alberta, and
Saskatchewan. Beef cattle
graze on the ranches
of Alberta and British
Columbia. Fruits,
especially apples,
flourish in the sheltered
southern valleys of British
Columbia, and Pacific
salmon, and herring are
caught off the west coast.

LAND USE

Pasture 5% — Cropland 4%

Forest 38%

Other (including mountains) 53%

FARMING AND LAND USE

- 🐄 Cattle
- 🐟 Fishing
- 🌾 Cereals
- 🍎 Fruit
- 🌲 Timber
- ● Major conurbation

- Pasture
- Cropland
- Forest
- Mountain region
- Barren
- Tundra

INDUSTRY

The major industries in the prairie provinces
are related to agriculture, such as meat-
processing in Manitoba. Alberta has
huge reserves of fossil fuels, and the
other provinces are rich in minerals,
including zinc, nickel, silver, and
uranium. British Columbia's
economy depends on
manufacturing, especially
automobiles, chemicals, and
machinery, along
with paper and
timber industries.

STRUCTURE OF
INDUSTRY (Canada)

Primary 3%
Services 66%

Manufacturing 31%

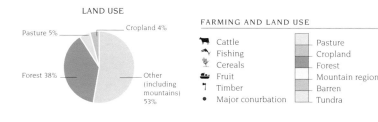

INDUSTRY

- 🚗 Car manufacturing
- ⚗ Chemicals
- ⚙ Engineering
- 📦 Food processing
- △ Metal refining
- ◊ Oil and gas
- 🅰 Mining
- 🌲 Timber processing
- ⦿ Tourism
- ▪ Major industrial center / area
- — Major road

THE LANDSCAPE

The prairie provinces are mostly flat. Occasionally, the
level plains are broken up by river valleys such as that
of the Qu'Appelle in Saskatchewan. In the west, the
jagged peaks and steep passes of the Rocky Mountains
are covered in snow for months on end. West of the
Rockies, the land descends sharply toward the coast of
British Columbia. The far north is covered by dense
forests and many glacial lakes.

The Arctic
Most of Canada's northern
islands are within the
Arctic Circle. They are
covered by ice year-round.

Mount Logan (B 5)
Mount Logan is Canada's
tallest peak. It rises 19,551 ft.

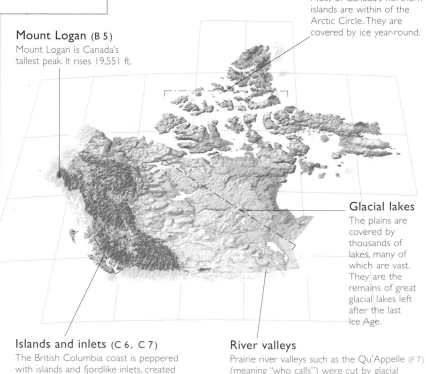

Glacial lakes
The plains are
covered by
thousands of
lakes, many of
which are vast.
They are the
remains of great
glacial lakes left
after the last
Ice Age.

ENVIRONMENTAL ISSUES

Across the north of the region, the ground is permanently
frozen. This is called permafrost. Building on this frozen
surface is very difficult, because the heat from houses or
roads can cause the ground to melt, and subside.
Many of the extensive forests in
British Columbia are used for
commercial lumbering. The
province produces more than
half of Canada's timber.

ENVIRONMENTAL
ISSUES

- 🌳 Lumbering activity
- ▦ Permafrost zone
- ● Major industrial center

Islands and inlets (C 6, C 7)
The British Columbia coast is peppered
with islands and fjordlike inlets, created
by the force of the Pacific Ocean.

River valleys
Prairie river valleys such as the Qu'Appelle (F 7)
(meaning "who calls") were cut by glacial
meltwater thousands of years ago.

POPULATION

Most of the people in western Canada live near the Canada/US border, taking advantage of the warmer climate and convenient transportation routes. In the cold, forested north, the population is sparse, with only a few people per 40 sq miles – many of them Native Americans such as the Inuit.

CLIMATE

Parts of northern Canada are frozen all year round. The prairie provinces and British Columbia have warm summers and cold winters.

January

July

TEMPERATURE AND PRECIPITATION

More than 68°F	23 to 32°F
59 to 68°F	14 to 23°F
50 to 59°F	5 to 14°F
41 to 50°F	Less than 5°F
32 to 41°F	4 — Precipitation (in)

NORTH AMERICA
Western Canada

Edmonton
Saskatoon
Winnipeg
Vancouver
Calgary
Regina

URBAN/RURAL POPULATION DIVISION

Vancouver 20%
Other towns and cities 37%
Edmonton 10.6%
Calgary 9.4%
Rural population 23%

INHABITANTS PER SQ MILE

More than 30
3–30
Less than 3
• Major city

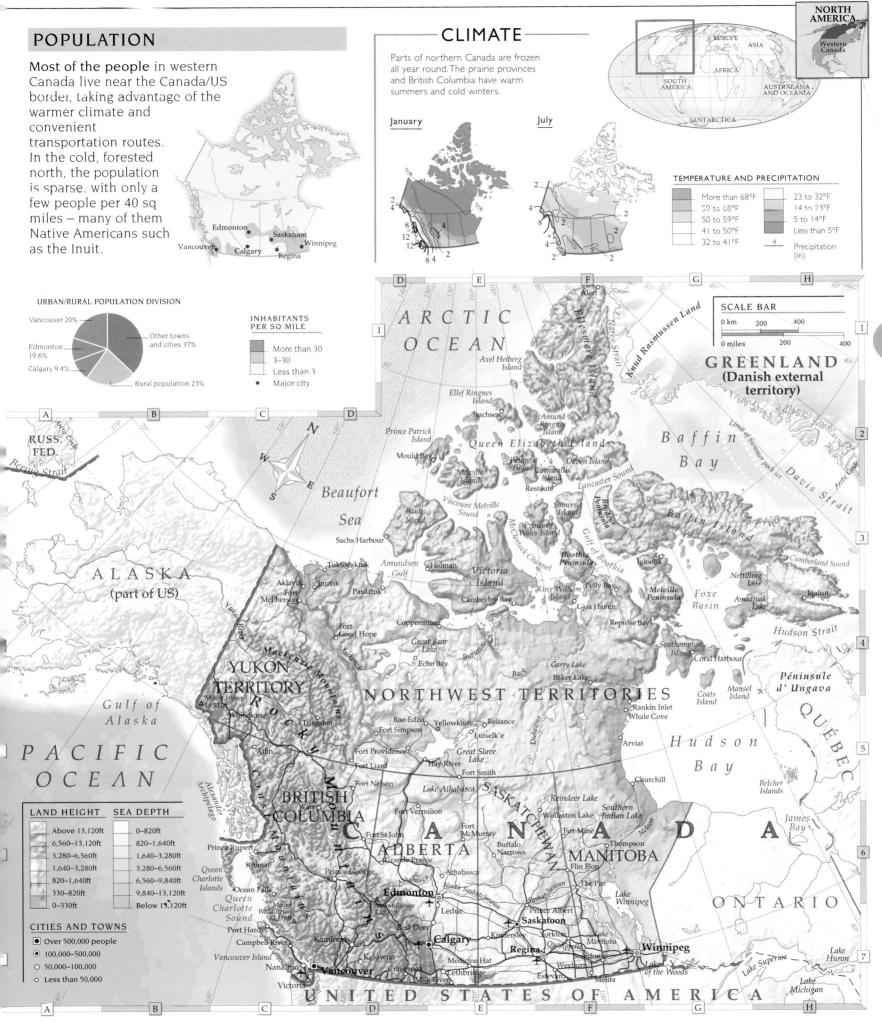

SCALE BAR
0 km 200 400
0 miles 200 400

GREENLAND
(Danish external territory)

ARCTIC OCEAN

Alert
Ellesmere Island
Axel Heiberg Island
Knud Rasmussen Land
Naves Strait
Isachsen
Ellef Ringnes Island
Amund Ringnes Island
Prince Patrick Island
Queen Elizabeth Islands
Baffin Bay
Mould Bay
Bathurst Island
Cornwallis Island
Devon Island
Melville Island
Resolute
Lancaster Sound
Viscount Melville Sound
Somerset Island
Prince of Wales Island
Baffin Island
Cumberland Sound

RUSS. FED.
Bering Strait
Arctic Circle

Beaufort Sea

Banks Island
Amundsen Gulf
Holman
Victoria Island
M'Clintock Channel
King William Island
Boothia Peninsula
Gulf of Boothia
Brodeur Peninsula
Igloolik
Nettilling Lake
Amadjuak Lake
Iqaluit

Sachs Harbour
Tuktoyaktuk
Aklavik
Inuvik
Fort McPherson
Paulatuk
Coppermine
Cambridge Bay
Pelly Bay
Melville Peninsula
Gjoa Haven
Foxe Basin
Repulse Bay
Hudson Strait

ALASKA (part of US)

Yukon River
Fort Good Hope
Great Bear Lake
Echo Bay
Burnside
Back
Garry Lake
Baker Lake
Coats Island
Mansel Island
Péninsule d' Ungava

Gulf of Alaska

Mackenzie Mountains
YUKON TERRITORY
Mount Logan △19,551ft
Whitehorse
Tungsten
NORTHWEST TERRITORIES
Rae-Edzo
Yellowknife
Reliance
Southampton Island
Coral Harbour
Rankin Inlet
Whale Cove

PACIFIC OCEAN

Atlin
Fort Simpson
Fort Providence
Great Slave Lake
Lutselk'e
Dubawnt
Arviat
Hudson Bay
QUÉBEC

Fort Liard
Hay River
Fort Smith
Churchill
Belcher Islands
James Bay

LAND HEIGHT | SEA DEPTH

LAND HEIGHT	SEA DEPTH
Above 13,120ft	0–820ft
6,560–13,120ft	820–1,640ft
3,280–6,560ft	1,640–3,280ft
1,640–3,280ft	3,280–6,560ft
820–1,640ft	6,560–9,840ft
330–820ft	9,840–13,120ft
0–330ft	Below 13,120ft

Fort Nelson
Lake Athabasca
Reindeer Lake
Southern Indian Lake
Fort McMurray
Wollaston Lake
Fox Mine
Thompson
ONTARIO

BRITISH COLUMBIA
Ware
Fort Vermilion
Fort St John
Buffalo Narrows
MANITOBA
Flin Flon
The Pas
Lake Winnipeg
Prince Rupert
Kitimat
Grande Prairie
ALBERTA
Athabasca
CANADA
SASKATCHEWAN
Nelson

Queen Charlotte Islands
Ocean Falls
Prince George
Athabasca
North Saskatchewan
Prince Albert
Saskatchewan

Queen Charlotte Sound
Mount Waddington △13,166ft
Mount Robson 12,972ft
Edmonton
Leduc
Red Deer
Saskatoon
Flin Flon
Lake Manitoba
Lake Winnipeg

Port Hardy
Campbell River
Kamloops
Calgary
Kindersley
Yorkton
Brandon
Winnipeg
Lake Superior
Lake Huron

Vancouver Island
Nanaimo
Vancouver
Kelowna
Cranbrook
Medicine Hat
Regina
Qu'Appelle
Weyburn
Lake of the Woods
Lake Michigan
Victoria
Milk River
Lethbridge
Estevan
Melita

CITIES AND TOWNS

◉ Over 500,000 people
⊙ 100,000–500,000
○ 50,000–100,000
○ Less than 50,000

UNITED STATES OF AMERICA

EASTERN CANADA

NEW BRUNSWICK, NEWFOUNDLAND AND LABRADOR,
NOVA SCOTIA, ONTARIO, PRINCE EDWARD ISLAND, QUÉBEC

The first towns built by European settlers grew
up in the maritime provinces, close to the rich
fishing grounds of the Atlantic Ocean. In recent
years, people have migrated to cities along the
St. Lawrence River and near the Great Lakes.
Although most Canadians speak English, people
in Québec speak mainly French and have sought
independence from the rest of Canada.

INDUSTRY

In the maritime provinces the traditional fishing industry
has declined, causing unemployment.
However, Newfoundland has a thriving
food processing industry. Ontario and
Québec have a wide range of
industries, including the
generation of hydroelectricity,
mining, and chemicals,
car manufacturing and fruit
canning in the great cities.
Large amounts of wood pulp
and paper are also produced.

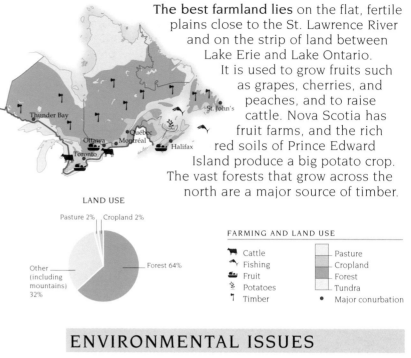

STRUCTURE
OF INDUSTRY

Primary 3%
Services 66%
Manufacturing 31%

INDUSTRY

- 🚗 Car manufacturing
- Chemicals
- Fish processing
- Food processing
- Hydroelectric power
- △ Metal refining
- Mining
- Timber processing
- High-tech industry
- Tourism
- •̣ Major industrial center / area
- — Major road

FARMING AND LAND USE

The best farmland lies on the flat, fertile
plains close to the St. Lawrence River
and on the strip of land between
Lake Erie and Lake Ontario.
It is used to grow fruits such
as grapes, cherries, and
peaches, and to raise
cattle. Nova Scotia has
fruit farms, and the rich
red soils of Prince Edward
Island produce a big potato crop.
The vast forests that grow across the
north are a major source of timber.

LAND USE

Pasture 2%   Cropland 2%

Other
(including
mountains)
32%

Forest 64%

FARMING AND LAND USE

- 🐄 Cattle
- Fishing
- Fruit
- Potatoes
- Timber
- Pasture
- Cropland
- Forest
- Tundra
- • Major conurbation

ENVIRONMENTAL ISSUES

Acid rain caused by emissions from factories in the US
and along the St. Lawrence River destroys forests and
kills marine life. Several huge new hydroelectric power
projects are planned for James Bay on Hudson Bay,
which will flood huge areas of land. Overfishing
in the Atlantic has led to
limits being set on the
number of fish that
can be caught.

ENVIRONMENTAL
ISSUES

- Depleted fish stocks
- Major dam
- Urban air pollution
- Affected by acid rain
- • Major industrial center

THE LANDSCAPE

A huge, ancient mass of rock called the Canadian Shield lies
beneath much of eastern Canada. It is covered by low hills, rocky
outcrops, thousands of lakes, and huge areas of forest. Much of
the Canadian Shield is permanently frozen. The St. Lawrence
River flows out of Lake Ontario and into the Atlantic Ocean.
It is surrounded by rolling hills and
flat areas of very fertile farmland.

Scoured by ice
About 20,000 years ago, Labrador and
northern Québec were completely covered
by ice. The glaciers scraped hollows in the
rock beneath. When the ice melted, lakes
were left in the hollows that remained.

Lake Superior (B 5)
Lake Superior is the largest freshwater lake in
the world. It covers an area of 32,150 sq
miles and lies between Canada and the USA.

St. Lawrence River (E 5)
The St. Lawrence River is 2,350 miles
long. Parts of it have become silted up,
causing it to be braided into many
different channels. Between December
and mid-April the river freezes over.

Highlands
The highlands of New
Brunswick, Nova Scotia,
and Newfoundland are
the most northerly
part of the Appalachian
mountain chain.

The Bay of Fundy (F 5)
This bay has the world's highest tides. It is shaped like a funnel, and as the Atlantic flows into
it, the ever narrowing shores cause the water level to rise 20–50 ft at every high tide.

NORTH AMERICA
Eastern Canada

POPULATION

Colonists from both France and Britain settled in Canada from the early 1600s onward. Ontario and the maritime provinces are English speaking. Québec is the center of French settlement; 75% of the people there have French as a first language. Most people in eastern Canada now live in large towns and cities close to the St. Lawrence River.

URBAN/RURAL POPULATION DIVISION

Toronto 20.2%
Montréal 16%
Ottawa 4.8%
Other towns and cities 35%
Rural population 24%

INHABITANTS PER SQ MILE

- More than 260
- 130–260
- 3–130
- Less than 3
- ■ Capital city
- ● Major city

CLIMATE

Winters are very cold, but warm winds from the Gulf of Mexico can bring hot summers to southern Ontario and the areas bordering the St. Lawrence River.

TEMPERATURE AND PRECIPITATION

- More than 68°F
- 59 to 68°F
- 50 to 59°F
- 41 to 50°F
- 32 to 41°F
- 23 to 32°F
- 5 to 23°F
- -13 to 5°F
- Less than -13°F
- —4— Precipitation (in)

January

July

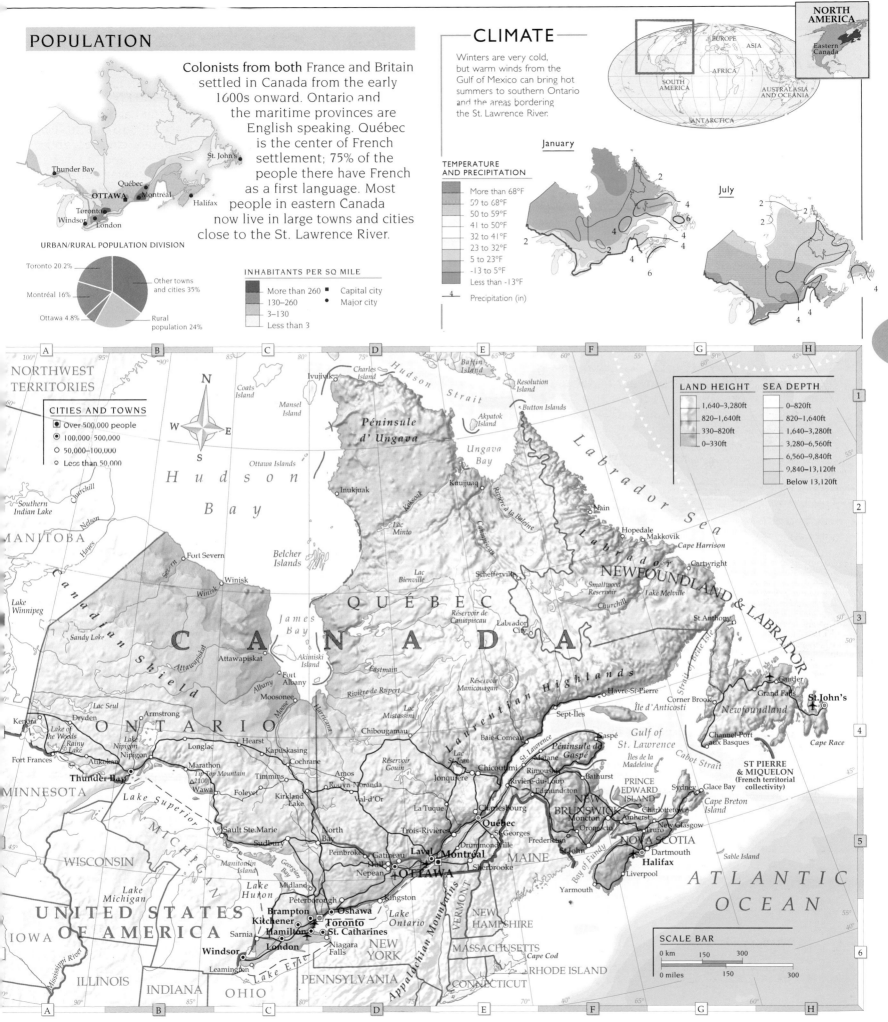

CITIES AND TOWNS
- ● Over 500,000 people
- ● 100,000–500,000
- ○ 50,000–100,000
- ○ Less than 50,000

LAND HEIGHT
- 1,640–3,280ft
- 820–1,640ft
- 330–820ft
- 0–330ft

SEA DEPTH
- 0–820ft
- 820–1,640ft
- 1,640–3,280ft
- 3,280–6,560ft
- 6,560–9,840ft
- 9,840–13,120ft
- Below 13,120ft

SCALE BAR
0 km 150 300
0 miles 150 300

THE PHYSICAL US

The United States of America covers the broad central portion of North America, from the northern border with Canada to Mexico in the dry desert south, and includes the mountainous northwestern state of Alaska and the distant volcanic islands of Hawaii. The US has large areas of fertile land at its heart, flanked by the high Rocky Mountains in the west and the ancient Appalachians in the east.

2,807 miles
1,548 miles

CROSS SECTION THROUGH THE US

Cascade Range | Rocky Mountains | Great Plains | Mississippi Basin | Bars and spits on East Coast

W — 2,807 miles — E

The highest points in the US are found in the wide belt of mountains in the west. Rising from the sea are the coastal ranges of the Cascades and Sierra Nevada, while the Rocky Mountains are farther inland. The terrain drops away to the east, down across the Great Plains and Mississippi Basin, toward the Appalachians and the East Coast.

THE LANDSCAPE OF THE US

Coastal mountains rise from the Pacific coast, dropping inland to the deserts and salt lakes of the Great Basin. The high Rocky Mountains are new mountains, formed by the collision of two of Earth's tectonic plates. Much of the central US is flat, consisting of a series of undulating, often virtually featureless plains known as the Great Plains. The Appalachian Mountains in the East are much older, lower, and more eroded than the Rockies. The Great Lakes, the world's largest freshwater lakes, lie on the US–Canada border.

HAWAII

Niihau · Kauai
Oahu · Molokai
Lanai · Maui
Kahoolawe · Red Hill 10,023ft
Hawaii
Mauna Kea 13,797ft
Mauna Loa 13,678ft
PACIFIC OCEAN

0 km 200
0 miles 200

ARCTIC OCEAN
RUSSIAN FEDERATION
Chukchi Sea
Colville River
Brooks Range
ALASKA
Yukon River
CANADA
Saint Lawrence Island
Bering Strait
Kuskokwim Mts
Mount McKinley (Denali) 20,322ft
Alaska Range
Bering Sea
Nunivak Island
Coast Mountains
Attu Island
Pribilof Islands
Kodiak Island
PACIFIC OCEAN
Aleutian Islands
Shumagin Islands
Amchitka Island
Andreanof Islands
Unalaska Island
Umnak Island
Alaska Peninsula

0 km 600
0 miles 600

LAND HEIGHT

Above 13,120ft
6,560–13,120ft
3,280–6,560ft
1,640–3,280ft
820–1,640ft
330–820ft
0–330ft
Below sea level

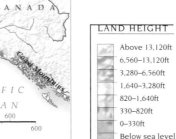

1 ALASKA

Alaska's far north is frozen solid for most of the year. Rivers can flow only during the short summer, when heat from the weak sun melts the surface ice.

2 DESERTS

The Great Basin in the Rocky Mountains is made up of many shallow, salty lakes, deserts, and scrubby vegetation like tumbleweed.

3 MOUNTAINS

The Rocky Mountains form a spine running up the western side of the US. The mountains continue north through Canada, into Alaska.

SCALE BAR

0 km 100 200
0 miles 100 200

NORTH AMERICA

USA

CLIMATE

The climate of the US is generally temperate and continental – with warm summers and cold winters. Humid, subtropical climates occur only in Hawaii and the Florida keys. In contrast, much of Alaska has a freezing arctic climate. On the Pacific Coast, warm, moist air from the ocean creates a milder climate, but the coastal mountains prevent this air from reaching the interior – making most of the central US very dry. Extreme weather events are common in the central US, including sudden tornadoes, blizzards, and hailstorms.

CLIMATE
Subarctic
Cool continental
Temperate
Warm temperate
Semiarid
Arid
Tropical

Wettest place
Waialeale, Kauai, Hawaii
Annual rainfall 460in

Coldest place
Prospect Creek, Alaska
Temp. -80°F

Hottest and driest place
Death Valley (California, USA)
Temp. 134°F
Annual rainfall 1.63in

EXTREME WEATHER EVENTS

Symbols indicate climatic extremes

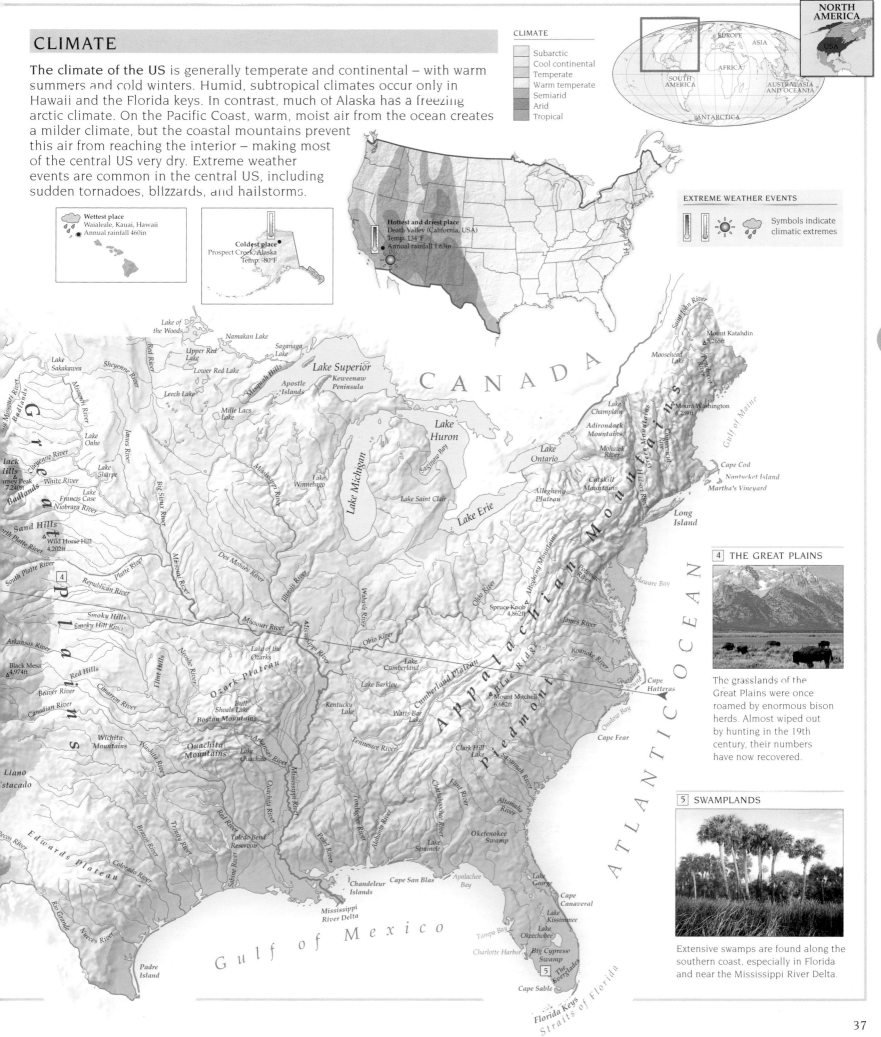

4 THE GREAT PLAINS

The grasslands of the Great Plains were once roamed by enormous bison herds. Almost wiped out by hunting in the 19th century, their numbers have now recovered.

5 SWAMPLANDS

Extensive swamps are found along the southern coast, especially in Florida and near the Mississippi River Delta.

UNITED STATES OF AMERICA

From a sparsely populated "unknown" territory in the 16th century, the US has built on its natural strengths – immense tracts of fertile land and great mineral resources – to become the world's most powerful nation. Its global success was fueled by a hardworking immigrant population, exploiting their land of opportunity and sustained by the ideals of liberty and democracy that continue to bind the American people.

WASHINGTON, DC

Washington, DC is the administrative capital of the US. All national government is based here, centered on the White House, an 18th-century building on Pennsylvania Avenue that is the official residence of the US president. Congress, composed of the Senate and the House of Representatives, meets in the Capitol.

THE FIFTY STATES

The US is a federation of 50 states. Following the 1776 Revolutionary War, 13 former colonies formed the core of the new nation. Expansion continued southward and westward, aided by the Louisiana Purchase in 1803, which added former French lands to the Union. By 1867, with the purchase of Alaska, the modern shape of the US was nearly complete. Alaska and Hawaii were admitted as states in 1959.

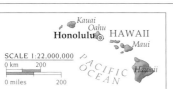

NEW YORK

The first skyscrapers in New York were built at the beginning of the 20th century. The intricate Manhattan skyline has become a symbol of US urban culture throughout the world.

STARS AND STRIPES

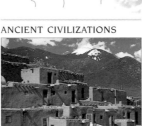

The 13 stripes of the US flag represent the 13 colonies that formed the first states of the Union. Each star symbolizes one of the current states; as states are admitted to the union, the number of stars increases.

ANCIENT CIVILIZATIONS

Evidence of some of the oldest cultures in the US can still be found in the Southwest. Peoples such as the Hopi and Hohokam farmed and built settlements (pueblos) here.

POPULATION

The US has the most varied population in the world. The original native population has been swollen by peoples from all corners of Europe, many seeking a new life away from poverty and persecution; by Africans whose ancestors were brought to the US as slaves; and during the later half of the 20th century, by people from South America, the Caribbean, and many parts of Asia – particularly the countries on the edge of the Pacific Ocean.

ALASKA

HAWAII

Largest city
NEW YORK
7.3 million people

NORTH
AMERICA

EUROPE
ASIA
AFRICA
AUSTRALASIA
AND OCEANIA
SOUTH
AMERICA
ANTARCTICA
USA

POPULATION DENSITY
(People per sq mile)

Below 25	130–259	650–1,299
26–129	260–649	Above 1,300

ALL AMERICANS

These children are all American citizens, regardless of their race, culture, or their parents' nationality. They show the diversity of the US, whose many different peoples came to North America for a variety of reasons.

THE GOOD LIFE

Since the beginning of the 1980s many people have moved to the northwest Pacific states, Oregon and Washington, drawn by a more leisurely lifestyle and proximity to the magnificent countryside.

URBAN DECAY

As industry and middle-class people have moved out of city centers into suburban areas, many inner cities have become run down, with restricted health services and delapidated amenities.

STANDARDS OF LIVING

Cheap and abundant food, spacious homes equipped with labor-saving devices, and easy access to beautiful scenery for leisure activities enable many people in the US to enjoy the highest standard of living in the world. In some inner-city areas, however, unemployment has led to poverty and homelessness with related social problems. Illegal immigrants, members of minority ethnic groups, and certain isolated rural dwellers are among the less privileged people in the US.

SCALE 1:15,500,000

0 km   200   400
0 miles   200   400

POPULATION
- Above 500,000
- 100,000 to 500,000
- 50,000 to 100,000
- Below 50,000

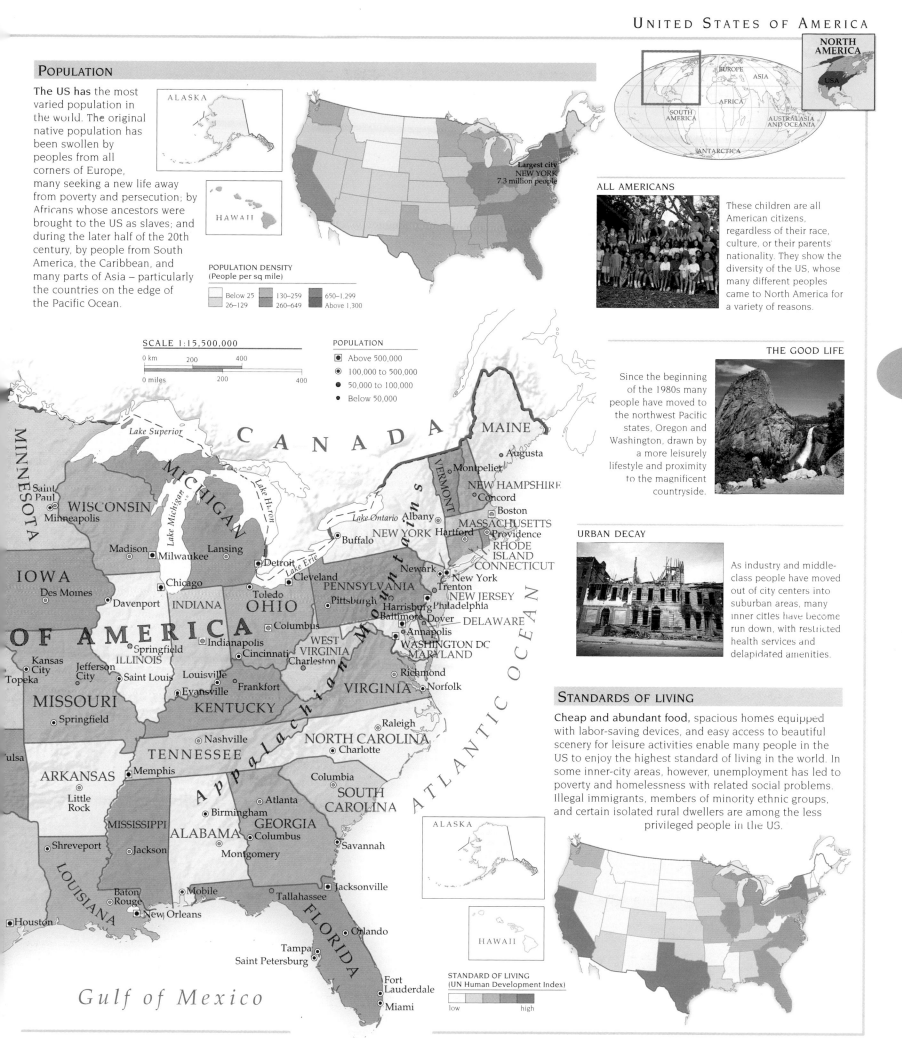

CANADA

MAINE
Augusta
Montpelier
VERMONT
NEW HAMPSHIRE
Concord
Boston
Albany
MASSACHUSETTS
Hartford
Providence
RHODE
ISLAND
CONNECTICUT
Newark
New York
Trenton
NEW JERSEY
Harrisburg
Philadelphia
Pittsburgh
Baltimore
Dover
DELAWARE
Annapolis
WASHINGTON DC
MARYLAND
Richmond
Norfolk

Lake Superior
MINNESOTA
Saint Paul
WISCONSIN
Minneapolis
MICHIGAN
Lake Michigan
Lake Huron
Madison
Lansing
Milwaukee
Detroit
Lake Erie
Lake Ontario
Buffalo
NEW YORK
Cleveland
IOWA
Chicago
Des Moines
Davenport
INDIANA
OHIO
PENNSYLVANIA
OF AMERICA
Columbus
Springfield
Indianapolis
ILLINOIS
Cincinnati
WEST VIRGINIA
Kansas City
Jefferson City
Saint Louis
Louisville
Charleston
Frankfort
Springfield
Evansville
KENTUCKY
VIRGINIA
MISSOURI
Appalachian Mountains
Topeka
Raleigh
Nashville
NORTH CAROLINA
TENNESSEE
Charlotte
Tulsa
ARKANSAS
Memphis
Columbia
Little Rock
Atlanta
SOUTH CAROLINA
MISSISSIPPI
Birmingham
GEORGIA
ALABAMA
Columbus
Shreveport
Jackson
Savannah
Montgomery
LOUISIANA
Baton Rouge
Mobile
Jacksonville
Tallahassee
New Orleans
Houston
FLORIDA
Orlando
Tampa
Saint Petersburg
Fort Lauderdale
Miami

ATLANTIC OCEAN

Gulf of Mexico

ALASKA

HAWAII

STANDARD OF LIVING
(UN Human Development Index)

low   high

US: THE NORTHEASTERN STATES

CONNECTICUT, DELAWARE, MAINE, MASSACHUSETTS, NEW HAMPSHIRE, NEW JERSEY, NEW YORK, PENNSYLVANIA, RHODE ISLAND, VERMONT

The dynamic 200-year boom of the northeastern states has been the result of a combination of factors. Between 1855 and 1924, over 20 million people poured into the region from all over the world, hoping to build a new life. Natural resources, including coal and iron, fueled new industries and fertile farmland provided food for the region's growing population. The "gateway" cities of the Atlantic seaboard, New York and Boston, enabled manufacturers to export their goods worldwide.

INDUSTRY

Boston, New York, and Philadelphia are international centers of industry and commerce. Electronics and communications are growing throughout the Northeast alongside traditional industries such as fishing and wood products. Tourism is vital for the northeastern states, particularly along the Atlantic coast.

STRUCTURE OF INDUSTRY

Manufacturing 27%
Primary 4%
Services 69%

INDUSTRY

- Chemicals
- Engineering
- Food processing
- Iron and steel
- Pharmaceuticals
- Textiles
- Timber processing
- Defense
- Finance
- High-tech
- Research and development
- Tourism

■ Major industrial center / area
— Major road

FARMING AND LAND USE

The varied landscape of the northeastern states supports a great range of farming. Livestock, including cattle, horses, poultry, and pigs, are raised throughout the region. The main crops are fruits and vegetables. Fishing is important, especially off the Atlantic coast of Maine.

FARMING AND LAND USE

- Cattle
- Pigs
- Poultry
- Fishing
- Cereals
- Cranberries
- Fruit
- Maple syrup
- Timber

Cropland
Forest
Pasture
• Major conurbation

LAND USE

Pasture 6%
Cropland 14%
Other 16 %
Forest 64%

THE LANDSCAPE

The Appalachian and Adirondack Mountains form a barrier between the marshy lowlands of the Atlantic coast and the lowlands farther west. The interior consists of rolling hills, fertile valleys, and thousands of lakes created by the movement of glaciers.

Appalachians (E 3)
The Appalachian Mountains, which run through most of this region, are the eroded remnants of peaks that were once much higher.

Rocky coastline (G 3)
The coast of Maine is made up of rocky bays, islands, and inlets. If the shoreline were stretched out, it would be 2,500 miles long.

Adirondacks (E 3)
The Adirondacks are a broad, wide mountain range, formed when older rocks were forced into a "dome" shape by movements in the Earth's crust many millions of years ago.

ENVIRONMENTAL ISSUES

The high level of industry and the large population puts great pressure on the environment. Air pollution from automobiles and industry led to poor air quality in many cities and caused acid rain. The problem is worse toward the Great Lakes, where severe lake pollution has occurred.

ENVIRONMENTAL ISSUES

 Urban air pollution

Affected by acid rain
Severely affected by acid rain

Polluted rivers
Sea/lake pollution
Severe sea/lake pollution

• Major industrial center

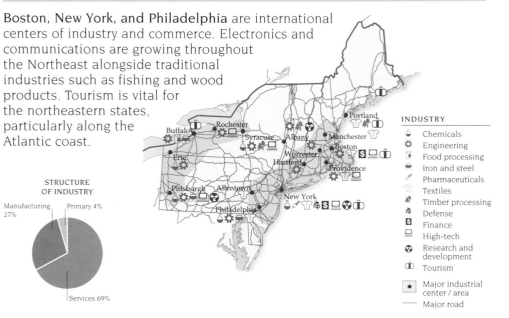

Long Island Sound (F 5)
Long Island Sound is a river valley that was drowned by rising sea levels.

Finger Lakes (D 3)
The long, narrow Finger Lakes lie in upper New York state. They were cut by glaciers.

Delaware Bay (D 6)
Deep bays such as Delaware Bay are often surrounded by salt marshes and barrier beaches that create ideal breeding conditions for a wide variety of birds and animals.

POPULATION

The areas along the eastern seaboard were settled by some of the earliest European colonists. The Northeast is now one of the most densely populated parts of the US. A few of the largest cities in the US, such as New York and Philadelphia, are in this region, but in the six states known as New England many towns and cities have populations of less than 30,000 inhabitants.

CLIMATE

Although the climate is mild during the spring and fall, summers can be hot and extremely humid, while winters are often very cold with heavy snowfall.

NORTH AMERICA
US: The Northeastern States

January

July

INHABITANTS PER SQ MILE

- More than 520
- 260–520
- 130–260
- 65–130
- Less than 65
- • Major city

URBAN/RURAL POPULATION DIVISION

New York 14.5%
Philadelphia 3%
Baltimore 1.5%
Rural population 21%
Other towns and cities 60%

TEMPERATURE AND PRECIPITATION

- More than 68°F
- 59 to 68°F
- 32 to 41°F
- 23 to 32°F
- 14 to 23°F
- Less than 14°F
- 4 Precipitation (in)

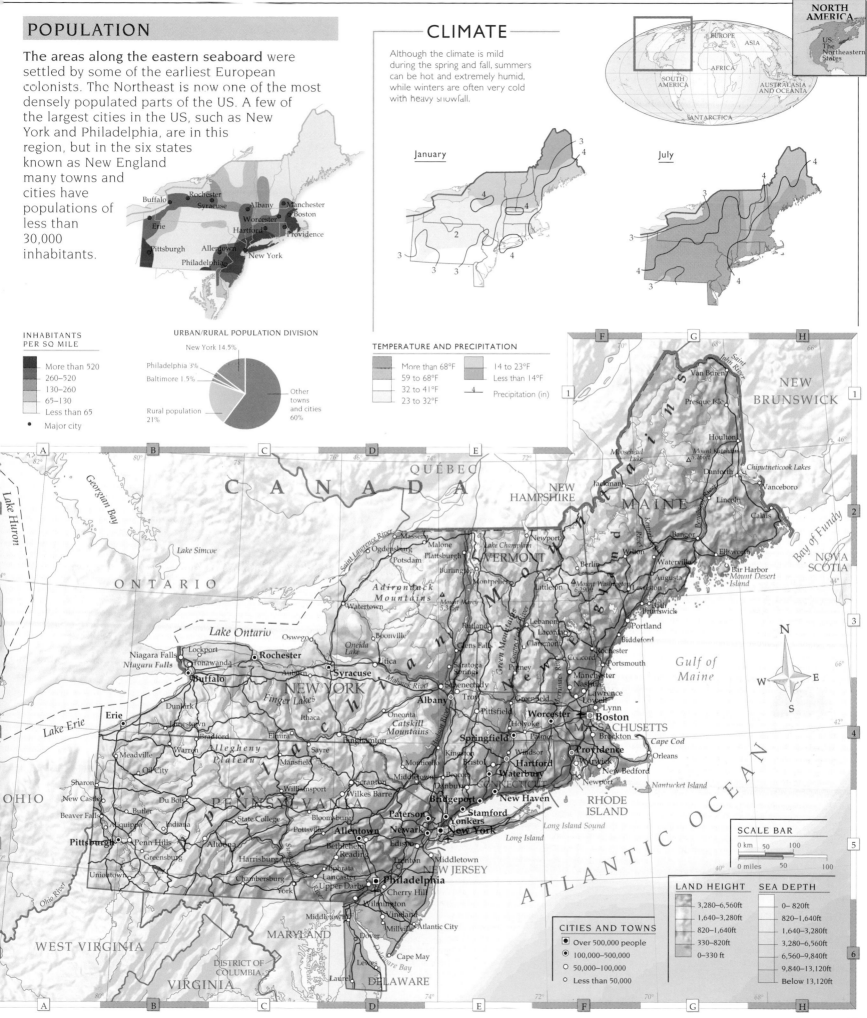

SCALE BAR
0 km 50 100
0 miles 50 100

LAND HEIGHT
- 3,280–6,560ft
- 1,640–3,280ft
- 820–1,640ft
- 330–820ft
- 0–330 ft

SEA DEPTH
- 0– 820ft
- 820–1,640ft
- 1,640–3,280ft
- 3,280–6,560ft
- 6,560–9,840ft
- 9,840–13,120ft
- Below 13,120ft

CITIES AND TOWNS
- ■ Over 500,000 people
- ◉ 100,000–500,000
- ◎ 50,000–100,000
- ○ Less than 50,000

US: THE SOUTHERN STATES

ALABAMA, ARKANSAS, DISTRICT OF COLUMBIA, FLORIDA, GEORGIA, KENTUCKY, LOUISIANA, MARYLAND, MISSISSIPPI, NORTH CAROLINA, SOUTH CAROLINA, TENNESSEE, VIRGINIA, WEST VIRGINIA

The southern states suffered great devastation and poverty as a result of the Civil War (1861–65). Recovery has come with the discovery and exploitation of resources and the development of major commercial and industrial centers. Yet these states retain the vibrant mix of cultures that reflect their French, Spanish, and English heritage.

INDUSTRY

Tourism is a major industry in the "sunbelt" states, especially Florida, and many people move to the area when they retire to enjoy the climate. Oil and gas are extracted along the coast of the Gulf of Mexico, and there are many related chemical industries. Textiles are still produced in North and South Carolina, but aerospace and other high-tech industries have been established as well.

STRUCTURE OF INDUSTRY

Primary 5%
Services 65%
Manufacturing 30%

INDUSTRY

- ✈ Aerospace
- ⚗ Chemicals
- ⚙ Engineering
- 🏭 Food processing
- ⚒ Iron and steel
- 👕 Textiles
- ⛏ Coal
- 🛢 Oil and gas
- 💻 High-tech
- ☢ Research and development
- 🎫 Tourism
- ▫ Major industrial center / area
- — Major road

POPULATION

Creoles, descended from Spanish and French colonizers, and Cajuns, of French-Canadian ancestry, live in the south of this region. Florida has a large Hispanic population, increased by migration from the Caribbean. In the early 20th century, five million black people, the descendants of slaves, left the South for cities in the North.

INHABITANTS PER SQ MILE

- More than 520
- 260–520
- 130–260
- 65–130
- Less than 65
- ■ Capital city
- ● Major city

URBAN/RURAL POPULATION DIVISION

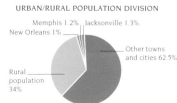

Memphis 1.2%   Jacksonville 1.3%
New Orleans 1%
Other towns and cities 62.5%
Rural population 34%

FARMING AND LAND USE

Cotton is still the South's main crop, but many old cottonfields are now pastures where all types of livestock are raised. Florida is famous for citrus fruits, while Georgia is renowned for peanuts. Sugarcane, soybeans, tobacco, corn, fruits, and rice are grown in other areas.

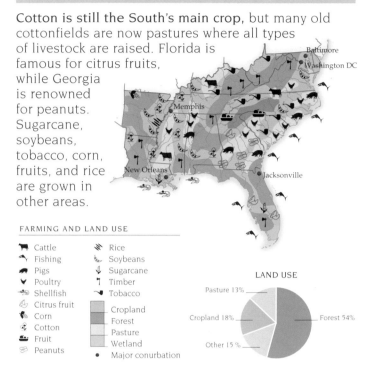

FARMING AND LAND USE

- 🐄 Cattle
- 🎣 Fishing
- 🐖 Pigs
- 🦃 Poultry
- 🦐 Shellfish
- 🍋 Citrus fruit
- 🌽 Corn
- Cotton
- 🍓 Fruit
- Peanuts
- 🐟 Rice
- Soybeans
- Sugarcane
- Timber
- Tobacco
- Cropland
- Forest
- Pasture
- Wetland
- ● Major conurbation

LAND USE

Pasture 13%
Cropland 18%
Forest 54%
Other 15%

THE LANDSCAPE

The South is a land of contrasts, the uplands of the Appalachians, the foothills of the Piedmont, and low-lying coastal regions are all featured. The interior lowlands are drained by the Mississippi. Florida is dotted with thousands of lakes and is home to The Everglades, a giant sawgrass swamp.

Mississippi River (C 4)
A major transportation artery, the Mississippi was an essential route in opening up the interior region. With its main tributary, the Missouri, it is nearly 3,800 miles long, making it the world's third-longest river.

Kentucky Bluegrass (E 2)
The gently rolling bluegrass landscape of northern Kentucky is ideal horse- and livestock-raising country.

Barrier beaches (I 3)
Sandy barrier beaches and islands line the eastern and southern coasts, along with sheltered lagoons and salt marshes.

Thermal springs (B 4)
Hot Springs National Park in Arkansas has 47 thermal springs and is a popular tourist and health resort. Visitors relax here in the hot water that trickles from the hillsides.

Tennessee River (D 4)
The Tennessee River is 625 miles long. Dams along the river generate hydro-electricity to provide most of the region's energy needs.

Limestone caves (E 4)
Cathedral Caverns in Alabama is a collection of enormous limestone caves. The main entrance is more than 1,000 ft high and 150 ft wide.

The Everglades (G 8)
The Everglades cover 5,000 sq miles and support abundant wild animals and plants, many unique to the area.

ENVIRONMENTAL ISSUES

Factories in the Great Lakes region have contributed to the large blanket of acid rain across the northern part. Toward the south, hurricanes sweep in from the Atlantic Ocean and Gulf of Mexico during the hurricane season, which lasts from May to October each year.

ENVIRONMENTAL ISSUES

- - - - Path of recent, devastating hurricane
▨ Affected by acid rain
━━ Polluted river

NORTH AMERICA

US: The Southern States

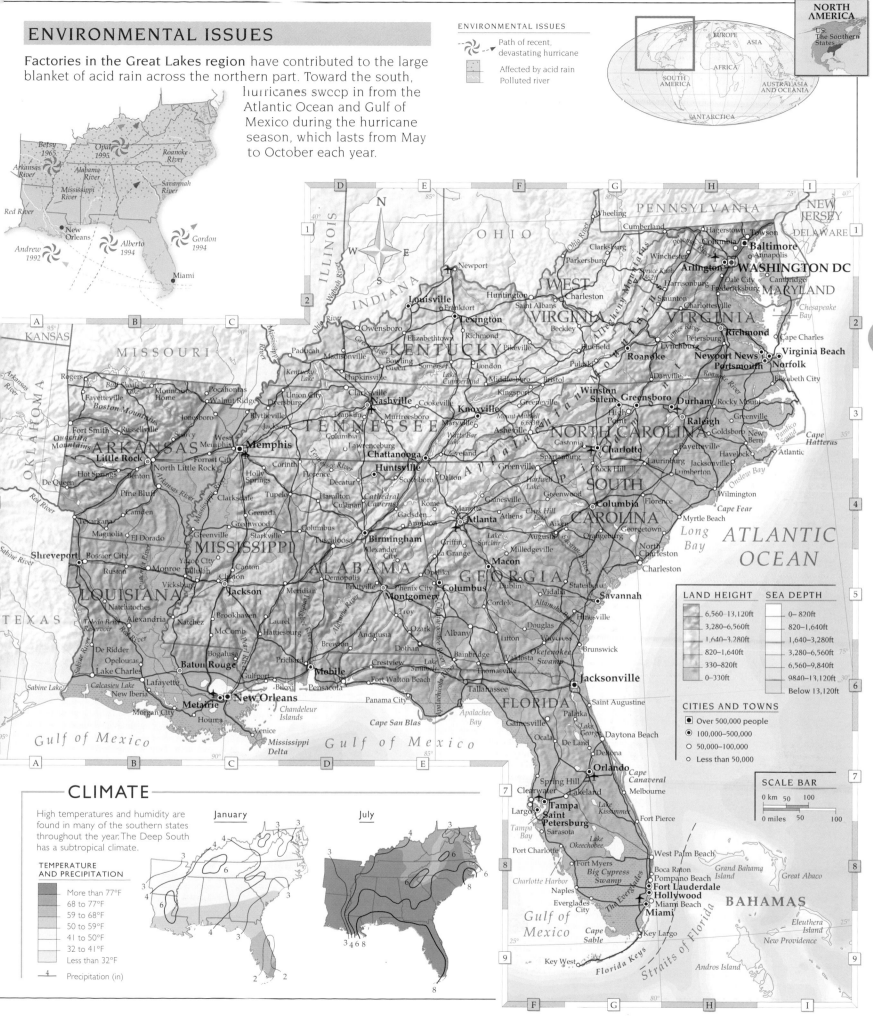

CLIMATE

High temperatures and humidity are found in many of the southern states throughout the year. The Deep South has a subtropical climate.

TEMPERATURE AND PRECIPITATION

- More than 77°F
- 68 to 77°F
- 59 to 68°F
- 50 to 59°F
- 41 to 50°F
- 32 to 41°F
- Less than 32°F

—4— Precipitation (in)

January

July

LAND HEIGHT
- 6,560–13,120ft
- 3,280–6,560ft
- 1,640–3,280ft
- 820–1,640ft
- 330–820ft
- 0–330ft

SEA DEPTH
- 0–820ft
- 820–1,640ft
- 1,640–3,280ft
- 3,280–6,560ft
- 6,560–9,840ft
- 9840–13,120ft
- Below 13,120ft

CITIES AND TOWNS
- ■ Over 500,000 people
- ◉ 100,000–500,000
- ◎ 50,000–100,000
- ○ Less than 50,000

SCALE BAR
0 km 50 100
0 miles 50 100

US: THE GREAT LAKES STATES

ILLINOIS, INDIANA, MICHIGAN, OHIO, WISCONSIN

Good transportation links, excellent farmland, and a wealth of natural resources drew settlers from Europe and the south and east of the US to the Great Lakes states during the late 19th century. By the 1930s, they had become one of the world's most prosperous industrial and agricultural regions. In recent years, the decline in traditional heavy industries has hit some cities hard, leading to unemployment and a rising crime rate.

POPULATION

The Great Lakes states are one of the most densely populated parts of the US. Many of the largest cities in this region – Chicago, Detroit, and Milwaukee – grew up on the banks of the lakes and are connected to each other and the rest of the US by an impressive road and rail network.

INHABITANTS PER SQ MILE

- More than 520
- 260–520
- 130–260
- 65–130
- Less than 65
- ● Major city

URBAN/RURAL POPULATION DIVISION

- Detroit 2.4%
- Chicago 7%
- Indianapolis 1.6%
- Other towns and cities 63%
- Rural population 26%

CLIMATE

Plentiful rainfall waters the agricultural lands. In winter, strong winds sweep across the lakes, and water close to the shore may freeze.

January

July

TEMPERATURE AND PRECIPITATION

- More than 77°F
- 68 to 77°F
- 59 to 68°F
- 32 to 41°F
- 23 to 32°F
- 14 to 23°F
- Less than 14°F
- —4— Precipitation (in)

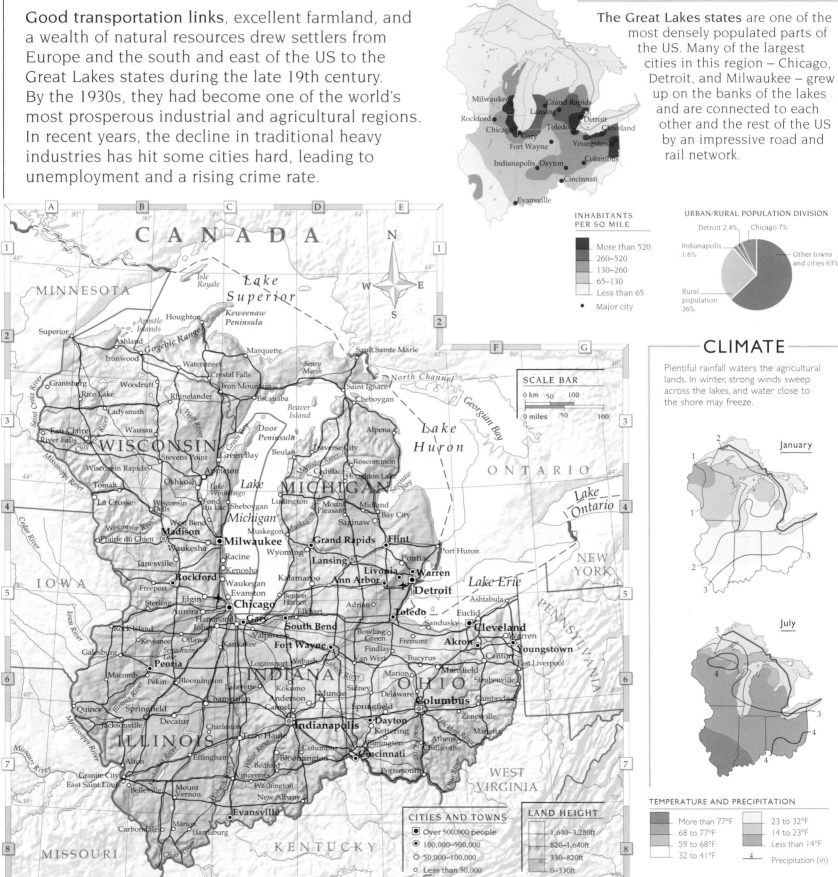

SCALE BAR

0 km 50 100

0 miles 50 100

CITIES AND TOWNS

- ■ Over 500,000 people
- ● 100,000–500,000
- ◉ 50,000–100,000
- ○ Less than 50,000

LAND HEIGHT

- 1,640–3,280ft
- 820–1,640ft
- 330–820ft
- 0–330ft

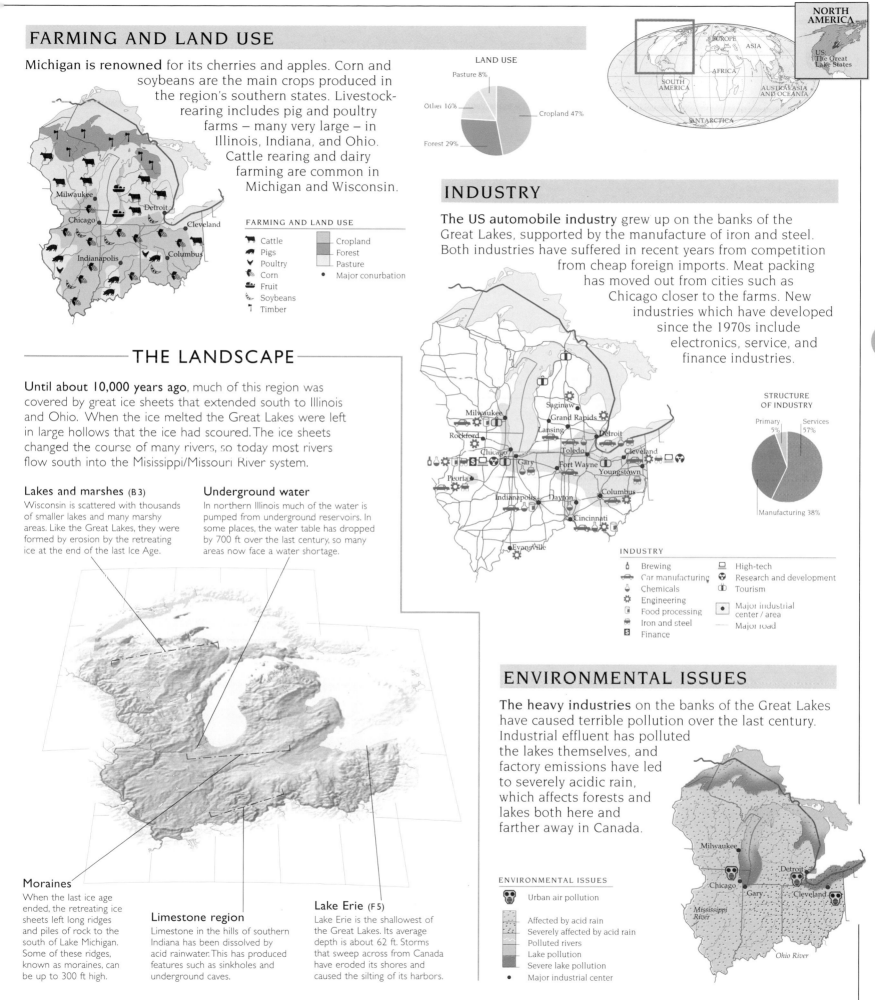

FARMING AND LAND USE

Michigan is renowned for its cherries and apples. Corn and soybeans are the main crops produced in the region's southern states. Livestock-rearing includes pig and poultry farms – many very large – in Illinois, Indiana, and Ohio. Cattle rearing and dairy farming are common in Michigan and Wisconsin.

NORTH AMERICA

US: The Great Lake States

EUROPE ASIA
AFRICA
SOUTH AMERICA AUSTRALASIA AND OCEANIA
ANTARCTICA

LAND USE
Pasture 8%
Other 10%
Cropland 47%
Forest 29%

FARMING AND LAND USE
- Cattle
- Pigs
- Poultry
- Corn
- Fruit
- Soybeans
- Timber
- Cropland
- Forest
- Pasture
- Major conurbation

Milwaukee, Detroit, Chicago, Cleveland, Indianapolis, Columbus

INDUSTRY

The US automobile industry grew up on the banks of the Great Lakes, supported by the manufacture of iron and steel. Both industries have suffered in recent years from competition from cheap foreign imports. Meat packing has moved out from cities such as Chicago closer to the farms. New industries which have developed since the 1970s include electronics, service, and finance industries.

STRUCTURE OF INDUSTRY
Primary 5%
Services 57%
Manufacturing 38%

Milwaukee, Saginaw, Grand Rapids, Rockford, Lansing, Detroit, Chicago, Toledo, Cleveland, Gary, Fort Wayne, Youngstown, Peoria, Indianapolis, Dayton, Columbus, Cincinnati, Evansville

INDUSTRY
- Brewing
- Car manufacturing
- Chemicals
- Engineering
- Food processing
- Iron and steel
- Finance
- High-tech
- Research and development
- Tourism
- Major industrial center / area
- Major road

THE LANDSCAPE

Until about 10,000 years ago, much of this region was covered by great ice sheets that extended south to Illinois and Ohio. When the ice melted the Great Lakes were left in large hollows that the ice had scoured. The ice sheets changed the course of many rivers, so today most rivers flow south into the Misissipp/Missouri River system.

Lakes and marshes (B 3)
Wisconsin is scattered with thousands of smaller lakes and many marshy areas. Like the Great Lakes, they were formed by erosion by the retreating ice at the end of the last Ice Age.

Underground water
In northern Illinois much of the water is pumped from underground reservoirs. In some places, the water table has dropped by 700 ft over the last century, so many areas now face a water shortage.

Moraines
When the last ice age ended, the retreating ice sheets left long ridges and piles of rock to the south of Lake Michigan. Some of these ridges, known as moraines, can be up to 300 ft high.

Limestone region
Limestone in the hills of southern Indiana has been dissolved by acid rainwater. This has produced features such as sinkholes and underground caves.

Lake Erie (F 5)
Lake Erie is the shallowest of the Great Lakes. Its average depth is about 62 ft. Storms that sweep across from Canada have eroded its shores and caused the silting of its harbors.

ENVIRONMENTAL ISSUES

The heavy industries on the banks of the Great Lakes have caused terrible pollution over the last century. Industrial effluent has polluted the lakes themselves, and factory emissions have led to severely acidic rain, which affects forests and lakes both here and farther away in Canada.

Milwaukee, Chicago, Gary, Detroit, Cleveland
Mississippi River
Ohio River

ENVIRONMENTAL ISSUES
- Urban air pollution
- Affected by acid rain
- Severely affected by acid rain
- Polluted rivers
- Lake pollution
- Severe lake pollution
- Major industrial center

US: THE CENTRAL STATES

IOWA, KANSAS, MINNESOTA, MISSOURI, NEBRASKA, NORTH DAKOTA, OKLAHOMA, SOUTH DAKOTA

The prairie states of the central US became one of America's richest agricultural regions in the mid-19th century. Despite the "Dustbowl" crisis of the 1930s, which led many farmers to leave their ruined lands, agriculture is still crucial to the economy, and most people still live in rural areas rather than large cities.

FARMING AND LAND USE

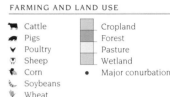

Wheat and corn grow on the fertile plains. Kansas is the leading grower of wheat in the entire US, while Iowa is the leader in corn, soybeans, and livestock. Irrigation projects to combat drought are crucial in large areas. Livestock – including cattle in vast herds; pigs, particularly in Iowa, the Dakotas, and Nebraska; sheep; and turkeys – are raised throughout these states.

LAND USE

Other 11%
Forest 11%
Pasture 34%
Cropland 44%

FARMING AND LAND USE

- Cattle
- Pigs
- Poultry
- Sheep
- Corn
- Soybeans
- Wheat
- Cropland
- Forest
- Pasture
- Wetland
- Major conurbation

INDUSTRY

Industries related to agriculture, such as food processing and the production of farm machinery, are traditional in these states but high-tech industries – such as aeronautical engineering – are increasing and large aerospace plants are found in Wichita and Saint Louis. Oil and gas are extracted in great quantities toward the south of the region, especially in Oklahoma and Kansas.

INDUSTRY

- ✈ Aerospace
- 🚗 Car manufacturing
- ⚗ Chemicals
- ⚙ Engineering
- 🍴 Food processing
- Iron and steel
- 👕 Textiles
- ⬦ Oil and gas
- S Finance
- Major industrial center / area
- Major road

STRUCTURE OF INDUSTRY

Primary 9%
Services 60%
Manufacturing 31%

THE LANDSCAPE

Most of the eastern edge of this region is marked by the Mississippi River, while the Missouri bisects it, running from northwest to southeast. The Great Plains cover most of this area, gradually rising toward the Rocky Mountains at the far western edge of the Central States.

The Badlands (A 4)
The Badlands cover an area of about 2,000 sq miles in South Dakota. Heavily eroded by wind and water, almost nothing grows there.

Minnesota
Minnesota is filled with lakes, hills strewn with boulders, and mineral-rich deposits that have been left behind by the scouring movement of glaciers.

Chimney Rock (A 5)
Chimney Rock stands 500 ft above the plains. It is a remnant of an ancient land surface that was eroded by the North Platte River.

ENVIRONMENTAL ISSUES

Intensive agriculture requires large quantities of water to grow crops. Overintensive use of the land has destroyed the balance of soil and water in the past, leading to fertile farmland being turned into useless areas of "Dustbowl." These states have a great underground store of water known as the Ogallala Aquifer, but overextraction for irrigation is reducing the amount of available water.

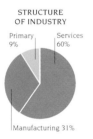

James River
Minneapolis
Saint Paul
Niobrara River
Platte River
Missouri River
Mississippi River
Kansas City
Ogallala Aquifer
Saint Louis
Arkansas River

ENVIRONMENTAL ISSUES

- Urban air pollution
- Affected by acid rain
- Aquifer
- Polluted river
- Risk of desertification
- Major industrial center

Great Plains (D 7)
Little more than a century ago the great flat plains that cover most of these states were home to wild grasses and massive herds of buffalo. In areas where lack of water has made farming impossible, large tracts of land are being allowed to return to grassland.

Great Salt Plains (D 7)
These arid salt plains cover about 45 sq miles of northern Oklahoma. An ancient salt lake once occupied the area. When the salt evaporated, only the salt flats were left.

POPULATION

The inhabitants are largely the descendants of Europeans who came to the region in the late 1800s. The entire region is primarily rural, with enormous tracts of land devoted to growing crops. North Dakota has no city with a population greater than 100,000.

URBAN/RURAL POPULATION DIVISION

Saint Louis 1.8% Kansas City 2.2%
Minneapolis 1.5%
Rural population 41%
Other towns and cities 53.5%

NORTH AMERICA

US: The Central States

INHABITANTS PER SQ MILE

- More than 130
- 65–130
- Less than 65
- • Major city

CLIMATE

The Central States have a continental climate, with hot, dry summers and long, cold winters. Unreliable rainfall can be a problem for farmers on the Great Plains.

January

July

TEMPERATURE AND PRECIPITATION

More than 77°F	23 to 32°F
68 to 77°F	14 to 23°F
59 to 68°F	5 to 14°F
50 to 59°F	Less than 5°F
41 to 50°F	4 Precipitation (in)
32 to 41°F	

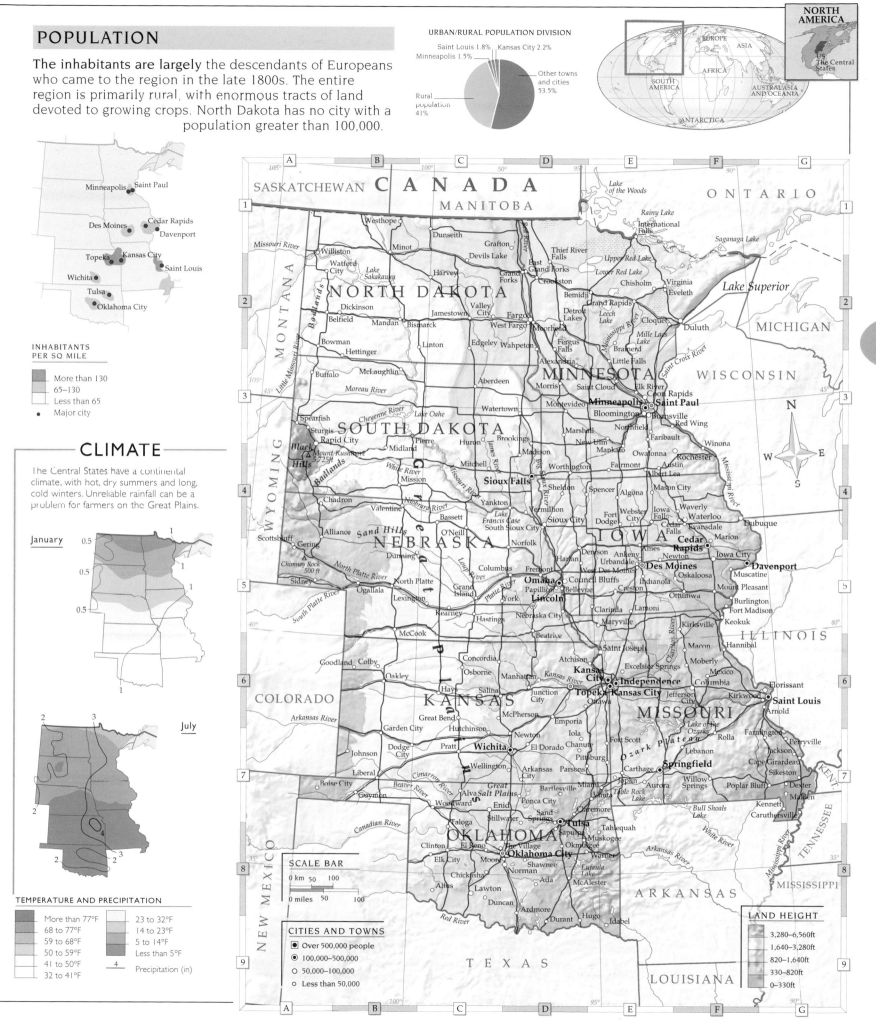

SASKATCHEWAN CANADA MANITOBA ONTARIO

Lake of the Woods

Rainy Lake

International Falls

Saganaga Lake

Lake Superior

MONTANA

Westhope Dunseith Grafton Thief River Falls

Williston Minot Devils Lake Upper Red Lake Virginia Eveleth

Missouri River Watford City Harvey Grand Forks Crookston Chisholm

Lake Sakakawea East Grand Forks Lower Red Lake Cloquet MICHIGAN

NORTH DAKOTA Bemidji Grand Rapids Duluth

Dickinson Jamestown Valley City Fargo Detroit Lakes Leech Lake

Belfield Mandan Bismarck West Fargo Moorhead Mille Lacs Lake

Bowman Linton Edgeley Wahpeton Fergus Falls Brainerd WISCONSIN

Hettinger Alexandria Little Falls

Buffalo McLaughlin Aberdeen Morris MINNESOTA Saint Croix River

Moreau River Watertown Saint Cloud Elk River

SOUTH DAKOTA Montevideo Minneapolis Saint Paul Coon Rapids Burnsville

Spearfish Bloomington Northfield Red Wing

Sturgis Rapid City Pierre Marshall New Ulm Faribault Winona

Black Hills Mount Rushmore 5,725ft Midland Brookings Madison Mankato Owatonna Rochester

Badlands Mitchell Worthington Fairmont Albert Lea Austin Mason City

White River Mission Sheldon Spencer Algona Waverly

Chadron Yankton Vermillion Fort Dodge Webster City Iowa Falls Waterloo Evansdale Dubuque

Valentine Bassett Lake Francis Case South Sioux City Sioux City Cedar Falls Marion

NEBRASKA O'Neill Norfolk IOWA Cedar Rapids Iowa City

Scottsbluff Alliance Sand Hills Denison Ankeny Ames Newton Davenport

Gering Dunning Columbus Fremont Harlan West Des Moines Des Moines Muscatine

Chimney Rock 500 ft North Platte River Loup River Grand Island Omaha Council Bluffs Indianola Mount Pleasant

Sidney Ogallala North Platte York Papillion Bellevue Creston Oskaloosa Burlington

Lexington Platte River Lincoln Ottumwa Fort Madison

Kearney Hastings Nebraska City Clarinda Lamoni Keokuk

McCook Maryville Kirksville ILLINOIS

Beatrice Hannibal

Goodland Colby Concordia Atchison Saint Joseph Macon Moberly

Oakley Osborne Manhattan Excelsior Springs Mexico

COLORADO Hays Salina Kansas River Kansas City Independence Columbia Florissant

KANSAS Junction City Topeka Kansas City Jefferson City Kirkwood Saint Louis

Arkansas River Great Bend McPherson Ottawa MISSOURI Arnold

Garden City Hutchinson Emporia Lake of the Ozarks

Dodge City Pratt Newton Iola Fort Scott Ozark plateau Rolla Farmington

Johnson Wichita El Dorado Chanute Lebanon Jackson Perryville

Liberal Wellington Pittsburg Carthage Springfield Cape Girardeau

Arkansas City Parsons Joplin Aurora Willow Springs Sikeston

Boise City Cimarron River Bartlesville Miami Table Rock Lake Poplar Bluff Dexter

Guymon Beaver River Great Salt Plains Ponca City Bull Shoals Lake Kennett Malden

Woodward Alva Enid Sand Springs Tahlequah White River Caruthersville

Taloga Stillwater Tulsa Sapulpa Muskogee KENTUCKY

Clinton El Reno The Village Okmulgee Warner Arkansas River TENNESSEE

OKLAHOMA Moore Oklahoma City Eufaula Lake ARKANSAS MISSISSIPPI

Elk City Chickasha Shawnee McAlester

Altus Lawton Ada Duncan

Ardmore Durant Hugo Idabel

Red River LOUISIANA

TEXAS

NEW MEXICO

SCALE BAR

0 km 50 100

0 miles 50 100

CITIES AND TOWNS

- ▣ Over 500,000 people
- ◉ 100,000–500,000
- ○ 50,000–100,000
- ∘ Less than 50,000

LAND HEIGHT

- 3,280–6,560ft
- 1,640–3,280ft
- 820–1,640ft
- 330–820ft
- 0–330ft

US: THE SOUTHWESTERN STATES

ARIZONA, NEW MEXICO, TEXAS

Large parts of the southwestern states were purchased from Mexico in 1848. This land of expansive plateaus, spectacular canyons, prairies, and deserts is home to several distinct peoples, whose customs and traditions are still practiced. The Navaho and Hopi own one-third of the land in Arizona, and the ruins of thousand-year-old cliff dwellings built by the Anasazi people are still preserved there today.

ENVIRONMENTAL ISSUES

Desertification is a serious problem in the southwestern states. Lack of water combined with intensive farming has allowed soils to erode. Drought is held at bay by irrigation, but falling water table levels are a cause for concern. New Mexico was the site for many of the earliest nuclear weapons tests, and some places remain contaminated.

ENVIRONMENTAL ISSUES

- Urban air pollution
- Former nuclear test site
- Desert area
- Risk of desertification
- Polluted river
- • Major industrial center

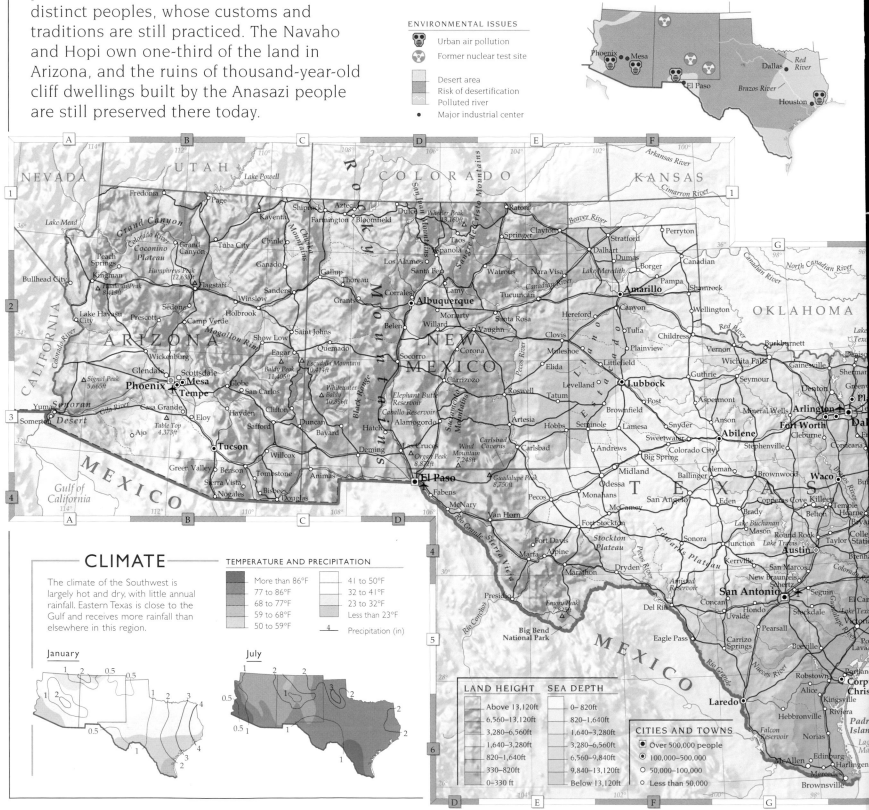

CLIMATE

The climate of the Southwest is largely hot and dry, with little annual rainfall. Eastern Texas is close to the Gulf and receives more rainfall than elsewhere in this region.

January

July

TEMPERATURE AND PRECIPITATION

- More than 86°F
- 77 to 86°F
- 68 to 77°F
- 59 to 68°F
- 50 to 59°F
- 41 to 50°F
- 32 to 41°F
- 23 to 32°F
- Less than 23°F
- 4 Precipitation (in)

LAND HEIGHT | SEA DEPTH

LAND HEIGHT	SEA DEPTH
Above 13,120ft	0– 820ft
6,560–13,120ft	820–1,640ft
3,280–6,560ft	1,640–3,280ft
1,640–3,280ft	3,280–6,560ft
820–1,640ft	6,560–9,840ft
330–820ft	9,840–13,120ft
0–330 ft	Below 13,120ft

CITIES AND TOWNS
- ■ Over 500,000 people
- ◉ 100,000–500,000
- ○ 50,000–100,000
- ○ Less than 50,000

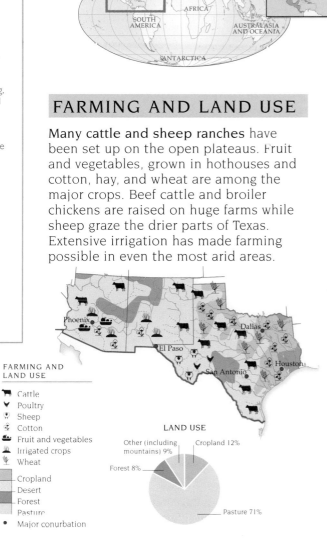

THE LANDSCAPE

The arid, mountainous Colorado Plateau covers nearly half of Arizona, dipping toward the south to form desert basins. Parts of northern New Mexico are forested, but the south consists primarily of semiarid plains. Eastern Texas is bordered by the waters of the Gulf of Mexico, and the farmland of this area is well watered. Western Texas is covered by the Llano Estacado and, in the south, much of the land is arid.

Big Bend (E5)
Big Bend National Park gets its name from the 90° bend that the Rio Grande makes there.

Invading sea
The crust of southeastern Texas is warping, causing the land to subside and allowing the sea to invade. Hurricanes make the situation worse.

Grand Canyon (B1)
The Grand Canyon is a dramatic gorge cut in the rock by the Colorado River. It is about 217 miles long, 418 miles wide, and up to one mile deep.

Carlsbad Caverns (B3)
Carlsbad Caverns are a series of underground caves, consisting of a three-level chain of limestone chambers studded with towering stalactites and stalagmites. They are millions of years old.

Rio Grande (G5)
The Rio Grande, or "Great River" forms all of the border between Texas and Mexico. It flows from its source high up in the Rocky Mountains, to the Gulf of Mexico.

INDUSTRY

Mining and related industries are one of the most important sources of income in the Southwest. Great deposits of oil lie under about 65% of Texas; copper and coal are mined in Arizona and New Mexico. Defense-related industries, including NASA have encouraged the development of many high-tech companies in Texas – and high-tech is also growing in larger cities such as Santa Fe and Phoenix.

SCALE BAR
0 km 100
0 miles 100

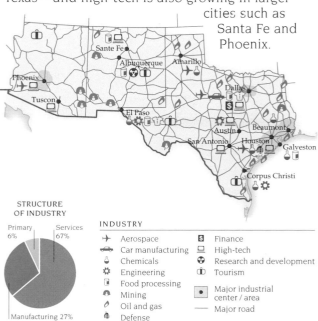

STRUCTURE OF INDUSTRY
Primary 6%
Services 67%
Manufacturing 27%

INDUSTRY
- ✈ Aerospace
- 🚗 Car manufacturing
- ⚗ Chemicals
- ⚙ Engineering
- 🍲 Food processing
- ⛏ Mining
- 🛢 Oil and gas
- Defense
- 💲 Finance
- 🖥 High-tech
- Research and development
- Tourism
- ▪ Major industrial center / area
- — Major road

FARMING AND LAND USE

Many cattle and sheep ranches have been set up on the open plateaus. Fruit and vegetables, grown in hothouses and cotton, hay, and wheat are among the major crops. Beef cattle and broiler chickens are raised on huge farms while sheep graze the drier parts of Texas. Extensive irrigation has made farming possible in even the most arid areas.

FARMING AND LAND USE
- Cattle
- Poultry
- Sheep
- Cotton
- Fruit and vegetables
- Irrigated crops
- Wheat
- Cropland
- Desert
- Forest
- Pasture
- ● Major conurbation

LAND USE
Other (including mountains) 9%
Cropland 12%
Forest 8%
Pasture 71%

POPULATION

The descendants of Mexican and Spanish settlers and numerous groups of Native Americans live in the southwestern states. The great cities of Texas grew up on income from cattle-ranching and the oil industry. Much of Arizona and New Mexico is sparsely populated, but today people are moving to these states to escape the cold winters elsewhere.

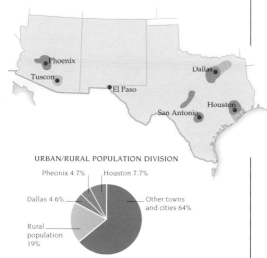

INHABITANTS PER SQ MILE
- More than 130
- 65–130
- Less than 65
- ● Major city

URBAN/RURAL POPULATION DIVISION
Pheonix 4.7%
Houston 7.7%
Dallas 4.6%
Other towns and cities 64%
Rural population 19%

US: THE MOUNTAIN STATES

COLORADO, IDAHO, MONTANA, NEVADA, UTAH, WYOMING

These states are home to some of the nation's most fantastic landscapes: endless treeless plains, craggy peaks, incredible desert landforms, and the salt flats of Utah. Although this was one of the last regions of the US to be settled, great mineral reserves have been exploited here in recent years, and new industries have grown up in some of the larger cities. Utah is the headquarters of the Mormon religion.

INDUSTRY

Rich mineral reserves, including coal, oil, and gas, are mined throughout the region and forests are a source of good-quality timber. In the larger cities of Colorado and Utah, growing industries include high-tech computer firms. Many tourists are drawn to this region to ski in the resorts of Colorado and to explore the wilderness.

STRUCTURE OF INDUSTRY

Manufacturing 23%
Primary 7%
Services 70%

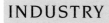

INDUSTRY

- 🝊 Chemicals
- 📦 Food processing
- ⚊ Textiles
- ⚒ Coal
- ⛏ Mining
- 🛢 Oil and gas
- 🪵 Timber processing
- ♠ Gambling
- 💻 High-tech
- ☢ Research and development
- ⚓ Tourism
- • Major industrial center / area
- — Major road

FARMING AND LAND USE

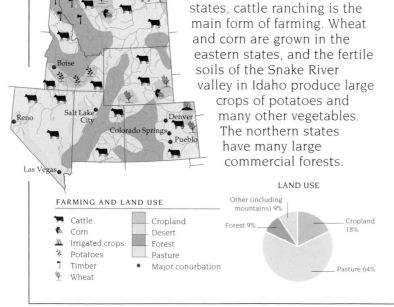

In the southern mountain states, cattle ranching is the main form of farming. Wheat and corn are grown in the eastern states, and the fertile soils of the Snake River valley in Idaho produce large crops of potatoes and many other vegetables. The northern states have many large commercial forests.

FARMING AND LAND USE

- 🐄 Cattle
- 🌽 Corn
- 🌾 Irrigated crops
- 🥔 Potatoes
- 🌲 Timber
- 🌾 Wheat

Cropland
Desert
Forest
Pasture
• Major conurbation

LAND USE

Other (including mountains) 9%
Forest 9%
Cropland 18%
Pasture 64%

POPULATION

Colorado, with the growing city of Denver, is the most populous of the mountain states. In other states, people have settled close to sources of water such as Great Salt Lake in Utah. Many towns have less than 10,000 people and are far apart.

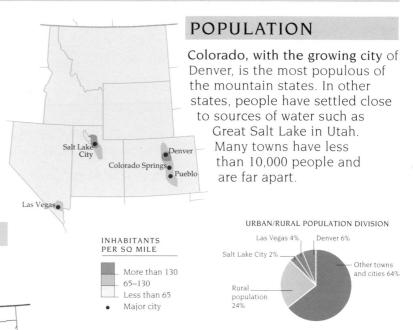

INHABITANTS PER SQ MILE
- More than 130
- 65–130
- Less than 65
- • Major city

URBAN/RURAL POPULATION DIVISION

Las Vegas 4%
Denver 6%
Salt Lake City 2%
Other towns and cities 64%
Rural population 24%

THE LANDSCAPE

The great Rocky Mountains and many smaller mountain ranges cover almost all of this region. Only eastern Montana is not mountainous. Here western parts of the Great Plains rise to meet the mountains. Parts of the southern mountain states are very arid with spectacular scenery, including blocklike *mesas*, formed by erosion.

Continental Divide
From this watershed, crossing the Lewis Range, rivers flow in different directions across North America. Some flow east to Hudson Bay, some south to the Gulf of Mexico and others west to the Pacific Ocean.

Yellowstone National Park (D 3)
Yellowstone was set up in 1872 as the first national park in the US. Water from hot springs has deposited minerals as it cools, forming white rock terraces close to the springs.

Snake River (C 4)

Great Plains (E 2)

North Platte River (F 4)

Artificial lake (C 7)
Lake Mead – more than 177 miles long, is one of the largest artificial lakes in the world. It was formed in 1936, when the Hoover Dam was built across the Colorado River.

Great Salt Lake (C 5)

Mountainous state
Colorado has more than 1,500 peaks more than 9,840 ft high – this is six times the number of high mountains found in the Swiss Alps.

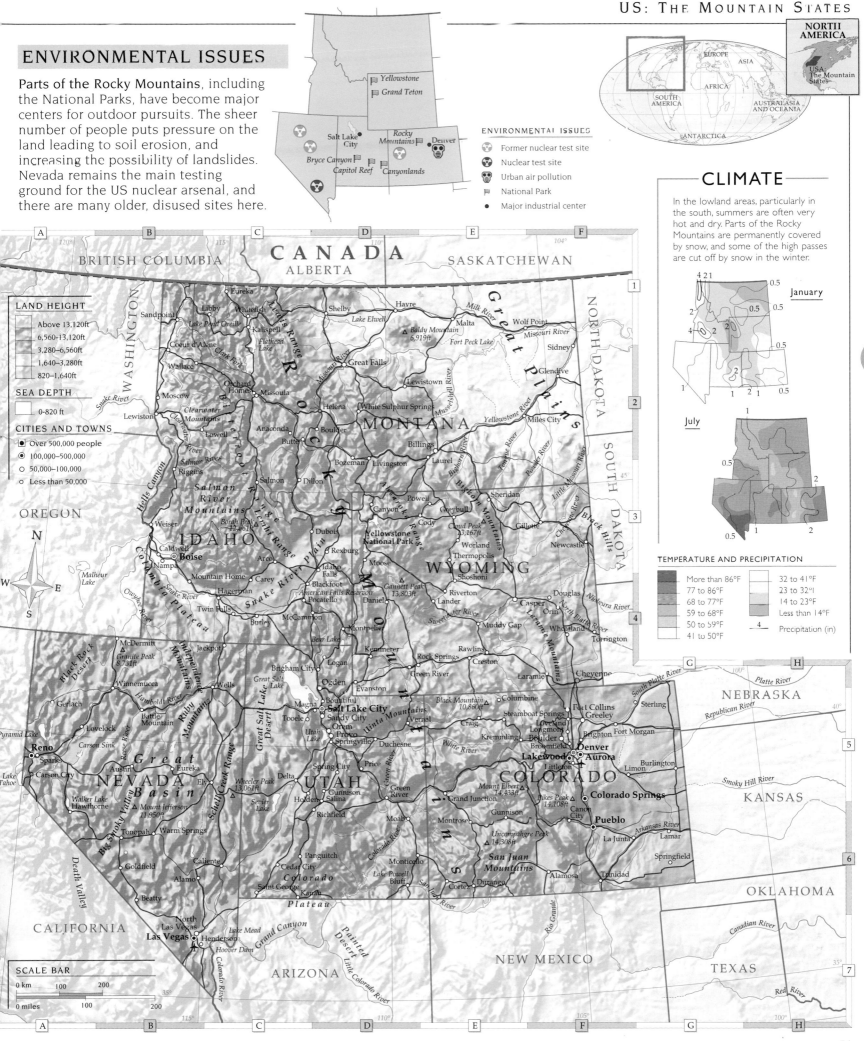

ENVIRONMENTAL ISSUES

Parts of the Rocky Mountains, including the National Parks, have become major centers for outdoor pursuits. The sheer number of people puts pressure on the land leading to soil erosion, and increasing the possibility of landslides. Nevada remains the main testing ground for the US nuclear arsenal, and there are many older, disued sites here.

ENVIRONMENTAL ISSUES

- Former nuclear test site
- Nuclear test site
- Urban air pollution
- National Park
- Major industrial center

NORTH AMERICA

USA: The Mountain States

CLIMATE

In the lowland areas, particularly in the south, summers are often very hot and dry. Parts of the Rocky Mountains are permanently covered by snow, and some of the high passes are cut off by snow in the winter.

January

July

TEMPERATURE AND PRECIPITATION

More than 86°F	32 to 41°F
77 to 86°F	23 to 32°F
68 to 77°F	14 to 23°F
59 to 68°F	Less than 14°F
50 to 59°F	—4— Precipitation (in)
41 to 50°F	

LAND HEIGHT
- Above 13,120ft
- 6,560–13,120ft
- 3,280–6,560ft
- 1,640–3,280ft
- 820–1,640ft

SEA DEPTH
- 0–820 ft

CITIES AND TOWNS
- Over 500,000 people
- 100,000–500,000
- 50,000–100,000
- Less than 50,000

SCALE BAR

0 km   100   200

0 miles   100   200

51

US: THE PACIFIC STATES

CALIFORNIA, OREGON, WASHINGTON

The earliest European visitors to the West Coast were fur-trappers and miners, but the Gold Rush of 1849 brought in the first major wave of settlers. Drawn by tales of the beautiful scenery, pleasant climate, and fertile valleys, more people arrived on the newly built railroads. People from all over the world are still moving into this region, seeking jobs in the dynamic economy and the famous laid-back lifestyle.

INDUSTRY

The Pacific States are the center of the high-tech computer industry with Silicon Valley between San Francisco and San Jose, and electronics industries growing in Portland and Seattle. Other major industries include research and development for the defense industry, filmmaking in Los Angeles, food processing and lumbering. Tourism is well developed throughout the Pacific States.

STRUCTURE OF INDUSTRY

Primary 6%
Services 68%
Manufacturing 25%

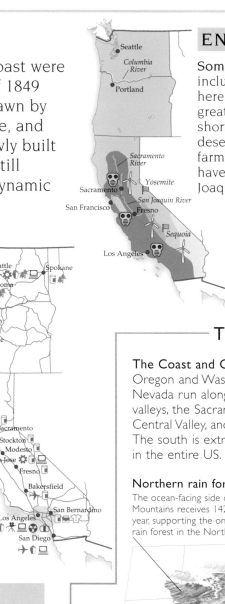

INDUSTRY

- ✈ Aerospace
- ⚗ Chemicals
- ⚙ Engineering
- ▣ Food processing
- ⚒ Iron and steel
- ⚓ Shipbuilding
- ▼ Textiles
- ⚜ Timber processing
- ✹ Film industry
- ▭ High-tech
- ⊛ Research and development
- ⌖ Tourism
- ⊡ Major industrial center / area
- — Major road

FARMING AND LAND USE

California's Central Valley and the river valleys of Washington and Oregon provide ideal conditions for a wide range of fruit and vegetables, including citrus fruit and grapes. Poultry farming is widespread in the northwest and there are many large cattle ranches. Millions of acres of commercial forest are located in this region.

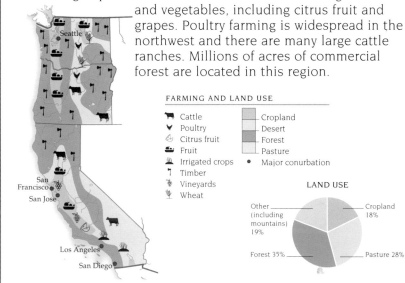

FARMING AND LAND USE

- 🐂 Cattle
- ⌄ Poultry
- 🍊 Citrus fruit
- 🍓 Fruit
- ⚒ Irrigated crops
- 🌲 Timber
- 🌾 Vineyards
- 🌿 Wheat
- Cropland
- Desert
- Forest
- Pasture
- ● Major conurbation

LAND USE

Other (including mountains) 19%
Cropland 18%
Forest 35%
Pasture 28%

ENVIRONMENTAL ISSUES

Some of the great national parks of the US, including Yosemite and Sequoia, are found here. The immense numbers of visitors put great pressure on the landscape. Water is in short supply in large parts of California, and desertification, caused by overintense farming methods, is a problem. Wind farms have been set up on the hills above the San Joaquin valley to provide alternative energy.

ENVIRONMENTAL ISSUES

- ⚑ National park
- ☠ Urban air pollution
- ⚡ Wind farm
- Desert area
- Risk of desertification
- Severe risk of desertification
- Polluted rivers
- ● Major industrial center

THE LANDSCAPE

The Coast and Cascade ranges run north–south through Oregon and Washington while further south, the high Sierra Nevada run along California's eastern fringes. Two broad valleys, the Sacramento and San Joaquin, are known as the Central Valley, and form a trough beneath the Sierra Nevada. The south is extremely dry – Death Valley is the hottest place in the entire US.

Northern rain forest (B 2)
The ocean-facing side of the Olympic Mountains receives 142 in of rain every year, supporting the only true temperate rain forest in the Northern Hemisphere.

Hells Canyon (D 3)
Hells Canyon is North America's deepest gorge. Running through part of Oregon, it was created as the Snake River cut down through the land.

Volcanic eruption (B 2)
Mount St. Helens erupted in 1980, killing 57 people and destroying a vast area.

San Andreas Fault
The San Andreas Fault runs for 650 miles underneath California. When both sides of the fault move at different rates, tremors and earthquakes result.

Hottest place (D 7)
In 1913, Death Valley set the record for the highest temperature ever recorded in the US, at 134° F.

NORTH AMERICA

US: The Pacific States

CLIMATE

Coastal northern California, Washington, and Oregon have a mild climate and plentiful rainfall. Farther south, temperatures rise and there is little rain.

January

July

TEMPERATURE AND PRECIPITATION

More than 86°F
77 to 86°F
68 to 77°F
59 to 68°F
50 to 59°F
41 to 50°F
32 to 41°F
23 to 32°F
Less than 23°F

— 4 — Precipitation (in)

POPULATION

California has the most diverse population in the entire US and is one of the most populated states. Oregon and Washington are far less densely populated, but increasing numbers of people are moving into the Northwest and to cities such as Seattle. Los Angeles is one of the world's most sprawling urban centers.

INHABITANTS PER SQ MILE

More than 520
260–520
130–260
65–130
Less than 65

● Major city

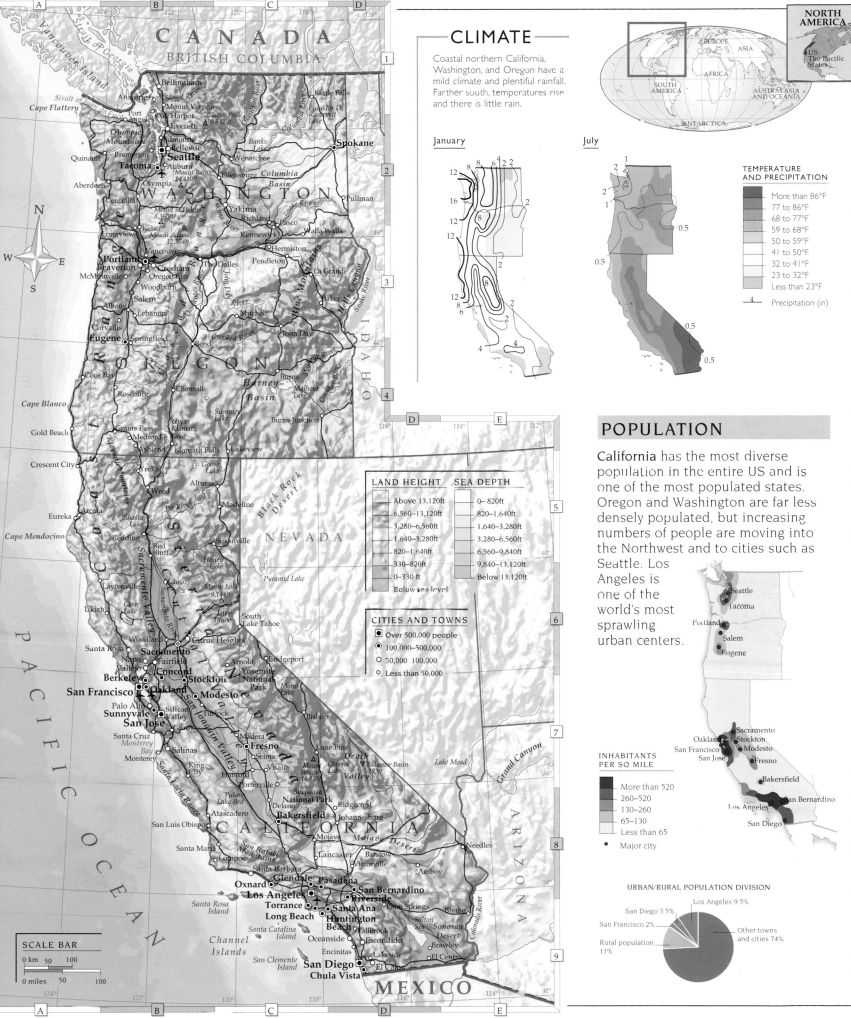

LAND HEIGHT

Above 13,120ft
6,560–13,120ft
3,280–6,560ft
1,640–3,280ft
820–1,640ft
330–820ft
0–330 ft
Below sea level

SEA DEPTH

0– 820ft
820–1,640ft
1,640–3,280ft
3,280–6,560ft
6,560–9,840ft
9,840–13,120ft
Below 13,120ft

CITIES AND TOWNS

■ Over 500,000 people
● 100,000–500,000
○ 50,000 100,000
○ Less than 50,000

SCALE BAR

0 km 50 100

0 miles 50 100

URBAN/RURAL POPULATION DIVISION

Los Angeles 9.5%
San Diego 3.5%
San Francisco 2%
Rural population 11%
Other towns and cities 74%

ALASKA

A **magnificent land** of mountains, forests, and snowfields, with rich oil and mineral reserves, Alaska was purchased from Russia for $1 million in 1867. Just over half a million people live here, many drawn by the oil industry. Some of Alaska's native peoples like the Aleuts and Inupiaq still live by hunting and fishing.

ENVIRONMENTAL ISSUES

Much of northern Alaska is covered by permafrost (permanently frozen ground). The Trans-Alaskan Pipeline, which brings oil from Prudhoe Bay to Valdez, was built above ground to stop the permafrost melting. A number of major oil spills have threatened Alaska's unique environment.

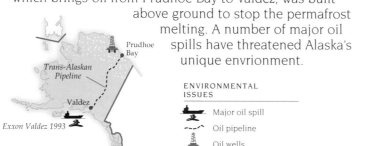

ENVIRONMENTAL ISSUES

- 🚢 Major oil spill
- ┉ Oil pipeline
- ⛽ Oil wells
- ▦ Permafrost zone
- ● Major town

INDUSTRY

The **Alaskan economy** is dominated by the oil business. The oilfields of Alaska are of a similar size to those in the Persian Gulf. Minerals including gold are mined in the mountains, and paper products are exported to countries on the Pacific Rim.

INDUSTRY

- 🝆 Chemicals
- ⛏ Mining
- 🛢 Oil and gas
- 🏭 Timber processing
- ▪ Major industrial center
- — Major road

FARMING AND LAND USE

Salmon are caught in great numbers in the waters of the north Pacific. Much of the state – more than 5.5 million acres – is covered by forest which is commercially lumbered. Most food must be imported, although fruit is grown in hothouses near the larger cities.

FARMING AND LAND USE

- 🐟 Fishing
- 🍎 Fruit
- 🌲 Timber
- Barren
- Forest
- Mountains
- Tundra
- ● Major conurbation

CLIMATE

Parts of northern Alaska are frozen year-round and can be cut off entirely in the winter. Summers are milder – especially in the Aleutians.

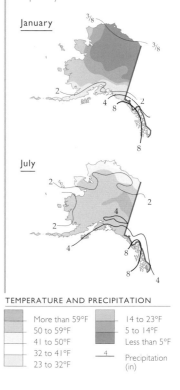

January

July

TEMPERATURE AND PRECIPITATION

- More than 59°F
- 50 to 59°F
- 41 to 50°F
- 32 to 41°F
- 23 to 32°F
- 14 to 23°F
- 5 to 14°F
- Less than 5°F
- —4— Precipitation (in)

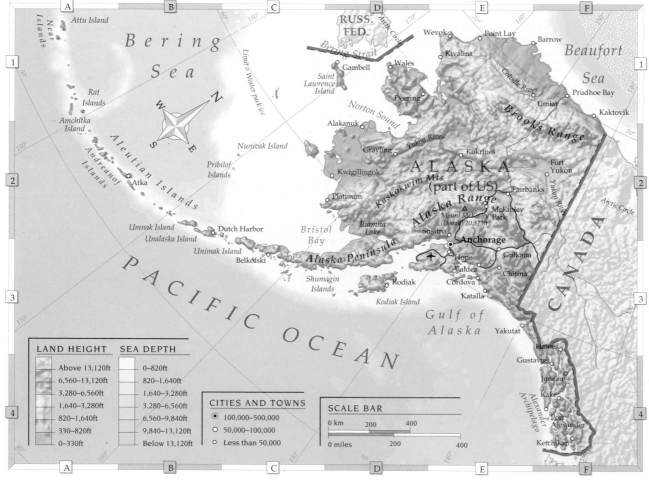

LAND HEIGHT
- Above 13,120ft
- 6,560–13,120ft
- 3,280–6,560ft
- 1,640–3,280ft
- 820–1,640ft
- 330–820ft
- 0–330ft

SEA DEPTH
- 0–820ft
- 820–1,640ft
- 1,640–3,280ft
- 3,280–6,560ft
- 6,560–9,840ft
- 9,840–13,120ft
- Below 13,120ft

CITIES AND TOWNS
- ◉ 100,000–500,000
- ○ 50,000–100,000
- ○ Less than 50,000

SCALE BAR

0 km   200   400

0 miles   200   400

HAWAII

Hawaii is the 50th US state. It lies far from the mainland in the middle of the Pacific Ocean. The volcanoes that form the island chain are still active, and eruptions are frequent. The islands' indigenous peoples are Polynesians, but continued immigration means that they now make up only 2% of the population.

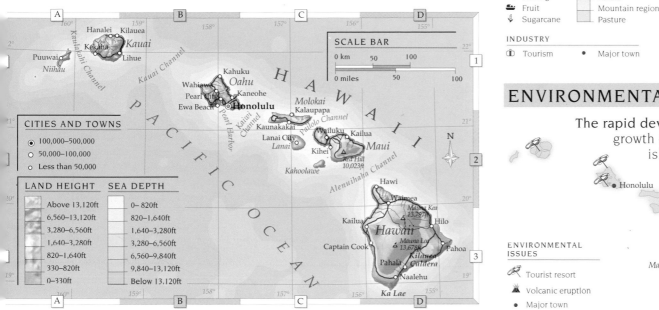

CITIES AND TOWNS
- ◉ 100,000–500,000
- ◎ 50,000–100,000
- ○ Less than 50,000

LAND HEIGHT
- Above 13,120ft
- 6,560–13,120ft
- 3,280–6,560ft
- 1,640–3,280ft
- 820–1,640ft
- 330–820ft
- 0–330ft

SEA DEPTH
- 0–820ft
- 820–1,640ft
- 1,640–3,280ft
- 3,280–6,560ft
- 6,560–9,840ft
- 9,840–13,120ft
- Below 13,120ft

SCALE BAR
0 km 50 100
0 miles 50 100

INDUSTRY AND LAND USE

Tourism is the most important industry in Hawaii, employing more than half the population. The naval base at Pearl Harbor also provides jobs for numerous people. The many large plantations grow sugarcane, bananas, and tropical fruit for export.

FARMING AND LAND USE
- Cattle
- Fishing
- Fruit
- Sugarcane
- Cropland
- Forest
- Mountain region
- Pasture

INDUSTRY
- ⊕ Tourism
- ● Major town

ENVIRONMENTAL ISSUES

The rapid development of tourism and the growth of resorts are destroying the islands' unique flora and fauna. The frequent volcanic eruptions may threaten the many tourist areas.

ENVIRONMENTAL ISSUES
- Tourist resort
- Volcanic eruption
- ● Major town

Mauna Loa – 1984
Kilauea – 1983

US OVERSEAS TERRITORIES

America's overseas territories have traditionally been seen as strategically or economically important. In most cases, the local population has been given a say in deciding whether it wants to govern itself. A US commonwealth territory has a greater level of independence than a US unincorporated or external territory. The US has 13 overseas territories: the four largest are shown here.

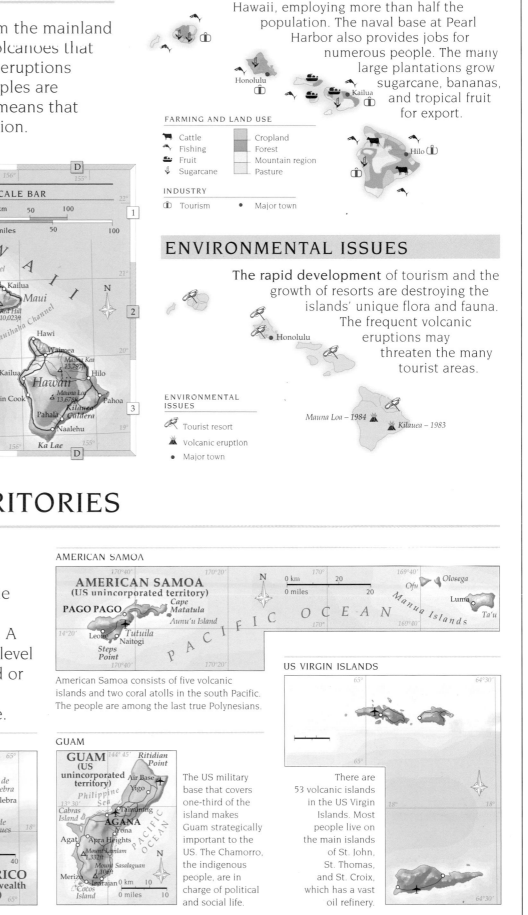

AMERICAN SAMOA

American Samoa consists of five volcanic islands and two coral atolls in the south Pacific. The people are among the last true Polynesians.

PUERTO RICO

The large island of Puerto Rico has a population of more than 3.5 million people. In recent years there have been campaigns to make it the 51st US state.

PUERTO RICO (US commonwealth territory)

GUAM

The US military base that covers one-third of the island makes Guam strategically important to the US. The Chamorro, the indigenous people, are in charge of political and social life.

US VIRGIN ISLANDS

There are 53 volcanic islands in the US Virgin Islands. Most people live on the main islands of St. John, St. Thomas, and St. Croix, which has a vast oil refinery.

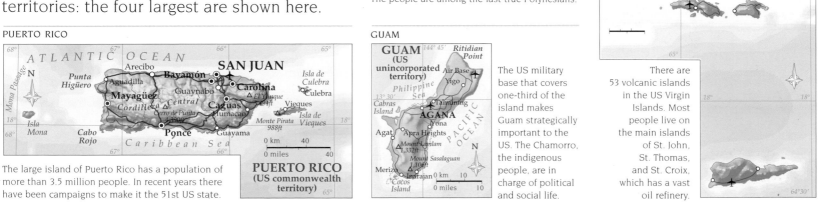

MEXICO

Mexico is a large country with a rich mixture of traditions and cultures. The ancient civilization of the Aztecs that flourished here was crushed by Spanish invaders in the 16th century. Spain ruled Mexico until its independence in 1836, and today the country has the world's largest and fastest-growing Spanish-speaking population. Mexico is mostly dry and mountainous, and farmland is limited, so the country has to import most of the basic foods it needs to feed its people.

FARMING AND LAND USE

Most of the land suitable for farming is planted with corn – a big part of the Mexican diet. Along the Gulf coast coffee, sugarcane, and cotton are grown on plantations for export. Parts of the dry north are irrigated to grow cotton, but most of the land is taken up by large cattle ranches. Fishing, especially for shellfish such as lobster and shrimp is important in coastal areas.

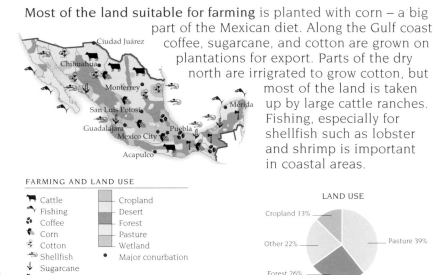

FARMING AND LAND USE

- Cattle
- Fishing
- Coffee
- Corn
- Cotton
- Shellfish
- Sugarcane
- Timber
- Cropland
- Desert
- Forest
- Pasture
- Wetland
- Major conurbation

LAND USE

Cropland 13%
Other 22%
Pasture 39%
Forest 26%

THE LANDSCAPE

Much of Mexico is made up of a high plateau. The climate there is very dry and varies between true desert in the north, and semidesert farther south. The plateau is separated from the coastal plains by two long, rugged mountain chains: the Eastern Sierra Madre and the Western Sierra Madre. Toward the south, the mountain ranges join, meeting in the region of high volcanic peaks that surround Mexico City.

Baja (Lower) California (B 3)
This long and very dry peninsula separates the Gulf of California from the Pacific Ocean. The Gulf was formed after the last Ice Age, when the sea rose to flood a major rift valley.

The Rio Grande (D 2)
This river flows from Colorado in the US and forms much of Mexico's northern border. It crosses a vast arid area on its way to the Gulf of Mexico.

Earthquakes and volcanoes
Volcanic activity is common in Mexico. Popocatépetl (F 5) and Volcán El Chichónal (G 5) have erupted recently, and Mexico City was hit by a devastating earthquake in 1985.

Eastern Sierra Madre (D 5)

Yucatan Peninsula (H 4)
The Yucatan Peninsula is a low, wide tableland, formed by layers of limestone. Limestone absorbs water, so there are few rivers on the peninsula, and the tropical rain forests found there are fed mainly by streams and underground water.

Western Sierra Madre (C 3)

POPULATION

Most of the north is sparsely populated due to the hot, dry climate and lack of cultivable farmland. As people have migrated from the countryside in search of work, the cities have grown dramatically; almost 75% of Mexicans now live in urban areas. Mexico City is home to almost a quarter of the population and is one of the world's largest cities.

INHABITANTS PER SQ MILE

- More than 520
- 260–520
- 130–260
- Less than 130
- ■ Capital city
- • Major city

URBAN/RURAL POPULATION DIVISION

Mexico City 21.6%
Guadalajara 2.4%
Monterrey 2%
Rural population 26%
Other towns and cities 48%

ENVIRONMENTAL ISSUES

Fast, unplanned growth has led to poor sanitation and water supplies in Mexico City, while the wall of mountains that surrounds the city traps pollution from cars and factories, giving it some of the world's worst air pollution. Much of Mexico's tropical rainforest has been felled, leading to increased soil erosion. Land clearance farther north is also causing desertification.

ENVIRONMENTAL ISSUES

- Volcanic eruption
- Urban air pollution
- Risk of desertification
- Deforested areas
- Remaining tropical forests
- • Major industrial center

Guadalajara
Nevado de Colima 1994
Mexico City
Popocatépetl 1994
Volcán El Chichónal 1994

INDUSTRY

Oil and gas on the Gulf coast are the biggest source of income. Mexico is also rich in other minerals; it is the world's top silver producer. Manufacturing is centered around Mexico City and along the US border, where mainly foreign-owned factories assemble products for export. Tourism is increasing throughout Mexico.

Tijuana
Mexicali
Ciudad Juárez
Chihuahua
Nuevo Laredo
Piedras Negras
Reynosa
Torreón
Monterrey
Tampico
Mérida
San Luis Potosí
Guadalajara
Veracruz
Mexico City
Manzanillo
Puebla
Minatitlán
Oaxaca
Salina Cruz

STRUCTURE OF INDUSTRY

Primary 8%
Services 64%
Manufacturing 28%

INDUSTRY

- Car manufacturing
- Electronics
- Engineering
- Food processing
- Iron and steel
- Oil refining
- Textiles
- Mining
- Oil and gas
- Tourism
- Major industrial center / area
- Major road

CLIMATE

Northern Mexico and the peninsula of Baja California are dry, hot, and largely desert. Toward the south, rainfall increases, especially in July. Moist, warm conditions allow rain forests to grow.

January

July

TEMPERATURE AND PRECIPITATION

More than 86°F
77 to 86°F
68 to 77°F
59 to 68°F
50 to 59°F
41 to 50°F
Less than 41°F

4 — Precipitation (in)

ALABAMA
GEORGIA
MISSISSIPPI
FLORIDA
TEXAS
LOUISIANA
UNITED STATES OF AMERICA
ARIZONA
NEW MEXICO

Red River
Sabine River
Mississippi River
Mississippi Delta

Ciudad Juárez
Nogales
Agua Prieta
Samalayuca
Cananea
Nuevo Casas Grandes
Magdalena
Cumpas
El Sueco
Ojinaga
Acuña
Piedras Negras
aborca
San Pedro de la Cueva
El Sáuz
Boquillas
San Miguel
Hermosillo
Chihuahua
Nueva Rosita
Isla Tiburón
Cuauhtémoc
Delicias
Camargo
Sabinas
Nuevo Laredo
la Ángel la Guarda
Guaymas
Empalme
Esperanza
Jiménez
Santa Barbara
Sabinas Hidalgo
Ciudad Miguel Alemán
Padre Island
San Ignacio
Ciudad Obregón
Navojoa
San Francisco del Oro
Hidalgo del Parral
Reynosa
Matamoros
San
Huatabampo
Santa Barbara
Gómez Palacio
San Pedro
Monclova
Monterrey
Saltillo
Montemorelos
Linares
Laguna Madre
San Blas
Ciudad Lerdo
Torreón
Parras
Los Mochis
Guasave Guamúchil
Navolato
Miguel Asúa
Juan Aldama
Ciudad Victoria
Isla Magdalena
Culiacán
Río Grande
Ciudad Mante
Ciudad Madero
Isla Santa Margarita
El Dorado
Durango
Fresnillo
Tampico
Panuco
La Paz
Zacatecas
Guadalupe
San Luis Potosí
Ciudad Valles
Santa Genoveva Miraflores 7,894ft
Mazatlán
Villanueva
Laguna de Tamiahua
San Lucas Cape
Escuinapa
Aguascalientes
Jalpa
Río Verde
Dolores
Tamazunchale
Tuxpán
Papantla
Acaponeta
Tuxpan
Lagos de Moreno
León
Guanajuato
Poza Rica
Tepic
Tlaltenango
Querétaro
Tulancingo
Isla San Juanito
Pachuca
Isla María Madre
Guadalajara
Irapuato
Isla María Magdalena
Chapala
Lago de Chapala
Teziutlán
Xalapa
Isla María Cleofas
Puerto Vallarta
Tlaquepaque
Morelia
MEXICO CITY
Veracruz
Zamora de Hidalgo
Toluca
Perote
Alvarado
Ciudad Guzmán
Tuxpan
Cuernavaca
Puebla
Córdoba
Coatzacoalcos
Colima
Uruapan
Zacatepec
Tehuacán
Minatitlán
Manzanillo
Tecomán
Aguililla
Presa del Infiernillo
Taxco
Iguala
Cuautla
San Andrés Tuxtla
Volcán El Chichonal
San Cristóbal de Las Casas
Lázaro Cárdenas
Ixtapa
Río Balsas
Chilpancingo
Oaxaca
Ixtepec
Matías Romero
Chiapa de Cerzo
Comitán
Tecpan
Sierra Madre del Sur
Ixtepec
Presa de la Angostura
Acapulco
Pinotepa Nacional
Tehuantepec
Juchitán
Pijijiapán
Isthmus of Tehuantepec
Salina Cruz
Arriaga
Mahuatlán
Puerto Escondido
Puerto Ángel
Gulf of Tehuantepec
Escuintla
Huixtla
Tapachula
Ciudad Hidalgo
GUATEMALA
HONDURAS
EL SALVADOR

Gulf of Mexico
Yucatan Channel
Río Lagartos
Cancún
Progreso
Tizimín
Isla Cozumel
Mérida
Motul
Umán
Valladolid
Ticul
Peto
Oxkutzcab
Campeche
Yucatan Peninsula
Felipe Carrillo Puerto
Champotón
Chetumal
Bay of Campeche
Laguna de Términos
Frontera
Comalcalco
Villahermosa
Carmen
Francisco Escárcega
Macuspana
BELIZE

Tropic of Cancer

LAND HEIGHT
- Above 13,120ft
- 6,560–13,120ft
- 3,280–6,560ft
- 1,640–3,280ft
- 820–1,640ft
- 330–820ft
- 0–330ft

SEA DEPTH
- 0–820ft
- 820–1,640ft
- 1,640–3,280ft
- 3,280–6,560ft
- 6,560–9,840ft
- 9,840–13,120ft
- Below 13,120ft

CITIES AND TOWNS
- Over 500,000 people
- 100,000–500,000
- 50,000–100,000
- Less than 50,000

Islas Revillagigedo (part of Mexico)
Isla San Benedicto
Isla Roca Partida
Isla Socorro
Sierra Madre
Western Sierra Madre
Eastern Sierra Madre
California
Bahía de La Paz
Pacific Ocean
Gulf of Honduras

SCALE BAR
0 km 200
0 miles 200

CENTRAL AMERICA

BELIZE, COSTA RICA, EL SALVADOR, GUATEMALA, HONDURAS, NICARAGUA, PANAMA

Central America lies on a narrow bridge of land which links North and South America. All the countries here, except Belize, were once governed by Spain. Today, most of their people are *mestizos* – a mix of the original Maya Indian inhabitants and Spanish settlers. The hot, steamy climate is ideal for growing tropical crops, such as coffee and bananas, which are exported worldwide.

FARMING AND LAND USE

About half of all the agricultural products grown here are exported. The Pacific coast has fertile, well-watered land suitable for growing cotton and sugarcane. In the central highlands are big coffee plantations and ranches where beef cattle are raised. Bananas grow well along the humid Caribbean coastal plain, and shrimp and lobster are caught offshore.

FARMING AND LAND USE

- 🐂 Cattle
- 🦪 Shellfish
- 🍌 Bananas
- ☕ Coffee
- 🌽 Corn
- ❀ Cotton
- ⚘ Sugarcane
- ⚑ Timber

- ■ Cropland
- ■ Forest
- ■ Pasture
- • Major conurbation

Guatemala City
Tegucigalpa
San Salvador
Managua
San José
Colón
Panama City

LAND USE

Pasture 28%
Forest 40%
Cropland 14%
Other 18%

ENVIRONMENTAL ISSUES

Central America's rain forests are rapidly being cut down for timber and to make way for farmland and land for building. Over half of Guatemala's forests have been felled, mostly in the last 30 years. The situation is also bleak in Honduras, Costa Rica, and Nicaragua. Central America lies in a volcanically active zone, and the line of volcanoes running through the region have erupted many times this century.

Volcán Tacaná 1986
Volcán de Fuego 1974
Volcán de Izalco 1958
Volcán Cerro Negro 1995
Volcán Concepcion 1986
Volcán Arenal 1995

ENVIRONMENTAL ISSUES
- ▲ Volcanic eruption
- ■ Deforested areas
- ■ Remaining forests

POPULATION

Central America's people live mainly in the valleys of the central highlands or along the Pacific coastal plains. Despite the threat of volcanic eruptions and earthquakes, towns and cities were developed in these areas because of the fertile volcanic soils found there. Just over half the population still lives in rural areas, mostly in small villages or remote settlements, but the cities have expanded rapidly and overcrowding has become a serious problem.

BELMOPAN
GUATEMALA CITY
TEGUCIGALPA
SAN SALVADOR
MANAGUA
SAN JOSÉ
PANAMA CITY

INHABITANTS PER SQ MILE
- ■ More than 130
- ■ 52–130
- ■ Less than 52
- ■ Capital city

URBAN/RURAL POPULATION DIVISION

San Salvador 3.3%
Tegucigalpa 3.2%
Managua 3.5%
Other towns and cities 37%
Rural population 53%

THE LANDSCAPE

The Sierra Madre in the north and the Cordillera Central to the south form a mountainous ridge that stretches down most of Central America. Along the Pacific coast north of Panama is a belt of more than 40 active volcanoes. The mountains are broken by valleys and basins with large, fertile areas of rich, volcanic soil.

Sierra Madre (A 3)

Coral reef (C 2)
Off the coast of Belize is a 180-mile-long coral reef – the second longest in the world. Its waters contain spectacular marine life. In places, the reef has become built up into dozens of small sandy islands called cayes.

The Mosquito Coast (E 4)
The Mosquito Coast is a remote area of tropical rain forests, lagoons, and rivers lined with mangroves. Most of it is uninhabited by humans, but there is a huge variety of animal species, including monkeys and alligators.

Lake Nicaragua (E 5)
This large freshwater lake contains about 400 islands, some of which are active volances like Volcán Concepcion. The lake is also home to the world's only freshwater sharks.

Cordillera Central (G 6)

Panama Canal (H 6)
The Panama Canal links the Atlantic and Pacific oceans along a distance of 51 miles. Half of its route passes through Lake Gatún, a freshwater lake that acts as a reservoir for the canal, providing water to operate the locks.

MEXICO
Yucat
Carmeli
Río Usumacinta
La Libe
Sayax
Barillas
Chi
Jacaltenango
Chajul
Cobán
Huehuetenango
Nebaj
Rabin
Volcán Tacaná 13,428
Santa Cruz del Quiché
Sal.
San Marcos
Quezaltenango
GUATEMALA CITY
Champerico
Escui
San José
E

NORTH
AMERICA

Central
America

CLIMATE

Temperatures are high all year round, although in January
the Caribbean side of Central America is cooler and
wetter than the Pacific side. Summers are generally much
wetter, especially in the Sierra Madre in Guatemala and
on the Pacific coasts of Costa Rica and Panama.

**TEMPERATURE
AND PRECIPITATION**

More than 77°F
68 to 77°F
Less than 68°F
Precipitation (mm)

January

July

INDUSTRY

Coffee, fish, and timber processing, fruit
exporting, and textile-weaving are typical of
the small-scale industries found in Central
America. Most industries are based in the
capital cities and larger towns. In Panama,
many people work at the Panama Canal, which
is one of the world's busiest shipping routes.
The country is also a major financial center,
with many banking and insurance companies.

INDUSTRY

- Chemicals
- Coffee processing
- Fish processing
- Food processing
- Textiles
- Banana exporting
- Timber processing
- Finance
- Major industrial center / area
- Major road

STRUCTURE OF INDUSTRY

Primary 18%
Services 60%
Manufacturing 22%

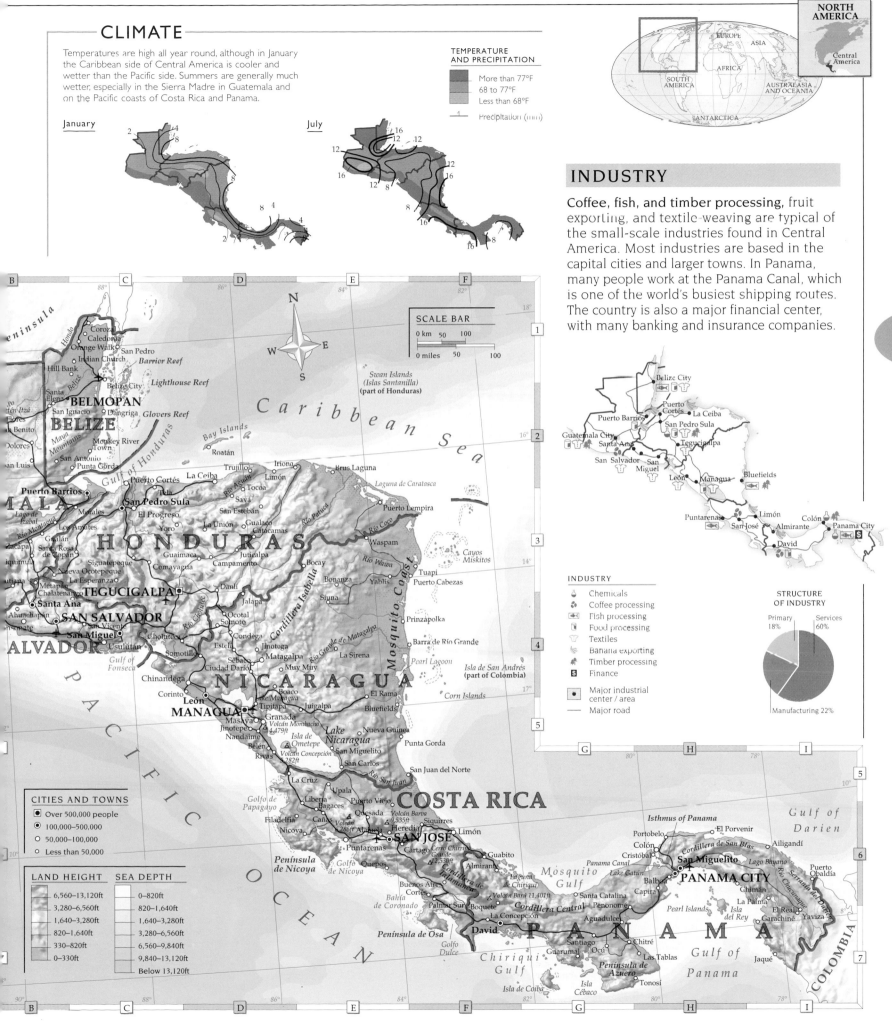

CITIES AND TOWNS

- Over 500,000 people
- 100,000–500,000
- 50,000–100,000
- Less than 50,000

LAND HEIGHT

- 6,560–13,120ft
- 3,280–6,560ft
- 1,640–3,280ft
- 820–1,640ft
- 330–820ft
- 0–330ft

SEA DEPTH

- 0–820ft
- 820–1,640ft
- 1,640–3,280ft
- 3,280–6,560ft
- 6,560–9,840ft
- 9,840–13,120ft
- Below 13,120ft

SCALE BAR

0 km   50   100
0 miles   50   100

THE CARIBBEAN

The Caribbean Sea is enclosed by an arc of many hundreds of islands, islets, and offshore reefs that reach from Florida in the US, round to Venezuela in South America. From 1492, Spain, France, Britain, and the Netherlands claimed the islands as colonies. Most of the islands' original inhabitants were wiped out by disease and a wide mixture of peoples – of African, Asian, and European descent – now make up the population. The islands are prone to earthquakes, hurricanes, and volcanic eruptions.

THE LANDSCAPE

The Bahamas
The Bahamas are low-lying islands formed from limestone rock. Their coastlines are fringed by coral reefs, lagoons, and mangrove swamps. Some of the bigger islands are covered by forests.

The islands are formed from two main mountain chains: the Greater Antilles, which are part of a chain running from west to east, and the Lesser Antilles, which run from north to south. The mountains are now almost submerged under the Atlantic Ocean and Caribbean Sea. Only the higher peaks reach above sea level to form islands.

Hispaniola (F 4)
Two countries, Haiti and the Dominican Republic, occupy the island of Hispaniola. The land is mostly mountainous, broken by fertile valleys.

Cuba (C 3)
Cuba is the largest island in the Antilles. Its landscape is made up of wide, fertile plains with rugged hills and mountains in the southeast.

The Lesser Antilles
Most of these small volcanic islands have mountainous interiors. Barbados and Antigua and Barbuda are flatter, with some higher volcanic areas. Monserrat was evacuated in 1997, following volcanic eruptions on the island.

FARMING AND LAND USE

Agriculture is an important source of income, with over half of all produce exported. Many islands have fertile, well-watered land and large areas are set aside for commercial crops such as sugarcane, tobacco, and coffee. Some islands rely heavily on a single crop; in Dominica, bananas provide over half the country's income. Cuba is one of the world's biggest sugar producers.

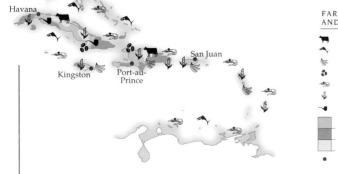

FARMING AND LAND USE	
Cattle	
Fishing	
Bananas	
Coffee	
Shellfish	
Sugarcane	
Tobacco	

Cropland
Forest
Pasture
• Major conurbation

ENVIRONMENTAL ISSUES

The islands of the Caribbean are often under threat from hurricane storm systems which sweep in from the Atlantic Ocean between May and October. The winds can reach speeds of up to 156 miles per hour, devastating everything that lies in their path and causing severe flooding. The storms themselves are enormous; a hurricane can extend outward for 406 miles from its calm center, which is known as the "eye."

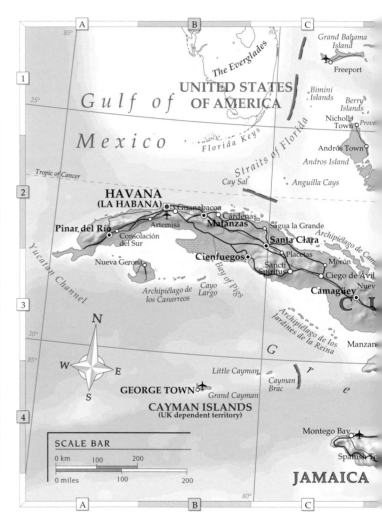

TOURISM

Tourism is thriving in the Caribbean, often bringing more income to the region than other, traditional industries. Long sandy beaches, clear, warm waters, and the climate are the main attractions. In Cuba and the Dominican Republic, tourism is expanding at some of the fastest rates in North America. As hotel complexes and new roads and airports are developed, the environment is often damaged. Local people who work in the industry often receive little of the extra cash brought in by the tourists.

TOURISM
Major tourist destinations

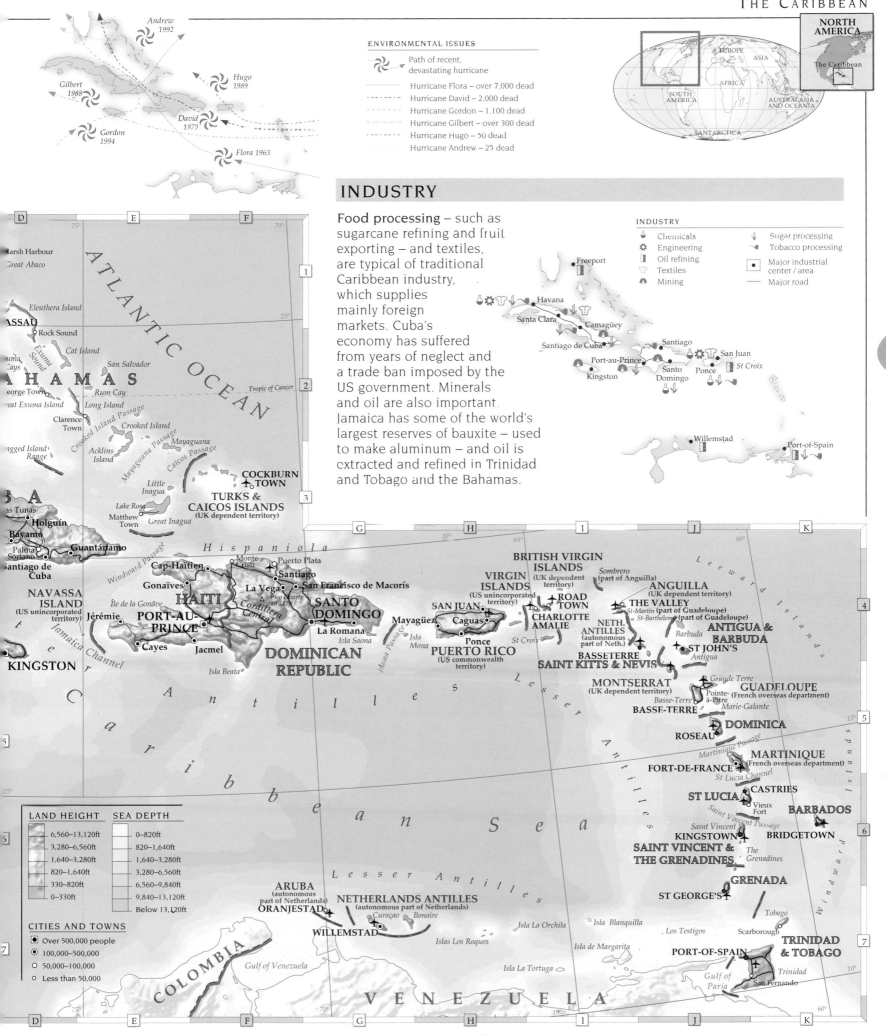

NORTH AMERICA

The Caribbean

ENVIRONMENTAL ISSUES

Path of recent, devastating hurricane

Hurricane Flora – over 7,000 dead
Hurricane David – 2,000 dead
Hurricane Gordon – 1,100 dead
Hurricane Gilbert – over 300 dead
Hurricane Hugo – 50 dead
Hurricane Andrew – 25 dead

Andrew 1992
Hugo 1989
Gilbert 1988
David 1979
Gordon 1994
Flora 1963

INDUSTRY

Food processing – such as sugarcane refining and fruit exporting – and textiles, are typical of traditional Caribbean industry, which supplies mainly foreign markets. Cuba's economy has suffered from years of neglect and a trade ban imposed by the US government. Minerals and oil are also important. Jamaica has some of the world's largest reserves of bauxite – used to make aluminum – and oil is extracted and refined in Trinidad and Tobago and the Bahamas.

INDUSTRY

Chemicals
Engineering
Oil refining
Textiles
Mining
Sugar processing
Tobacco processing
Major industrial center / area
Major road

Freeport
Havana
Santa Clara
Camagüey
Santiago de Cuba
Santiago
San Juan
St Croix
Port-au-Prince
Ponce
Kingston
Santo Domingo
Willemstad
Port-of-Spain

LAND HEIGHT
6,560–13,120ft
3,280–6,560ft
1,640–3,280ft
820–1,640ft
330–820ft
0–330ft

SEA DEPTH
0–820ft
820–1,640ft
1,640–3,280ft
3,280–6,560ft
6,560–9,840ft
9,840–13,120ft
Below 13,120ft

CITIES AND TOWNS
Over 500,000 people
100,000–500,000
50,000–100,000
Less than 50,000

Marsh Harbour
Great Abaco
Eleuthera Island
NASSAU
Rock Sound
Cat Island
San Salvador
Exuma Sound
Exuma Cays
George Town
Great Exuma Island
Long Island
Rum Cay
Tropic of Cancer
Clarence Town
Crooked Island
Crooked Island Passage
Acklins Island
Mayaguana Passage
Mayaguana
Ragged Island Range
Caicos Passage
Little Inagua
Lake Rosa
Matthew Town
Great Inagua
COCKBURN TOWN
TURKS & CAICOS ISLANDS (UK dependent territory)

ATLANTIC OCEAN
BAHAMAS

CUBA
as Tunas
Holguín
Bayamo
Palma Soriano
Guantánamo
Santiago de Cuba

Hispaniola
Monte Cristi
Puerto Plata
Cap-Haïtien
Santiago
Gonaïves
La Vega
San Francisco de Macorís
Pico Duarte 10,417ft
Cordillera Central
HAITI
SANTO DOMINGO
NAVASSA ISLAND (US unincorporated territory)
Jérémie
PORT-AU-PRINCE
La Romana
Isla Saona
Cayes
Jacmel
DOMINICAN REPUBLIC
Isla Beata
KINGSTON
Jamaica Channel
Windward Passage

Mayagüez
Isla Mona
Caguas
San Juan
PUERTO RICO (US commonwealth territory)
Ponce
Isla Mona
Mona Passage
St Croix

VIRGIN ISLANDS (US unincorporated territory)
ROAD TOWN
BRITISH VIRGIN ISLANDS (UK dependent territory)
Sombrero (part of Anguilla)
CHARLOTTE AMALIE
ANGUILLA (UK dependent territory)
THE VALLEY
St-Martin (part of Guadeloupe)
St-Barthélemy (part of Guadeloupe)
NETH. ANTILLES (autonomous part of Neth.)
Barbuda
ANTIGUA & BARBUDA
ST JOHN'S
Antigua
BASSETERRE
SAINT KITTS & NEVIS
MONTSERRAT (UK dependent territory)
Grande Terre
Pointe-à-Pitre
GUADELOUPE (French overseas department)
Basse-Terre
BASSE-TERRE
Marie-Galante
DOMINICA
ROSEAU
Martinique Passage
MARTINIQUE (French overseas department)
FORT-DE-FRANCE
St Lucia Channel
CASTRIES
Vieux Fort
ST LUCIA
BARBADOS
Saint Vincent Passage
KINGSTOWN
Saint Vincent
BRIDGETOWN
SAINT VINCENT & THE GRENADINES
The Grenadines
GRENADA
ST GEORGE'S

Leeward Islands
Windward Islands
Lesser Antilles
Greater Antilles

Caribbean Sea

Lesser Antilles
ARUBA (autonomous part of Netherlands)
ORANJESTAD
NETHERLANDS ANTILLES (autonomous part of Netherlands)
Curaçao
Bonaire
WILLEMSTAD
Isla La Orchila
Isla Blanquilla
Los Testigos
Tobago
Scarborough
TRINIDAD & TOBAGO
Isla Margarita
PORT-OF-SPAIN
Trinidad
San Fernando
Gulf of Paria
Isla La Tortuga

COLOMBIA
Gulf of Venezuela
Islas Los Roques

VENEZUELA

CONTINENTAL EUROPE

Europe is the world's second smallest continent, occupying the western tip of the vast Eurasian landmass. To the north and west are old highlands, with the high peaks of the Alps in the south. Most people live on the densely populated North European Plain, which extends from southern England, through northern France, across Germany into Russia.

CROSS-SECTION THROUGH EUROPE

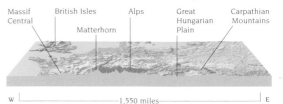

Massif Central | British Isles | Alps | Great Hungarian Plain | Carpathian Mountains

Matterhorn

W ——————1,550 miles—————— E

In the west, the land rises up from the Atlantic coast toward the Massif Central in France, and the high peaks of the Alps. Between the Alps and the Carpathian Mountains is the Great Hungarian Plain, where the Danube River flows on its way to the Black Sea.

PHYSICAL EUROPE

The ancient mountains of northwest Europe were scoured and smoothed by glaciers in the last Ice Age. The Alps are newer and more jagged – pushed up when Africa collided with Europe. In between is the North European Plain, where thick layers of fertile soils allow many different crops to be grown.

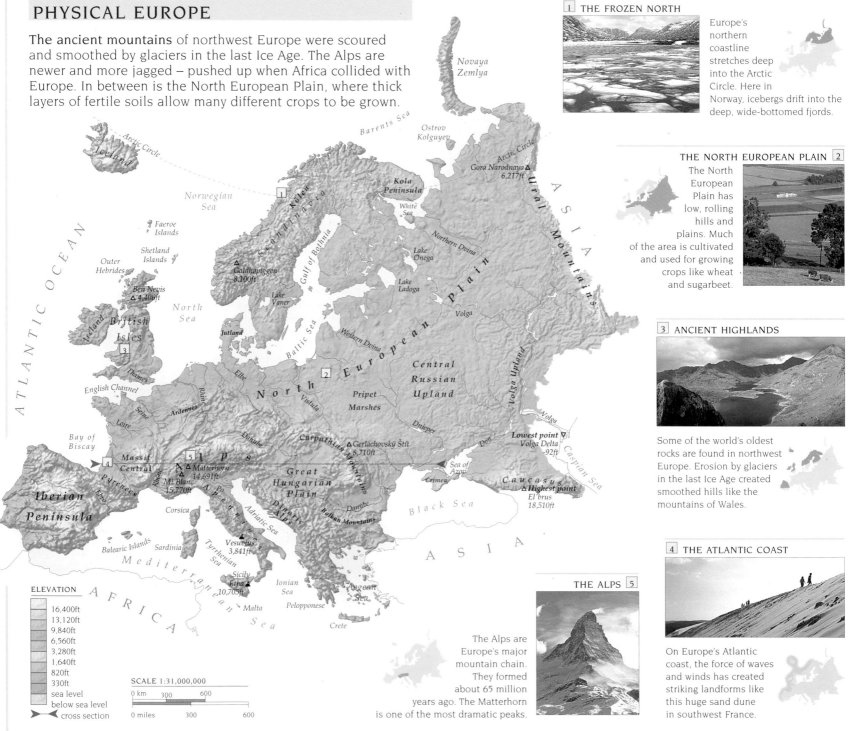

1 THE FROZEN NORTH

Europe's northern coastline stretches deep into the Arctic Circle. Here in Norway, icebergs drift into the deep, wide-bottomed fjords.

THE NORTH EUROPEAN PLAIN 2

The North European Plain has low, rolling hills and plains. Much of the area is cultivated and used for growing crops like wheat and sugarbeet.

3 ANCIENT HIGHLANDS

Some of the world's oldest rocks are found in northwest Europe. Erosion by glaciers in the last Ice Age created smoothed hills like the mountains of Wales.

4 THE ATLANTIC COAST

On Europe's Atlantic coast, the force of waves and winds has created striking landforms like this huge sand dune in southwest France.

THE ALPS 5

The Alps are Europe's major mountain chain. They formed about 65 million years ago. The Matterhorn is one of the most dramatic peaks.

Map labels:

Novaya Zemlya

Arctic Circle

Iceland

Barents Sea

Ostrov Kolguyev

Gora Narodnaya △ 6,217ft

Arctic Circle

Kola Peninsula

White Sea

Norwegian Sea

Faeroe Islands

Shetland Islands

Outer Hebrides

Scandinavia

Gulf of Bothnia

Lake Onega

Northern Dvina

ASIA

Ural Mountains

Galdhøpiggen 8,100ft

Lake Vaner

Lake Ladoga

Volga

Ben Nevis △ 4,400ft

North Sea

Ireland

British Isles

Jutland

Baltic Sea

Western Dvina

Central Russian Upland

ATLANTIC OCEAN

Thames

English Channel

Seine

Rhine

Ardennes

Elbe

North European Plain

Vistula

Pripet Marshes

Dnieper

Volga Upland

Volga

Loire

Danube

Lowest point Volga Delta -92ft

Caspian Sea

Bay of Biscay

Massif Central

Alps

Matterhorn 14,691ft

Mt. Blanc 15,770ft

Carpathian Mountains

Gerlachovský Štít 8,710ft

Don

Sea of Azov

Crimea

Caucasus △ Highest point El'brus 18,510ft

Pyrenees

Iberian Peninsula

Ebro

Apennines

Po

Great Hungarian Plain

Dinaric Alps

Danube

Balkan Mountains

Black Sea

Corsica

Adriatic Sea

ASIA

Balearic Islands

Sardinia

Tyrrhenian Sea

Vesuvius 3,841ft

Sicily Etna ▲ 10,705ft

Ionian Sea

Aegean Sea

Mediterranean Sea

Malta

Peloponnese

Crete

AFRICA

ELEVATION

16,400ft
13,120ft
9,840ft
6,560ft
3,280ft
1,640ft
820ft
330ft
sea level
below sea level
⋗ cross section

SCALE 1:31,000,000

0 km 300 600

0 miles 300 600

POLITICAL EUROPE

Europe's population increased rapidly during the 18th and 19th centuries, following the Industrial Revolution. In the 20th century, Europe suffered a series of wars that redrew the political map. From 1989 to 1991, communist governments in eastern Europe and the former Soviet Union collapsed, as political reform swept through the countries behind the "Iron Curtain." In western Europe, the 15 countries of the European Union are discussing closer political and economic ties.

POPULATION

Capital cities

- Above 500,000
- 100,000 to 500,000
- 50,000 to 100,000

SCALE 1:27,500,000

0 km   300   600

0 miles   300   600

REGIONAL IDENTITY

Throughout Europe, there is a growing call to recognize regional cultural identity. The Basque region, bordering southwest France and Spain, is one example.

RURAL LIFE

Away from Europe's bustling cities, traditional rural lifestyles survive. Here in the Republic of Ireland, a winter shelter is being made for cattle.

STANDARDS OF LIVING

Living standards are generally much lower in eastern Europe than in the wealthier west. Homelessness and unemployment are still common, even in the most prosperous countries.

POPULATION

More than 700 million people live in Europe, and its population is highly urbanized. In Belgium and the Netherlands, almost 90% of people live in cities. In the south and east, more people still live in rural areas. The northern countries have the smallest populations because much of the land is too cold to be habitable.

POPULATION DENSITY
(People per sq mile)

Below 129	260–389	520–779
130–259	390–519	Above 780

SPREADING CITIES

Rotterdam, in the Netherlands, is part of a conurbation, a large built-up area where several towns or cities have merged together to form a single urban area.

Largest city
MOSCOW
9.4 million people

STANDARD OF LIVING
(UN Human Development Index)

low   high

EUROPEAN GEOGRAPHY

Europe is blessed with a temperate climate, ample mineral reserves, and good transportation links. During the 18th and 19th centuries the continent was transformed, as new methods of production made industry and farming more efficient and productive. Today, in many countries, heavy industries have been replaced by high-tech and service industries. Agriculture is still important, and many crops thrive on Europe's fertile plains.

INDUSTRY

Western Europe has some of the world's wealthiest countries. In countries such as France, Germany, and the UK, traditional industries like iron and steel-making are now being replaced by light industries, such as electronics, and services like finance and insurance. In Eastern Europe, industry was subsidized by the communist governments for years. Many factories are old-fashioned and need investment to improve their equipment and production methods.

MINERAL RESOURCES

Europe has few sizable reserves of metallic minerals; most were used up by industry during the last century. Oil, gas, and coal are found in large quantities – gas in the North Sea and oil in the Volga basin. Coal, although abundant, is being steadily depleted.

MINERAL RESOURCES

- Bauxite
- Chromium
- Iron
- Manganese
- Nickel
- Uranium
- Oil/gas field
- Coal field

ECONOMIC ACTIVITY

- Aerospace
- Vehicle manufacturing
- Chemicals
- Coal
- Defense
- Electronics
- Engineering
- Finance
- Food processing
- High-tech industry
- Iron and steel
- Oil and gas
- Printing and publishing
- Textiles
- Timber processing

GNP per capita (US$)

- Below 1,999
- 2,000–4,999
- 5,000–9,999
- 10,000–19,999
- 20,000–24,999
- Above 25,000
- Industrial center

OIL AND GAS

Oil and gas reserves are plentiful in the Russian Federation. South of Rostov-on-Don, oil is pumped from the ground and piped to nearby refineries.

CAR MANUFACTURING

Germany is one of the world's largest manufacturers of cars. Companies like BMW, Mercedes-Benz, and Volkswagen export cars across the world.

FINANCE

London is one of the most important financial centers in the world. Many banks and financial institutions have their headquarters here. At the London Stock Exchange, people buy and sell stocks and shares.

Barents Sea

Norwegian Sea

RUSSIAN FEDERATION

ICELAND

North Sea

NORWAY
SWEDEN
FINLAND

Oslo
Stockholm
Gothenburg
Helsinki
St Petersburg
Perm'
Ufa
Yaroslavl'
ESTONIA
LATVIA
Moscow
Nizhniy Novgorod
Samara
LITHUANIA
Kaliningrad (part of Russ. Fed.)
Tula
Saratov

UNITED KINGDOM
Glasgow
Newcastle upon Tyne
Manchester
Birmingham
London
REPUBLIC OF IRELAND

DENMARK
Hamburg
Amsterdam
NETH.
Berlin
GERMANY
Cologne
BELG.
Brussels
LUX.
Frankfurt am Main
Paris
Stuttgart
Munich
Prague
CZECH REP.
POLAND
Warsaw
Kraków
BELARUS
Kiev
UKRAINE
Dnipropetrovs'k
Kryvvy Rih
Rostov-on-Don
Volgograd

FRANCE
Lyon
LIECH.
Zürich
SWITZ.
AUSTRIA
SLOVAKIA
HUNGARY
MOLDOVA
ROMANIA
Bilbao
Toulouse
Turin
Milan
SLVN.
CROATIA
BOSNIA AND HERZ.
SAN MARINO
Bucharest
Black Sea
PORTUGAL
Lisbon
SPAIN
Madrid
ANDORRA
Barcelona
ITALY
Naples
YUGOSLAVIA
BULGARIA
Sofia
MACED.
ALBANIA
Istanbul
TURKEY
GREECE
Athens

ATLANTIC OCEAN

Baltic Sea

ASIA

AFRICA
Mediterranean Sea
MALTA

CLIMATE

Europe's climate is temperate with few climatic extremes. In the far north, Europe extends into the Arctic Circle and the climate is so cold that the Baltic Sea freezes over in the winter. Toward the Atlantic coast in the west, the climate becomes wetter and warmer because of a warm ocean current, known as the Gulf Stream. Countries such as Italy and Spain that border the Mediterranean Sea have long, hot summers and low rainfall, which can sometimes lead to such problems as drought.

EXTREME WEATHER EVENTS

Symbols indicate climatic extremes

CLIMATE

- Tundra
- Subarctic
- Cool continental
- Temperate/humid
- Mediterranean
- Semiarid

Coldest place UST'SHCHUGOR (Russ. Fed.) Temp. -67°F

Driest place ASTRAKHAN' (Russ. Fed.) Annual rainfall 6 in

Hottest place SEVILLE (Spain) Temp. 122°F

Wettest place CRKVICE (Bos. & Herz.) Annual rainfall 183 in

THE MEDITERRANEAN CLIMATE

The mild, warm climate around the Mediterranean Sea allows olives, citrus fruits, and grapes to thrive. Long, sunny days also help the fruits ripen. Grapes are harvested and crushed to make many different wines.

LAND USE AND AGRICULTURE

Europe's agricultural heart is the North European Plain, where fertile soils and ample rainfall allow a variety of crops to be grown. Wheat is the main grain crop, and a wide range of fruit and vegetables are also grown. Dairy and beef cattle are raised for their milk and meat throughout Europe. In the south, the Mediterranean climate is ideal for citrus fruits and olives. Forests cover much of northern Scandinavia, while sheep farming is common in the hills of the British Isles.

CROPLANDS

Many different crops are grown on the North European Plain. Sunflowers, wheat, and sugar beets – used to make sugar – are among the main crops grown there.

FISHING

The north Atlantic Ocean provides a rich marine harvest for fishermen. High quality cod and mackerel are caught in the cold, nutrient-rich waters.

LAND USE AND AGRICULTURE

- Cattle
- Goats
- Pigs
- Reindeer
- Sheep
- Cereals
- Citrus fruits
- Fishing
- Fruit
- Olive oil
- Potatoes
- Root crops
- Shellfish
- Sunflowers
- Timber
- Vineyards

- Cropland
- Forest
- Ice cap
- Mountain region
- Pasture
- Tundra
- Wetland
- Major conurbation

DAIRY FARMING

Dairy farming is very common across northern Europe. Cows grazed on rich pastures produce milk used for making butter and cheese.

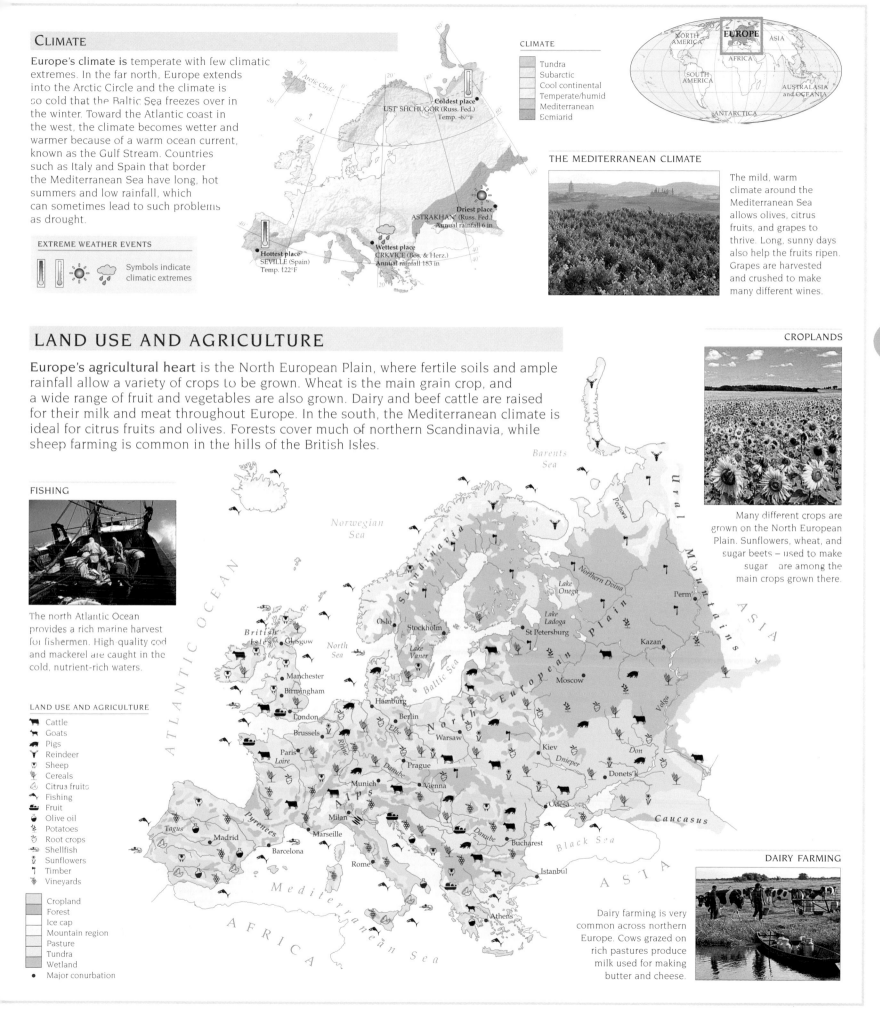

NORTHERN EUROPE

DENMARK, ESTONIA, FINLAND, ICELAND, LATVIA, LITHUANIA, NORWAY, SWEDEN

Denmark, Sweden, and Norway are together known as Scandinavia. These countries, along with the North Atlantic island of Iceland, have similar languages and cultures. Finland has a very different language and a separate identity from its Scandinavian neighbors. Estonia, Latvia, and Lithuania, known as the Baltic states, were part of the Soviet Union until 1989, when each became an independent country.

FARMING AND LAND USE

Southern Denmark and Sweden are the most productive areas, with pig farming, dairy farming, and crops such as wheat, barley, and potatoes. Sheep farming is important in southern Norway and Iceland. In the Baltic states, cereals, potatoes, and sugar beets are the main crops, and cattle graze on damp pasture.

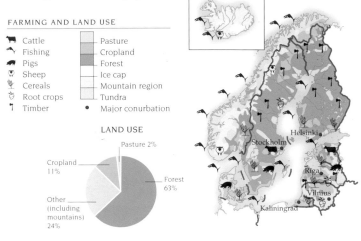

FARMING AND LAND USE

- 🐄 Cattle
- 🐟 Fishing
- 🐖 Pigs
- 🐑 Sheep
- 🌾 Cereals
- 🥕 Root crops
- 🌲 Timber
- Pasture
- Cropland
- Forest
- Ice cap
- Mountain region
- Tundra
- • Major conurbation

LAND USE

Pasture 2%
Cropland 11%
Other (including mountains) 24%
Forest 63%

INDUSTRY

In Scandinavia, many natural resources are used in industry: timber for paper and furniture; iron ore for steel and cars; and fish and natural gas from the seas. Hydroelectric power is generated by water flowing down steep mountain slopes. The Baltic states still rely on Russia to supply their raw materials and energy.

INDUSTRY

- 🚗 Car manufacturing
- 🧪 Chemicals
- ⚙️ Engineering
- 🐟 Fish processing
- Hydroelectric power
- ⚓ Shipbuilding
- 🌲 Timber processing
- 🏛 Tourism

- ▪ Major industrial center / area
- — Major road

STRUCTURE OF INDUSTRY

Primary 4%
Services 65%
Manufacturing 31%

THE LANDSCAPE

The north and west of Scandinavia is extremely rugged and mountainous, with landscapes eroded by ice. In the south of Scandinavia the land is flatter, with fertile soils deposited by glaciers. Much of Finland, Norway, and Sweden is covered by dense forests. The Baltic states are much lower, with rounded hills and many lakes and marshes.

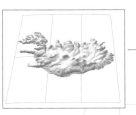

The land of ice and fire.
Iceland is one of the world's most active volcanic areas. There are about 200 volcanoes on the island, along with bubbling hot springs, mud-holes, and geysers that spurt boiling water and steam high into the air.

POPULATION

The population is distributed mainly along the warmer and flatter southern and coastal areas. Population totals and densities are low for all of the countries, and Iceland has the lowest population density in Europe, with just eight people per sq mile. Many Scandinavians have holiday homes on the islands, along the lake shores, or in coastal areas.

INHABITANTS PER SQ MILE

- More than 520
- 260–520
- 130–260
- Less than 130

- ▪ Capital city
- • Major city

URBAN/RURAL POPULATION DIVISION

Helsinki 1.8%
Stockholm 2.5%
Oslo 1.7%
Other towns and cities 64%
Rural population 30%

Fjords
Norway has many fjords: deep, wide valleys, drowned by seawater when the ice melted at the end of the last Ice Age.

Baltic Sea (D 7)
Ships from Finland, Sweden, and the Baltic states use the Baltic Sea as their route to the north Atlantic Ocean. In winter, much of the sea is frozen.

Glacial lakes
Finland and Sweden have many thousands of lakes. During the last Ice Age, glaciers scoured hollows that filled with water when the ice melted.

Courland Spit (D 7)
This wide sandspit runs for 62 miles along the Baltic coast of Lithuania and the Russian enclave of Kaliningrad. It encloses a huge lagoon.

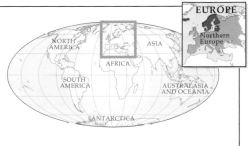

ENVIRONMENTAL ISSUES

Northern Europe has been badly affected by industrial pollution from other parts of Europe. Polluted air moves north and mixes with the rain to create acid rain. This poisons forests and lakes, destroying the plants and animals living in them. In Norway and Sweden, electricity is produced by dams that obtain from the plentiful water supply. Hydro-electric power is a clean, alternative energy source.

ENVIRONMENTAL ISSUES

- Major dams
- Urban air pollution
- Volcanic eruption
- Affected by acid rain
- Sea pollution
- Major industrial center

CLIMATE

Warm ocean currents flowing north along the coasts of Norway and Iceland make the climate mild and wet. Away from the sea, the climate is generally colder and drier.

January

July

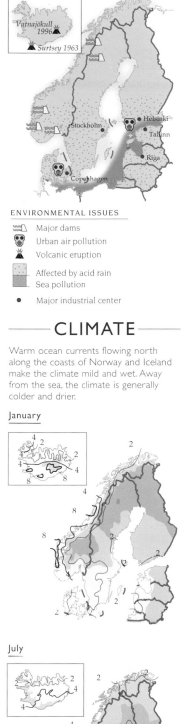

TEMPERATURE AND PRECIPITATION

More than 59°F	23 to 32°F
50 to 59°F	14 to 23°F
41 to 50°F	5 to 14°F
32 to 41°F	Less than 5°F

4 — Precipitation (in)

ICELAND

Norwegian Sea

Bolungarvík, Raufarhöfn, Ísafjördhur, Siglufjördhur, Húsavík, Akureyri, Stykkishólmur, Seydhisfjördhur, Neskaupstadhur, *Faxaflói*, **REYKJAVIK**, Selfoss, Djúpivogur, Thorláksfhöfn, Hvannadalshnúkur 6,953ft, *Surtsey*, Vestmannaeyjar

ATLANTIC OCEAN

SCALE BAR

LAND HEIGHT
- 6,560–13,120ft
- 3,280–6,560ft
- 1,640–3,280ft
- 820–1,640ft
- 330–820ft
- 0–330ft

SEA DEPTH
- 0–160ft
- 160–330ft
- 330–820ft
- 820–1,640ft
- 1,640–3,280ft
- 3,280–6,560ft
- Below 6,560ft

CITIES AND TOWNS
- Over 500,000 people
- 100,000–500,000
- 50,000–100,000
- Less than 50,000

THE LOW COUNTRIES

BELGIUM, LUXEMBOURG, NETHERLANDS

Belgium, Luxembourg, and the Netherlands are called the Low Countries because most of their land is flat and low-lying. Much of the Netherlands lies below sea level, and over hundreds of years the Dutch have built dikes and dams to prevent flooding, and have pumped water off large areas of land to reclaim them from the sea. The Low Countries are Europe's most densely populated countries, but most of their people have a high living standard.

ENVIRONMENTAL ISSUES

Huge land reclamation projects in the Netherlands, such as the IJsselmeer project, have created some new land for agricultural use, and also for houses, roads, and open spaces. Heavy industry has caused serious air pollution in cities such as Amsterdam and Rotterdam, and added to Europe's acid rain problem.

ENVIRONMENTAL
ISSUES

- 😷 Urban air pollution
- Built-up areas
- Reclaimed land
- Polluted river
- • Major industrial center

CLIMATE

The Low Countries share a similar climate, with mild winters and warm summers. Only in the upland Ardennes region does rainfall increase and temperatures decrease.

January

July

TEMPERATURE
AND PRECIPITATION

- More than 59°F
- 50 to 59°F
- 41 to 50°F
- 32 to 41°F
- Less than 32°F

4 — Precipitation (in)

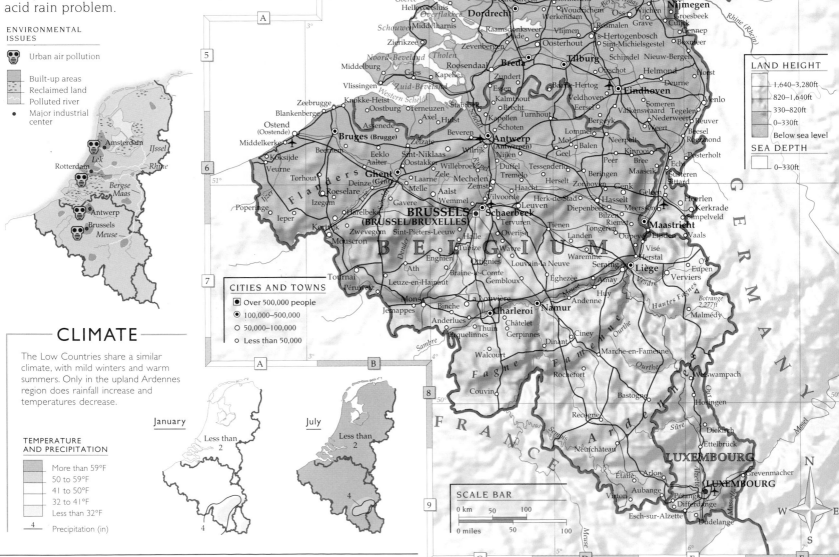

NETHERLANDS'
TWO CAPITALS
AMSTERDAM - capital
THE HAGUE - seat of government

LAND HEIGHT
- 1,640–3,280ft
- 820–1,640ft
- 330–820ft
- 0–330ft
- Below sea level

SEA DEPTH
- 0–330ft

CITIES AND TOWNS
- ■ Over 500,000 people
- ◉ 100,000–500,000
- ○ 50,000–100,000
- ○ Less than 50,000

SCALE BAR
0 km   50   100
0 miles   50   100

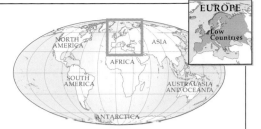

EUROPE
Low
Countries

POPULATION

More than 25 million people live in the Low Countries, and nine out of every ten people live in a town or city. The largest urban area – known as the *Randstad Holland* – is in the Netherlands. It runs in an unbroken line from Rotterdam in the south, to Amsterdam in the west. Even most rural areas in the Low Countries are densely populated.

INHABITANTS PER SQ MILE

- More than 520
- 260–520
- 130–260
- 0–130

- ■ Capital city
- ● Major city

Groningen
AMSTERDAM
THE HAGUE
Randstad Holland
Utrecht
Rotterdam
Arnhem
Ghent
Antwerp
BRUSSELS
Liège
Charleroi
LUXEMBOURG

URBAN/RURAL POPULATION DIVISION

- Amsterdam 2.8%
- Brussels 3.9%
- Rotterdam 2.3%
- Rural population 8%
- Other towns and cities 83%

FARMING AND LAND USE

The Low Countries' fertile soils and flat plains provide excellent conditions for farming. The main crops grown are barley, potatoes, and flax for making linen. In the Netherlands, much farmland is used for dairy farming. The country is also famous for growing flowers, which are exported around the world. Flowers and vegetables are grown either in open fields or in enormous greenhouses, which allow production year-round.

Amsterdam
The Hague
Rotterdam
Brussels

LAND USE

- Forest 16%
- Other (including urban) 29%
- Pasture 26%
- Cropland 29%

FARMING AND LAND USE

- 🐄 Cattle
- 🐖 Pigs
- 🌾 Cereals
- 🌷 Flowers
- 🌱 Sugar beets

- Pasture
- Cropland
- Forest
- Wetland
- ● Major conurbation

THE LANDSCAPE

The Low Countries are largely flat and low-lying. The ancient hills of the Ardennes, in the far southeast, are the only higher region. They rise to heights of more than 1,640 ft. Two major rivers – the Meuse and the Rhine – flow across the Low Countries to their mouths in the North Sea. At the coast, the Rhine deposits large quantities of sediment to form a delta.

Polders

In the Netherlands, land has been reclaimed from the sea since the Middle Ages by building dikes and drainage ditches. These areas of land are called polders. They are very fertile.

Rhine River (E4)

The River Rhine erodes and carries large amounts of sediment along its course. When it reaches the Netherlands it divides into three rivers. As they approach the North Sea, the rivers slow down, depositing the sediment to form a delta.

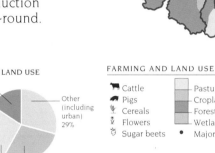

Low-lying Netherlands

Over two-thirds of the Netherlands lies at or below sea level. This makes flooding a constant threat in coastal areas.

INDUSTRY

The Low Countries are an important center for the high-tech and electronics industries. Good transportation links to the rest of Europe allow them to sell their products in other countries. The built-up area stretching from Amsterdam in the Netherlands to Antwerp in Belgium has the greatest number of factories. Luxembourg is also an important banking center; many international banks have their headquarters in its capital city.

STRUCTURE OF INDUSTRY

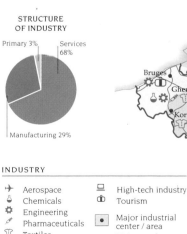

- Primary 3%
- Services 68%
- Manufacturing 29%

Groningen
Amsterdam
Enschede
The Hague
Utrecht
Nijmegen
Rotterdam
Breda
Tilburg
Eindhoven
Bruges
Ghent
Antwerp
Kortrijk
Brussels
Liège
Charleroi
Namur
Luxembourg

INDUSTRY

- ✈ Aerospace
- ⚗ Chemicals
- ⚙ Engineering
- ⚗ Pharmaceuticals
- ⊤ Textiles
- Ⓢ Finance
- 💻 High-tech industry
- ⚓ Tourism
- ■ Major industrial center / area
- — Major road

Flanders (B 6)

The plains of Flanders in western Belgium have fertile soils which were deposited by glaciers during the last Ice Age. They provide excellent land for growing crops.

Heathlands

The heathlands on the Dutch-Belgian border have thin, sandy soils. The only plants that grow well here are heathers and gorse.

Ardennes (D 8)

The hills of the Ardennes were formed over 300 million years ago. They have many deep valleys, which have been eroded by rivers like the Meuse.

THE BRITISH ISLES

UNITED KINGDOM, REPUBLIC OF IRELAND

The British Isles lie off the northwest coast of mainland Europe. They are made up of two large islands and more than 5,000 smaller ones. Politically, the region is divided into two countries: the United Kingdom – England, Wales, Scotland, and Northern Ireland – and the Republic of Ireland. Geographically, the British Isles are divided between highlands to the north and west, and lowlands to the south and east.

THE LANDSCAPE

Low rolling hills, high moorlands, and small fields with high hedges are all typical of the British Isles. Ireland is known as the Emerald Isle because heavy rainfall gives it a lush, green appearance. Scotland and Wales are mountainous; the rocks forming the mountains there are some of the oldest in the world.

Indented coastlines
The west coast of the British Isles faces the Atlantic Ocean, and more than 1,860 miles of open sea to the North American continent. Storms and high waves constantly batter the hard, rocky coastline, giving it a jagged outline.

Ben Nevis (C 4)
This mountain is the highest point in the British Isles. It is 4,406 ft above sea level.

The Lake District (D 5)
The Lake District National Park has England's highest peak, Scafell Pike, at 3,209 ft, its deepest lake, Wast Water (260 ft), and its largest lake, Windermere (10 miles long).

The Pennines (D 6)
The Pennines are a chain of high hills, topped by moorland. They run for more than 250 miles, and are known as the "backbone of England."

The Burren (A 6)
The Burren is a large area of limestone in the west of Ireland. Its flat surfaces are known as limestone "pavements." There are also many caves and sinkholes in the area.

Rias
Rias are river valleys that have been drowned by rising sea levels. The southern coast of southwest England has many good examples.

The Fens (E 6)
This is the flattest area in England. Much of the land here has been reclaimed from the sea.

FARMING AND LAND USE

The English lowlands and the wide, flat stretches of land in East Anglia are the agricultural heartland of the United Kingdom. The country is no longer self-sufficient in food, but wheat, potatoes and other vegetables, and fruits, are widely grown. In Ireland, and in central and southern England, dairy and beef cattle feed off grassy pastures. In the hilly and mountainous areas, sheep farming is more usual.

FARMING AND LAND USE

- Cattle
- Sheep
- Cereals
- Market gardening
- Root crops
- Pasture
- Cropland
- Forest
- Mountain region
- Major conurbation

LAND USE

- Cropland 24%
- Pasture 50%
- Other (including urban) 17%
- Forest 9%

INDUSTRY

The United Kingdom's traditional industries, such as coal mining, iron- and steel-making, and textiles, have declined in recent years. Today, newer industries make cars, chemicals, and electronic and high-tech goods. Service industries, especially banking and insurance, have grown in importance. The country's most valuable natural resource is its large North Sea oil and gas fields.

INDUSTRY

- ✈ Aerospace
- 🚗 Car manufacturing
- Chemicals
- ⚙ Engineering
- Textiles
- S Finance
- High-tech industry
- Tourism
- ▪ Major industrial center / area
- — Major road

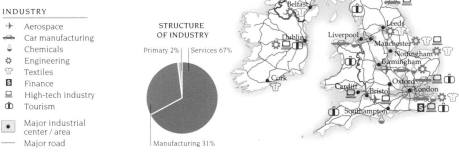

STRUCTURE OF INDUSTRY

- Primary 2%
- Services 67%
- Manufacturing 31%

POPULATION

The United Kingdom is densely populated, with most of the people living in urban areas. The southeast is the most crowded part of the country. The Scottish Highlands are less populated today than they were 200 years ago. Ireland is still mainly rural, with many Irish people making their living from farming.

URBAN/RURAL POPULATION DIVISION

- London 11.4%
- Birmingham 3.8%
- Manchester 3.8%
- Rural population 13%
- Other towns and cities 68%

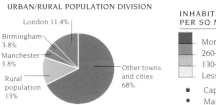

INHABITANTS PER SQ MILE

- More than 520
- 260–520
- 130–260
- Less than 130
- ▪ Capital city
- ● Major city

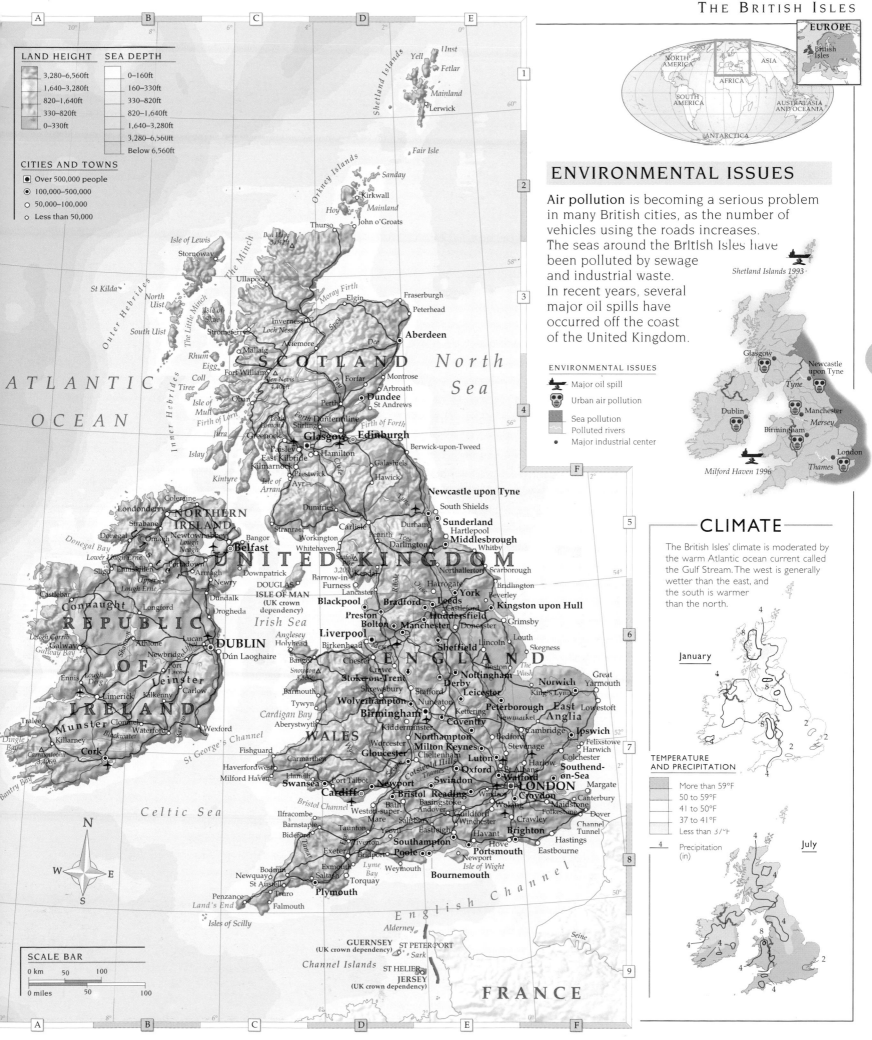

LAND HEIGHT
3,280–6,560ft
1,640–3,280ft
820–1,640ft
330–820ft
0–330ft

SEA DEPTH
0–160ft
160–330ft
330–820ft
820–1,640ft
1,640–3,280ft
3,280–6,560ft
Below 6,560ft

CITIES AND TOWNS
● Over 500,000 people
◉ 100,000–500,000
◎ 50,000–100,000
○ Less than 50,000

SCALE BAR
0 km   50   100
0 miles   50   100

EUROPE

NORTH AMERICA   ASIA
AFRICA
SOUTH AMERICA   AUSTRALASIA AND OCEANIA
ANTARCTICA

British Isles

ENVIRONMENTAL ISSUES

Air pollution is becoming a serious problem in many British cities, as the number of vehicles using the roads increases.
The seas around the British Isles have been polluted by sewage and industrial waste.
In recent years, several major oil spills have occurred off the coast of the United Kingdom.

Shetland Islands 1993

ENVIRONMENTAL ISSUES
✈ Major oil spill
☠ Urban air pollution
▮ Sea pollution
〰 Polluted rivers
● Major industrial center

Glasgow
Newcastle upon Tyne
Tyne
Dublin
Manchester
Mersey
Birmingham
London
Thames
Milford Haven 1996

CLIMATE

The British Isles' climate is moderated by the warm Atlantic ocean current called the Gulf Stream. The west is generally wetter than the east, and the south is warmer than the north.

January

July

TEMPERATURE AND PRECIPITATION
More than 59°F
50 to 59°F
41 to 50°F
37 to 41°F
Less than 37°F
4 — Precipitation (in)

FRANCE

ANDORRA, MONACO, FRANCE

France has helped shape the history and culture of Europe for centuries. Today, as a founder-member of the European Union, France is an avid supporter of the eventual political and economic integration of Europe's different countries. France is Western Europe's leading farming nation and one of the world's top industrial powers. Its cultural attractions and scenery draw tourists from around the world.

FARMING AND LAND USE

France is able to produce a variety of crops because of its rich soils and mild climate. Wheat is grown in many parts of the north, along with potatoes and other vegetables. Fields of corn and sunflowers and fruit orchards are found in the south, while grapes for the famous wine industry are grown across the country. Beef and dairy cattle are grazed on low-lying pasture.

FARMING AND LAND USE

- 🐂 Cattle
- 🌾 Cereals
- 🥕 Market gardening
- 🌱 Root crops
- 🍇 Vineyards

  Pasture
  Cropland
  Forest
  Mountain region
  Wetland
- • Major conurbation

LAND USE

- Cropland 35%
- Pasture 20%
- Forest 27%
- Other (including urban) 18%

THE LANDSCAPE

The north and west of France is made up of mainly flat, grassy plains or low hills. Wooded mountains line the country's borders in the south and east, and much of central France is taken up by the Massif Central, an enormous plateau cut by deep river valleys and scattered with extinct volcanoes. Three major rivers, the Loire, Seine, and Garonne, drain the lowland basins.

Paris Basin
The Paris Basin is a saucer-shaped hollow made up of layers of hard and soft rock, covered with very fertile soils. It runs across about 38,600 sq miles of northern France.

Alps (E 5)
The western end of the European Alpine mountain chain stretches into southeast France. The French Alps can be crossed by several passes, which give access to Italy and Switzerland.

Normandy
The coast of Normandy is lined with high chalk cliffs.

Pyrenees (C 7)
These mountains form a natural barrier between France and Spain. Several peaks reach heights of over 9,480 ft. The Pyrenees are difficult to cross, due to their height, and because they have few low passes.

Massif Central (D 5)
This vast granite plateau was formed over 200 million years ago. Volcanic activity here stopped only within the last 10,000 years, and the region's rounded hills are the worn-down remains of volcanic mountains.

Camargue (D 7)
The Camargue is an area of marshes, pastures, sand dunes, and salt flats at the mouth of the Rhône River. Rare animal and plant species are found there.

Mont Blanc (E 5)
This mountain in the French Alps is the tallest in Western Europe. It is 15,771 ft high.

INDUSTRY

France is one of the world's top manufacturing nations, with a variety of both traditional and high-tech industries. Cars, machinery, and electronic products are exported worldwide, along with luxury goods such as perfumes, fashions, and wines. Fossil fuels provide some energy, but France is currently the world's second-biggest producer of nuclear power.

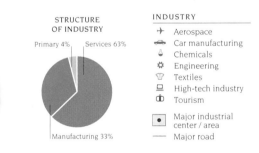

STRUCTURE OF INDUSTRY

- Primary 4%
- Services 63%
- Manufacturing 33%

INDUSTRY

- ✈ Aerospace
- 🚗 Car manufacturing
- ⚗ Chemicals
- ⚙ Engineering
- 👕 Textiles
- 💻 High-tech industry
- ⚓ Tourism

- ▣ Major industrial center / area
- — Major road

POPULATION

In the past 50 years, most people have moved from the countryside into urban areas. Paris and its suburbs, the industrial cities, and the Côte d'Azur in the southeast are the most economically developed parts of France and now have the biggest populations.

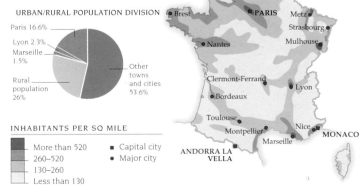

URBAN/RURAL POPULATION DIVISION

- Paris 16.6%
- Lyon 2.3%
- Marseille 1.5%
- Rural population 26%
- Other towns and cities 53.6%

INHABITANTS PER SQ MILE

- More than 520
- 260–520
- 130–260
- Less than 130

- ■ Capital city
- • Major city

ENVIRONMENTAL ISSUES

Many of France's coastal areas have been polluted by industry and tourism. The French government has recently introduced policies that aim to protect the country's environment. France's reliance on nuclear energy – 75% of its electricity is generated by nuclear power – causes it to suffer less from the pollution caused by burning fossil fuels than many other countries in Europe.

EUROPE
France

NORTH AMERICA
ASIA
AFRICA
SOUTH AMERICA
AUSTRALASIA AND OCEANIA
ANTARCTICA

ENVIRONMENTAL ISSUES

- Nuclear power station
- Sea pollution
- Polluted rivers
- Major industrial center

Seine
Paris
Loire
Saône
Lyon
Bordeaux
Garonne
Rhône
Marseille

CLIMATE

In winter, the coldest areas of France are the mountains of the Massif Central and the Alps. Summers are hottest on the Mediterranean coast.

TEMPERATURE AND PRECIPITATION

- More than 68°F
- 59 to 68°F
- 50 to 59°F
- 41 to 50°F
- 32 to 41°F
- 23 to 32°F
- Less than 23°F

— 4 Precipitation (in)

January

July

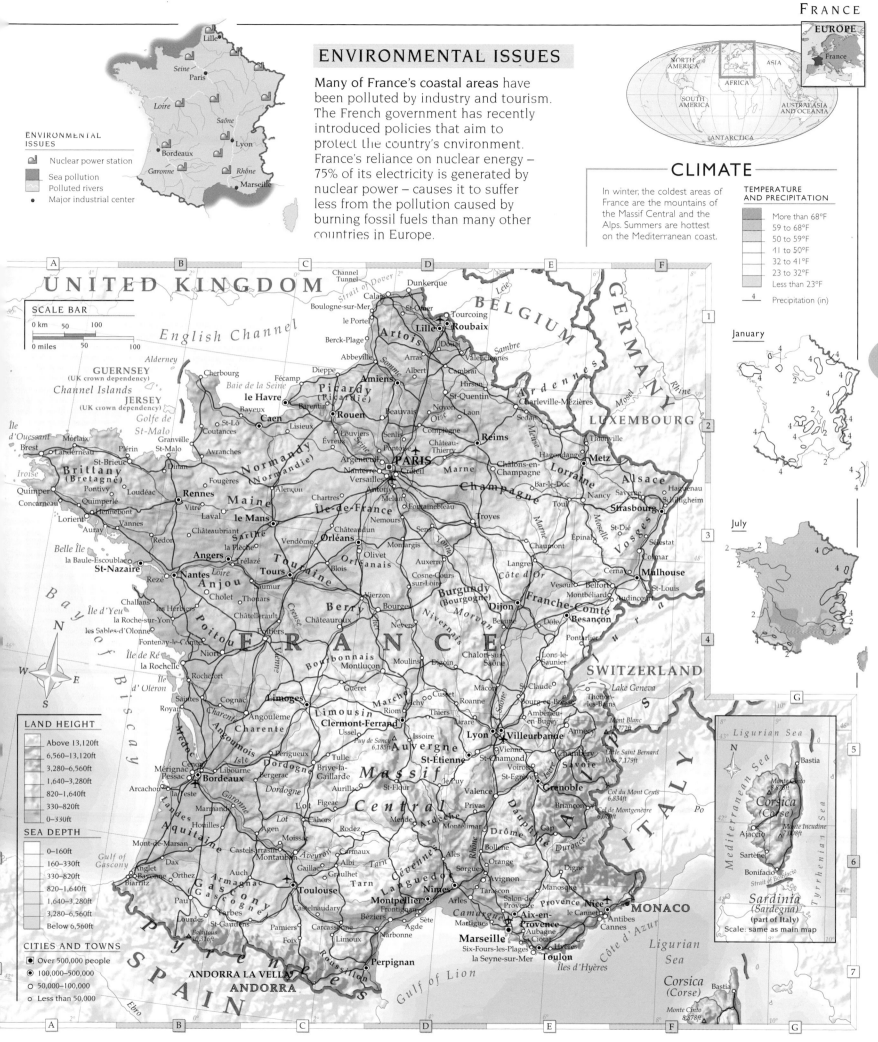

UNITED KINGDOM

SCALE BAR
0 km 50 100
0 miles 50 100

English Channel

GUERNSEY
(UK crown dependency)
Channel Islands
JERSEY
(UK crown dependency)

Alderney

BELGIUM
GERMANY
LUXEMBOURG
SWITZERLAND
ITALY
SPAIN
ANDORRA LA VELLA
ANDORRA

Channel Tunnel
Strait of Dover
Dunkerque
Calais
Boulogne-sur-Mer
le Portel
St-Omer
Tourcoing
Lille
Roubaix
Artois
Berck-Plage
Abbeville
Arras
Douai
Valenciennes
Cambrai
Picardy
(Picardie)
Amiens
Hirson
Charleville-Mézières
Sedan
Ardennes
Sambre
Meuse
Rhine
Mosel

Cherbourg
Baie de la Seine
Fécamp
Dieppe
le Havre
Bayeux
Caen
Barentin
Rouen
Beauvais
Noyon
St-Quentin
Laon
Reims
Châlons-en-Champagne
Thionville
Hagondange
Metz
Lorraine
Alsace
Haguenau
Mitiligheim
Strasbourg
Saverne
Nancy

Golfe de St-Malo
St-Lô
Coutances
Granville
St-Malo
Dinan
Avranches
Lisieux
Louviers
Évreux
Senlis
Pontoise
Compiègne
Château-Thierry
Bar-le-Duc
Toul
St-Dié
Sélestat
Colmar

Île d'Ouessant
Brest
Morlaix
Landerneau
Plérin
St-Brieuc
Quimper
Pontivy
Loudéac
Rennes
Fougères
Maine
Alençon
Chartres
Argenteuil
Nanterre
PARIS
Créteil
Versailles
Antony
Melun
Île-de-France
Fontainebleau
Marne
Champagne
Épinal
Chaumont
Langres
Vesoul
Vosges

Iroise
Concarneau
Quimperlé
Quimper
Pontivy
Hennebont
Vitré
Laval
le Mans
Sarthe
Châteaudun
Orléans
Montargis
Sens
Yonne
Auxerre
Côte d'Or
Cernay
Belfort
Mulhouse
St-Louis

Lorient
Auray
Vannes
Redon
Châteaubriant
la Flèche
Vendôme
Blois
Orléanais
Toul

Belle Île
la Baule-Escoublac
St-Nazaire
Rezé
Nantes
Angers
Trélazé
Tours
Touraine
Olivet
Saumur
Thouars
Cholet
Anjou
Loire
Vierzon
Bourges
Berry
Nivernais
Nevers
Morvan
Dijon
Franche-Comté
Montbéliard
Audincourt
Besançon
Dole
Pontarlier

Île d'Yeu
les Herbiers
Challans
la Roche-sur-Yon
Châtellerault
Poitou
Poitiers
Vienne
Châteauroux
Creuse
Bourbonnais
Montluçon
Moulins
Digoin
Chalon-sur-Saône
Lons-le-Saunier
SWITZERLAND

Île de Ré
la Rochelle
Fontenay-le-Comte
Niort
FRANCE
Marche
Montluçon
Vichy
Cusset
Roanne
Mâcon
St-Claude
Lake Geneva
Thonon-les-Bains

Bay of Biscay
Île d'Oléron
Rochefort
Saintes
Royan
Cognac
Angoulême
Charente
Limousin
Limoges
Guéret
Riom
Thiers
Lyon
Villeurbanne
Bourg-en-Bresse
Ambérieu-en-Bugey
Annecy
Mont Blanc
15,772ft

Médoc
Lesparre
Blaye
Libourne
Bergerac
Périgueux
Brive-la-Gaillarde
Tulle
Clermont-Ferrand
Ussel
Puy de Sancy
6,185ft
Issoire
Auvergne
St-Étienne
St-Chamond
Vienne
Voiron
St-Egrève
Chambéry
Savoie
le Petit Saint Bernard
Pass 7,179ft

Mérignac
Pessac
Bordeaux
Arcachon
la Teste
Aquitaine
Garonne
Marmande
Villeneuve
Agen
Lot
Figeac
Rodez
Aurillac
St-Flour
le Puy
Valence
Grenoble
Col du Mont Cenis
6,834ft
Briançon
Col de Montgenèvre
6,070ft
Po

Anglet
Bayonne
Biarritz
Mont-de-Marsan
Dax
Orthez
Hostens
Landes
Gascony
Gascogne
Lot
Cahors
Mende
Ardèche
Montélimar
Drôme
Bollène
Durance
Gap
Digne

Pau
Lourdes
Balaïtous
10,316ft
St-Gaudens
Auch
Armagnac
Castelsarrasin
Montauban
Aveyron
Gaillac
Albi
Tarn
Cévennes
Languedoc
Sorgues
Orange
Avignon
Tarascon
Salon-de-Provence
Manosque
Provence
Nice
Monaco
Antibes
Cannes

Tarbes
Castelnaudary
Toulouse
Carmaux
Graulhet
Nîmes
Arles
Camargue
Aix-en-Provence
le Cannet
Aubagne
Ciotat
Hyères
Côte d'Azur

Pamiers
Foix
Carcassonne
Limoux
Narbonne
Agde
Sète
Béziers
Frontignan
Montpellier
Martigues
Marseille
Six-Fours-les-Plages
la Seyne-sur-Mer
Toulon
Îles d'Hyères

Perpignan
Roussillon
Gulf of Lion
Ligurian Sea

PYRENEES
SPAIN
Ebro

LAND HEIGHT
- Above 13,120ft
- 6,560–13,120ft
- 3,280–6,560ft
- 1,640–3,280ft
- 820–1,640ft
- 330–820ft
- 0–330ft

SEA DEPTH
- 0–160ft
- 160–330ft
- 330–820ft
- 820–1,640ft
- 1,640–3,280ft
- 3,280–6,560ft
- Below 6,560ft

CITIES AND TOWNS
- ● Over 500,000 people
- ◉ 100,000–500,000
- ◎ 50,000–100,000
- ○ Less than 50,000

Ligurian Sea
Bastia
Corsica (Corse)
Monte Cinto
8,878ft
Ajaccio
Sartène
Monte Incudine
7,008ft
Bonifacio
Strait of Bonifacio
Mediterranean Sea
Tyrrhenian Sea
Sardinia (Sardegna)
(part of Italy)
Scale: same as main map

Corsica (Corse)
Bastia
Monte Cinto
8,878ft

SPAIN AND PORTUGAL

PORTUGAL, SPAIN

Spain and Portugal occupy the Iberian Peninsula, which is cut off from the rest of Europe by the Pyrenees. Over the centuries, Iberia has been invaded and settled by many different peoples. The Moors, who arrived from North Africa in the 8th century, ruled much of Spain for almost 800 years, and their influence can still be seen in Spanish culture. Portugal is one of the poorest countries in western Europe, but Spain's economy is rapidly expanding.

INDUSTRY

Madrid, Barcelona, and the northern ports are Spain's industrial centers. Here, iron ore from Spanish mines is used to make steel, and factories produce cars, machinery, and chemicals. Portugal exports textiles, clothing, and footwear, along with fish, such as sardines and tuna, caught off the Atlantic coast. In both countries, tourism is very important to the economy.

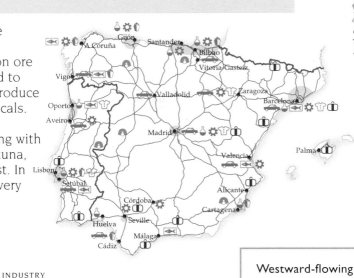

STRUCTURE OF INDUSTRY

Primary 5%
Services 62%
Manufacturing 33%

INDUSTRY

- 🚗 Car manufacturing
- ⚗ Chemicals
- ⚙ Engineering
- 🐟 Fish processing
- ⚓ Shipbuilding
- 👕 Textiles
- ⛏ Mining
- 🛆 Tourism
- ▪ Major industrial center / area
- — Major road

POPULATION

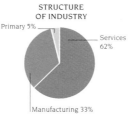

In the first half of the 20th century, most Spaniards lived in villages or small towns scattered around the country. Today, tourism and industry have drawn most of the population to the cities and coastal areas. Most Portuguese still live in rural areas along the coast or in the river valleys, but the cities are growing fast.

URBAN/RURAL POPULATION DIVISION

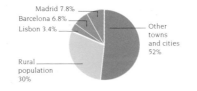

Madrid 7.8%
Barcelona 6.8%
Lisbon 3.4%
Other towns and cities 52%
Rural population 30%

INHABITANTS PER SQ MILE

- More than 520
- 260–520
- 130–260
- Less than 130
- ▪ Capital city
- ● Major city

FARMING AND LAND USE

Cereals, especially wheat and barley, are Iberia's chief crops. In the dry south of Spain, the land is irrigated to citrus fruits, particularly oranges, and a variety of vegetables. In both countries, olive trees and vineyards occupy large areas of land; olive oil and wine are important exports. Cork oak trees from Iberia's forests supply 80% of the world's cork.

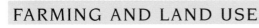

FARMING AND LAND USE

- 🐑 Sheep
- 🌾 Cereals
- 🍊 Citrus fruit
- 🫒 Olive oil
- 🍇 Vineyards
- 🌳 Cork
- Pasture
- Cropland
- Forest
- Mountain region
- ● Major conurbation

LAND USE

Other 10%
Cropland 39%
Forest 33%
Pasture 18%

THE LANDSCAPE

Most of inland Spain is taken up by the Meseta, a dry, almost treeless plateau surrounded by steep mountain ranges. The only lowlands, apart from narrow strips along the Mediterranean coast, are the valleys of the Ebro, Tagus, Guadiana, and Guadalquivir Rivers. Portugal's coast is lined by wide plains. Inland, the Tagus River divides the country in two. To the north the land is hilly and wooded; to the south it is low-lying and drier.

Westward-flowing rivers
The Duero, Tagus, and Guadalquivir Rivers flow across the Meseta on their courses to the Atlantic Ocean.

Ebro River (E 2)
The Ebro River carries vital irrigation water to Spain's northeastern plains before flowing into the Mediterranean Sea.

Cordillera Cantábrica (C 1)
These rugged, forested mountains rise on Spain's Atlantic coast. They form the northern edge of the Meseta.

The Pyrenees (F 2)
These high mountains form a natural boundary with France.

Duero River (D 2)

Tagus River (B 4)

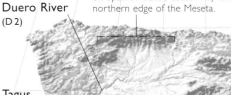

The Meseta
Much of this vast plateau of ancient rock is covered with dry, dusty high plains. It has thin soils and is mainly used to graze sheep and goats.

Sierra Morena (C 5)
The southern end of the Meseta is marked by this low range of mountains.

Guadalquivir Basin (C 5)
The Guadalquivir River has deposited layers of rich soil called alluvium on its floodplain, making this one of Spain's most fertile regions.

Mulhacén (D 5)
Mulhacén, in the snow-capped Sierra Nevada range in southern Spain, is 11,421 ft high. It is Iberia's tallest mountain.

ENVIRONMENTAL ISSUES

Soil erosion – where the top layer of soil has been worn away by wind and rain – has affected much of the Iberian Peninsula. This is caused by farming, combined with drought and deforestation. In Spain, a national tree-planting program has been started to combat this problem. Industrial and tourist development along the Mediterranean coast of Spain and in the Balearic Islands has damaged natural habitats on both land and sea.

ENVIRONMENTAL ISSUES
- Overbuilding
- Soil degradation
- Severe soil degradation
- Polluted rivers

Douro
Ebro
Costa Brava
Guadiana
Majorca
Segura
Ibiza
Guadalquivir
Costa Blanca
Costa del Sol

CLIMATE

Northern Spain is wetter and cooler than the south. On the central plateau, summers are very hot and dry, and winters often freezing. The north of Portugal is cooled by winds blowing off the Atlantic Ocean. The south is warmer, with dry, mild winters.

EUROPE
NORTH AMERICA
ASIA
AFRICA
SOUTH AMERICA
AUSTRALASIA AND OCEANIA
ANTARCTICA
Spain and Portugal

January

July

TEMPERATURE AND PRECIPITATION
- More than 77°F
- 68 to 77°F
- 59 to 68°F
- 50 to 59°F
- 41 to 50°F
- 32 to 41°F
- 23 to 32°F
- 14 to 23°F
- Less than 14°F

4 — Precipitation (in)

LAND HEIGHT
- 6,560–13,120ft
- 3,280–6,560ft
- 1,640–3,280ft
- 820–1,640ft
- 330–820ft
- 0–330ft

SEA DEPTH
- 0–820ft
- 820–1,640ft
- 1,640–3,280ft
- 3,280–6,560ft
- 6,560–9,840ft
- 9,840–13,120ft
- Below 13,120ft

CITIES AND TOWNS
- Over 500,000 people
- 100,000–500,000
- 50,000–100,000
- Less than 50,000

SCALE BAR
0 km   50   100
0 miles   50   100

GERMANY AND THE ALPINE STATES

AUSTRIA, GERMANY, LIECHTENSTEIN, SLOVENIA, SWITZERLAND

Germany lies at the heart of Europe and is the biggest industrial power in the continent. In 1945, Germany was divided into two separate countries, East and West Germany, which were reunited in 1990. To the south, the snow-capped peaks of the Alps, Europe's highest mountains, tower over the Alpine states – Switzerland, Austria, Liechtenstein, and the former Yugoslavian state of Slovenia.

INDUSTRY

Germany is a leading manufacturer of cars, chemicals, machinery, and transportation equipment. Switzerland and Liechtenstein make high-value products such as watches and pharmaceuticals and provide services such as banking. The Alpine states are a popular tourist location year-round.

INDUSTRY

- 🚗 Car manufacturing
- Chemicals
- ⚙ Engineering
- Iron and steel
- Shipbuilding
- Pharmaceuticals
- 💻 High-tech industry
- Tourism

- ▪ Major industrial center / area
- — Major road

STRUCTURE OF INDUSTRY

Primary 1%   Services 62%

Manufacturing 37%

POPULATION

Western and central Germany are the most densely populated areas in this region – particularly in and around the Rhine and Ruhr valleys, where there are many industries. In the south, the steep slopes of the Alps and permanent snow cover on the higher peaks means that most large towns and cities are in scattered lowland areas.

INHABITANTS PER SQ MILE

- More than 520
- 260–520
- 130–260
- Less than 130

- ▪ Capital city
- • Major city

URBAN/RURAL POPULATION DIVISION

Vienna 1.4%   Berlin 3.6%
Munich 1%
Rural population 18%
Other towns and cities 76%

FARMING AND LAND USE

Germany produces three-quarters of its own food. Crop farming is widespread, with cereals and root crops grown in flat, fertile areas. Cattle and pig farming supplies meat and dairy products. Across the Alps, the mountains limit farming, although grapes are grown on the warmer, south-facing slopes. The rich pastures of the lower slopes are used to graze beef and dairy cattle.

FARMING AND LAND USE

- Cattle
- Pigs
- Cereals
- Root crops
- Vineyards

- Pasture
- Cropland
- Forest
- Mountain region
- • Major conurbation

LAND USE

Forest 33%   Other (including mountains) 20%

Pasture 18%   Cropland 29%

THE LANDSCAPE

To the north, flat plains and heathlands surround the North Sea coast. Farther south are Germany's central uplands, which are lower and older than the jagged peaks of the Alps, which began to form about 65 million years ago. From its source in the Black Forest, the Danube River flows eastward across Germany and Austria on its course to the Black Sea. The other major river, the Rhine, flows northward.

Harz mountains (C 4)
These rugged, wooded mountains are much older than the Alps. They were formed over 300 million years ago.

Rhine River (B 5)
The Rhine is Germany's main waterway. It is an important transportation route to and from northern ports. It twists and turns across 820 miles of Europe, from its source in southeast Switzerland, to the North Sea.

Karst region (E 8)
Most of the water in this limestone region of Slovenia flows underground, through huge caves and caverns.

Danube River (B 7)
The Danube is Europe's second-longest river, flowing 1,765 miles.

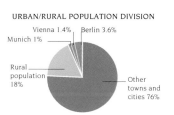

Lake Constance (B 7)
Lake Constance covers 210 sq miles and is Germany's largest lake, although its waters are shared by Austria and Switzerland.

Alps (C 8)
The Alps were formed when the African Plate collided with the Eurasian Plate, pushing up and crushing huge amounts of rock, to form mountains.

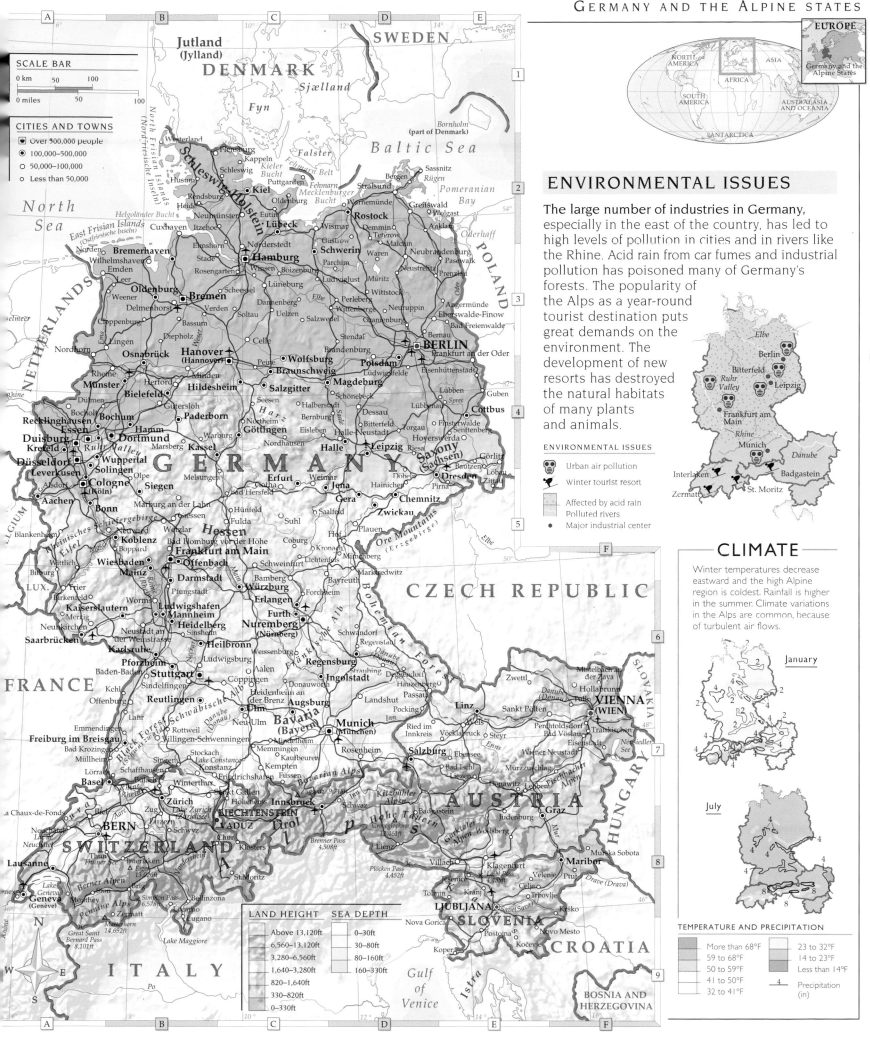

EUROPE
Germany and the Alpine States

ENVIRONMENTAL ISSUES

The large number of industries in Germany, especially in the east of the country, has led to high levels of pollution in cities and in rivers like the Rhine. Acid rain from car fumes and industrial pollution has poisoned many of Germany's forests. The popularity of the Alps as a year-round tourist destination puts great demands on the environment. The development of new resorts has destroyed the natural habitats of many plants and animals.

ENVIRONMENTAL ISSUES

- Urban air pollution
- Winter tourist resort
- Affected by acid rain
- Polluted rivers
- Major industrial center

CLIMATE

Winter temperatures decrease eastward and the high Alpine region is coldest. Rainfall is higher in the summer. Climate variations in the Alps are common, because of turbulent air flows.

January

July

TEMPERATURE AND PRECIPITATION

More than 68°F	23 to 32°F
59 to 68°F	14 to 23°F
50 to 59°F	Less than 14°F
41 to 50°F	
32 to 41°F	4 — Precipitation (in)

SCALE BAR

0 km 50 100
0 miles 50 100

CITIES AND TOWNS

- Over 500,000 people
- 100,000–500,000
- 50,000–100,000
- Less than 50,000

LAND HEIGHT

- Above 13,120ft
- 6,560–13,120ft
- 3,280–6,560ft
- 1,640–3,280ft
- 820–1,640ft
- 330–820ft
- 0–330ft

SEA DEPTH

- 0–30ft
- 30–80ft
- 80–160ft
- 160–330ft

ITALY

ITALY, SAN MARINO, VATICAN CITY

Italy has played an important role in Europe since the Romans based their mighty empire here over 2,000 years ago. The famous boot shape divides into two very different halves. Northern Italy has a varied range of industries and agriculture. Beautiful cities like Venice, Florence, and Rome draw tourists from all over the world. Southern Italy is poorer and less developed than the north, with a hotter, drier climate and less productive land.

THE LANDSCAPE

Italy is a peninsula jutting south from mainland Europe into the Mediterranean Sea. In northern and central Italy the land is mainly mountainous. Most of the flat land is in the Po Valley and along the eastern coast. Italy lies within an earthquake zone, which makes the land unstable, and there are also a number of active volcanoes.

Italian lakes
Great lakes like Garda (B3) and Como (B2) fill several south-facing valleys once occupied by glaciers.

The Dolomites (D2)
These high mountains are part of the same range as the Alps. They were formed 65 million years ago.

Po Valley (C2)
The basin of the Po River has the best soils in Italy. Rich alluvium is washed from the mountains by the river to form a wide plain.

The Apennines (C4)
This mountain range forms the "backbone" of Italy, dividing the rocky west coast from the flatter, sandy east coast.

Earthquakes
The southern Apennines, as well as coastal areas of southwestern Italy, often experience earthquakes and mudslides.

Tyrrhenian Sea (C6)
This sea, which divides the Italian mainland from Sardinia, is gradually filling with sediment from the rivers which flow into it.

Sardinia
The island of Sardinia is made from very old rocks that were thrust up to form mountains.

Sicily
Sicily is the largest island in the Mediterranean. It has a famous active volcano called Mount Etna and often experiences earthquakes.

Gulf of Taranto (F7)
During earthquakes, great blocks of land have broken away and sunk into the sea, forming the Gulf's square shape.

FARMING AND LAND USE

The Po Valley is a broad, flat plain in the north of Italy. It contains the most fertile land in the country, and wheat and rice are the main cereal crops grown here. Grapes for wine are grown everywhere in Italy. In much of the south, the land must be irrigated to support crops. Where there is enough water, citrus fruits, olives, and many kinds of tomatoes are grown.

LAND USE

Other 21%
Cropland 41%
Forest 23%
Pasture 15%

FARMING AND LAND USE
- Cattle
- Cereals
- Citrus fruits
- Olive oil
- Rice
- Vineyards
- Pasture
- Cropland
- Forest
- Mountain region
- Major conurbation

INDUSTRY

Italian industry is located mainly in the north. Design is extremely important to Italians, and they are proud of the elegant designs of their furniture, clothes, and shoes. Although many firms are small, they are very efficient. Italy has few mineral resources, so it needs to import raw materials to make cars, engines, and other high-tech products.

INDUSTRY
- Car manufacturing
- Chemicals
- Iron and steel
- Textiles
- Finance
- High-tech industry
- Tourism
- Major industrial center / area
- Major road

STRUCTURE OF INDUSTRY
Primary 3%
Services 66%
Manufacturing 31%

POPULATION

Most of Italy's population lives in the north, mainly in and around the Po Valley, which is home to over 25 million people. Most people here have a high standard of living. Southern Italy is much more rural: towns are smaller and life is often much harder.

URBAN/RURAL POPULATION DIVISION
Milan 1.5%
Rome 2.8%
Naples 1.2%
Rural population 31%
Other towns and cities 63.5%

INHABITANTS PER SQ MILE
- More than 520
- 260–520
- 130–260
- 0–130
- Capital city
- Major city

CLIMATE

Southeastern Europe's climate varies from north to south. Continental climates are found in the north; winters are cold and dry, while toward the south, winters are milder and summers much hotter. Europe's wettest place is found in the mountains in Bosnia and Herzegovina.

EUROPE
Southeast Europe

NORTH AMERICA • ASIA • AFRICA • SOUTH AMERICA • AUSTRALASIA AND OCEANIA • ANTARCTICA

January

July

TEMPERATURE AND PRECIPITATION
- More than 77°F
- 68 to 77°F
- 59 to 68°F
- 50 to 59°F
- 41 to 50°F
- 32 to 41°F
- 23 to 32°F
- Less than 23°F
- —4— Precipitation (in)

ENVIRONMENTAL ISSUES

Emissions from industry and traffic fumes have polluted the air in Athens and Zagreb. In Athens, smog caused by exhausts can become so severe on some days that the use of cars is banned. Earthquakes are common, Macedonia's capital city, Skopje, was badly hit in 1963, and Bulgaria's run-down Kozloduy nuclear power station lies within the earthquake zone.

Zagreb
Danube
Kozloduy
Skopje 1963
Salonica 1978
Athens

ENVIRONMENTAL ISSUES
- ◉ Catastrophic earthquake
- ⌖ Unstable nuclear reactor
- ☻ Urban air pollution
- ▒ Water pollution
- ░ Polluted river
- • Major town

CITIES AND TOWNS
- ■ Over 500,000 people
- ● 100,000–500,000
- ○ 50,000–100,000
- · Less than 50,000

LAND HEIGHT
- 6,560–13,120ft
- 3,280–6,560ft
- 1,640–3,280ft
- 820–1,640ft
- 330–820ft
- 0–330ft

SEA DEPTH
- 0–160ft
- 160–330ft
- 330–820ft
- 820–1,640ft
- 1,640–3,280ft
- 3,280–6,560ft
- Below 6,560ft

SCALE BAR
0 km 50 100
0 miles 50 100

AUSTRIA
SLOVENIA
ITALY
HUNGARY
Drava (Drau)
Mur
Sava
Drava
Danube (Duna)
Great Hungarian Plain
Mures
Varaždin
ZAGREB
Virovitica
Subotica
Kikinda
Osijek
Vojvodina
Vrbas
Zrenjanin
CROATIA
Papuk
Vukovar
Slavonski Brod
Novi Sad
Istra
Karlovac
Rijeka
Pula
Novi
Bihać
Bosanski
Banja Luka
Gradačac
Tuzla
Zemun
Vršac
Pančevo
ROMANIA
Ialomița
Danube (Dunăv)
San MARINO
Zadar
Dugi Otok
BOSNIA AND HERZEGOVINA
Zenica
Sava
BELGRADE (BEOGRAD)
Smederevo
Smederevska Palanka
Valjevo
SERBIA
Negotin
Bor
Danube (Dunav)
Silistra
Dulovo
Adriatic Sea
Dalmatia
SARAJEVO
Kraljevo
Kragujevac
Velika Morava
Vidin
Dimovo
Lom
Kozloduy
Ruse
Razgrad
Dobrich
Kavarna
Split
Mostar
Foča
Kruševac
Niš
Leskovac
Montana
Vratsa
Pleven
Veliko Turnovo
Shumen
Varna
Brač
Hvar
Vis
YUGOSLAVIA
BULGARIA
Gabrovo
Sliven
Black Sea
Korčula
Bijelo Polje
Kosovska Mitrovica
MONTENEGRO
Peć
Priština
Pernik
SOFIA (SOFIYA)
Kazanluk
Stara Zagora
Aytos
Burgas
Mljet
Dubrovnik
Palagruža
Nikšić
Podgorica
Kosovo
Kumanovo
Kyustendil
Blagoevgrad
Plovdiv
Pazardzhik
Khaskovo
Kurdzhali
Dimitrovgrad
Tsarevo
Scutari
Shkodër
Prizren
Gjilan
Đakovica
ALBANIA
SKOPJE
MACEDONIA
Rhodope Mountains
Musala 9,597ft
Petrich
Sandanski
Didymoteicho
Ergene Irmağı
TIRANA (TIRANË)
Durrës
Bitola
Prilep
Kičevo
Drama
Xanthi
Komotini
Kavala
Alexandroupoli
Sea of Marmara
Fier
Berat
Vlorë
Kozani
Giannitsa
Kilkis
Salonica (Thessaloniki)
Kalamaria
Chalkidiki
Thasos
Thracian Sea
Samothraki
TURKEY
Korçë
Lake Prespa
Katerini
Thermaic Gulf
Karyes
Neapoli
Mount Olympus
Sarti
Gjirokastër
Komitsa
Larisa
Myrina
Limnos
Agios Efstratios
Kalloni
Mytilini
Sarandë
Metsovo
Trikala
Karditsa
Volos
Alonnisos
Lesbos
Corfu (Kerkyra)
Ioannina
Igoumenitsa
Pindus Mountains
Northern Sporades
Skiros
Psara
Chios
Gediz Nehri
Corfu (Kerkyra)
Paxoi
Arta
Preveza
Karpenisi
Lamia
Kymi
Skyros
Euboea (Evvoia)
Chios
Lefkada
GREECE
Aegean Sea
Büyükmenderes Nehri
Vasiliki
Kefallinia
Nafpaktos
Aharhos
Chalkida
Patra
Gulf of Corinth
Lechaina
Isthmus of Corinth
Corinth (Korinthos)
ATHENS (ATHINA)
Piraeus (Peiraias)
Andros
Tinos
Samos
Ikaria
Agathonisi
Patmos
Leros
Poros
Keri
Naplio
Ermioni
Kea
Syros
Mykonos
Kythnos
Kalymnos
Zakynthos
Tripoli
Pyrgos
Alfeios
Leonidi
Serifos
Paros
Naxos
Amorgos
Dodecanese (Dodekanisos)
Nisyros
Rhodes (Rodos)
Kalamata
Sparti
Cyclades (Kyklades)
Sifnos
Milos
Thira
Anafi
Tilos
Chalki
Rhodes (Rodos)
Lindos
Koroni
Areopoli
Neapoli
Mirtoan Sea
Kythira
Antikythira
Sea of Crete (Kritiko Pelagos)
Karpathos
Saria
Karpathos
Ionian Sea (Ionio Nisoi)
Strait of Otranto
Drini i Zi
Chania
Rethymno
Irakleio
Lefka Ori
Agios Nikolaos
Tympaki
Crete (Kriti)
Kasos
Ionian Islands (Ionioi Nisoi)
Mediterranean Sea
MOLDOVA
UKRAINE

EASTERN EUROPE

BELARUS, MOLDOVA, ROMANIA, UKRAINE

Much of Eastern Europe, which extends north from the Danube River and the Black Sea, is covered by open grasslands called steppe. Ukraine's excellent farmland and large mineral reserves make it one of the strongest new countries to emerge from the former Soviet Union. Moldova and Belarus were also part of the USSR until they became independent in 1991. Romania was a strict communist regime from 1945 until 1989.

POPULATION

Most Romanians live in Bucharest, the capital, or in other cities and towns. In Ukraine, two-thirds of the population lives in cities in the Donbass industrial area. Most people in Belarus are city dwellers. Moldova is the most rural country in Eastern Europe; half its people live in the countryside and make their living from farming.

URBAN/RURAL POPULATION DIVISION

Bucharest 2.5% Kiev 3.2%
Dnipropetrovs'k 1.3%
Rural population 36%
Other towns and cities 57%

INHABITANTS PER SQ MILE
- More than 520
- 260–520
- 130–260
- Less than 130
- ■ Capital city
- ● Major city

INDUSTRY

In Ukraine, most industry is based around the country's mineral reserves. The Donbass region has Europe's largest coalfield and is an important center for iron and steel production. The main industries of Belarus are chemicals, machine building, and food-processing. Romania's manufacturing industries are growing, with the help of foreign investment.

INDUSTRY
- 🚗 Car manufacturing
- 🧪 Chemicals
- ⚙ Engineering
- Food processing
- Iron and steel
- 👕 Textiles
- Coal
- Mining
- Oil and gas
- ⚓ Tourism
- ▣ Major industrial center / area
- — Major road

STRUCTURE OF INDUSTRY
Primary 20% Manufacturing 47%
Services 33%

THE LANDSCAPE

Flat or rolling grasslands, marshes, and river flood plains cover almost all of Ukraine and Belarus. The Carpathian Mountains cross the southwestern corner of Ukraine and continue in a large arc-shaped chain of high peaks at the heart of Romania. Along the southern part of this chain, the Carpathians are called the Transylvanian Alps.

Pripet Marshes (C3)
The Pripet Marshes in Belarus and Ukraine form the largest area of marshland in Europe.

The steppes
The steppes are great, wide grasslands that are found across eastern Europe and central Asia. Over 70% of the Ukrainian landscape is steppe. Little rain falls throughout the steppes.

FARMING AND LAND USE

The black soils found across much of Ukraine are very fertile and the country is a big producer of cereals, sugar beets, and sunflowers, which are grown for their oil. In Moldova and southern Romania, the warm summers are ideal for growing grapes for wine, along with sunflowers and a variety of vegetables. Cattle and pigs are farmed throughout Eastern Europe.

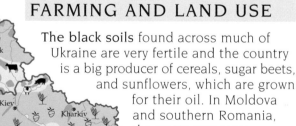

LAND USE
Other 11%
Forest 24%
Pasture 15%
Cropland 50%

FARMING AND LAND USE

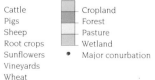
- 🐄 Cattle
- 🐖 Pigs
- 🐑 Sheep
- Root crops
- Sunflowers
- Vineyards
- Wheat
- Cropland
- Forest
- Pasture
- Wetland
- ● Major conurbation

Carpathian Mountains (C5)
The Carpathians are the largest mountain range in Eastern Europe. They are a rich source of timber and minerals.

Dnieper (E4) and Dniester (D5) Rivers
The Dnieper and Dniester run south and east toward the Black Sea. They flow slowly across huge areas of low-lying land.

The Crimea (F6)
This peninsula divides the Sea of Azov from the Black Sea. The steep mountains of Kryms'ki Hory run along the southeastern coast of the Crimea.

CLIMATE

January

July

The climate is continental, with warm, dry summers and very cold, dry winters. Temperatures are higher along the fringes of the Black Sea, while the Carpathian Mountains are colder and wetter all year round.

TEMPERATURE AND PRECIPITATION

- More than 68°F
- 59 to 68°F
- 50 to 59°F
- 41 to 50°F
- 32 to 41°F
- 23 to 32°F
- Less than 23°F

4 — Precipitation (in)

ENVIRONMENTAL ISSUES

The worst nuclear accident in history happened at Chernobyl nuclear power plant in northern Ukraine in 1986. Around 70% of the nuclear fallout was received by Belarus, contaminating its farmland, forests, and water supplies. Four million Ukrainians still live in dangerously radioactive areas.

ENVIRONMENTAL ISSUES

- Destroyed nuclear reactor
- Urban air pollution
- Levels of nuclear fallout
  - Very high
  - High
  - Moderate
- Polluted river
- Major industrial center

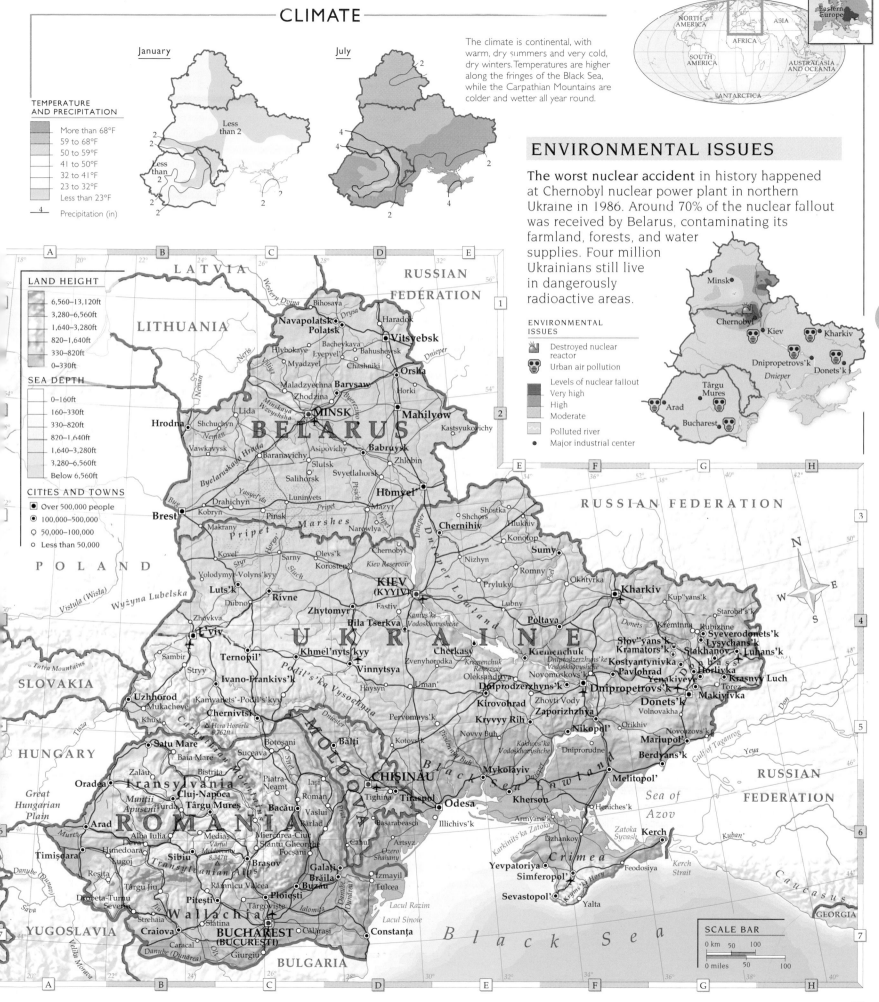

LAND HEIGHT

- 6,560–13,120ft
- 3,280–6,560ft
- 1,640–3,280ft
- 820–1,640ft
- 330–820ft
- 0–330ft

SEA DEPTH

- 0–160ft
- 160–330ft
- 330–820ft
- 820–1,640ft
- 1,640–3,280ft
- 3,280–6,560ft
- Below 6,560ft

CITIES AND TOWNS

- ■ Over 500,000 people
- ◉ 100,000–500,000
- ◎ 50,000–100,000
- ○ Less than 50,000

SCALE BAR

0 km 50 100

0 miles 50 100

EUROPEAN RUSSIA

RUSSIAN FEDERATION

European Russia is separated from the Asiatic part of the Russian Federation by the Ural Mountains. It is home to two-thirds of the country's population. Russia was the largest and most powerful republic of the communist Soviet Union, which collapsed in 1991. New businesses were set up when communism ended, but many old state industries closed down, causing unemployment and further hardship for many people.

INDUSTRY

European Russia is rich in natural resources. Minerals are mined on the Kola Peninsula and in the Urals, while dense forests are felled and processed in many of the larger northern cities. The Volga basin is one of Europe's largest sources of oil and gas. Moscow and the cities near the Volga are centers of skilled labor for a wide range of manufacturing industries like cars, chemicals, and heavy engineering and steel production.

INDUSTRY

🚗 Car manufacturing	🛢 Oil and gas
⚗ Chemicals	🌲 Timber processing
⚙ Engineering	
🏭 Iron and steel	▣ Major industrial center/area
👕 Textiles	— Major road
⛏ Mining	

FARMING AND LAND USE

Russia's best farmland lies within this region. Big crops of wheat, barley and oats, potatoes and sunflowers are produced in the fertile black soil that forms a thick band across the country to the south of Moscow. The far north is cold and frozen, with bare mountains and tundra making cultivation impossible. Farther south there are extensive forests, and rough pastures that are used for herding and hunting.

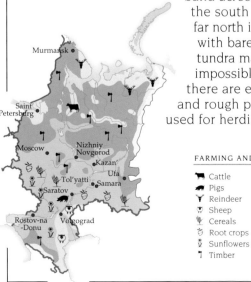

FARMING AND LAND USE

🐄 Cattle		▨ Barren land
🐖 Pigs		▨ Cropland
🦌 Reindeer		▨ Forest
🐑 Sheep		▨ Mountain region
🌾 Cereals		▨ Pasture
🌱 Root crops		▨ Tundra
🌻 Sunflowers		▨ Wetland
🌲 Timber		● Major conurbation

POPULATION

Three-quarters of European Russia's people live in towns and cities, most in a broad band stretching south from St. Petersburg to Moscow, and eastward to the Urals. The capital, Moscow, and St. Petersburg are very crowded cities. Living conditions there are cramped, with two families often sharing one apartment. The southeast is also heavily populated. Over 12 million people live in the cities and towns that line the banks of the Volga River.

INHABITANTS PER SQ MILE

▨	More than 260
▨	130–260
▨	30–130
▨	Less than 30
■	Capital city
●	Major city

THE LANDSCAPE

European Russia lies on the North European Plain, a huge, rolling lowland with wide river basins. The northern half of the plain, which was once covered by glaciers, has many lakes and swamps. The Volga River drains much of the plain as it flows south to the Caspian Sea. The Caucasus and Ural Mountains form natural boundaries in the south and east.

Northern European Russia (C 3)
Northern European Russia reaches into the Arctic Circle. It is a region of pine and birch forests, marshes, and tundra. There are also tens of thousands of lakes, including the biggest in Europe, Ladoga, which covers about 6,830 sq miles.

Ural Mountains (E 5)
The Ural Mountains run from north to south, stretching almost 2,500 miles.

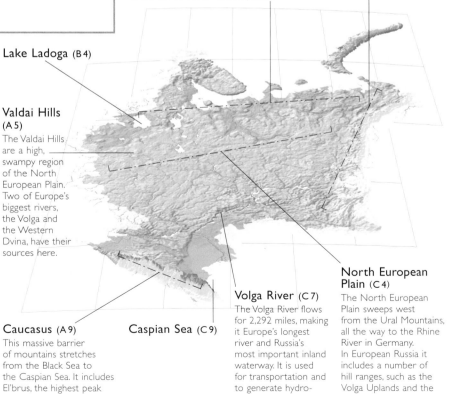

Lake Ladoga (B 4)

Valdai Hills (A 5)
The Valdai Hills are a high, swampy region of the North European Plain. Two of Europe's biggest rivers, the Volga and the Western Dvina, have their sources here.

Caucasus (A 9)
This massive barrier of mountains stretches from the Black Sea to the Caspian Sea. It includes El'brus, the highest peak in Europe, at 18,510 miles.

Caspian Sea (C 9)

Volga River (C 7)
The Volga River flows for 2,292 miles, making it Europe's longest river and Russia's most important inland waterway. It is used for transportation and to generate hydro-electric power.

North European Plain (C 4)
The North European Plain sweeps west from the Ural Mountains, all the way to the Rhine River in Germany. In European Russia it includes a number of hill ranges, such as the Volga Uplands and the Central Russian Upland.

ENVIRONMENTAL ISSUES

The many factories in European Russia have caused widespread pollution, and in most industrial cities air quality is poor. Several of Russia's older nuclear power plants have been declared unsafe, but are yet to be shut down. Waste from these power plants, as well as from nuclear submarines, has for many years been dumped in the Barents Sea and off Novaya Zemlya.

ENVIRONMENTAL
ISSUES

- Nuclear waste dump site
- Unstable nuclear reactor
- Urban air pollution
- Polluted rivers
- Major industrial center

CLIMATE

Winters are extremely cold and dry; temperatures plunge well below freezing in the north and east. Summer brings much warmer and wetter weather, especially in the south, while along the northern coast it remains relatively cold. Rainfall is highest in the Caucasus.

January

July

TEMPERATURE
AND PRECIPITATION

More than 68°F
59 to 68°F
50 to 59°F
41 to 50°F
32 to 41°F
23 to 32°F
14 to 23°F
5 to 14°F
Less than 5°F

4 — Precipitation (in)

THE MEDITERRANEAN

The **Mediterranean Sea** separates Europe from Africa. It stretches more than 2,500 miles from east to west and is almost completely enclosed by land. Many great civilizations, including the Greek and Roman empires, grew up around the Mediterranean. It has been a crossroads of international trade routes for many centuries. More than 100 million people live in the 28 countries that border the sea, and their numbers are increased by the large crowds of tourists who regularly visit the area.

ENVIRONMENTAL ISSUES

Water pollution is widespread in the Mediterranean, especially near the large coastal resorts where raw sewage and industrial effluent is pumped out to sea, and often ends up on the beaches. Oil refining and oil spills have also increased pollution.

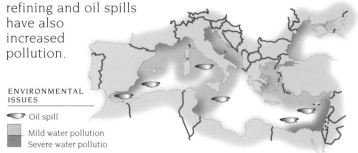

ENVIRONMENTAL ISSUES

⬯ Oil spill

　Mild water pollution
　Severe water pollutio

SCALE BAR

0 km 100 200

0 miles 100 200

MALTA

Victoria Nadur
Gozo Mgarr Comino
N
Mellieha
Mosta Naxxar St Julian's
Sliema
VALLETTA
Malta Paola
Rabat Birżebbuġa
0 km 10
0 miles 10

CYPRUS

Mediterranean Sea
Agialousa (Yenierenköy)
Lapithos Kyrenia
(Lapta) (Girne)
Morfou Kythrea
(Güzelyurt) (Degirmenlik)
Polis Famagusta (Ammochostos) (Gazimağusa)
NICOSIA
Larnaca (Larnaka)
Troodos Dhekelia Sovereign Base Area (to UK)
Pafos
Akrotiri Sovereign Base Area (to UK)
Limassol (Lemesos)
0 km 25
0 miles 25

TURKISH REPUBLIC OF NORTHERN CYPRUS (recognized only by Turkey)

Famagusta Bay

LAND HEIGHT	SEA DEPTH
Above 13,120ft	0–820ft
6,560–13,120ft	820–1,640ft
3,280–6,560ft	1,640–3,280ft
1,640–3,280ft	3,280–6,560ft
820–1,640ft	6,560–9,840ft
330–820ft	9,840–13,120ft
0–330ft	Below 13,120ft
Below sea level	

CITIES AND TOWNS

● Over 500,000 people
◉ 100,000–500,000
○ 50,000–100,000
○ Less than 50,000

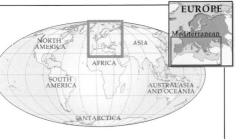

THE LANDSCAPE

The Mediterranean Sea would be an enormous lake if it were not for the Strait of Gibraltar, a narrow opening only 8 miles wide, which joins it to the Atlantic Ocean. The Mediterranean lies over the boundary of two continental plates. Where they meet, earthquakes and volcanoes are common.

Strait of Gibraltar

Sandy beaches
The Mediterranean coasts are bordered by several thousand miles of sandy beaches.

Shallow shelves
The area of water off the coast of Tunisia, and also the Adriatic Sea, are shallower than the rest of the Mediterranean.

Greek islands
Greece has thousands of islands that lie both in the Mediterranean and in the smaller Aegean Sea. Some of them are the remains of old volcanoes which have left black sand on the beaches.

Suez Canal
The Suez Canal links the Mediterranean to the Gulf of Suez and the Red Sea. Before it was built, ships had to sail around all of Africa to reach Asia.

Atlas Mountains
The rugged Atlas Mountains run through most of Morocco and Algeria. They form a barrier between the Mediterranean coast and the Sahara, which lies to the south.

TOURISM

The tourist industry in and around the Mediterranean is one of the most highly developed in the world. More than half the world's income from tourism is generated here. Resorts have grown up along the northwest coast of Africa, and in Egypt, southern Spain, France, Italy, Greece, and Turkey. Tourism brings huge economic benefits, but the ever-increasing number of visitors has also damaged the environment.

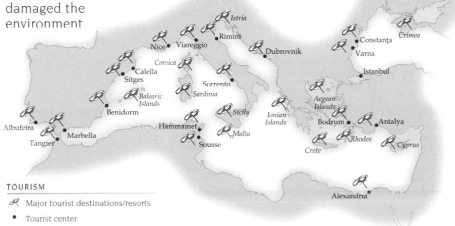

TOURISM

- Major tourist destinations/resorts
- Tourist center

INDUSTRY

The Mediterranean has a large fishing industry, although most of the fishing is small-scale. Tuna and sardines are caught throughout the region, and mussels are farmed off the coast of Italy. Fish canning and packing take place at most of the larger ports. Small oil and gas reserves are extracted off the coast of North Africa and near Greece, Spain, and Italy.

INDUSTRY

- Fishing ports
- Oil and gas
- Major city

CONTINENTAL ASIA

Asia is the world's largest continent, and has the greatest range of physical extremes. Some of the highest, lowest, and coldest places on Earth are found in Asia: Mount Everest in the Himalayas is the highest, the Dead Sea in the west is the lowest, and the frozen wastes of northern Siberia are among the coldest. More people live in Asia than on any other continent – 1.2 billion of them in China, and 940 million in India.

4,040 miles

6,030 miles

CROSS SECTION THROUGH ASIA

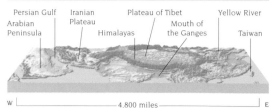

Persian Gulf   Iranian   Plateau of Tibet   Yellow River
Arabian   Plateau   Mouth of   Taiwan
Peninsula   Himalayas   the Ganges

W ◄——————— 4,800 miles ———————► E

The Arabian Peninsula and the mountainous Iranian Plateau are divided by the Persian Gulf, fed by the Tigris and Euphrates Rivers. Farther east, the land begins to rise, the mountains spreading north to the Plateau of Tibet, and south to the Himalayas. The plains to the south of the Himalayas are drained by the Indus and Ganges, and to the east of the Plateau of Tibet by the Yellow River.

PHYSICAL ASIA

Northern Asia is made up of old mountains and ancient, stable plateaus. The jagged Himalayan mountains dominate the central part of the continent, along with the Plateau of Tibet, which stretches north into China. In Southeast Asia, there are many islands. Volcanoes and earthquakes are common, and some of the islands are volcanically formed.

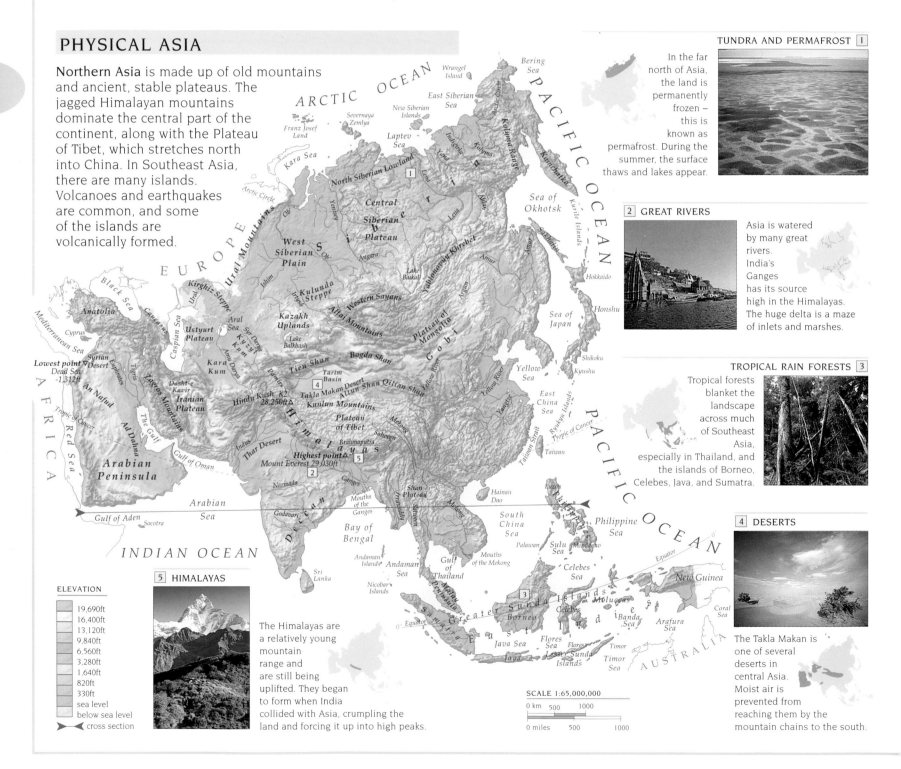

TUNDRA AND PERMAFROST 1

In the far north of Asia, the land is permanently frozen – this is known as permafrost. During the summer, the surface thaws and lakes appear.

2 GREAT RIVERS

Asia is watered by many great rivers. India's Ganges has its source high in the Himalayas. The huge delta is a maze of inlets and marshes.

TROPICAL RAIN FORESTS 3

Tropical forests blanket the landscape across much of Southeast Asia, especially in Thailand, and the islands of Borneo, Celebes, Java, and Sumatra.

4 DESERTS

The Takla Makan is one of several deserts in central Asia. Moist air is prevented from reaching them by the mountain chains to the south.

5 HIMALAYAS

The Himalayas are a relatively young mountain range and are still being uplifted. They began to form when India collided with Asia, crumpling the land and forcing it up into high peaks.

ELEVATION

| 19,690ft |
| 16,400ft |
| 13,120ft |
| 9,840ft |
| 6,560ft |
| 3,280ft |
| 1,640ft |
| 820ft |
| 330ft |
| sea level |
| below sea level |

✕ cross section

SCALE 1:65,000,000

0 km   500   1000

0 miles   500   1000

POLITICAL ASIA

Asia is a continent of many contrasts: in its lands, its peoples, and its traditions. The break-up of the Soviet Union, which once stretched south from Russia to Iran, produced the new central Asian republics of Kazakhstan, Kyrgyzstan, Tajikistan, Turkmenistan, and Uzbekistan. The countries in southwest Asia are mainly Muslim, but are divided by religious differences and conflicts. India is the world's largest democracy, while China is a communist power with restricted access to the rest of the world.

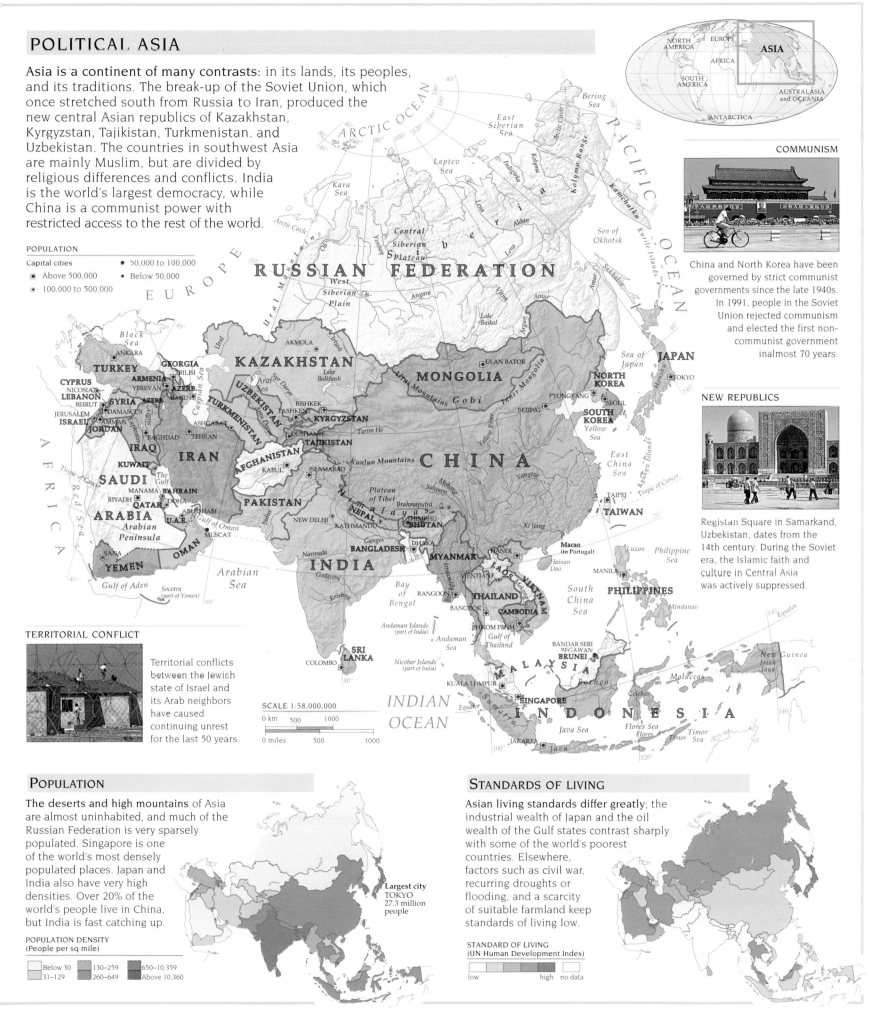

POPULATION

Capital cities
- Above 500,000
- 100,000 to 500,000
- 50,000 to 100,000
- Below 50,000

COMMUNISM

China and North Korea have been governed by strict communist governments since the late 1940s. In 1991, people in the Soviet Union rejected communism and elected the first non-communist government in almost 70 years.

NEW REPUBLICS

Registan Square in Samarkand, Uzbekistan, dates from the 14th century. During the Soviet era, the Islamic faith and culture in Central Asia was actively suppressed.

TERRITORIAL CONFLICT

Territorial conflicts between the Jewish state of Israel and its Arab neighbors have caused continuing unrest for the last 50 years.

SCALE 1:58,000,000

0 km 500 1000

0 miles 500 1000

POPULATION

The deserts and high mountains of Asia are almost uninhabited, and much of the Russian Federation is very sparsely populated. Singapore is one of the world's most densely populated places. Japan and India also have very high densities. Over 20% of the world's people live in China, but India is fast catching up.

Largest city
TOKYO
27.3 million
people

POPULATION DENSITY
(People per sq mile)

- Below 30
- 31–129
- 130–259
- 260–649
- 650–10,359
- Above 10,360

STANDARDS OF LIVING

Asian living standards differ greatly; the industrial wealth of Japan and the oil wealth of the Gulf states contrast sharply with some of the world's poorest countries. Elsewhere, factors such as civil war, recurring droughts or flooding, and a scarcity of suitable farmland keep standards of living low.

STANDARD OF LIVING
(UN Human Development Index)

low   high   no data

ASIAN GEOGRAPHY

Asia's forbidding mountain ranges, barren deserts, and fertile plains have affected the way in which people settled the continent. Intensive agriculture is found in the more fertile areas, and the largest concentrations of people grew up near fertile land and close to great rivers. Asia's mineral wealth has brought people to the more inhospitable parts of the continent: the deserts of southwest Asia for oil, and frozen Siberia for oil, gas, and minerals.

INDUSTRY

Many people in Asia still rely on agriculture as a source of income, and some countries have very few industries. Heavy industry dominates eastern China and Russia, but Japan is the most industrially productive country. In recent years, booming "tiger" economies have developed in countries such as Taiwan, that border the Pacific Ocean.

MINERAL RESOURCES

Over half of the world's oil and gas reserves are in Asia, most importantly around the Gulf and in western Siberia. Coal in Siberia and China has provided power for steel industries. Metallic minerals are also abundant: tin in Southeast Asia, and platinum and nickel in Siberia.

MINERAL RESOURCES

- Chromium
- Tin
- Nickel
- Iron
- Platinum
- Gold
- Lead
- Oil/gas field
- Coal field

OIL AND GAS

The discovery of oil in the Gulf has generated enormous wealth, and produced rapid industrial and social change in countries such as Saudi Arabia, U.A.E., and Kuwait that control the oil supplies.

HIGH-TECH INDUSTRIES

Japan is a world-leading producer of electronic and high-tech goods like computers, cameras, and hi-fi equipment. Taiwan, South Korea, and Singapore also produce electronic goods.

INDUSTRY

✈ Aerospace	⚒ Coal
🍶 Brewing	🖳 Electronics
🚗 Car/vehicle manufacturing	⚙ Engineering
⚙ Cement	Ⓢ Finance
⚗ Chemicals	🗎 Food processing
	🖥 High-tech industry
	🏭 Iron and steel
	⛏ Mining
	🛢 Oil and gas
	⚗ Pharmaceuticals
	🗐 Printing and publishing
	⚓ Shipbuilding
	🧵 Textiles
	🌲 Timber processing

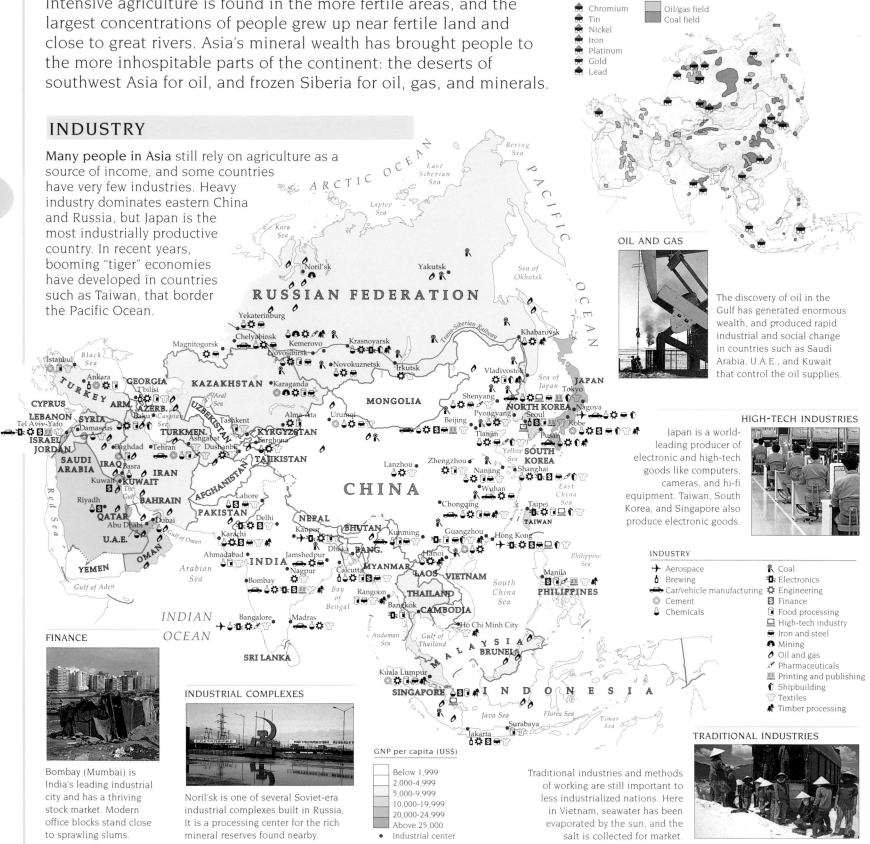

FINANCE

Bombay (Mumbai) is India's leading industrial city and has a thriving stock market. Modern office blocks stand close to sprawling slums.

INDUSTRIAL COMPLEXES

Noril'sk is one of several Soviet-era industrial complexes built in Russia, It is a processing center for the rich mineral reserves found nearby.

GNP per capita (US$)

- Below 1,999
- 2,000-4,999
- 5,000-9,999
- 10,000-19,999
- 20,000-24,999
- Above 25,000
- • Industrial center

TRADITIONAL INDUSTRIES

Traditional industries and methods of working are still important to less industrialized nations. Here in Vietnam, seawater has been evaporated by the sun, and the salt is collected for market.

CLIMATE

Most of Asia has a continental climate, apart from coastal areas. Without the moderating effects of the ocean, temperatures can soar during the day and plummet at night, while rainfall is generally low – producing several large deserts. Temperatures as low as −90°F have been recorded in the frozen wastes of Siberia, while the islands in southeast Asia have tropical climates. Southern and eastern Asia are also affected by a seasonal wind called the monsoon. This originates in the Indian Ocean and brings heavy rainfall and high winds, often devastating small coastal and low-lying villages and towns.

EXTREME WEATHER EVENTS

Symbols indicate climatic extremes

CLIMATE

Tundra
Subarctic
Cool continental
Warm temperate
Mediterranean
Semiarid
Arid
Humid equatorial
Tropical
Hot humid

Coldest place
VERKHOYANSK (Russ. Fed.)
Temp -90°F

Hottest place
TIRAT TSVI (Israel)
Temp 129°F

Wettest place
CHERRAPUNJI (India)
Annual rainfall 45in

Driest place
ADEN (Yemen)
Annual rainfall 3/16in

RAIN FORESTS

The tropical climate across the islands of southeast Asia produces warm, humid conditions in which rain forests flourish. Each island provides a slightly different habitat, so the animals and plants that have evolved on one island may be very different to those on the next.

LAND USE AND AGRICULTURE

Large expanses of Asia are uncultivated because the soil is too poor, or the climate is too cold or dry for crops to grow. The Plateau of Tibet, much of Siberia, and the Arabian Peninsula have limited agriculture. Some of the most fertile land is found in eastern China and India, where rice is a staple. Elsewhere, cash crops are grown for profit, such as dates in southwest Asia; rubber in Southeast Asia; tea in India, China, and Sri Lanka; and coconuts throughout the island archipelago of Southeast Asia.

LAND USE AND AGRICULTURE

- Cattle
- Goats
- Pigs
- Sheep
- Cereals
- Coconuts
- Corn
- Cotton
- Dates
- Fishing
- Fruit
- Jute
- Peanuts
- Rice
- Root crops
- Rubber
- Shellfish
- Sugarcane
- Soya beans
- Tea
- Timber

- Mountains
- Cropland
- Desert
- Forest
- Pasture
- Wetland
- Major conurbation

RICE

China is the world's largest producer of rice, which is grown in muddy fields called paddy fields. Water buffaloes are used to plow the ground before planting.

COTTON

Uzbekistan is the world's fourth-largest producer of cotton. Water has been diverted from nearby rivers to water the crops, which has led to the drying up of the Aral Sea.

DATES

Dates have been cultivated on the Arabian Peninsula since ancient times. They are an important cash crop, grown for export in dry sandy areas where few other crops can grow.

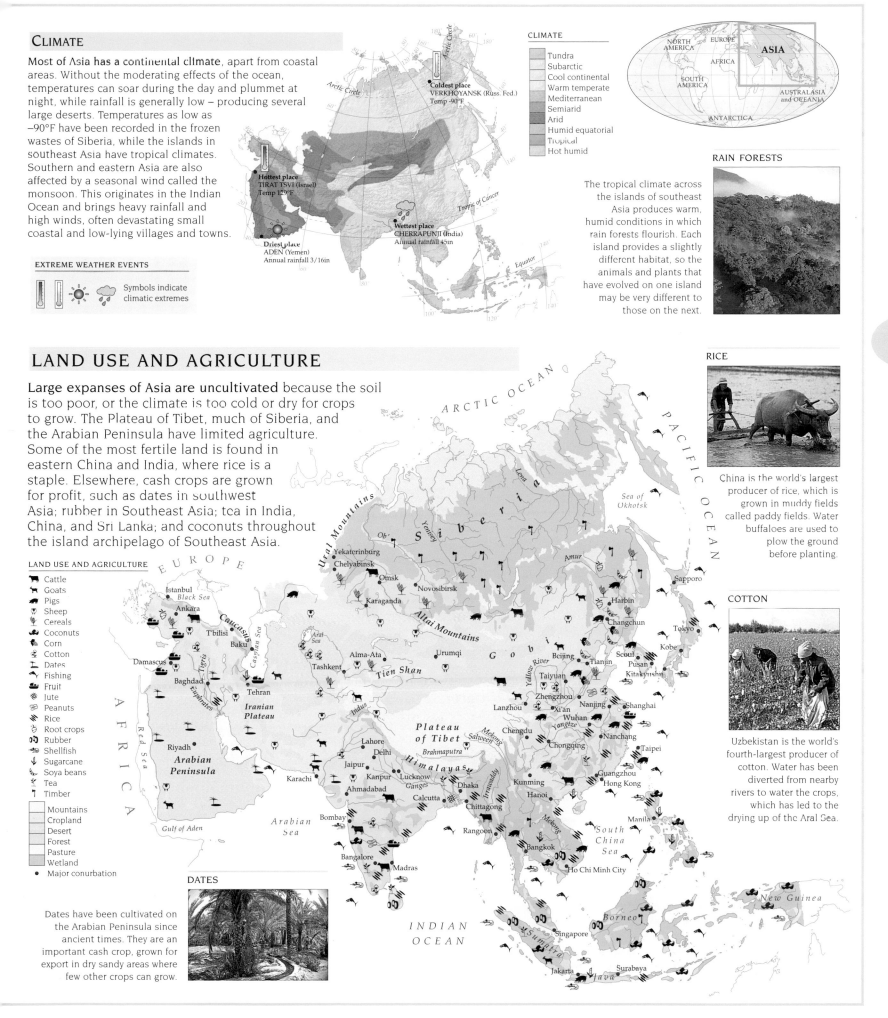

RUSSIA AND KAZAKHSTAN

Russia lies partly in Europe but mostly in Asia. The land to the east of the Ural Mountains is called Siberia. This immense stretch of grasslands, thick, evergreen forest, and tundra is crossed by giant rivers. Vast areas of Siberia are almost untouched by human activity, yet in the industrial regions set up under communism (1922–1991), air, water, and soil are heavily polluted with harmful substances. Along with the former Soviet state of Kazakhstan, Siberia is rich in a huge variety of minerals.

INDUSTRY

The discovery of gold in the 19th century opened Siberia up to economic and industrial development. Later, vast reserves of oil, coal, and gas were found, especially in the west, which is now the main center for oil extraction. Gold and diamonds are mined in the east. In Kazakhstan, mining and other industries are growing with the help of foreign investors.

STRUCTURE OF INDUSTRY

Primary 9%
Services 53%
Manufacturing 38%

INDUSTRY

- Car manufacturing
- Chemicals
- Engineering
- Iron and steel
- Textiles
- Mining
- Oil and gas
- Timber manufacturing
- Major industrial center / area
- Major road

LAND HEIGHT
- Above 13,120ft
- 6,560–13,120ft
- 3,280–6,560ft
- 1,640–3,280ft
- 820–1,640ft
- 330–820ft
- 0–330ft
- Below sea level

SEA DEPTH
- 0–820ft
- 820–1,640ft
- 1,640–3,280ft
- 3,280–6,560ft
- 6,560–9,840ft
- 9,840–13,120ft
- Below 13,120ft

SCALE BAR
0 km 200 400
0 miles 200 400

CITIES AND TOWNS
- Over 500,000 people
- 100,000–500,000
- 50,000–100,000
- Less than 50,000

THE LANDSCAPE

East of the Ural Mountains lies the West Siberian Plain – the world's largest area of flat ground. The plain gradually rises to the Central Siberian Plateau and then again to highlands in the southeast. Great coniferous forests called *taiga* stretch across most of this land. The far north of Siberia extends into the Arctic Circle. Here the landscape is made up of frozen plains called tundra. Much of Kazakhstan is covered by huge rolling grasslands, or steppe. In the south are arid sandy deserts.

Tundra and *taiga*

Stubby birch trees, dwarf bushes, moss and lichen huddle close to the ground in the frozen tundra wastes of northern Russia. They lie between the permanent ice and snow of the Arctic, and the thick *taiga* forests which cover an area greater than the Amazon rain forest.

The Caspian Sea (A 5)
The Caspian Sea covers 143,243 sq miles and is the world's largest expanse of inland water. It is fed by the Volga and Ural Rivers, which flow in from the plains of the north.

West Siberian Plain (D 4)
This vast, flat expanse is covered with a network of marshes and streams. The Ob' River, which winds its way north across the plains, is frozen for up to half the year.

Lake Baikal (F 5)
Lake Baikal is the deepest lake in the world, and the largest freshwater one – it is more than 1 mile deep and covers 12,500 sq miles. It is fed by 336 rivers and contains around 20% of all the fresh water in the world.

CLIMATE

Russia and Kazakhstan have continental climates, and their distance from seas and oceans means that temperatures fluctuate wildly, both daily and seasonally. Temperatures in eastern Siberia have been known to reach -90°F.

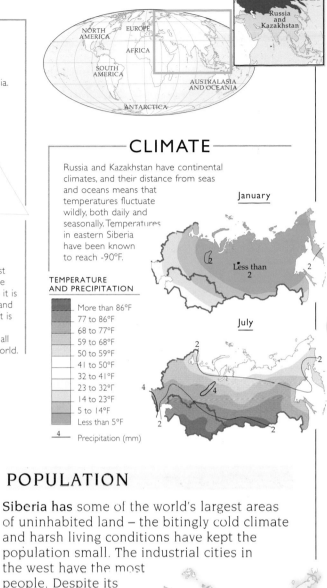

January

July

TEMPERATURE AND PRECIPITATION
- More than 86°F
- 77 to 86°F
- 68 to 77°F
- 59 to 68°F
- 50 to 59°F
- 41 to 50°F
- 32 to 41°F
- 23 to 32°F
- 14 to 23°F
- 5 to 14°F
- Less than 5°F

—4— Precipitation (mm)

FARMING AND LAND USE

Siberia's harsh climate has restricted farming to the south, where there are a few areas warm enough to grow cereal crops such as wheat and oats and to raise cattle on the small pockets of pasture. The rest of the region is used for hunting, herding reindeer, and forestry – the *taiga* forests contain the world's largest timber reserves. In Kazakhstan, big herds of cattle, goats, and sheep are raised for wool and meat, and wheat is cultivated in the fertile north.

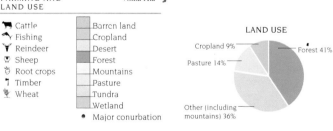

FARMING AND LAND USE
- Cattle
- Fishing
- Reindeer
- Sheep
- Root crops
- Timber
- Wheat
- Barren land
- Cropland
- Desert
- Forest
- Mountains
- Pasture
- Tundra
- Wetland
- Major conurbation

LAND USE
- Cropland 9%
- Pasture 14%
- Forest 41%
- Other (including mountains) 36%

POPULATION

Siberia has some of the world's largest areas of uninhabited land – the bitingly cold climate and harsh living conditions have kept the population small. The industrial cities in the west have the most people. Despite its huge size, Kazakhstan has only 17 million people, most of whom live in urban areas.

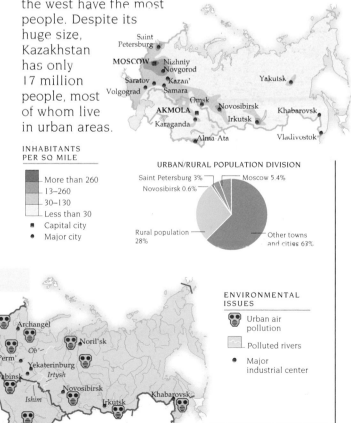

INHABITANTS PER SQ MILE
- More than 260
- 13–260
- 30–130
- Less than 30
- ■ Capital city
- ● Major city

URBAN/RURAL POPULATION DIVISION
- Saint Petersburg 3%
- Novosibirsk 0.6%
- Moscow 5.4%
- Rural population 28%
- Other towns and cities 63%

ENVIRONMENTAL ISSUES

Decades of industrial development during the communist regime brought new industries to undeveloped parts of the region, such as Siberia. This industrial development has led to environmental degradation on a massive scale: river, air, and land pollution in Russia is among the worst in the world.

ENVIRONMENTAL ISSUES
- Urban air pollution
- Polluted rivers
- ● Major industrial center

TURKEY AND THE CAUCASUS

ARMENIA, AZERBAIJAN, GEORGIA, TURKEY

Turkey and the Caucasus lie partly in Europe, and partly in Asia. Turkey has a long Islamic tradition, and although the country is now a secular (nonreligious) one, most Turks are Muslims. Turkey is becoming more industrialized, although half of its workforce is still employed in agriculture. The ancient countries of the Caucasus were under Russian rule for 70 years, until 1991. They are home to more than 50 different ethnic groups.

INDUSTRY

Turkey has a wide range of industries and growing trade links with Europe. Azerbaijan has large oil reserves and is able to export oil. The other states use imported fuel and hydroelectric power generated by their rushing rivers. Georgia produces industrial machinery and chemicals. Armenia's economy is recovering from civil war and earthquake damage.

FARMING AND LAND USE

With its warm climate and good soils, Turkey is able to produce all of its own food. Cattle and goats are kept on the central plateau. Along the Mediterranean coast, farmers grow olives, figs, grapes, and peaches. Hazelnuts are cultivated along the shores of the Black Sea. Across the Caucasus, the limited fertile land is used to grow wine grapes, tobacco, and cotton.

FARMING AND LAND USE

- 🐄 Livestock
- 🐟 Fishing
- Cotton
- 🍓 Fruit
- Hazelnuts
- Root crops
- Tobacco
- Vineyards
- Pasture
- Cropland
- Forest
- • Major conurbation

STRUCTURE OF INDUSTRY

Primary 18%
Services 51%
Manufacturing 31%

INDUSTRY

- ⚙ Cement manufacturing
- 🜀 Chemicals
- ✿ Engineering
- Food processing
- Textiles
- ⚓ Oil field
- Tourism
- ▣ Major industrial center / area
- — Major road

LAND USE

Other 26%
Cropland 31%
Forest 25%
Pasture 18%

THE LANDSCAPE

A huge semiarid plateau called Anatolia runs across the center of Turkey. It is rimmed by several mountain ranges along the Black Sea coast and the steep Taurus Mountains in the south. A narrow strip of lowland separates the Caucasus and the Lesser Caucasus mountains in the northeast.

Anatolia
Anatolia has large areas of soft limestone rock. Over a long period of time, layers of rock have been worn away by water to produce strange landscapes with caves and tall, isolated rock pinnacles.

Caucasus Mountains (H1)

Lesser Caucasus (H2)

Earthquakes
In 1988, 25,000 people were killed in an earthquake in the west of Armenia.

Between two continents
The city of Istanbul (B2) in Turkey is divided in two by a narrow channel of water called the Bosporus. One part of the city is in Europe, the other in Asia. The two parts are linked by bridges.

Taurus Mountains (D5)
The Taurus Mountains were formed around 60 to 65 million years ago. Weathering has formed caves and deep gorges.

Lake Van (H4)
Lake Van is one of the shallow salt lakes found in Anatolia. Salt lakes develop in hot, dry areas where large quantities of water evaporate, leaving behind salty deposits.

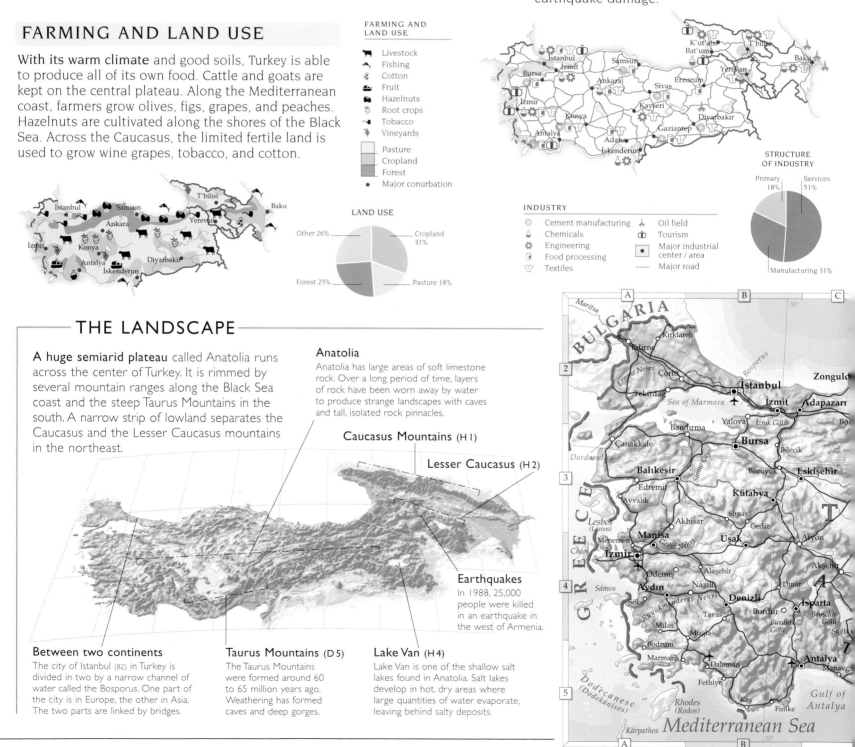

ASIA

Turkey & the Caucasus

POPULATION

Over 60% of Turks live in large towns or cities, mostly in the western half of the country. The eastern and southeastern parts of Anatolia are home to the Kurdish people. The Caucasian republics became more industrialized under Russian rule, and today, over half of their people live in urban places.

URBAN/RURAL POPULATION DIVISION

INHABITANTS PER SQ MILE

- More than 520
- 260–520
- 130–260
- Less than 130
- ■ Capital city
- ● Major city

Istanbul 10.3%
Baku 2.4%
Ankara 2.3%
Other towns and cities 46%
Rural population 39%

ENVIRONMENTAL ISSUES

Turkey has built many large dams to use water from rivers – especially the Euphrates – to irrigate its farmland. Syria and Iraq, which lie downstream, have opposed the dams, because they will have less water flowing into their countries. In Armenia, a nuclear power plant that was closed after being damaged in the 1988 earthquake has reopened, although it is still unsafe.

Atatürk Dam
Euphrates

ENVIRONMENTAL ISSUES

- Major dam
- Unstable nuclear power station
- Urban air pollution
- ● Major industrial center

CLIMATE

Winters are coldest in the Caucasus Mountains and in Anatolia, while the shores of the Mediterranean and Black Seas remain mild. Summers are hottest around the edge of the Mediterranean and near Turkey's border with Syria and Iraq.

January

July

TEMPERATURE AND PRECIPITATION

- More than 86°F
- 77 to 86°F
- 68 to 77°F
- 59 to 68°F
- 50 to 59°F
- 41 to 50°F
- 32 to 41°F
- 23 to 32°F
- 14 to 23°F
- Less than 14°F
- —4— Precipitation (in)

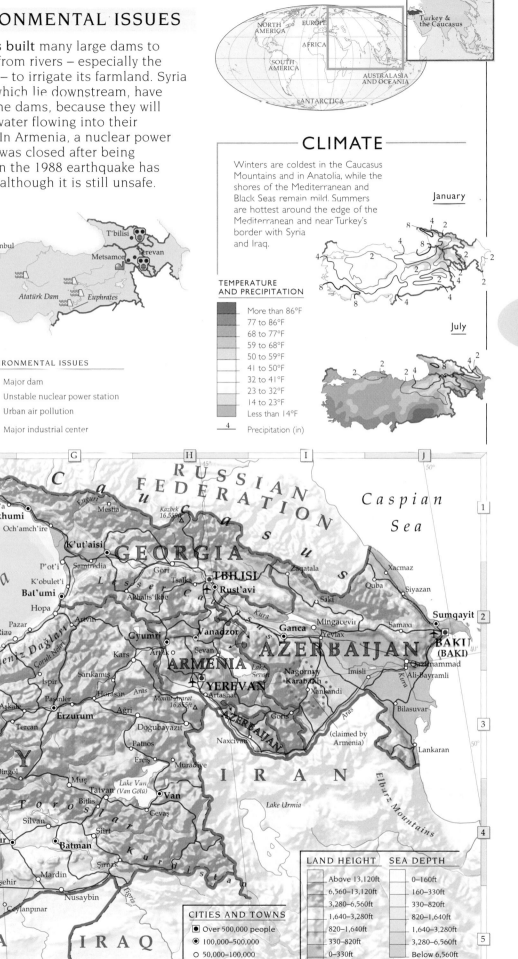

SCALE BAR
0 km 75 150
0 miles 75 150

CITIES AND TOWNS
- ■ Over 500,000 people
- ● 100,000–500,000
- ○ 50,000–100,000
- ○ Less than 50,000

LAND HEIGHT
- Above 13,120ft
- 6,560–13,120ft
- 3,280–6,560ft
- 1,640–3,280ft
- 820–1,640ft
- 330–820ft
- 0–330ft
- Below sea level

SEA DEPTH
- 0–160ft
- 160–330ft
- 330–820ft
- 820–1,640ft
- 1,640–3,280ft
- 3,280–6,560ft
- Below 6,560ft

SOUTHWEST ASIA

BAHRAIN, IRAN, IRAQ, ISRAEL, JORDAN, KUWAIT, LEBANON, OMAN, QATAR, SAUDI ARABIA, SYRIA, UNITED ARAB EMIRATES, YEMEN

Most of southwest Asia is barren desert, yet the world's first cities originated here over 5,000 years ago. It was the birthplace of three major religions: Islam, Judaism, and Christianity. In recent years, the discovery of oil has brought great wealth to much of the region, but it has also been torn by civil wars and conflicts between neighboring countries. Most people here are Muslims, although Israel is the world's only Jewish state.

ENVIRONMENTAL ISSUES

Water shortages are common because of the hot, dry climate and the lack of rivers. Desalination plants convert seawater into freshwater, and are found along the Red Sea and Gulf coasts. Lack of water also makes the risk of desertification greater. Iran has had many catastrophic earthquakes; in 1978 an earthquake killed 25,000 people.

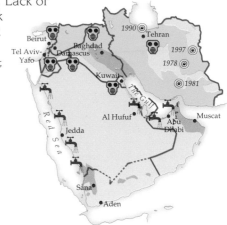

ENVIRONMENTAL ISSUES

- Area with many desalination plants
- ◉ Catastrophic earthquake
- Urban air pollution
- Existing desert
- Risk of desertification
- • Major industrial center

INDUSTRY

Oil has made the previously poor Arab states very wealthy. It and natural gas continue to be the main sources of income for many of the countries here. Other industries are being developed to support the region's economies when these resources run out. Iran is famous for its carpets, which are woven from wool or silk.

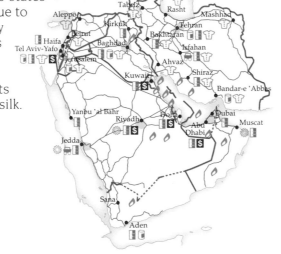

INDUSTRY
- ⚙ Cement manufacturing
- Food processing
- Iron and steel
- Oil refining
- ▽ Textiles
- Oil and gas
- S Finance

- ▪ Major industrial center / area
- — Major road

STRUCTURE OF INDUSTRY

Primary 10%
Services 49%
Manufacturing 41%

THE LANDSCAPE

Great desert plateaus, both sandy and rocky, cover much of southwest Asia. On the enormous Arabian Peninsula, which covers an area almost the size of India, narrow, sandy plains along the Red Sea and south coast rise to dry mountains. In the center is a vast, high plateau that slopes gently down to the flat shores of the Gulf. The mountainous areas of Iran experience frequent earthquakes.

Wadis
Valleys or riverbeds, called *wadis*, are found in the Saudi Arabian desert. They are usually dry, but after heavy rains, they are briefly filled by fast flowing rivers.

Syrian Desert (B 2)
The Syrian Desert extends from the Jordan valley in the west to the fertile plains of the Tigris and Euphrates Rivers in the east. It is mainly a rocky desert, because the sand has been swept away by winds and occasional heavy rainstorms.

Oases
Oases are areas within a desert where water is available for plants and human use. They are usually formed when a fault, or split, in the rock allows water to come to the surface. Oases can be no bigger than a few palm trees or cover several hundred sq miles.

FARMING AND LAND USE

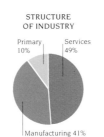

The best farmland is found along the Mediterranean coast and in the fertile valleys of the Tigris, Euphrates and Jordan Rivers. Wheat is the main cereal crop, and cotton, dates, and citrus and orchard fruits are grown for export. Elsewhere, modern irrigation techniques have created patches of fertile land in the desert. Dates, wheat, and coffee are cultivated in the oases and along the Gulf coast.

LAND USE

Forest 5%
Pasture 36%
Cropland 7%
Other (including desert) 52%

FARMING AND LAND USE
- 🐐 Goats
- 🐟 Fishing
- 🐑 Sheep
- 🍊 Citrus fruits
- ☕ Coffee
- 🌿 Cotton
- 🌴 Dates
- 🍎 Fruit
- 🌾 Wheat

- Cropland
- Desert
- Forest
- Pasture
- Wetland
- • Major conurbation

Dead Sea (A 2)
This large lake on the border between Israel and Jordan is the lowest point on the Earth's surface – its shores lie 1,286 ft below sea level. It is also the world's saltiest body of water, and cannot sustain any life.

Ar Rub' al Khali (D 5)
The Ar Rub' al Khali desert, also known as the "Empty Quarter," is the largest uninterrupted stretch of sand on Earth. It covers some 250,000 sq miles and is one of the world's driest and most hostile deserts.

Iranian Plateau (E 3)
Central Iran is taken up by a vast, semiarid plateau, that rises steeply from the coastal lowlands bordering the Gulf. It is ringed by the high Zagros and Elburz mountains.

POPULATION

Desert has kept much of the population clustered along the coastal areas and rivers or around the oases. Most people live in the cities, some of which are the fastest growing in the world. Oman and Yemen have mainly rural populations, and in Saudi Arabia, small groups of Bedouin tribespeople roam the desert with their animals.

URBAN/RURAL POPULATION DIVISION

Riyadh 1%
Baghdad 3%   Tehran 5%

Rural population 39%

Other towns and cities 52%

INHABITANTS PER SQ MILE

- More than 520
- 260–520
- 130–260
- Less than 130

■ Capital city
● Major city

CLIMATE

Most of the region receives very little rain, apart from a few isolated pockets. Temperatures soar during July, but in January they are much cooler, especially in the north.

TEMPERATURE AND PRECIPITATION

- More than 86°F
- 77 to 86°F
- 68 to 77°F
- 59 to 68°F
- 50 to 59°F
- 41 to 50°F
- 32 to 41°F
- Less than 32°F

4 Precipitation (in)

January

July

ASIA
Southwest Asia

CITIES AND TOWNS
- ■ Over 500,000 people
- ● 100,000–500,000
- ◐ 50,000–100,000
- ○ Less than 50,000

LAND HEIGHT	SEA DEPTH
Above 13,120ft	0–820ft
6,560–13,120ft	820–1,640ft
3,280–6,560ft	1,640–3,280ft
1,640–3,280ft	3,280–6,560ft
820–1,640ft	6,560–9,840ft
330–820ft	9,840–13,120ft
0–330ft	Below 13,120ft
Below sea level	

SCALE BAR

0 km 100 200
0 miles 100 200

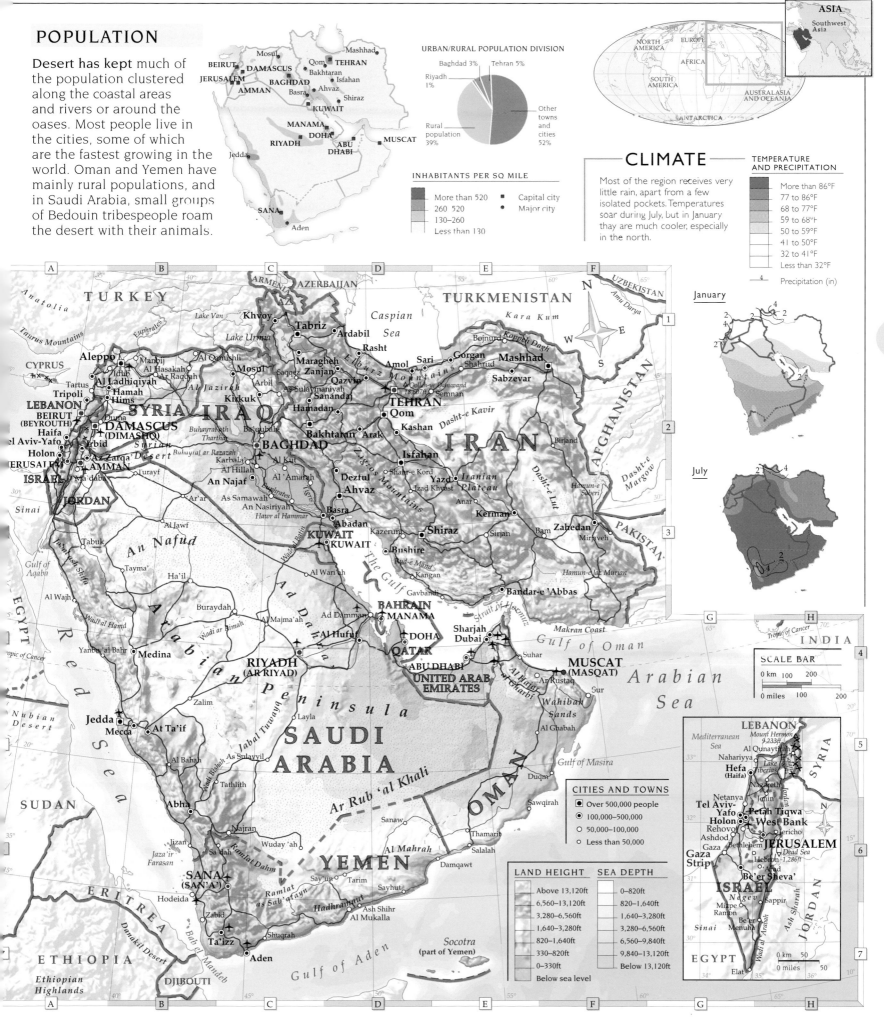

CENTRAL ASIA

AFGHANISTAN, KYRGYZSTAN, TAJIKISTAN, TURKMENISTAN, UZBEKISTAN

Central Asia is a land of hot, dry deserts and high, rugged mountains. It lies on the ancient Silk Road, an important trade route between China and Europe for over 400 years, until the 15th century. All of the countries here, except for Afghanistan, were part of the Soviet Union from the 1920s until 1991, when they gained independence. Since then, their people have reestablished their local languages and Islamic faith, which were restricted under Russian rule.

INDUSTRY

Fossil fuels, especially coal, natural gas, and oil, are extracted and processed throughout Central Asia. Agriculture supplies the raw materials for many industries, including food and textile processing, and the manufacture of leather goods and clothing. The region is famous for its colorful traditional carpets, hand-woven from the wool of the Karakul sheep. The Fergana Valley, southeast of Tashkent, is the main industrial area.

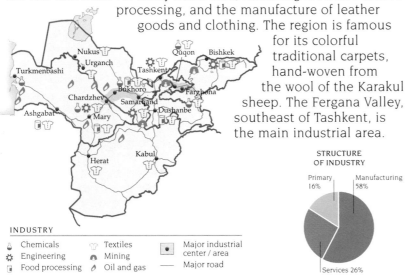

INDUSTRY

- ⚗ Chemicals
- ⚙ Engineering
- ▤ Food processing
- 👕 Textiles
- ⛏ Mining
- ⬧ Oil and gas
- ▪ Major industrial center / area
- — Major road

STRUCTURE OF INDUSTRY
- Primary 16%
- Manufacturing 58%
- Services 26%

POPULATION

The peoples of Central Asia are mostly rural farmers, living in the river valleys and in oases. There are few large cities. A few still lead a traditional nomadic lifestyle, moving from place to place with their animals in search of new pastures. Large areas of Afghanistan, the western deserts, and the mountain regions in the east, are virtually uninhabited.

INHABITANTS PER SQ MILE
- More than 260
- 130–260
- 30–130
- Less than 30
- ▪ Capital city
- ● Major city

URBAN/RURAL POPULATION DIVISION
- Kabul 2.9%
- Tashkent 3%
- Bishkek 1.1%
- Rural population 62%
- Other towns and cities 31%

FARMING AND LAND USE

Farming is concentrated around the fertile river valleys in the east, like the Fergana Valley. A variety of cereals and fruits – including peaches, melons, and apricots – are grown. In drier areas, animal breeding is important, with goats, sheep, and cattle supplying wool, meat, and hides. Big crops of cotton, which is a major export, are produced on land irrigated by the Amu Darya River.

FARMING AND LAND USE
- 🐂 Cattle
- 🐐 Goats
- 🐑 Sheep
- Cotton
- 🍇 Fruit
- 🌾 Wheat
- Cropland
- Desert
- Mountains
- Pasture
- Wetland
- ● Major conurbation

LAND USE
- Forest 4%
- Cropland 9%
- Pasture 41%
- Other (including mountains and deserts) 45%

THE LANDSCAPE

Two of the world's great deserts, the Kara Kum and the Kyzyl Kum, cover much of the western portion of Central Asia. In the east, a belt of high mountain ranges – the Hindu Kush, the Tien Shan, and the Pamirs – tower above the land. Few rivers cross the deserts, apart from the Amu Darya, which flows from the Pamirs to the shrinking Aral Sea.

Aral Sea (D 1)
The Aral Sea was once the fourth largest lake in the world, but it has shrunk by 40% since 1960. Diversion of its water for irrigation has made the lake shallower, so its waters evaporate faster.

Kara Kum (D 3)
The sandy desert of the Kara Kum occupies over 70% of Turkmenistan. Its surface consists of wind-shaped dunes and depressions. Human settlement is limited to the desert's fringes.

Tien Shan (H 2)

Fergana Valley (G 3)
Stresses and strains in the Earth created the Fergana Valley, a deep depression encircled by high mountains. The valley's fertile soils are irrigated by water from the Syr Darya River, and underground sources.

Amu Darya River (E 3)

Hindu Kush (G 4)

Pamirs (G 4)
The Pamirs lie mainly in Tajikistan. Their highest point, at 24,590 ft, is Communism Peak, so named because it was the highest peak in the former Soviet Union.

ENVIRONMENTAL ISSUES

The Aral Sea is rapidly drying up, because the rivers feeding it are being diverted to irrigate cottonfields. Central Asia is a very dry area, and desertification is a constant threat, especially in Afghanistan. Severe urban and industrial air pollution is a legacy from the communist era, when heavy industries were established in the countries here.

ENVIRONMENTAL ISSUES

- 🏭 Urban air pollution
- Existing desert
- Risk of desertification
- Severe risk of desertification
- Polluted river
- • Major industrial center

CLIMATE

Central Asia's climate is strongly inflenced by its position deep within Asia, far from the moderating effects of the oceans. Winters are cold, summers are very hot everywhere. Rainfall is virtually nonexistent all year round.

January

July

TEMPERATURE AND PRECIPITATION
- More than 86°F
- 77 to 86°F
- 41 to 50°F
- 32 to 41°F
- Less than 32°F

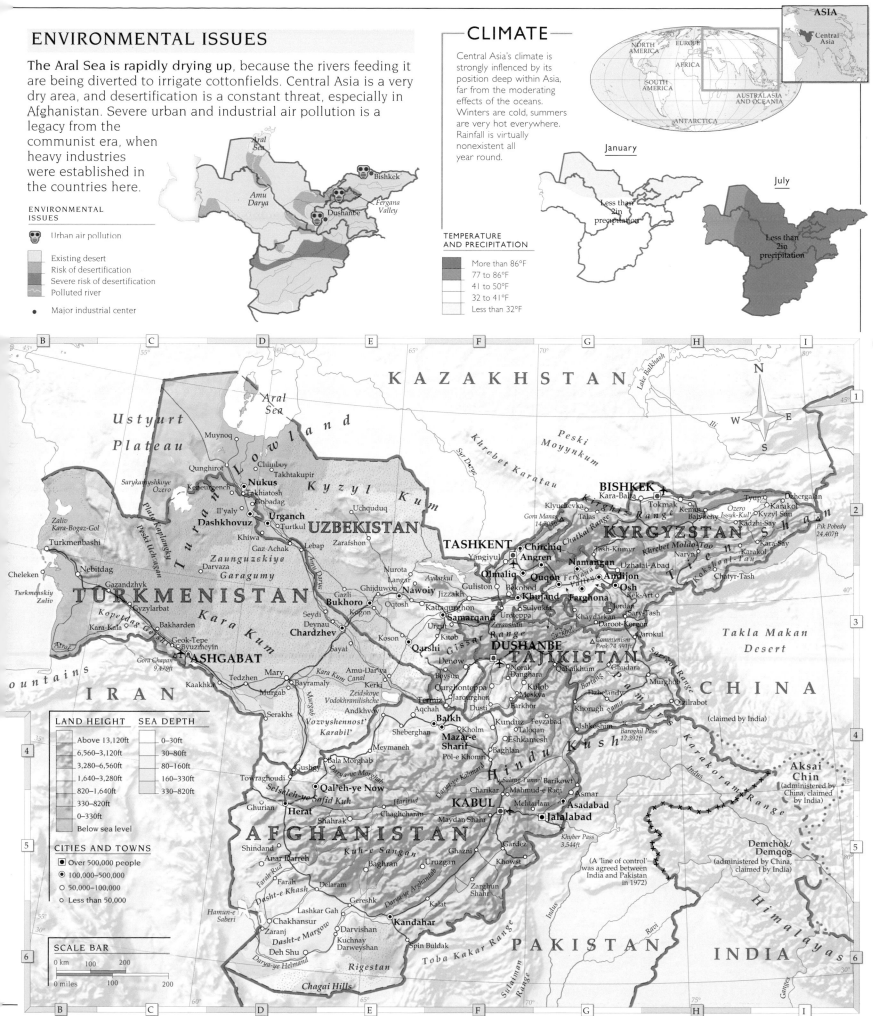

LAND HEIGHT
- Above 13,120ft
- 6,560–3,120ft
- 3,280–6,560ft
- 1,640–3,280ft
- 820–1,640ft
- 330–820ft
- 0–330ft
- Below sea level

SEA DEPTH
- 0–30ft
- 30–80ft
- 80–160ft
- 160–330ft
- 330–820ft

CITIES AND TOWNS
- Over 500,000 people
- 100,000–500,000
- 50,000–100,000
- Less than 50,000

SCALE BAR
0 km 100 200
0 miles 100 200

JAPAN AND KOREA

JAPAN, NORTH KOREA, SOUTH KOREA

Japan is a curved chain of over 4,000 islands in the Pacific Ocean. To the west, Korea juts out from northern China. Japan has few natural resources, but it has become one of the world's most successful industrial nations, due to investment in new technology and a highly efficient workforce. North Korea is a communist state with limited contact with the outside world, while South Korea is a democracy with major international trade links.

FARMING AND LAND USE

Modern farming methods allow Japan to grow much of its own food, despite a shortage of farmland. Rice is the main crop grown throughout the region. Japan has a large fishing fleet; the Japanese eat more fish than any other nation. In North Korea, farming is controlled by the government.

FARMING AND LAND USE

- 🐄 Cattle
- 🐟 Fishing
- 🐖 Pigs
- 🍐 Fruit
- 🌾 Rice
- 🫘 Soybeans
- 🌱 Tea
- Cropland
- Forest
- Pasture
- ● Major conurbation

LAND USE

- Pasture 1%
- Cropland 14%
- Other (including mountains) 30%
- Forest 55%

POPULATION

Most of Japan's 125 million people live in crowded cities on the coasts of the four main islands. The Kanto Plain around Tokyo is Japan's biggest area of flat land, and the most populous part of the country. In South Korea, a quarter of the population lives in the capital, Seoul. Most North Koreans live on the coastal plains.

INHABITANTS PER SQ MILE

- More than 520
- 260–520
- 130–260
- Less than 130
- ■ Capital city
- ● Major city

URBAN/RURAL POPULATION DIVISION

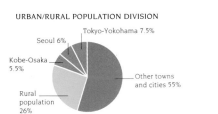

- Tokyo-Yokohama 7.5%
- Seoul 6%
- Kobe-Osaka 5.5%
- Rural population 26%
- Other towns and cities 55%

THE LANDSCAPE

Most of Japan is covered by forested mountains and hills, among which are many short, fast-flowing rivers and small lakes. Only about a quarter of the land is suitable for building and farming, and new land has been created by cutting back hillsides and reclaiming land from the sea. North and South Korea are mostly mountainous, with some coastal plains.

Hokkaido, Honshu, Shikoku, and Kyushu
Japan's four main islands were formed when two giant plates making up the Earth's crust collided, making their edges buckle upward.

T'aebaek-sanmaek (C 5)
This wooded mountain range forms the "backbone" of the Korean peninsula. It runs from north to south close to the east coast.

Tsunamis
Huge sea waves called tsunamis frequently threaten the east coast of Japan. They are set off by submarine earthquakes. The waves increase in size as they near the shore and can flood coastal areas and sink ships.

Earthquakes
In Japan, earthquakes are part of everyday life. The islands lie on a fault line, and earthquake tremors occur, on average, 5,000 times a year. Most of these are mild and may go unnoticed, but there is a constant threat of disaster.

Volcanoes
Japan's mountain ranges are studded with volcanoes, 60 of which are still active. Mount Fuji is a 12,388-ft snow-capped volcano and the highest mountain in Japan. It last erupted in 1707.

INDUSTRY

Japan is a world leader in high-tech electronic goods like computers, televisions and cameras, as well as cars. South Korea also has a thriving economy. It produces ships, cars, high-tech goods, shoes, and clothes for worldwide export. Both countries have to import most of their raw materials and energy. North Korea has little trade with other countries, but it is rich in minerals such as coal and silver.

STRUCTURE OF INDUSTRY

- Primary 3%
- Services 57%
- Manufacturing 40%

INDUSTRY

- 🚗 Car manufacturing
- Chemicals
- ⚙️ Engineering
- Food processing
- Iron and steel
- Shipbuilding
- 👕 Textiles
- 🅂 Finance
- 💻 High-tech
- Research and Development
- ● Major industrial center / area
- — Major road

ENVIRONMENTAL ISSUES

Industrial pollution from Korea and China has produced acid rain, and pollution in Japanese cities has led to people wearing masks to filter the air. Russia regularly dumps nuclear waste into the Sea of Japan. In 1995, an earthquake caused great destruction to the city of Kobe.

ENVIRONMENTAL ISSUES

⊙ Catastrophic earthquake

☢ Nuclear waste dump site

😷 Urban air pollution

⬚ Affected by acid rain

• Major industrial center

Sea of Japan

Seoul

Tokyo

Kobe 1995

Osaka

CLIMATE

Korea has hot summers and dry, very cold winters, especially in the north, where snow is common. In Japan, winters are less cold than on the Asian mainland; summers are hot, wet, and humid.

January

Less than 2

July

TEMPERATURE AND PRECIPITATION

More than 68°F	32 to 41°F
59 to 68°F	23 to 32°F
50 to 59°F	Less than 23°F
41 to 50°F	4 Precipitation (in)

ASIA
Japan and Korea

NORTH AMERICA · EUROPE · AFRICA · SOUTH AMERICA · AUSTRALASIA AND OCEANIA · ANTARCTICA

Map (Japan)

Sea of Okhotsk

Kurile Islands (administered by Russian Federation, claimed by Japan)

La Perouse Strait
Rebun-to
Wakkanai
Rishiri-to
Monbetsu
Abashiri
Nayoro
Shibetsu
Kitami
Nemuro

Hokkaido
Asahikawa
Takikawa
△ Asahi-dake 7,514ft
Akkeshi
Otaru
Ebetsu
Obihiro
Kushiro
Iwanai
Sapporo
Chitose
△ Horoshiri-dake 6,733ft
Tomakomai
Noboribetsu
Muroran
Okushiri-to
Uchiura-wan
Hakodate

Tsugaru-kaikyo
Aomori
Hachinohe
Goshogawara
Kuji
Hirosaki
Odate
Iwate
Miyako
Noshiro
Gojome
Morioka

JAPAN

Akita
Honjo
Yokote
Kesennuma
Shizugawa
Sakata
Shinjo
Fukukawa
Tsuruoka
Ishinomaki
Sendai
Yamagata
Soma
Fukushima
Haramachi
Niigata
Sado
Sendai-wan
Koriyama
Nagaoka
Inawashiro-ko
Sukagawa
Iwaki
Joetsu
Itoigawa
Honshu
Utsunomiya
Hitachi
Toyama-wan
Shim
Maebashi
Owani
Mito
Takaoka
Nagano
Kawagoe
Kasumiga-ura
Kanazawa
Toyama
Kanto Plain
Choshi
Komatsu
Matsumoto
TOKYO
Hida-sanmyaku
Chiba
Fukui
Kofu
Kawasaki
Tsuruga
Mount Fuji 12,389ft
Yokohama
Gifu
Nakatsugawa
Boso-hanto
Shizuoka
Ogaki
Toyota
Izu-hanto
Nagoya
Okazaki
O-shima
Hamamatsu
Nii-jima
Suruga-wan
Miyako-jima
Kozu-shima
Mikura-jima
Izu-shoto
Hachijo-jima

Korea map

SCALE BAR
0 km 100 200
0 miles 100 200

CHINA

RUSS. FED.

Hoeryong
Najin
Paektu-san 9,023ft △
Ch'ongjin
Hyesan
Huich'ang
Kilchu
Kanggye
Kimch'aek
Ch'osan
Pukch'ong
Huich'on
Sinp'o
Namsan-ni
Hamhung
Sinuiju
NORTH KOREA
Chongju
Anju
Yonghung
Wonsan
Sunch'on
East Korea Bay
Sinmi-do
PYONGYANG
Kosong
Sokch'o
Namp'o
(North and South Korea have been divided by a ceasefire agreement since 1953)
Changyon
Korea Bay
Haeju
Kaesong
Kangnung
Liancourt Rocks (claimed by Japan and South Korea)
Ongjin
Ch'unch'on
Tonghae
Wonju
Inch'on
SEOUL (SŎUL)
Suwon
Ch'onan
Ch'ungju
Andong
Taejon
P'ohang
SOUTH KOREA
Kunsan
Taegu
Ulsan
Yellow Sea
Namwon
Masan
Pusan
Kwangju
Sunch'on
Mokp'o
Koje-do
Namhae-do
Kogum-do
Tsushima

Sea of Japan

Matsue
Yonago
Tottori
Gotsu
Hamada
Chugoku-sanchi
Himeji
Kyoto
Masuda
Kurashiki
Otsu
Kobe
Tsu
Nagato
Okayama
Takamatsu
Ise
Hiroshima
Kure
Iwakuni
Tokushima
Osaka
Wakayama
Yamaguchi
Niihama
Gobo
Shingu
Shimonoseki
Horu
Matsuyama
Kii-suido
Ube
Iyo-nada
Kochi
Shikoku
Kitakyushu
Oita
Tosa-wan
Fukuoka
Nakamura
Kurume
Sukumo
Saga
Bungo-suido
Omuta
Kumamoto
Sasebo
Yatsushiro
Nagasaki
Nobeoka
Amakusa-nada
Miyazaki
Miyakonojo
Sendai
Kagoshima
Kyushu
Koshikijima-retto
Shibushi-wan

PACIFIC OCEAN

Sea of Japan

Inset (Ryukyu Islands)

0 km 200
0 miles 200
Kyushu
Osumi-shoto
East China Sea
Satsunan-shoto
Naze
Amami-gunto
Amami o-shima
Ryukyu Islands (part of Japan)
Okinawa
Naha
Okinawa-shoto
Senkaku-shoto
Sakishima-shoto
Ishigaki-jima
Iriomote-jima
East China Sea
Philippine Sea
Cheju Strait
Cheju-do
Goto-retto
Chin-do
Ko-saki
Iki
Fukuoka
Korea Strait
Namhae-do

LAND HEIGHT
6,560–13,120ft
3,280–6,560ft
1,640–3,280ft
820–1,640ft
330–820ft
0–330ft

SEA DEPTH
0–820ft
820–1,640ft
1,640–3,280ft
3,280–6,560ft
6,560–9,840ft
9,840–13,120ft
Below 13,120ft

CITIES AND TOWNS
■ Over 500,000 people
◉ 100,000–500,000
○ 50,000–100,000
∘ Less than 50,000

EAST ASIA

CHINA, MONGOLIA, TAIWAN

China is the world's third-largest country and its most populous – over one billion people live there. Under its communist government, which came to power in 1949, China has become a major industrial nation, but most of its people still live and work on the land as they have for thousands of years. Taiwan also has a booming economy and exports its products around the world. Mongolia is a vast, remote country with a small population, many of whom are nomads.

INDUSTRY

Chemicals, iron and steel, engineering, and textiles are the main industries in China's east coast cities, and in industrial centers like Shenyang. Shanghai, Hong Kong, and Beijing are also important financial centers. In the interior, large deposits of coal support the heavy industries in major cities such as Chengdu and Wuhan. Taiwan specializes in textiles and shoe manufacture, along with electronic goods. Mongolia's economy is mainly agricultural.

STRUCTURE OF INDUSTRY

Services 21%
Manufacturing 47%
Primary 32%

INDUSTRY

- 🚗 Car manufacturing
- 🧪 Chemicals
- ⚡ Electronics
- ⚙ Engineering
- 🍴 Food processing
- 🏭 Iron and steel
- ⚓ Shipbuiding
- 👕 Textiles
- ⛏ Coal
- 🅂 Finance
- ■ Major industrial center / area
- — Major road

POPULATION

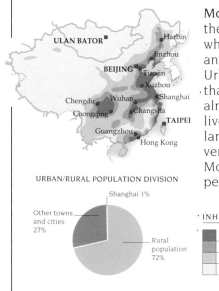

URBAN/RURAL POPULATION DIVISION

Shanghai 1%
Other towns and cities 27%
Rural population 72%

INHABITANTS PER SQ MILE

- More than 520
- 260–520
- 130–260
- Less than 130
- ■ Capital city
- ● Major city

Most of China's people live in the eastern part of the country, where the climate, landscape and soils are most favorable. Urban areas there house more than 250 million people, but almost 75% of the population lives in villages and farms the land. Taiwan's lowlands are very densely populated. In Mongolia, about 50% of the people live in the countryside.

FARMING AND LAND USE

FARMING AND LAND USE

- 🐟 Fishing
- 🐖 Pigs
- 🐑 Sheep
- 🐄 Corn
- ✿ Cotton
- 🐟 Fruit
- 〰 Rice
- 🌱 Soybeans
- ⬇ Sugarcane
- 🌾 Wheat
- Cropland
- Desert
- Forest
- Mountain region
- Pasture
- ● Major conurbation

Despite its size, about 90% of China is unsuitable for farming. Either the soils and climate are poor, or the landscape is too mountainous. In the north and west, most farmers make their living by herding animals. On the fertile eastern plains, soybeans, wheat, corn, and cotton are grown. Farther south, rice becomes the main crop, and pigs are raised in large numbers.

LAND USE

Cropland 7%
Pasture 42%
Other (including mountains) 24%
Forest 27%

THE LANDSCAPE

China's landscape is divided into three areas. The vast Plateau of Tibet in the southwest is the highest and largest plateau on Earth. It contains both dry deserts and pockets of pasture surrounded by high mountains. Northwest China has dry highlands. The great plains of eastern China were formed from soils deposited by rivers like the Yellow River over thousands of years. Most of Mongolia is dry, grassland steppe and cold, arid desert.

Tien Shan mountains (B 2)

The Tien Shan, or "Heavenly Mountains" reach heights of 24,393 ft. They surround fields of permanent ice and spectacular glaciers.

Gobi (E 2) and Takla Makan (B 3) deserts

The arid landscapes of the Gobi and Takla Makan deserts are made up of bare rock surfaces and huge areas of shifting sand dunes. They are hot in summer, but unlike most other deserts, are extremely cold in winter.

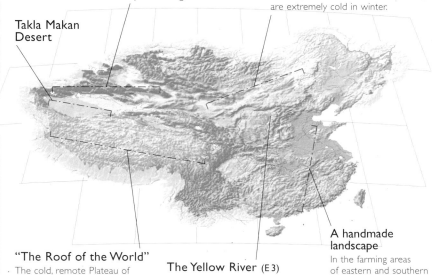

Takla Makan Desert

A handmade landscape

In the farming areas of eastern and southern China, terraces have been carved into the hillsides to make them flat enough to grow rice and other crops. This method of farming has been used for over 7,000 years.

"The Roof of the World"

The cold, remote Plateau of Tibet averages 13,000 ft in height. Many of China's great rivers have their sources here. The world's highest human settlement, a town called Wenquan, is found in the east of the plateau. It lies 16,729 ft above sea level.

The Yellow River (E 3)

The Yellow River (Huang He) is the world's muddiest river, carrying hundreds of truckloads of sediment to the sea every minute. The river has burst its banks many times throughout history, causing enormous damage and claiming millions of human lives.

FARMING AND LAND USE

The staple crop here is rice, which grows in low-lying flooded fields called paddies, or on terraces cut into the hillsides. Sugarcane, coconuts, bananas, and pineapples are widely grown as cash crops, and Malaysia produces 25% of the world's rubber. Freshwater and marine fish are caught in large quantities; fish is one of the main foods in this region.

FARMING AND LAND USE

- Cattle
- Fishing
- Shellfish
- Coconuts
- Fruit
- Rice
- Rubber
- Sugarcane
- Timber

- Cropland
- Forest
- Pasture
- Wetland
- Major conurbation

LAND USE

- Pasture 4%
- Cropland 21%
- Other 24%
- Forest 51%

CLIMATE

Southeast Asia's climate is strongly affected by the monsoon, which brings warm, humid air and high rainfall to mainland Southeast Asia during July and to maritime southeast Asia during January.

January

July

TEMPERATURE AND PRECIPITATION

- More than 86°F
- 68 to 86°F
- 50 to 68°F
- Less than 50°F
- 4 — Precipitation (in)

ASIA
Southeast Asia

LAND HEIGHT
- Above 13,120ft
- 6,560–13,120ft
- 3,280–6,560ft
- 1,640–3,280ft
- 820–1,640ft
- 330–820ft
- 0–330ft

SEA DEPTH
- 0–820ft
- 820–1,640ft
- 1,640–3,280ft
- 3,280–6,560ft
- 6,560–9,840ft
- 9,840–13,120ft
- Below 13,120ft

CITIES AND TOWNS
- Over 500,000 people
- 100,000–500,000
- 50,000–100,000
- Less than 50,000

109

CONTINENTAL SOUTH AMERICA

The towering peaks of the Andes stand high above the western side of the South America. They act as a barrier to the sparsely inhabited interior of the continent, which includes the dense rain forest of the Amazon Basin – one of the Earth's last great wildernesses. Most people live on South America's coastal fringes. Brazil is both the largest country and the most populous. Over half of the continent's land area and half of its people are found there.

3,100 miles
4,750 miles

CROSS SECTION ACROSS SOUTH AMERICA

Andes | Amazon River | Guiana Highlands | Mouths of the Amazon | Brazilian Highlands

W — 3,360 miles — E

The high peaks of the Andes rise up from a narrow strip of land bordering the Pacific Ocean. East of the Andes, the land flattens into a broad, shallow basin into which the Amazon River flows. To the north are the older Guiana Highlands where rock has been eroded to form flat-topped "table" mountains.

PHYSICAL SOUTH AMERICA

Ancient masses of rocks, like the Guiana and Brazilian highlands, which are known as shields, form the core of South America. The Andes are the solid backbone of the continent. They are relatively young, formed by collisions between different plates of the Earth's crust. The major rivers: the Paraná and the mighty Amazon, flow in deep depressions to the east of the mountains.

ELEVATION

19,960ft
16,400ft
13,120ft
9,840ft
6,560ft
3,280ft
1,640ft
820ft
330ft
sea level
below sea level
◀ cross section

SCALE 1:40,000,000

0 km 400 800
0 miles 400 800

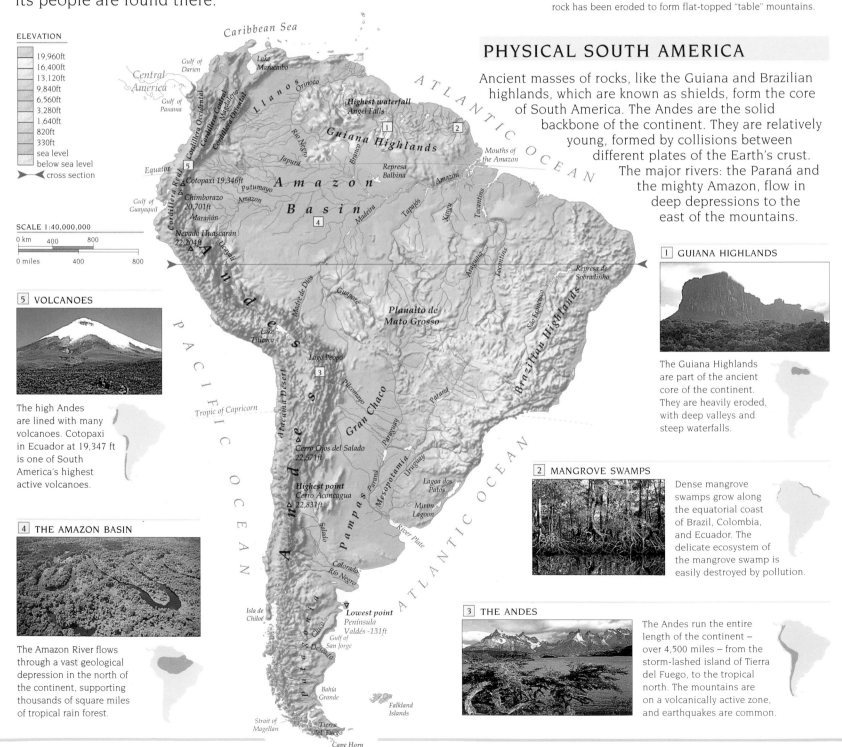

Caribbean Sea
Central America
Gulf of Darien
Gulf of Panama
Lake Maracaibo
Llanos
Orinoco
Cordillera Occidental
Cordillera Central
Cordillera Magdalena
Cordillera Oriental
Highest waterfall Angel Falls
Guiana Highlands
ATLANTIC OCEAN
Rio Negro
Japura
Branco
Represa Balbina
Mouths of the Amazon
Equator
Cotopaxi 19,346ft
Putumayo
Amazon
Amazon Basin
Amazon
Madeira
Tapajós
Xingu
Tocantins
Chimborazo 20,701ft
Marañón
Cordillera Real
Gulf of Guayaquil
Nevado Huascarán 22,204ft
Ucayali
Madre de Dios
Guaporé
Araguaia
Tocantins
Tocantins
São Francisco
Represa de Sobradinho
Planalto de Mato Grosso
Brazilian Highlands
Lake Titicaca
Lago Poopó
Atacama Desert
Andes
Pilcomayo
Tropic of Capricorn
PACIFIC OCEAN
Cerro Ojos del Salado 22,571ft
Gran Chaco
Paraguay
Paraná
Paraná
Mesopotamia
Uruguay
Lagoa dos Patos
Mirim Lagoon
Highest point Cerro Aconcagua 22,831ft
Pampas
ATLANTIC OCEAN
Salado
River Plate
Colorado
Rio Negro
Isla de Chiloé
Patagonia
Chico
Gulf of San Jorge
Deseado
▼ **Lowest point** Península Valdés -131ft
Bahía Grande
Strait of Magellan
Tierra del Fuego
Cape Horn
Falkland Islands

5 VOLCANOES

The high Andes are lined with many volcanoes. Cotopaxi in Ecuador at 19,347 ft is one of South America's highest active volcanoes.

4 THE AMAZON BASIN

The Amazon River flows through a vast geological depression in the north of the continent, supporting thousands of square miles of tropical rain forest.

1 GUIANA HIGHLANDS

The Guiana Highlands are part of the ancient core of the continent. They are heavily eroded, with deep valleys and steep waterfalls.

2 MANGROVE SWAMPS

Dense mangrove swamps grow along the equatorial coast of Brazil, Colombia, and Ecuador. The delicate ecosystem of the mangrove swamp is easily destroyed by pollution.

3 THE ANDES

The Andes run the entire length of the continent – over 4,500 miles – from the storm-lashed island of Tierra del Fuego, to the tropical north. The mountains are on a volcanically active zone, and earthquakes are common.

POLITICAL SOUTH AMERICA

In the 17th century, explorers from Spain and Portugal claimed most of South America for their rulers in Europe. Their influences are still strong today: Brazilians speak Portuguese, while much of the rest of the continent is Spanish-speaking. The small nations of the north Suriname and Guyana, were Dutch and British colonies, and French Guiana is a French overseas department. The mix of peoples is mainly European, Native American, and African. Some native peoples still live in the dense Amazon rain forest.

BORDER DISPUTES

Many of South America's borders have been, or remain, disputed. Bolivia is landlocked as a result of a dispute with Chile in 1883, when it lost its lands bordering the Pacific Ocean.

TRANSPORTATION LINKS

The Pan American Highway is a vital transportation link, running from the far south of the continent, northward along the Pacific coast. Its route takes it through sparsely populated areas like the Atacama Desert

POPULATION

Many South American countries have a similar pattern of population distribution. The largest concentrations of people are found near the coasts. Migration to the coastal cities has led to rocketing population figures and growing social problems. São Paulo is now the world's third-largest city after Mexico City and Tokyo; its outskirts are fringed with sprawling, shanty town suburbs, known as *favelas*.

URBAN GROWTH

Urban growth has transformed São Paulo into a major population and industrial center. Its rapid growth has created many problems, such as traffic congestion, overcrowding, and inadequate sewerage.

SCALE 1:35,000,000

0 km   400   800

0 miles   400   800

POPULATION

Capital cities
- ◉ Above 500,000
- ◉ 100,000 to 500,000
- ■ 50,000 to 100,000
- ● Below 50,000

Other cities
- ▣ Above 500,000
- ○ 50,000 to 100,000

STANDARDS OF LIVING

There are many inequalities in living standards across South America. Argentina's wealth and strong economy means its living standards are well above those of Guyana and Bolivia, which have weak economies and are heavily reliant upon trade in raw materials. The booming black-market drugs trade increases crime and corruption.

Largest city
SÃO PAULO
15 million people

POPULATION DENSITY
(People per sq mile)

- Below 13
- 13–29
- 30–39
- 40–51
- 52–77
- Above 78

STANDARD OF LIVING
(UN Human Development Index)

low   high   no data

111

SOUTH AMERICAN GEOGRAPHY

Agriculture is still the most common form of employment in South America. Cattle and cash crops of coffee, cocoa, and, in some places, coca for cocaine, provide the main sources of income. Brazil has the greatest range of industries, followed by Argentina, Venezuela, and Chile. The large coastal cities such as Rio de Janeiro, Lima, and Buenos Aires are where most of the jobs are found. This encourages people to migrate from the country to the city, in search of employment.

INDUSTRY

Brazil is the continent's leading industrial producer, and São Paulo is the major industrial city. Manufactured products include iron and steel, automobiles, chemicals, textiles, and meat and leather products from the continent's vast cattle herds. In the mountains of Bolivia and Colombia, coca plants are grown to make cocaine, which has created a black market for this illegal drug.

OIL AND GAS

Under the waters of Lake Maracaibo, Venezuela, lie some of South America's biggest oil reserves. Oil exploitation has brought great wealth to Venezuela. The money has helped the country to build new roads and develop other industries.

INDUSTRIAL CENTER

São Paulo, Brazil, is the largest city in South America and a leading industrial center. A wide range of goods is manufactured here, including automobiles, chemicals, textiles, and electronic products. São Paulo is also a leading financial center. Hundreds of people flock to the city daily in search of work.

TRADE AND EXPORTS

The Chilean port of Valparaíso ships many different products out of South America. Trade is growing with Japan and other countries around the Pacific Ocean.

MINERAL RESOURCES

South America's mineral resources are highly localized. Few countries have both fossil fuels and metallic ores. The richest oilfields are in the north, especially in Venezuela. Coal, however, is scarce. When the Andes were formed, heat helped create the many metallic minerals that are mined today.

MINERAL RESOURCES
- Bauxite
- Copper
- Iron
- Lead
- Silver
- Tin
- Oil/Gas field
- Coal field

COPPER MINES

Metallic mineral reserves are abundant in the Andes. Chuquicamata, northern Chile, is one of the world's largest copper mines.

INDUSTRY
- ✈ Aerospace
- 🍺 Brewing
- 🚙 Car/vehicle manufacturing
- ⚗ Chemicals
- ⛏ Coal
- ⚡ Electronics
- ⚙ Engineering
- $ Finance
- 🐟 Fish processing
- 🍴 Food processing
- 💻 High-tech industry
- 🚆 Iron and steel
- △ Metal refining
- ⚕ Narcotics
- 🛢 Oil and gas
- ✎ Pharmaceuticals
- 🖨 Printing and publishing
- ⚓ Shipbuilding
- 👕 Textiles
- 🌲 Timber processing
- 🚬 Tobacco processing

GNP per capita (US$)
- Below 499
- 500–999
- 1,000–1,499
- 1,500–2,999
- 3,000–5,999
- Above 6,000
- • Industrial center

CLIMATE

South America has four main climatic regions: tropical, arid, temperate, and the cold climate of the far south. The Amazon Basin, covered by massive rain forests, and the Guiana Highlands have a humid, tropical climate that allows vegetation to flourish. West of the Andes the climate tends to be very dry. Moist air flowing west from the Atlantic Ocean is prevented from reaching the shores of the Pacific Ocean by the Andes, and rain falls before it can pass over the mountains. This creates arid deserts like the Atacama.

EXTREME WEATHER EVENTS

Symbols indicate climatic extremes

Wettest place
QUIBDO (Colombia)
Annual rainfall 354in

Driest place
ARICA (Chile)
Annual rainfall 1⁄4in

Hottest place
RIVADAVIA (Argentina)
Temp 120°F

Coldest place
SARMIENTO (Argentina)
Temp -27°F

Equator
Tropic of Capricorn

CLIMATE

- Subarctic
- Cool continental
- Warm temperate
- Semiarid
- Arid
- Temperate
- Tropical
- Humid equatorial

NORTH AMERICA EUROPE ASIA
AFRICA
SOUTH AMERICA
AUSTRALASIA and OCEANIA
ANTARCTICA

PATAGONIAN ICEFIELDS

Toward the south of the continent, the climate becomes very cold. Large expanses of ice, forming glaciers, are found in southern Patagonia and on islands such as Tierra del Fuego at the tip of South America.

LAND USE AND AGRICULTURE

Many plants now found throughout the world originated in South America, like the tomato, potato, and cassava. Today, coffee, cocoa, rubber, soybeans, corn, and sugarcane are widely cultivated, and grapes are grown in sheltered valleys in the Andes. Much of the Amazon Basin is covered by dense rain forest and is unsuitable for cultivation, although some farmers practice "slash and burn" techniques to make land for crops and cattle farming, which destroy ancient forest.

LAND USE AND AGRICULTURE

- Cattle
- Pigs
- Sheep
- Bananas
- Corn
- Citrus fruits
- Coca
- Cocoa
- Cotton
- Coffee
- Fishing
- Oil palms
- Peanuts
- Rubber
- Shellfish
- Soybeans
- Sugarcane
- Vineyards
- Wheat

- Barren land
- Cropland
- Desert
- Forest
- Mountain region
- Pasture
- Wetland
- • Major conurbation

COFFEE

South America, and Brazil in particular, is a major producer of coffee. The plants thrive in the rich red soils of southern Brazil and are grown on huge plantations on the mountain slopes.

LOCAL MARKETS

At traditional markets such as this one in Ecuador, high in the Andes, local people trade fruit, vegetables, and goods such as clothing, rugs, and blankets. Some goods produced by Ecuadorean Indians are now exported worldwide.

CATTLE

The vast plains of the Pampas, to the west of Buenos Aires, support large herds of cattle. Meat processing and canning is a major industry in Argentina, Paraguay, and Uruguay.

NARCOTICS

Coca, grown in forest clearings in remote mountain areas, is used to make the drug cocaine. Government troops burn any coca plants they discover to discourage production.

NORTHERN SOUTH AMERICA

BRAZIL, COLOMBIA, ECUADOR, GUYANA, PERU,
SURINAME, VENEZUELA

High mountains, rain forests, and hot, grassy plains
cover much of northern South America. From the 16th
century, after the conquest of the Incas, the western
countries were ruled by Spain. Brazil was governed by
Portugal, Guyana by Britain, and Suriname by the
Dutch. The more recent history of some of these
countries has included periods of civil war and military
rule. Most are still troubled by widespread poverty.

FARMING AND LAND USE

The variety of climates allows a wide
range of crops, including sugarcane,
cocoa, and bananas, to be grown
for export. Coffee is the most
important cash crop; Brazil is
the world's leading coffee grower.
Cattle are farmed on the plains
of Colombia, Venezuela, and
southern Brazil. Much of the good
farmland is owned by a few rich
landowners: many peasant farmers
do not have enough land to make a living.

FARMING AND LAND USE

🐂 Cattle	⬇ Sugarcane
🐟 Fishing	⬆ Timber
🐐 Goats	▢ Cropland
🐑 Sheep	▢ Forest
🍌 Bananas	▢ Mountain region
🍈 Cocoa	▢ Pasture
☕ Coffee	▢ Wetland
Rubber	• Major conurbation

LAND USE

Cropland 6%
Other (including mountains) 15%
Pasture 23%
Forest 56%

INDUSTRY

Important oil reserves are found in
Venezuela and parts of the Amazon
Basin; Venezuela is one of the world's
top oil producers. Brazil's cities have
a wide range of industries including
chemicals, clothes and shoes,
and textiles. Metallic minerals,
particularly iron ore, are mined
throughout the area and specially built
industrial centers like Ciudad Guayana
have been developed to refine them.

STRUCTURE OF INDUSTRY

Primary 11%
Services 50%
Manufacturing 39%

INDUSTRY

🜁 Chemicals	⛽ Oil
🥫 Food processing	🪵 Timber processing
Iron and steel	🏛 Tourism
△ Metal refining	
▽ Textiles	▣ Major industrial center / area
⛏ Mining	— Major road

POPULATION

Most of the population lives in urban
areas. Many cities are extremely
overcrowded, with poor housing.
São Paulo in Brazil is one of
the world's fastest-growing
cities. The rain forests of
the interior and high Andes
are sparsely populated. The
few Native American peoples
live in remote areas.

INHABITANTS PER SQ MILE

■ More than 520	■ Capital city
■ 260–520	• Major city
■ 130–260	
▢ 30–130	
▢ Less than 30	

URBAN/RURAL POPULATION DIVISION

Rio de Janeiro 4.6%
São Paulo 8.4%
Lima 3%
Rural population 24%
Other towns and cities 60%

THE LANDSCAPE

The Andes run down the western side of South
America. There are many volcanoes among their peaks,
and earthquakes are common. The tropical rain forests
surrounding the Amazon River take up most of western
Brazil. Huge, dry, flat grasslands called *llanos* cover
central Venezuela and part of eastern Colombia.

Angel Falls (D 2)
Venezuela's Angel Falls is the
world's highest waterfall. Twenty
times as high as Niagara Falls, it
drops 3,215 ft from a spectacular
plateau deep in the Guiana Highlands.

Amazon River (D 4)
The Amazon is the longest
river in South America, and
the second longest in
the world. It flows over
4,000 miles from the
Peruvian Andes to the
coast of Brazil. One-fifth of
the world's freshwater is
carried by the river.

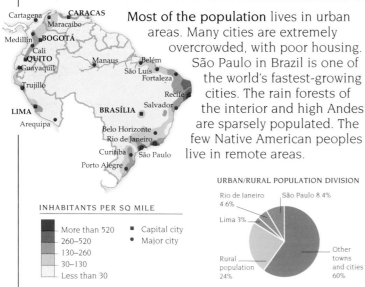

Andes (B 5)
The snow-capped
Andes are the
longest mountain
range on Earth.
They stretch
4,500 miles down
the whole length
of South America.

Lake Titicaca (C 6)
South America's
largest lake is the
highest navigable
lake in the world
at 12,500 ft
above sea level.
It lies across the
border between
Peru and Bolivia.

Pantanal (E 6)
This is the largest area of
wetlands in the world. It spreads
across 50,000 sq miles of Brazil.
Many hundreds of plant and
animal species are found here.

Amazon rain forest (D 4)
The enormous rain forest
surrounding the Amazon
River and its tributaries
covers 2,510,000 sq miles,
an area almost as big as
Australia. It is estimated
that at least half of all
known living species
are found in the forest.

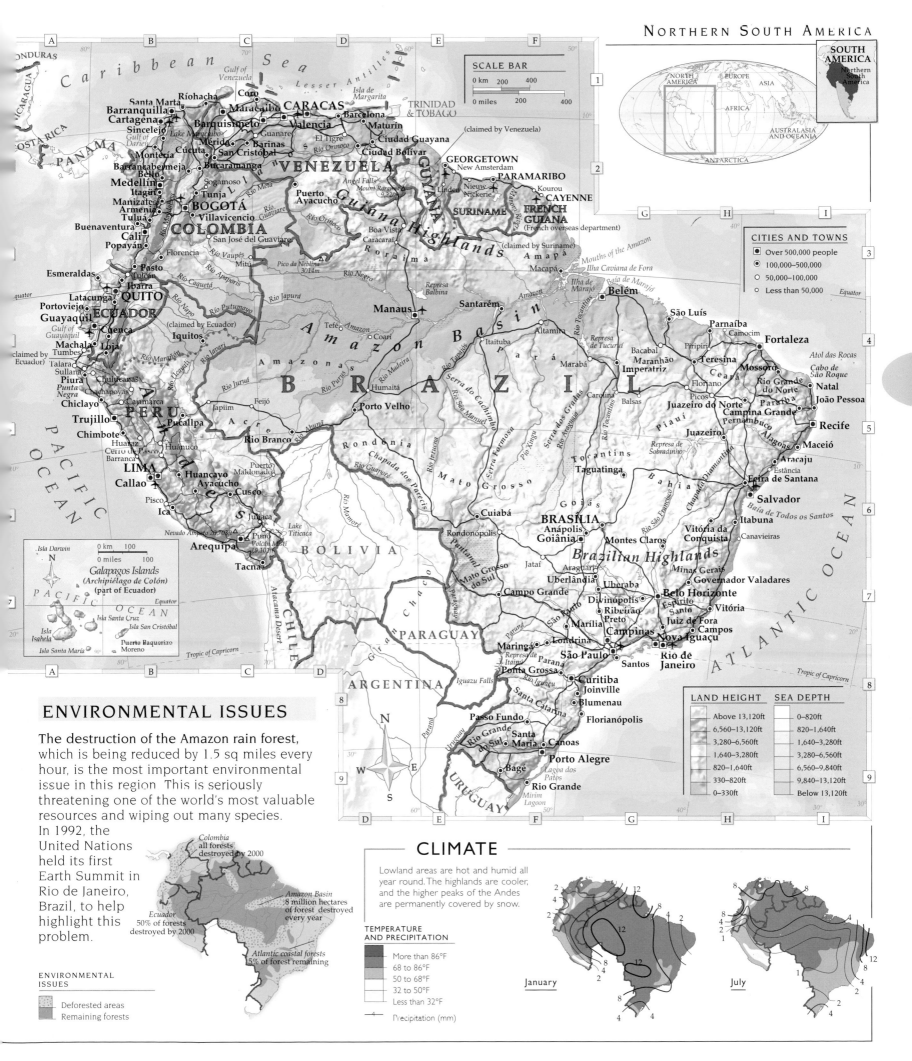

SOUTH AMERICA
Northern South America

SCALE BAR
0 km 200 400
0 miles 200 400

(claimed by Venezuela)

CITIES AND TOWNS
■ Over 500,000 people
● 100,000–500,000
◐ 50,000–100,000
○ Less than 50,000

Galapagos Islands
(Archipiélago de Colón)
(part of Ecuador)
0 km 100
0 miles 100

LAND HEIGHT
Above 13,120ft
6,560–13,120ft
3,280–6,560ft
1,640–3,280ft
820–1,640ft
330–820ft
0–330ft

SEA DEPTH
0–820ft
820–1,640ft
1,640–3,280ft
3,280–6,560ft
6,560–9,840ft
9,840–13,120ft
Below 13,120ft

ENVIRONMENTAL ISSUES

The destruction of the Amazon rain forest, which is being reduced by 1.5 sq miles every hour, is the most important environmental issue in this region. This is seriously threatening one of the world's most valuable resources and wiping out many species. In 1992, the United Nations held its first Earth Summit in Rio de Janeiro, Brazil, to help highlight this problem.

Colombia
all forests
destroyed by 2000

Amazon Basin
8 million hectares
of forest destroyed
every year

Ecuador
50% of forests
destroyed by 2000

Atlantic coastal forests
5% of forest remaining

ENVIRONMENTAL
ISSUES
Deforested areas
Remaining forests

CLIMATE

Lowland areas are hot and humid all year round. The highlands are cooler, and the higher peaks of the Andes are permanently covered by snow.

TEMPERATURE
AND PRECIPITATION
More than 86°F
68 to 86°F
50 to 68°F
32 to 50°F
Less than 32°F
Precipitation (mm)

January

July

SOUTHERN SOUTH AMERICA

ARGENTINA, BOLIVIA, CHILE, PARAGUAY, URUGUAY

The southern half of South America forms a long, narrow cone, with landscapes ranging from barren desert in the west to frozen glaciers in the far south. The whole area was governed by Spain until the early 19th century, and Spanish is still the main language spoken, although the few remaining Native American groups use their own languages. Most people now live in vast cities such as Buenos Aires and Santiago.

POPULATION

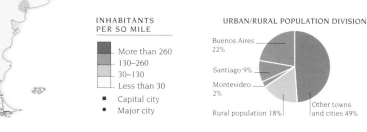

Since the 1950s, there has been a tremendous move from the countryside to the cities. In Argentina, Chile, and Uruguay more than 80% of the people are now city dwellers. The capital cities of all these countries have grown enormously – Buenos Aires holds a third of Argentina's population, and more than half of Uruguay's people live in the capital, Montevideo.

INHABITANTS PER SQ MILE
- More than 260
- 130–260
- 30–130
- Less than 30
- ■ Capital city
- ● Major city

URBAN/RURAL POPULATION DIVISION
- Buenos Aires 22%
- Santiago 9%
- Montevideo 2%
- Rural population 18%
- Other towns and cities 49%

INDUSTRY

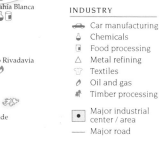

Rich deposits of minerals – especially copper – in the Andes have led to the development of large metal refining industries in Chile. The capital cities, Buenos Aires and Santiago, are home to a wide range of industries, and Argentina is an important producer of processed foods like canned beef. There are fewer industries in the south, although oil and gas are extracted in southern Argentina and Chile.

INDUSTRY
- 🚗 Car manufacturing
- Chemicals
- Food processing
- △ Metal refining
- Textiles
- Oil and gas
- Timber processing
- ▣ Major industrial center / area
- — Major road

STRUCTURE OF INDUSTRY
- Primary 6%
- Services 64%
- Manufacturing 30%

THE LANDSCAPE

Southern South America's landscape varies from tropical forest and dry desert in the north to subarctic conditions in the south. The towering Andes divide Chile from Argentina. East of the Andes lie forests and rolling grasslands. To the west is a thin coastal strip. The wet, windswept, freezing southern tip of the continent has volcanoes alongside glaciers and fjords.

Gran Chaco (C3)
This huge stretch of forest and grassland runs from Bolivia, through Paraguay and into Argentina. The south and east provide grazing for cattle.

Paraná River (C4)
South America's second-longest river is the Paraná. It stretches 2,610 miles from the Brazilian Highlands, finally flowing into the Plate River near Buenos Aires in Argentina.

Iguazu Falls (D4)
The Iguazu River drops 262 m over the Iguazu Falls. When the river is at its fullest, the water flowing over the falls could fill six Olympic swimming pools every second.

Atacama Desert (A3)
The Atacama Desert in northern Chile is the driest place on Earth. In some parts, rain has not fallen for hundreds of years.

Pampas (B5)
The grassy plains in central Argentina – known as the Pampas – cover 251,000 sq miles. The western part is semidesert, but the east gets plenty of rain.

Chile
The far south of Chile has a dramatic landscape of fjords, lakes, jagged mountain peaks, and spectacular glaciers.

Patagonia (B8)
The high, windswept plateau of Patagonia covers 297,000 sq miles of southern Argentina. The south is dry and freezing cold, with very little vegetation.

ENVIRONMENTAL ISSUES

Many of southern South America's rivers are polluted, particularly close to Buenos Aires. The Itaipú Dam on the Paraná River is the world's largest hydroelectric power plant. Deforestation is a persistent problem. In Bolivia, forests are being cut down at a record rate of 494,000 acres a year. Air quality in Buenos Aires and Santiago is poor, especially in Santiago, which is surrounded by mountains, making it difficult for pollution to escape.

ENVIRONMENTAL ISSUES
- 〰 Major dam
- 💀 Urban air pollution
- Deforested areas
- Polluted river
- ● Major industrial center

PERU

BRAZIL

BOLIVIA

PARAGUAY

ARGENTINA

URUGUAY

CHILE

LAND HEIGHT

Above 13,120ft
6,560–13,120ft
3,280–6,560ft
1,640–3,280ft
820–1,640ft
330–820ft
0–330ft

SEA DEPTH

0–820ft
820–1,640ft
1,640–3,280ft
3,280–6,560ft
6,560–9,840ft
9,840–13,120ft
Below 13,120ft

CITIES AND TOWNS

■ Over 500,000 people
◉ 100,000–500,000
○ 50,000–100,000
○ Less than 50,000

BOLIVIA'S TWO CAPITALS

LA PAZ – legislative and
administrative capital

SUCRE – legal capital

CLIMATE

Temperature patterns are similar in January
and July; warmer to the north and east, colder
to the south and west, although January is
much warmer than July. Temperatures are
always low, high in the Andes.

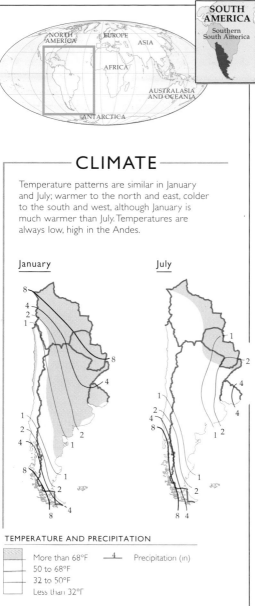

January

July

TEMPERATURE AND PRECIPITATION

More than 68°F
50 to 68°F
32 to 50°F
Less than 32°F

——4—— Precipitation (in)

SCALE BAR

0 km   200   400

0 miles   200   400

FALKLAND ISLANDS
(UK dependent territory)

FARMING AND LAND USE

The enormous grasslands to the east
of the Andes provide good grazing for
cattle and sheep, and Argentina is
one of the world's leading suppliers
of meat, milk, and hides. The
country is also an important grower
of wheat and fruit. Chile grows
grapes for its successful wine
industry, and for eating; it is also the
world's top producer of fishmeal.
The illegal growing of coca, used to
make the drug cocaine, is a major
source of income in Bolivia.

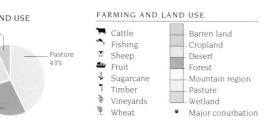

LAND USE

Cropland 7%
Pasture 43%
Other (including mountains) 23%
Forest 27%

FARMING AND LAND USE

Cattle
Fishing
Sheep
Fruit
Sugarcane
Timber
Vineyards
Wheat

Barren land
Cropland
Desert
Forest
Mountain region
Pasture
Wetland
● Major conurbation

CONTINENTAL AFRICA

Africa is the second-largest continent in the world. Its dramatic landscapes include arid deserts, humid rain forests, and the valleys of the east African rift – where humans may have first evolved. Today, there are 53 separate countries in Africa, and its people speak a rich variety of languages. The world's highest temperatures have been recorded in Africa's deserts.

4,510 miles
4,737 miles

CROSS SECTION THROUGH AFRICA

Niger Delta
Congo Basin
Great Rift Valley
Ethiopian Highlands
Lake Victoria
Horn of Africa

W — 3,230 miles — E

In the west, the Niger River flows into the Atlantic Ocean through the swampy Niger Delta. Farther east is the immense Congo Basin, where the Congo River winds its way through thick rain forests. In the east is the Great Rift Valley and the Ethiopian Highlands. The Horn of Africa is Africa's most easterly point.

1 DESERTS

The Sahara covers much of north Africa. One-quarter of the desert is sandy dunes; the remainder consists of bare, rocky plains and mountainous outcrops. Other large deserts include the Namib and the Kalahari in the south.

2 GREAT RIFT VALLEY

Cracks beneath the Earth formed this valley, which runs from Lake Nyasa to the Red Sea. It is thought that East Africa – the Horn – will eventually split from the rest of Africa.

4 RAIN FORESTS

Dense rain forests grow near the Equator, where rainfall is plentiful. Here, it is hot and humid enough for large areas of vegetation to flourish.

PHYSICAL AFRICA

Northern and southern Africa are both very hot and dry, with huge expanses of barren desert lying over raised platforms of rock called plateaus. Near the equator there are large areas of tropical rain forest. In east Africa, cracks in the continent form a string of flat-bottomed, steep-sided rift valleys, many of which contain vast lakes.

3 SAVANNA

Vast areas of sub-Saharan Africa are covered with grass and scrubland, known as savanna. Many of Africa's largest animals, such as elephants, live here.

ELEVATION

16,400ft
13,120ft
9,840ft
6,560ft
3,280ft
1,640ft
820ft
330ft
sea level
below sea level
cross section

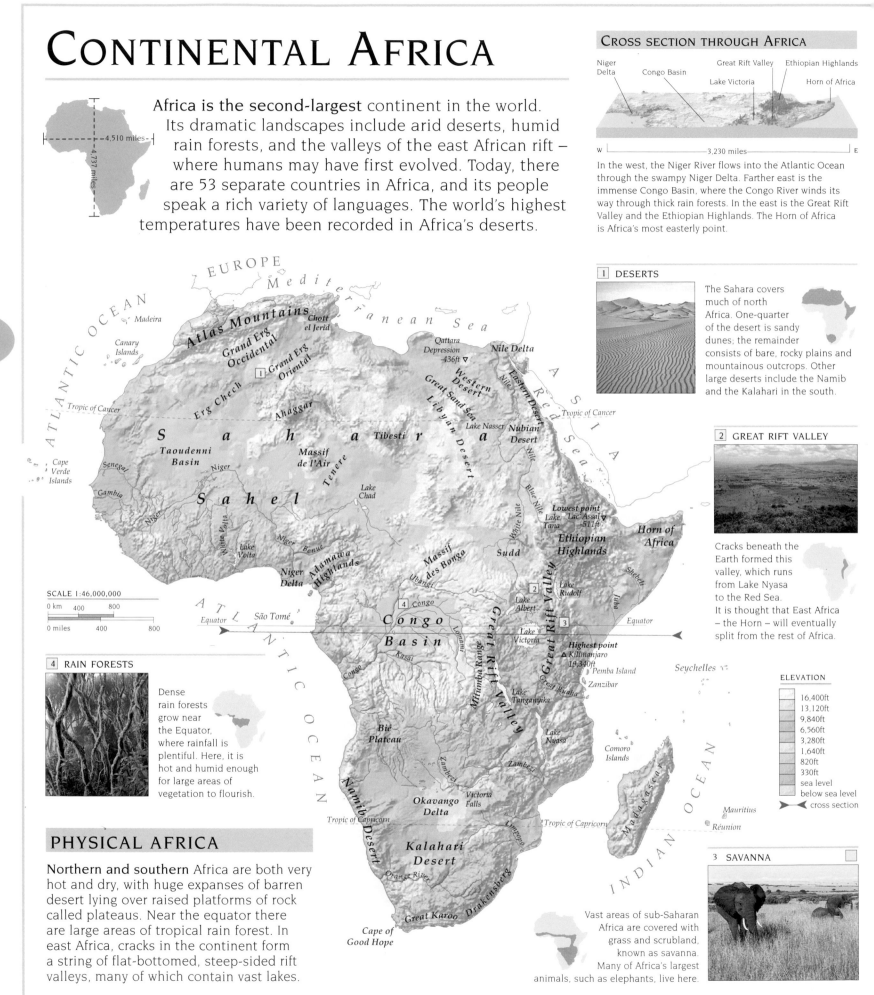

SCALE 1:46,000,000
0 km 400 800
0 miles 400 800

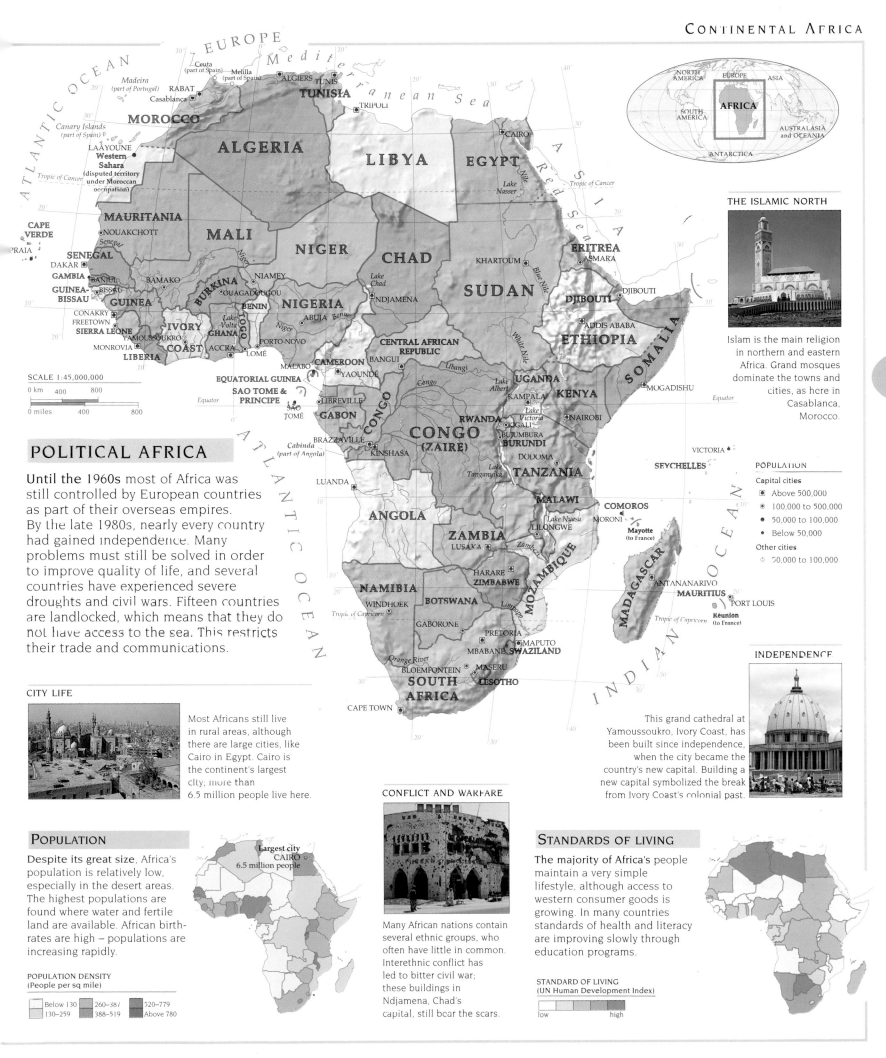

THE ISLAMIC NORTH

Islam is the main religion in northern and eastern Africa. Grand mosques dominate the towns and cities, as here in Casablanca, Morocco.

POPULATION

Capital cities
- ◉ Above 500,000
- ◉ 100,000 to 500,000
- ● 50,000 to 100,000
- ● Below 50,000

Other cities
- ○ 50,000 to 100,000

POLITICAL AFRICA

Until the 1960s most of Africa was still controlled by European countries as part of their overseas empires. By the late 1980s, nearly every country had gained independence. Many problems must still be solved in order to improve quality of life, and several countries have experienced severe droughts and civil wars. Fifteen countries are landlocked, which means that they do not have access to the sea. This restricts their trade and communications.

SCALE 1:45,000,000

0 km   400   800

0 miles   400   800

CITY LIFE

Most Africans still live in rural areas, although there are large cities, like Cairo in Egypt. Cairo is the continent's largest city; more than 6.5 million people live here.

INDEPENDENCE

This grand cathedral at Yamoussoukro, Ivory Coast, has been built since independence, when the city became the country's new capital. Building a new capital symbolized the break from Ivory Coast's colonial past.

POPULATION

Despite its great size, Africa's population is relatively low, especially in the desert areas. The highest populations are found where water and fertile land are available. African birth-rates are high – populations are increasing rapidly.

POPULATION DENSITY
(People per sq mile)

Largest city
CAIRO
6.5 million people

- Below 130
- 130–259
- 260–387
- 388–519
- 520–779
- Above 780

CONFLICT AND WARFARE

Many African nations contain several ethnic groups, who often have little in common. Interethnic conflict has led to bitter civil war; these buildings in Ndjamena, Chad's capital, still bear the scars.

STANDARDS OF LIVING

The majority of Africa's people maintain a very simple lifestyle, although access to western consumer goods is growing. In many countries standards of health and literacy are improving slowly through education programs.

STANDARD OF LIVING
(UN Human Development Index)

low   high

AFRICAN GEOGRAPHY

Africa's massive reserves of minerals, including oil, gold, copper, and diamonds, are among the largest in the world. Mining is a very important industry for many countries and has provided money for growth and development. Many different types of crops can be grown in Africa's wide range of environments. Rubber, bananas, and oil palms are grown for export in the Tropics, and east Africa is especially famous for its tea and coffee.

INDUSTRY

Most African industries are based on processing raw materials such as food crops or mineral ores. Some African countries depend on one product or crop for most of their income, but in many larger cities different industries are developing. Northern Africa, Nigeria, and South Africa have the widest range of industries.

MINERAL RESOURCES

The southern countries, in particular South Africa, have large reserves of diamonds, gold, uranium, and copper. The large copper deposits in Congo (Zaire) and Zambia are known as the "copper belt." Oil and gas are extracted in Algeria, Angola, Egypt, Libya, and Nigeria.

MINING

The world's largest uranium mine is in Namibia. Uranium is used to fuel nuclear power plants, and is also mined in Niger and South Africa.

MINERAL RESOURCES

- Bauxite
- Copper
- Diamonds
- Iron
- Phosphates
- Gold
- Uranium
- Oil/gas field
- Coal field

OIL AND GAS

In the desert wastes of Algeria, a drilling rig searches for new sources of oil in the rich north African oilfields. There are several large oil fields in the Niger delta and North Africa.

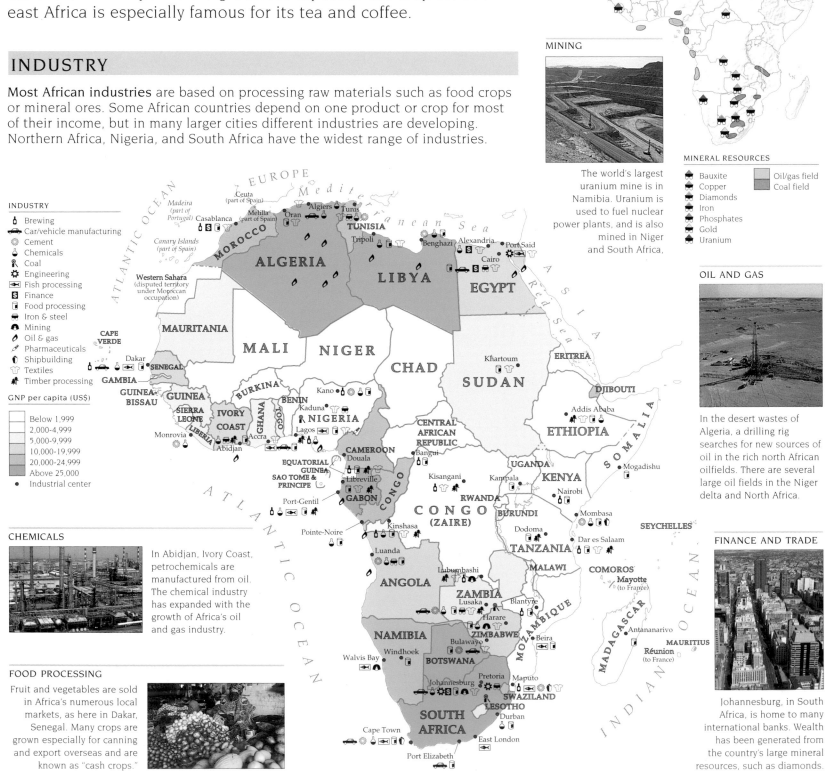

INDUSTRY

- Brewing
- Car/vehicle manufacturing
- Cement
- Chemicals
- Coal
- Engineering
- Fish processing
- Finance
- Food processing
- Iron & steel
- Mining
- Oil & gas
- Pharmaceuticals
- Shipbuilding
- Textiles
- Timber processing

GNP per capita (US$)

- Below 1,999
- 2,000-4,999
- 5,000-9,999
- 10,000-19,999
- 20,000-24,999
- Above 25,000
- • Industrial center

CHEMICALS

In Abidjan, Ivory Coast, petrochemicals are manufactured from oil. The chemical industry has expanded with the growth of Africa's oil and gas industry.

FOOD PROCESSING

Fruit and vegetables are sold in Africa's numerous local markets, as here in Dakar, Senegal. Many crops are grown especially for canning and export overseas and are known as "cash crops."

FINANCE AND TRADE

Johannesburg, in South Africa, is home to many international banks. Wealth has been generated from the country's large mineral resources, such as diamonds.

CLIMATE

Africa is the world's hottest continent: temperatures of more than 122°F have been recorded in the Sahara. The northern coast has a hot, dry climate with little rainfall. Farther inland, the Sahara is extremely arid, with strong, dry winds. South of the Sahara is the Sahel, where cutting down trees for fuel has turned farmland into desert. Close to the equator there is more rainfall, and huge rain forests can grow in western and central Africa. In the south, the climate is much drier, and drought is a problem.

EXTREME WEATHER EVENTS

Symbols indicate climatic extremes

Coldest place
IFRANE (Morocco)
Temp. -11°F

Hottest place
AL 'AZIZIYAH (Libya)
Temp. 136°F

Driest place
WADI HALFA (Sudan)
Annual rainfall 1/8in

Wettest place
CAPE DEBUNDSHA (Cameroon)
Annual rainfall 405in

Tropic of Cancer

Equator

Tropic of Capricorn

CLIMATE

- Warm temperate
- Mediterranean
- Semiarid
- Arid
- Humid equatorial
- Tropical

THE ENCROACHING DESERT

Africa has three main desert areas: the Sahara in the north and the Namib and Kalahari deserts in the south. They are a mixture of sandy dunes and bare, rocky plateaus. At the desert's edges, low rainfall and land clearance is causing the deserts to expand into areas that were once grassland.

LAND USE AND AGRICULTURE

The quality of land and the amount of rainfall has a great impact on the type of farming. In the mountain regions of countries such as Rwanda, Uganda, and Kenya, tea and coffee are grown. In the north, there is not enough water to produce staple crops such as wheat for all the population, but "cash crops" such as citrus fruits, dates, and olives are grown for export. Subtropical west Africa grows peanuts, cocoa, and coffee. In the southern part of the continent, South Africa grows many different crops: citrus fruits are grown for export, as well as grapes, which are used to make wine.

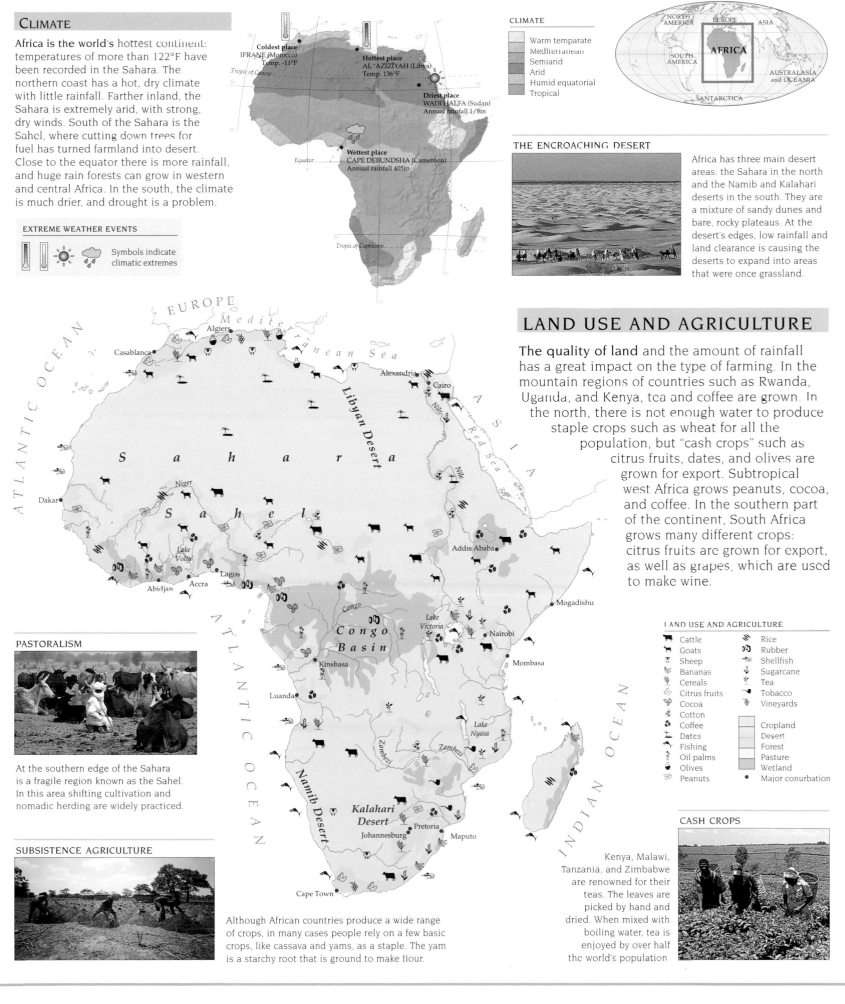

PASTORALISM

At the southern edge of the Sahara is a fragile region known as the Sahel. In this area shifting cultivation and nomadic herding are widely practiced.

SUBSISTENCE AGRICULTURE

Although African countries produce a wide range of crops, in many cases people rely on a few basic crops, like cassava and yams, as a staple. The yam is a starchy root that is ground to make flour.

LAND USE AND AGRICULTURE

- Cattle
- Goats
- Sheep
- Bananas
- Cereals
- Citrus fruits
- Cocoa
- Cotton
- Coffee
- Dates
- Fishing
- Oil palms
- Olives
- Peanuts
- Rice
- Rubber
- Shellfish
- Sugarcane
- Tea
- Tobacco
- Vineyards

- Cropland
- Desert
- Forest
- Pasture
- Wetland
- Major conurbation

CASH CROPS

Kenya, Malawi, Tanzania, and Zimbabwe are renowned for their teas. The leaves are picked by hand and dried. When mixed with boiling water, tea is enjoyed by over half the world's population.

NORTH AFRICA

ALGERIA, EGYPT, LIBYA, MOROCCO, TUNISIA.

Sandwiched between the Mediterranean and the Sahara, North Africa has a history dating back to the dawn of civilization. About 6,000 years ago, settlements were established along the banks of the Nile River. Since then, waves of settlers, including Romans, Arabs, and Turks, have brought a mix of different cultures to the area. In the 19th century, Spain, France, and Britain claimed colonies in the region, but today North Africa is independent, although Western Sahara is occupied by Morocco.

FARMING AND LAND USE

Most farming in North Africa is restricted to the fertile Mediterranean coastal strip, and the banks of the Nile where it relies heavily on irrigation. In spite of these seemingly inhospitable conditions, the region is a major producer of dates, which grow in desert oases, and of cork, made from the bark of the cork oak tree. A wide variety of other crops is also grown, including grapes, olives, and cotton.

FARMING AND LAND USE

- Fishing
- Goats
- Sheep
- Cork
- Cotton
- Dates
- Olives
- Vineyards

- Cropland
- Desert
- Forest
- Pasture

• Major conurbation

LAND USE

Forest 3%
Pasture 9%
Cropland 12%
Other (including desert) 76%

CLIMATE

Most of north Africa is desert, and the climate is harsh. Rainfall is scarce, and drought is common. Temperatures are freezing at night, scorching by day and have been known to climb to over 120°F.

January

July

whole area has below 1in rainfall

TEMPERATURE AND PRECIPITATION

- More than 95°F
- 86 to 95°F
- 77 to 86°F
- 68 to 77°F
- 59 to 68°F
- 50 to 59°F
- 41 to 50°F
- Less than 41°F

4 — Precipitation (in)

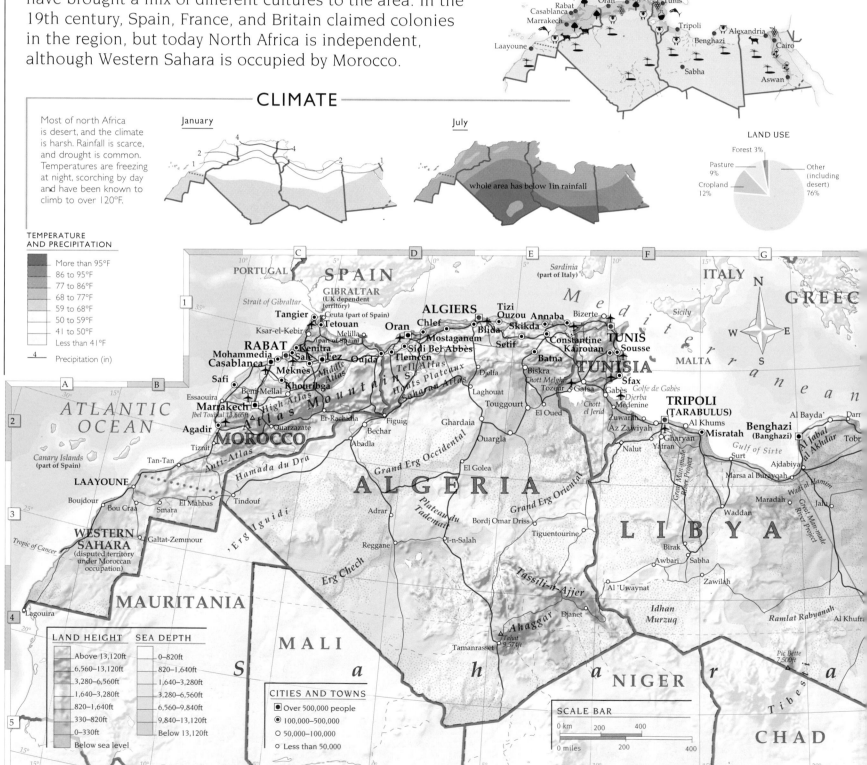

LAND HEIGHT
- Above 13,120ft
- 6,560–13,120ft
- 3,280–6,560ft
- 1,640–3,280ft
- 820–1,640ft
- 330–820ft
- 0–330ft
- Below sea level

SEA DEPTH
- 0–820ft
- 820–1,640ft
- 1,640–3,280ft
- 3,280–6,560ft
- 6,560–9,840ft
- 9,840–13,120ft
- Below 13,120ft

CITIES AND TOWNS
- ■ Over 500,000 people
- ⊙ 100,000–500,000
- ○ 50,000–100,000
- ○ Less than 50,000

SCALE BAR

0 km   200   400

0 miles   200   400

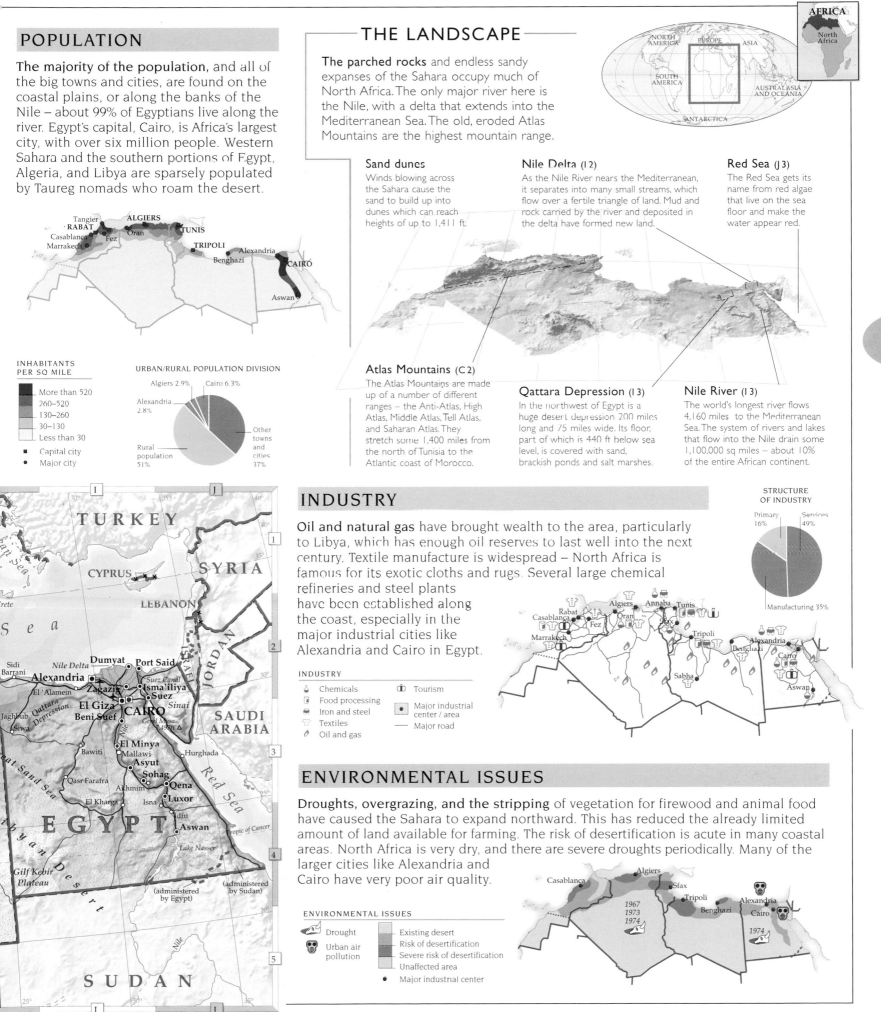

AFRICA
North Africa

POPULATION

The majority of the population, and all of the big towns and cities, are found on the coastal plains, or along the banks of the Nile – about 99% of Egyptians live along the river. Egypt's capital, Cairo, is Africa's largest city, with over six million people. Western Sahara and the southern portions of Egypt, Algeria, and Libya are sparsely populated by Taureg nomads who roam the desert.

Tangier · RABAT · ALGIERS · TUNIS · Casablanca · Fez · Oran · TRIPOLI · Marrakech · Benghazi · Alexandria · CAIRO · Aswan

INHABITANTS PER SQ MILE

- More than 520
- 260–520
- 130–260
- 30–130
- Less than 30

■ Capital city
● Major city

URBAN/RURAL POPULATION DIVISION

- Algiers 2.9%
- Cairo 6.3%
- Alexandria 2.8%
- Rural population 51%
- Other towns and cities 37%

THE LANDSCAPE

The parched rocks and endless sandy expanses of the Sahara occupy much of North Africa. The only major river here is the Nile, with a delta that extends into the Mediterranean Sea. The old, eroded Atlas Mountains are the highest mountain range.

Sand dunes
Winds blowing across the Sahara cause the sand to build up into dunes which can reach heights of up to 1,411 ft.

Nile Delta (I2)
As the Nile River nears the Mediterranean, it separates into many small streams, which flow over a fertile triangle of land. Mud and rock carried by the river and deposited in the delta have formed new land.

Red Sea (J3)
The Red Sea gets its name from red algae that live on the sea floor and make the water appear red.

Atlas Mountains (C2)
The Atlas Mountains are made up of a number of different ranges – the Anti-Atlas, High Atlas, Middle Atlas, Tell Atlas, and Saharan Atlas. They stretch some 1,400 miles from the north of Tunisia to the Atlantic coast of Morocco.

Qattara Depression (I3)
In the northwest of Egypt is a huge desert depression 200 miles long and 75 miles wide. Its floor, part of which is 440 ft below sea level, is covered with sand, brackish ponds and salt marshes.

Nile River (I3)
The world's longest river flows 4,160 miles to the Mediterranean Sea. The system of rivers and lakes that flow into the Nile drain some 1,100,000 sq miles – about 10% of the entire African continent.

INDUSTRY

Oil and natural gas have brought wealth to the area, particularly to Libya, which has enough oil reserves to last well into the next century. Textile manufacture is widespread – North Africa is famous for its exotic cloths and rugs. Several large chemical refineries and steel plants have been established along the coast, especially in the major industrial cities like Alexandria and Cairo in Egypt.

STRUCTURE OF INDUSTRY

- Primary 16%
- Services 49%
- Manufacturing 35%

INDUSTRY

- 🜊 Chemicals
- 🗄 Food processing
- ⚒ Iron and steel
- ⵙ Textiles
- ⬮ Oil and gas
- 🎫 Tourism
- ◉ Major industrial center / area
- — Major road

ENVIRONMENTAL ISSUES

Droughts, overgrazing, and the stripping of vegetation for firewood and animal food have caused the Sahara to expand northward. This has reduced the already limited amount of land available for farming. The risk of desertification is acute in many coastal areas. North Africa is very dry, and there are severe droughts periodically. Many of the larger cities like Alexandria and Cairo have very poor air quality.

ENVIRONMENTAL ISSUES

- 🌊 Drought
- 😷 Urban air pollution
- Existing desert
- Risk of desertification
- Severe risk of desertification
- Unaffected area
- ● Major industrial center

WEST AFRICA

BENIN, BURKINA, CAMEROON, CENTRAL AFRICAN REPUBLIC, CHAD, EQUATORIAL GUINEA,
GAMBIA, GHANA, GUINEA, GUINEA-BISSAU, IVORY COAST, LIBERIA, MALI, MAURITANIA,
NIGER, NIGERIA, SAO TOME & PRINCIPE, SENEGAL, SIERRA LEONE, TOGO

West Africa's varied climate and agricultural and
mineral wealth have provided the foundation for
some of Africa's greatest civilizations, like those
of the Malinke and Asante people. The area remains
ethnically and culturally diverse today as well
as densely populated. Nigeria is the most populous
country in Africa. Since independence from European
colonial powers in the 1960s, political instability has
been a reality for many countries here.

INDUSTRY

Agricultural products still form the basis of most economies in
West Africa. Food processing is widespread – oil palms and
peanuts are processed for their valuable
vegetable oils. Oil
and gas are found
off the coast of
Ivory Coast and
around the Niger
delta, where a
large chemical
industry has
developed.

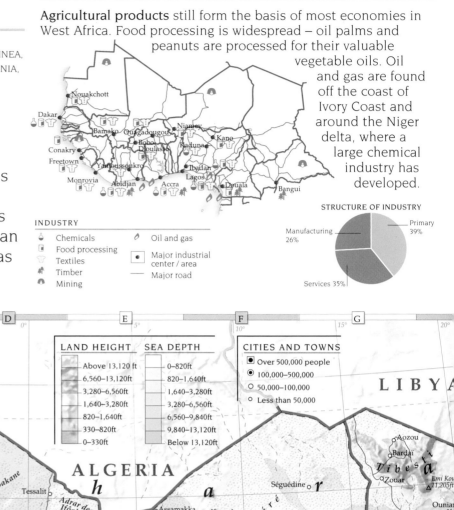

INDUSTRY

- Chemicals
- Food processing
- Textiles
- Timber
- Mining

○ Oil and gas
● Major industrial center / area
— Major road

STRUCTURE OF INDUSTRY

Manufacturing 26%
Primary 39%
Services 35%

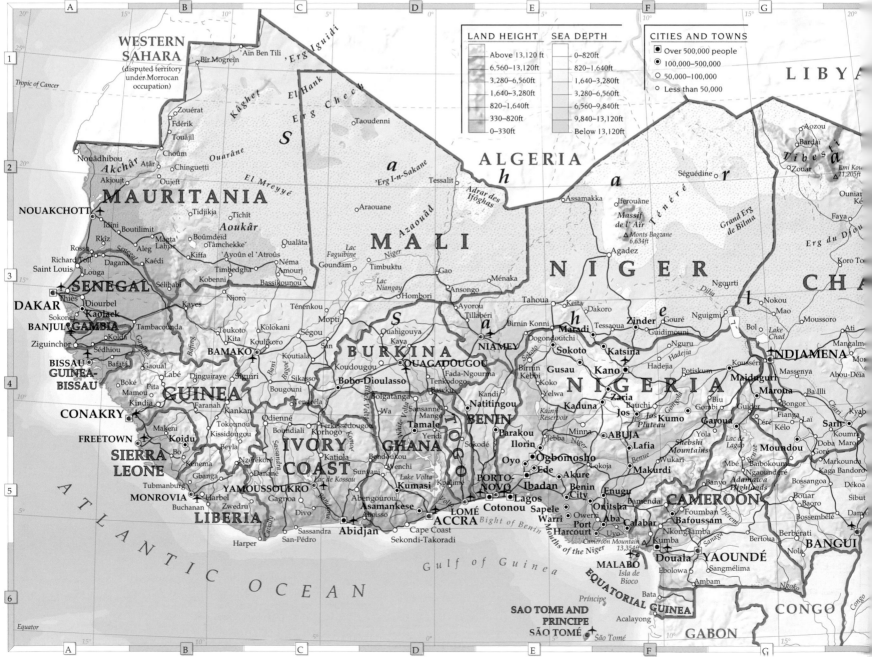

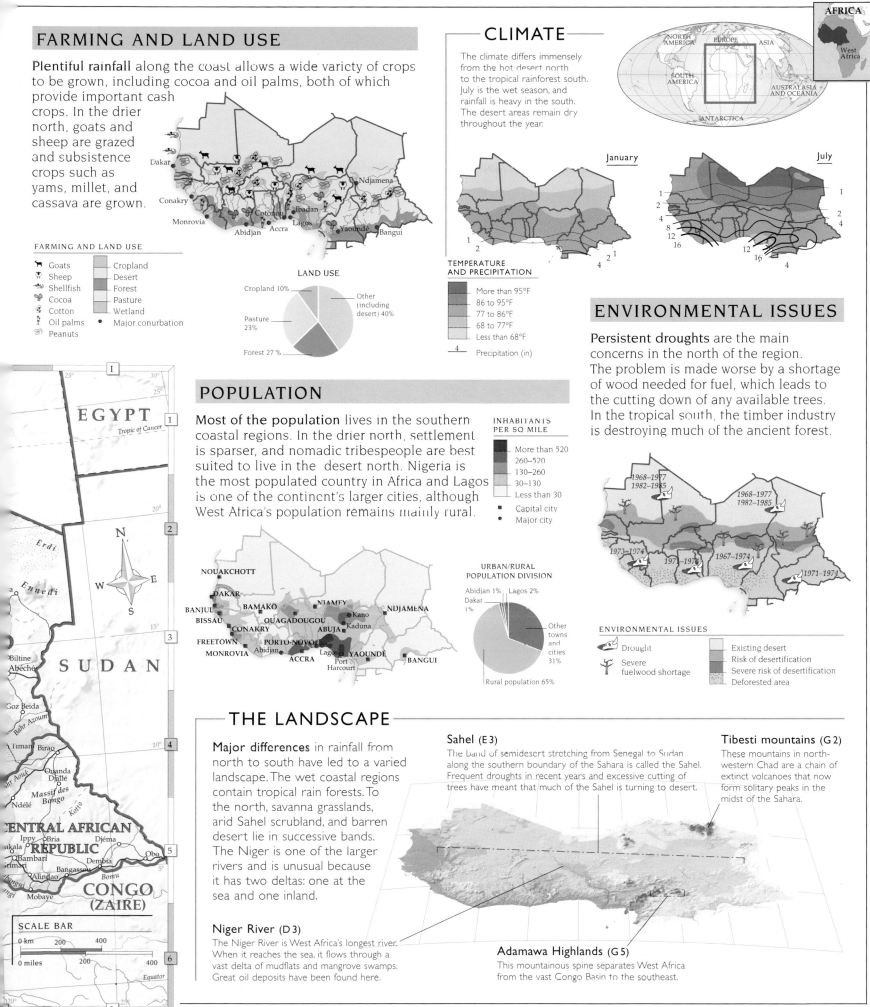

FARMING AND LAND USE

Plentiful rainfall along the coast allows a wide variety of crops to be grown, including cocoa and oil palms, both of which provide important cash crops. In the drier north, goats and sheep are grazed and subsistence crops such as yams, millet, and cassava are grown.

FARMING AND LAND USE

- 🐐 Goats
- 🐑 Sheep
- 🦪 Shellfish
- 🌰 Cocoa
- 🌿 Cotton
- 🌴 Oil palms
- 🥜 Peanuts

- Cropland
- Desert
- Forest
- Pasture
- Wetland
- • Major conurbation

LAND USE

- Cropland 10%
- Pasture 23%
- Forest 27 %
- Other (including desert) 40%

CLIMATE

The climate differs immensely from the hot desert north to the tropical rainforest south. July is the wet season, and rainfall is heavy in the south. The desert areas remain dry throughout the year.

January

July

TEMPERATURE AND PRECIPITATION

- More than 95°F
- 86 to 95°F
- 77 to 86°F
- 68 to 77°F
- Less than 68°F
- ——4—— Precipitation (in)

ENVIRONMENTAL ISSUES

Persistent droughts are the main concerns in the north of the region. The problem is made worse by a shortage of wood needed for fuel, which leads to the cutting down of any available trees. In the tropical south, the timber industry is destroying much of the ancient forest.

1968–1977 1982–1985
1968–1977 1982–1985
1971–1974
1971–1974
1967–1974
1971–1974

ENVIRONMENTAL ISSUES

- 🦴 Drought
- 🌴 Severe fuelwood shortage
- Existing desert
- Risk of desertification
- Severe risk of desertification
- Deforested area

POPULATION

Most of the population lives in the southern coastal regions. In the drier north, settlement is sparser, and nomadic tribespeople are best suited to live in the desert north. Nigeria is the most populated country in Africa and Lagos is one of the continent's larger cities, although West Africa's population remains mainly rural.

INHABITANTS PER SQ MILE

- More than 520
- 260–520
- 130–260
- 30–130
- Less than 30
- ■ Capital city
- • Major city

NOUAKCHOTT
DAKAR
BANJUL
BISSAU
BAMAKO
NIAMEY
NDJAMENA
CONAKRY
OUAGADOUGOU
ABUJA
Kano
Kaduna
FREETOWN
PORTO-NOVO
MONROVIA Abidjan
ACCRA Lagos YAOUNDÉ
Port BANGUI
Harcourt

URBAN/RURAL POPULATION DIVISION

- Abidjan 1%
- Dakar 1%
- Lagos 2%
- Other towns and cities 31%
- Rural population 65%

THE LANDSCAPE

Major differences in rainfall from north to south have led to a varied landscape. The wet coastal regions contain tropical rain forests. To the north, savanna grasslands, arid Sahel scrubland, and barren desert lie in successive bands. The Niger is one of the larger rivers and is unusual because it has two deltas: one at the sea and one inland.

Sahel (E 3)
The band of semidesert stretching from Senegal to Sudan along the southern boundary of the Sahara is called the Sahel. Frequent droughts in recent years and excessive cutting of trees have meant that much of the Sahel is turning to desert.

Tibesti mountains (G 2)
These mountains in north-western Chad are a chain of extinct volcanoes that now form solitary peaks in the midst of the Sahara.

Niger River (D 3)
The Niger River is West Africa's longest river. When it reaches the sea, it flows through a vast delta of mudflats and mangrove swamps. Great oil deposits have been found here.

Adamawa Highlands (G 5)
This mountainous spine separates West Africa from the vast Congo Basin to the southeast.

EGYPT
Tropic of Cancer
Erdi
Ennedi
SUDAN
Biltine
Abéché
Goz Beïda
Timan
Birao
Ouanda
Djallé
Massif des
Bongo
Ndélé
CENTRAL AFRICAN
REPUBLIC
Ippy Bria Djéma
Bambari
Dembia Obo
Bangassou
Alindao
Mobaye
CONGO
(ZAÏRE)

SCALE BAR

0 km 200 400

0 miles 200 400

Equator

EAST AFRICA

BURUNDI, DJIBOUTI, ERITREA, ETHIOPIA, KENYA, RWANDA, SOMALIA, SUDAN, TANZANIA, UGANDA

Much of East Africa is covered by long grass, scrub, and scattered trees, called savanna. This land is grazed by both domestic animals and a great variety of wild animals including lions, giraffes and elephants. The east of the region is known as the Horn of Africa, because it is shaped like an animal horn. Sudan, and the other countries there have recently been devastated by civil wars, and periods of drought and famine. In contrast, Kenya in the south is one of Africa's more stable and wealthy countries.

FARMING AND LAND USE

Much of the north and east is too dry for farming, but in Sudan, cotton is grown on land irrigated by the Nile River. The Lake Victoria basin and rich volcanic soils of the highlands in Kenya, Uganda, and Tanzania support staple food crops, and those grown for export, such as tea and coffee. Kenya also grows high-quality vegetables, like mangetout, and exports them by air to supermarkets abroad. Sheep, goats, and cattle are herded on the savanna.

FARMING AND LAND USE

- 🐂 Cattle
- 🐐 Goats
- 🐑 Sheep
- ☕ Coffee
- Cotton
- Dates
- Market gardening
- ⬇ Sugarcane
- 🌱 Sisal
- Tea

- Cropland
- Desert
- Forest
- Pasture
- Wetland
- ● Major conurbation

LAND USE

- Cropland 9%
- Pasture 40%
- Other 26%
- Forest 25%

INDUSTRY

East Africa has few mineral resources, and industry is mainly based on processing raw materials. Coffee, tea, sugarcane, and sisal, are harvested and processed before being exported. Textile production is widespread, but is only on a small scale. Tourism is increasingly important in Kenya and Tanzania; each year, many thousands of people visit the wildlife reserves there.

INDUSTRY

- ⚙ Cement manufacturing
- Chemicals
- Food processing
- Textiles
- Tourism

- ▪ Major industrial center / area
- — Major road

STRUCTURE OF INDUSTRY

- Primary 15%
- Services 46%
- Manufacturing 39%

THE LANDSCAPE

The south of East Africa is savanna grassland, broken by the rugged mountains – some of them active volcanoes – and large fresh and saltwater lakes that make up part of the Great Rift Valley. The Nile River has its source here, flowing through Lakes Victoria, Kyoga, and Albert as it takes much-needed water to the arid desert areas in the north.

Great Rift Valley (D 6) (D 4)

The Great Rift Valley is like a deep scar running 4,300 miles from north to south through East Africa. It has been formed by the movements of two of the Earth's plates over millions of years. If these movements continue, East Africa may eventually become an island, separated by the ocean from the rest of the continent.

Sudd (B 4)

The north of Sudan is rocky desert, but in the south, the waters of the White Nile run into a swampy area called the Sudd where much of its water disperses and evaporates.

Juba River (E 5)

This river rises in the highlands of Ethiopia and flows some 750 miles southwards to the Indian Ocean. It, and the Shebeli River, which joins it about 19 miles from the coast, are the only permanent rivers in Somalia.

Lake Victoria (C 5)

Lake Victoria is Africa's largest lake and the second largest freshwater lake in the world. It lies on the equator, between Kenya, Tanzania and Uganda, and covers 26,800 sq miles. Its only outlet is the Nile River in the north.

Kilimanjaro (D 6)

This old volcano, made up of alternating layers of lava and ash, is Africa's highest mountain, rising to 19,341 ft. Although it lies only three degrees from the Equator, its peak is permanently covered with snow.

ENVIRONMENTAL ISSUES

Rapid population growth has created a need for increasing amounts of land for farming. This, in addition to the need for firewood, has led to tree cover being stripped, allowing the soil to be washed or blown away. Over the past 25 years, East Africa has been stricken by many catastrophic droughts that have made desertification worse, and brought much human suffering.

1973
1980
1985–1986
1989

1973–1975
1980
1985
1989

1973–1975
1980
1986–1987
1989

1986

1973–1975
1980
1985
1989

1972–1974

1973–1974

1987
1989

ENVIRONMENTAL ISSUES

- Drought
- Severe firewood shortage

- Existing desert
- Risk of desertification
- Severe risk of desertification

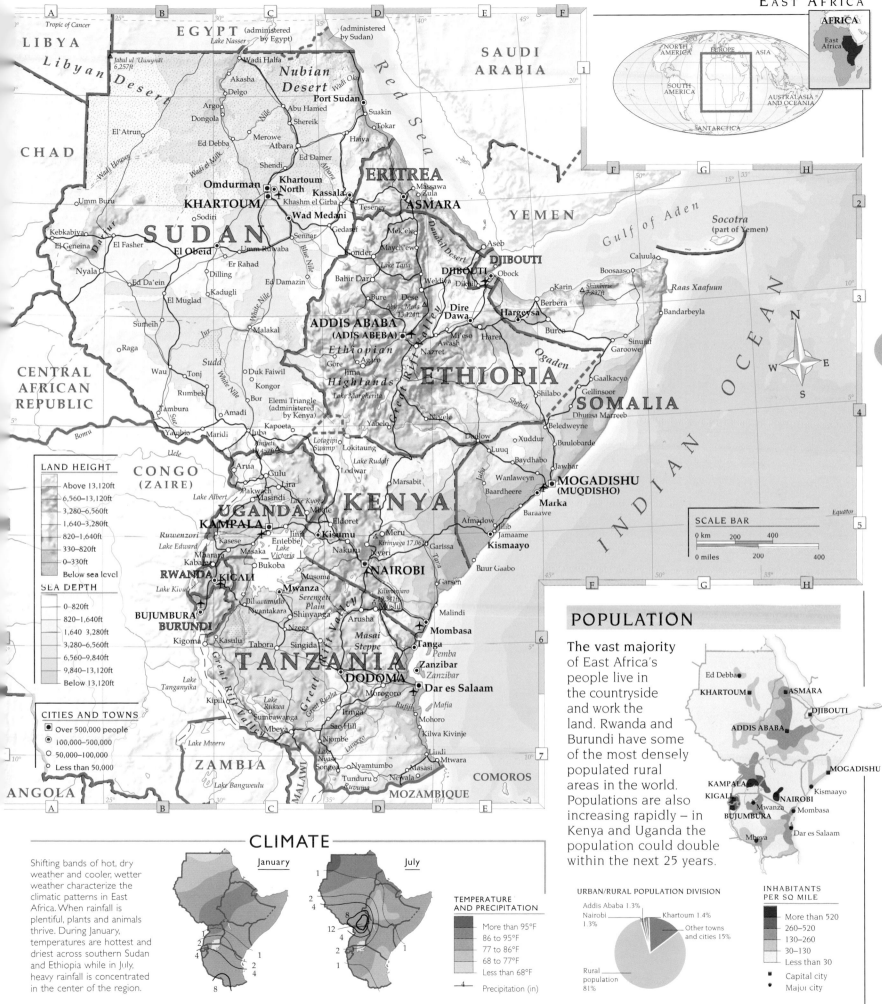

POPULATION

The vast majority of East Africa's people live in the countryside and work the land. Rwanda and Burundi have some of the most densely populated rural areas in the world. Populations are also increasing rapidly – in Kenya and Uganda the population could double within the next 25 years.

CLIMATE

Shifting bands of hot, dry weather and cooler, wetter weather characterize the climatic patterns in East Africa. When rainfall is plentiful, plants and animals thrive. During January, temperatures are hottest and driest across southern Sudan and Ethiopia while in July, heavy rainfall is concentrated in the center of the region.

SOUTHERN AFRICA

ANGOLA, BOTSWANA, COMOROS, CONGO, CONGO (ZAIRE), GABON, LESOTHO, MADAGASCAR, MALAWI, MOZAMBIQUE, NAMIBIA, SOUTH AFRICA, SWAZILAND, ZAMBIA, ZIMBABWE

Southern Africa contains the richest deposits of valuable minerals on the continent. South Africa is the wealthiest and most industrialized country in the region. Most of the surrounding countries rely on it for trade and work. Racial segregation under apartheid operated from 1948 until 1994, when South Africa held its first multiracial elections.

FARMING AND LAND USE

Most of southern Africa's farmers grow just enough food to feed their families, although much of the farmland is in the hands of a few wealthy landowners. In the tropical north, oil palms and rubber are grown on large commercial plantations. Fruits are cultivated in the south, and tea and coffee are important in the east. Cattle farming is widespread across the dry grasslands.

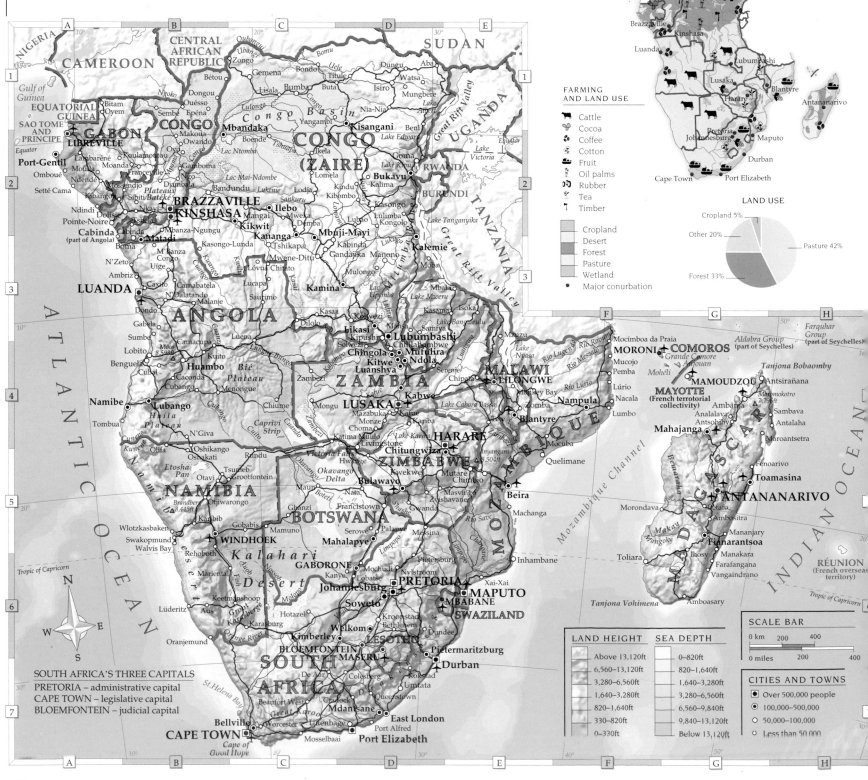

FARMING AND LAND USE

- 🐂 Cattle
- 🌿 Cocoa
- ☕ Coffee
- 🌱 Cotton
- 🍌 Fruit
- 🌴 Oil palms
- ♋ Rubber
- 🌿 Tea
- 🌲 Timber

LAND USE

- Cropland
- Desert
- Forest
- Pasture
- Wetland
- ● Major conurbation

Cropland 5%
Other 20%
Pasture 42%
Forest 33%

SOUTH AFRICA'S THREE CAPITALS
PRETORIA – administrative capital
CAPE TOWN – legislative capital
BLOEMFONTEIN – judicial capital

LAND HEIGHT	SEA DEPTH
Above 13,120ft	0–820ft
6,560–13,120ft	820–1,640ft
3,280–6,560ft	1,640–3,280ft
1,640–3,280ft	3,280–6,560ft
820–1,640ft	6,560–9,840ft
330–820ft	9,840–13,120ft
0–330ft	Below 13,120ft

SCALE BAR

0 km 200 400
0 miles 200 400

CITIES AND TOWNS
- ◼ Over 500,000 people
- ◉ 100,000–500,000
- ○ 50,000–100,000
- ○ Less than 50,000

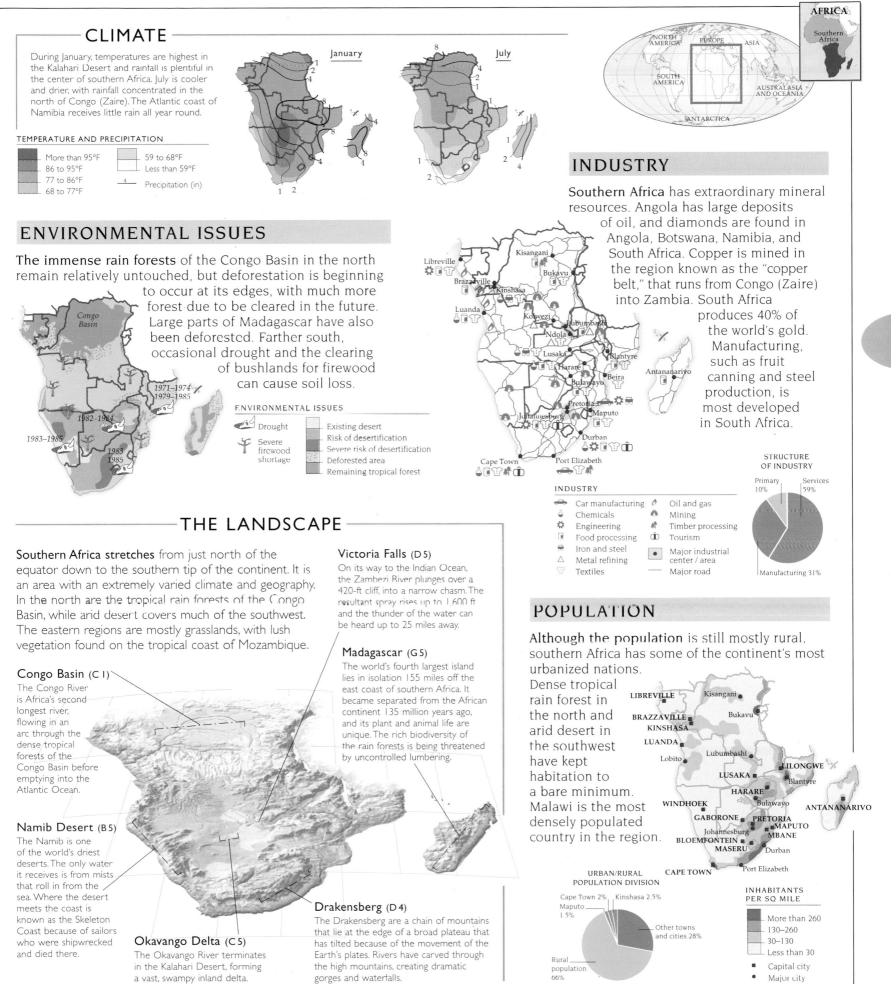

CLIMATE

During January, temperatures are highest in the Kalahari Desert and rainfall is plentiful in the center of southern Africa. July is cooler and drier, with rainfall concentrated in the north of Congo (Zaire). The Atlantic coast of Namibia receives little rain all year round.

January

July

TEMPERATURE AND PRECIPITATION

More than 95°F
86 to 95°F
77 to 86°F
68 to 77°F

59 to 68°F
Less than 59°F

— 4 — Precipitation (in)

ENVIRONMENTAL ISSUES

The immense rain forests of the Congo Basin in the north remain relatively untouched, but deforestation is beginning to occur at its edges, with much more forest due to be cleared in the future. Large parts of Madagascar have also been deforested. Farther south, occasional drought and the clearing of bushlands for firewood can cause soil loss.

Congo Basin

1971–1974
1979–1985

1982–1984

1983–1985

1983
1985

ENVIRONMENTAL ISSUES

Drought

Severe firewood shortage

Existing desert
Risk of desertification
Severe risk of desertification
Deforested area
Remaining tropical forest

THE LANDSCAPE

Southern Africa stretches from just north of the equator down to the southern tip of the continent. It is an area with an extremely varied climate and geography. In the north are the tropical rain forests of the Congo Basin, while arid desert covers much of the southwest. The eastern regions are mostly grasslands, with lush vegetation found on the tropical coast of Mozambique.

Congo Basin (C 1)
The Congo River is Africa's second longest river, flowing in an arc through the dense tropical forests of the Congo Basin before emptying into the Atlantic Ocean.

Namib Desert (B 5)
The Namib is one of the world's driest deserts. The only water it receives is from mists that roll in from the sea. Where the desert meets the coast is known as the Skeleton Coast because of sailors who were shipwrecked and died there.

Okavango Delta (C 5)
The Okavango River terminates in the Kalahari Desert, forming a vast, swampy inland delta.

Victoria Falls (D 5)
On its way to the Indian Ocean, the Zambezi River plunges over a 420-ft cliff, into a narrow chasm. The resultant spray rises up to 1,600 ft and the thunder of the water can be heard up to 25 miles away.

Madagascar (G 5)
The world's fourth largest island lies in isolation 155 miles off the east coast of southern Africa. It became separated from the African continent 135 million years ago, and its plant and animal life are unique. The rich biodiversity of the rain forests is being threatened by uncontrolled lumbering.

Drakensberg (D 4)
The Drakensberg are a chain of mountains that lie at the edge of a broad plateau that has tilted because of the movement of the Earth's plates. Rivers have carved through the high mountains, creating dramatic gorges and waterfalls.

INDUSTRY

Southern Africa has extraordinary mineral resources. Angola has large deposits of oil, and diamonds are found in Angola, Botswana, Namibia, and South Africa. Copper is mined in the region known as the "copper belt," that runs from Congo (Zaire) into Zambia. South Africa produces 40% of the world's gold. Manufacturing, such as fruit canning and steel production, is most developed in South Africa.

INDUSTRY

Car manufacturing
Chemicals
Engineering
Food processing
Iron and steel
Metal refining
Textiles

Oil and gas
Mining
Timber processing
Tourism
Major industrial center / area
Major road

STRUCTURE OF INDUSTRY

Primary 10%
Services 59%
Manufacturing 31%

POPULATION

Although the population is still mostly rural, southern Africa has some of the continent's most urbanized nations. Dense tropical rain forest in the north and arid desert in the southwest have kept habitation to a bare minimum. Malawi is the most densely populated country in the region.

URBAN/RURAL POPULATION DIVISION

Cape Town 2%
Maputo 1.5%
Kinshasa 2.5%
Other towns and cities 28%
Rural population 66%

INHABITANTS PER SQ MILE

More than 260
130–260
30–130
Less than 30

Capital city
Major city

AUSTRALASIA & OCEANIA

Australasia and Oceania encompasses the ancient landmass of Australia, the islands of New Zealand, and the scattering of thousands of small islands that stretch out into the Pacific Ocean. Indigenous peoples of the South Pacific, such as the Aborigines, Maoris, Polynesians, Micronesians, and Melanesians, inhabit the region. In Australia and New Zealand, they live alongside people of European origin who settled in the 18th century, and more recent arrivals from East and Southeast Asia.

PACIFIC ISLANDS

Micronesia is one of the Pacific's island nations, consisting of a group of volcanic islands, low-lying coral reefs, and lagoons. Many of the smaller Pacific islands are only a few feet above sea level.

LAND USE AND AGRICULTURE

Much of the center of Australia is a dry, barren desert and unsuitable for agriculture. At its fringes, sheep farming is practiced, and both Australia and New Zealand are massive producers of wool and lamb. The Pacific islands export many exotic fruits and crops – especially oil palms and coconut palms. Oil from the palms is processed and sold as well as the fruits themselves. Small-scale fishing is common, but larger operations are run by foreign fishing fleets, especially the Japanese, who fish for tuna in the deeper waters of the Pacific.

SHEEP FARMING

New Zealand and Australia are the world's biggest producers of wool. In New Zealand, sheep outnumber people by 20:1.

POPULATION

Capital cities
- ⊙ Above 500,000
- ⊙ 100,000 to 500,000
- • 50,000 to 100,000
- • Below 50,000

State capitals
- ⊙ Above 500,000
- ⊙ 100,000 to 500,000
- ○ 50,000 to 100,000

BORDERS

- full international border
- indication of maritime country extent
- indication of maritime dependent territory extent
- state border

SCALE 1:37,250,000

0 km 300 600

0 miles 300 600

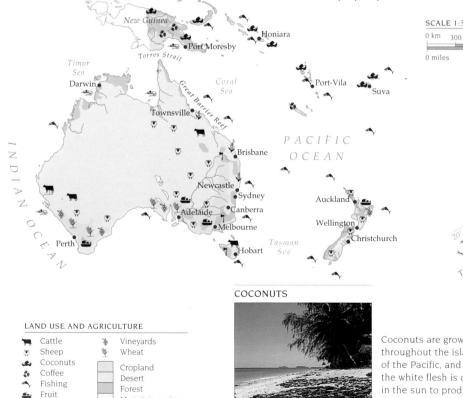

COCONUTS

Coconuts are grown throughout the islands of the Pacific, and the white flesh is dried in the sun to produce copra. Copra is a valuable export crop for many islands.

LAND USE AND AGRICULTURE

- 🐎 Cattle
- 🐂 Sheep
- 🥥 Coconuts
- ☕ Coffee
- 🎣 Fishing
- 🦐 Fruit
- 🐚 Shellfish
- ♇ Sugarcane
- 🌲 Timber
- 🍇 Vineyards
- 🌾 Wheat
- ▨ Cropland
- ▨ Desert
- ▨ Forest
- ▨ Mountain region
- ▨ Pasture
- • Major conurbation

MINERAL RESOURCES

Mineral resources are not widespread, but where they are found, they are in great abundance. Most of the small Pacific islands have no mineral resources, but Australia has enormous reserves of bauxite and iron ore, and also sizable reserves of gold and zinc. Copper is found in Papua New Guinea, and New Caledonia has large nickel reserves. There are ample supplies of fossil fuels, and although coal is plentiful in eastern Australia, oil and gas are found only in isolated pockets around Australia's coast.

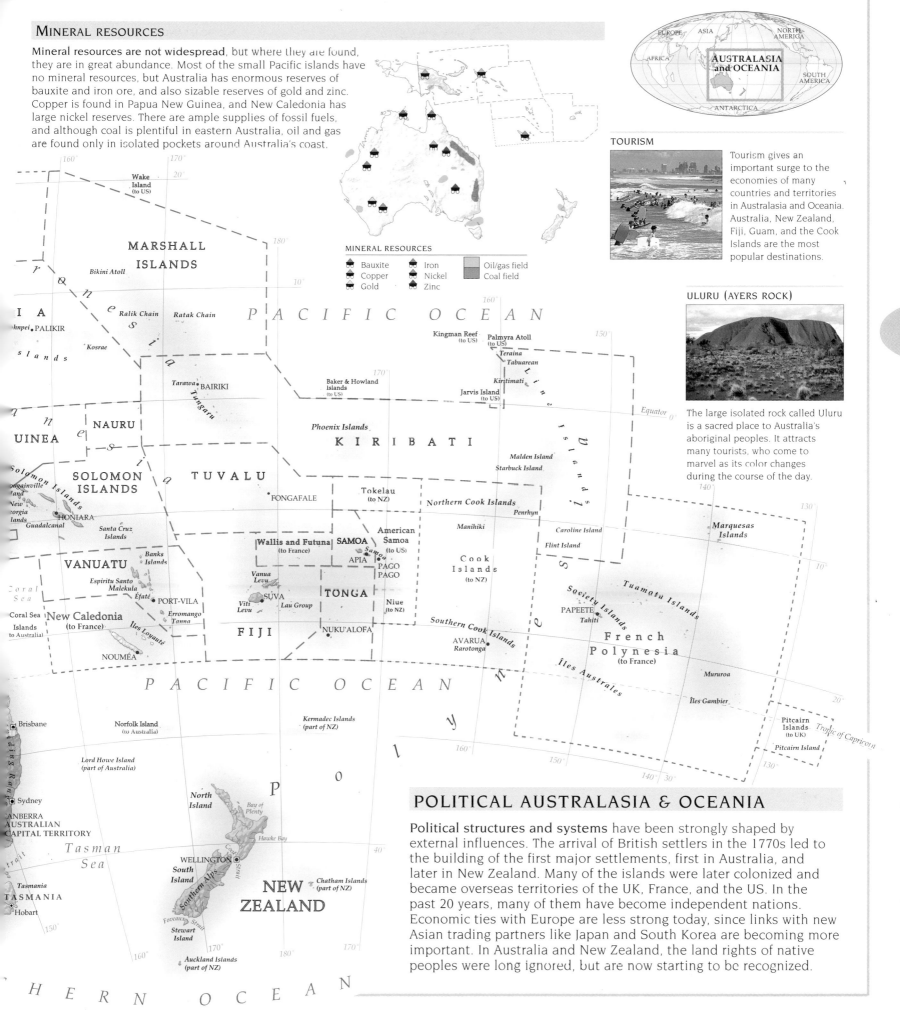

AUSTRALASIA and OCEANIA

MINERAL RESOURCES

Bauxite	Iron	Oil/gas field
Copper	Nickel	Coal field
Gold	Zinc	

TOURISM

Tourism gives an important surge to the economies of many countries and territories in Australasia and Oceania. Australia, New Zealand, Fiji, Guam, and the Cook Islands are the most popular destinations.

ULURU (AYERS ROCK)

The large isolated rock called Uluru is a sacred place to Australia's aboriginal peoples. It attracts many tourists, who come to marvel as its color changes during the course of the day.

POLITICAL AUSTRALASIA & OCEANIA

Political structures and systems have been strongly shaped by external influences. The arrival of British settlers in the 1770s led to the building of the first major settlements, first in Australia, and later in New Zealand. Many of the islands were later colonized and became overseas territories of the UK, France, and the US. In the past 20 years, many of them have become independent nations. Economic ties with Europe are less strong today, since links with new Asian trading partners like Japan and South Korea are becoming more important. In Australia and New Zealand, the land rights of native peoples were long ignored, but are now starting to be recognized.

AUSTRALIA

Australia is the world's sixth-largest country, and also the smallest, flattest continent, with the lowest rainfall. Most Australians are of European, mainly British, origin but in the past 50 years almost five million settlers from more than 200 countries have made Australia their home. The Aboriginal people, now only a tiny minority, were the first inhabitants. Recently, there have been several moves to restore their ancient lands.

INDUSTRY

Australia has one of the world's biggest mining industries. Bauxite, coal, copper, gold, and iron ore are mined and exported, especially to Japan. In the cities, service industries, particularly tourism, are growing fast; Australia's sunshine and dramatic scenery are attracting an increasing number of overseas visitors.

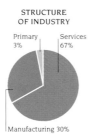

STRUCTURE OF INDUSTRY

Primary 3%
Services 67%
Manufacturing 30%

INDUSTRY

- Brewing
- Car manufacturing
- Chemicals
- Electronics
- Engineering
- Food processing
- Coal
- Mining
- Oil and gas
- Tourism
- Major industrial center / area
- Major road

POPULATION

Despite its vast size, Australia is sparsely populated. The desert outback, which covers most of the interior, is too dry and barren to support many people. About 70% of the population live in the cities and towns on the east and southeast coasts, and around Perth in the west.

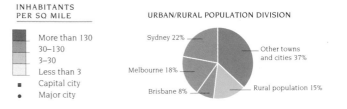

INHABITANTS PER SQ MILE

- More than 130
- 30–130
- 3–30
- Less than 3
- Capital city
- Major city

URBAN/RURAL POPULATION DIVISION

Sydney 22%
Melbourne 18%
Brisbane 8%
Other towns and cities 37%
Rural population 15%

FARMING AND LAND USE

Away from the coasts, much of the land is too dry for agriculture. Fields of sugarcane grow close the east coast, and grapes for the thriving wine industry are cultivated in the south and west, along with wheat. Vast numbers of cattle and sheep are raised for their meat and wool – both of which are major exports. They are grazed in the desert, on huge farms called "stations," and in more fertile areas.

FARMING AND LAND USE

- Cattle
- Sheep
- Wheat
- Sugarcane
- Timber
- Vineyards
- Cropland
- Desert
- Forest
- Pasture
- Major conurbation

LAND USE

Cropland 6%
Other (including desert) 21%
Forest 19%
Pasture 54%

THE LANDSCAPE

Most of Australia is dry, flat, and barren; all of the wetter, fertile land is found along its coastline. Huge sun-baked deserts, fringed by semiarid plains of scrub and grassland cover most of the west and center of the country. In the east, the land rises to the highlands of the Great Dividing Range, which run the whole length of the east coast. The tropical north coast has rainforests and

Blue Mountains (G 6)
The Blue Mountains lie toward the southern end of the Great Dividing Range. They get their name from the blue haze of oil droplets given off by the eucalyptus trees covering their slopes.

Great Barrier Reef (G 2)
This spectacular coral reef, which stretches for over 1,200 miles off the coast of Queensland, is the largest living structure on Earth. The reef has built up over millions of years and its waters are home to thousands of different species of coral and marine animals.

Uluru (Ayers Rock) (D 4)
Uluru is an enormous block of red sandstone, standing almost in the middle of Australia. It is the world's biggest free-standing rock – 5.8 miles around the base, and 2,844 ft high. It is the summit of a sandstone hill that is buried beneath the sands of the desert.

Simpson Desert (E 4)
The Simpson Desert covers around 50,000 sq miles. It contains long, parallel lines of sand dunes and is scattered with large salt pans and salt lakes, which were created when old rivers evaporated. They are now fed by the seasonal rains.

Murray River (F 5)
Together with its tributaries, the Murray River is Australia's main river system. It winds slowly westward for more than 1,562 miles from the Great Dividing Range to the Indian Ocean. It is fed by snow from mountains in the far southeast.

Great Dividing Range (H 5)
These highlands separate the desert regions from the fertile eastern plains. Rivers and streams have eroded them, creating deep valleys and gorges.

AUSTRALASIA
AND OCEANIA
Australia

ENVIRONMENTAL ISSUES

Australia's dry climate and low rainfall make it susceptible
to desertification. Around the edges of the large deserts –
especially in the north and
southeast – cattle grazing
and the removal of natural
vegetation are destroying
the natural habitat,
allowing the desert areas
to spread. During the
dry season, vegetation
becomes tinder-dry, and
bush fires are common,
burning huge tracts of land.

CLIMATE

Much of Australia's climate is
continental, and temperatures soar
during the day and fall rapidly at
night. The climate is also arid and
very little rain falls, apart from in
the summer months when the
north is affected by tropical storms.

January

July

TEMPERATURE
AND PRECIPITATION

More than 95°F
86 to 95°F
77 to 86°F
68 to 77°F
59 to 68°F
50 to 59°F
41 to 50°C
Less than 41°F
4 — Precipitation (in.)

ENVIRONMENTAL
ISSUES

✷ Area at risk
from bushfires

Existing desert
Risk of desertification
Severe risk of desertification

LAND HEIGHT   SEA DEPTH
6,560–13,120ft   0–820ft
3,280–6,560ft   820–1,640ft
1,640–3,280ft   1,640–3,280ft
820–1,640ft   3,280–6,560ft
330–820ft   6,560–9,840ft
0–330ft   9,840–13,120ft
Below sea level   Below 13,120ft

CITIES AND TOWNS
■ Over 500,000 people
◉ 100,000–500,000
◎ 50,000–100,000
○ Less than 50,000

SCALE BAR
0 km 100   200

0 miles 100   200

133

NEW ZEALAND

New Zealand is one of the most remote populated places in the world, and was one of the last places on Earth to be inhabited by people. The first people to settle on the islands were the Maori, a Polynesian people. When European settlers arrived during the 19th century, the Maori became a minority and today make up only about 9% of the population. With few people and rich natural resources, New Zealand's inhabitants have high living standards.

INDUSTRY

High-tech industries such as electronics and computing are growing in the major cities of Auckland and Wellington. Agricultural products such as meat, wool, and milk are still among New Zealand's major exports, and large pine forests supply wood for paper pulp and timber. The magnificent scenery and varied climate draw tourists from all over the world, especially for hiking and other special vacations.

STRUCTURE OF INDUSTRY

Primary 5%
Services 68%
Manufacturing 27%

INDUSTRY

♨	Chemicals
⊡	Electronics
⚙	Engineering
⊷	Fish processing
⎙	Food processing
⊤	Iron and steel
⊺	Textiles
♣	Timber
⊕	Tourism
▪	Major industrial center / area
—	Major road

POPULATION

Most of the population is descended from European settlers, although immigrants from Asia and the Pacific islands are increasing. More than one-third of New Zealand's 3.5 million people live in Auckland on North Island, which also has the largest Polynesian population of any city in the Pacific. Elsewhere, the population is clustered along the coasts, where the land is lower.

URBAN/RURAL POPULATION DIVISION

Auckland 27.2%
Other towns and cities 38%
Wellington 9.5%
Christchurch 9.3%
Rural population 16%

INHABITANTS PER SQ MILE

More than 130
30–130
3–30
Less than 3
■ Capital city
• Major city

ENVIRONMENTAL ISSUES

New Zealand is one of the world's least polluted countries, largely due to its small population and lack of heavy industries. Air quality is occasionally poor in Auckland and Christchurch. Environment-friendly geothermal energy is tapped to make electricity in the volcanic region of North Island. Recently, logging companies have begun to exploit the rich forest reserves, although this has been widely opposed.

ENVIRONMENTAL ISSUES

⊞	Geothermal power generation
⊛	Logging activity
⊗	Urban air pollution
•	Major industrial center

THE LANDSCAPE

Two large, mountainous islands form New Zealand's main land areas. A large crack or fault – the Alpine Fault, in the west of South Island – is the boundary between two plates in the Earth's crust. Land on either side of the fault tends to move, causing earthquakes. Volcanoes, many of them still active, are also found on both islands. South Island has many high peaks, several more than 10,000 ft high.

Geysers and boiling mud

Geysers occur when hot volcanic rocks come into contact with underground water. The water boils and turns to steam, forcing the water above it to burst through the Earth's surface into the air. There are many geysers and boiling mud pools in the areas around Rotorua and Taupo.

Northland (C 1)

This is a tropical region in the far northwest. Many of the inlets are fringed by mangrove swamps.

Mount Taranaki (C 4)

The dormant volcano of Mount Taranaki lies on New Zealand's North Island. It rises to a height of 8,261 ft.

Probable location of Alpine Fault

Lake Taupo (D 3)

New Zealand's largest lake, Lake Taupo, covers 234 sq miles of North Island. It lies in the crater of an extinct volcano.

Southern Alps

New Zealand's Southern Alps stretch more than 300 miles down the backbone of South Island. They were formed by the collision of the Indo-Australian and Pacific plates. Heavy snowfalls here, brought by westerly winds, feed the Fox Glacier, which moves at a speed of 1.5–15 ft a day.

FARMING AND LAND USE

Large areas of rich, sweet grasslands have made New Zealand one of the world's top regions for rearing sheep. There are almost 20 sheep for every person, grazing alongside about six million cattle. Fruits, including strawberries, apples, oranges, peaches, and the famous kiwi, are cultivated, particularly on South Island, and exported throughout the world. Fish caught off the Pacific coast are another important source of income.

AUSTRALASIA AND OCEANIA

EUROPE ASIA NORTH AMERICA
SOUTH AMERICA
ANTARCTICA
New Zealand

LAND USE

Other 8%
Cropland 14%
Forest 28%
Pasture 50%

FARMING AND LAND USE

- 🐄 Cattle
- Fishing
- 🐑 Sheep
- Fruit
- Timber
- Wheat

- Cropland
- Forest
- Mountains
- Pasture
- ● Major conurbation

CLIMATE

North Island has a generally warm climate that becomes tropical – hotter and more humid toward the far north. South Island is cooler and wetter. There may be heavy snowfall in winter, particularly in the highlands, and many mountains are permanently snow-capped.

TEMPERATURE AND PRECIPITATION

- More than 59°F
- 50 to 59°F
- 41 to 50°F
- 32 to 41°F
- 23 to 32°F
- Less than 23°F
- Precipitation (in)

January

July

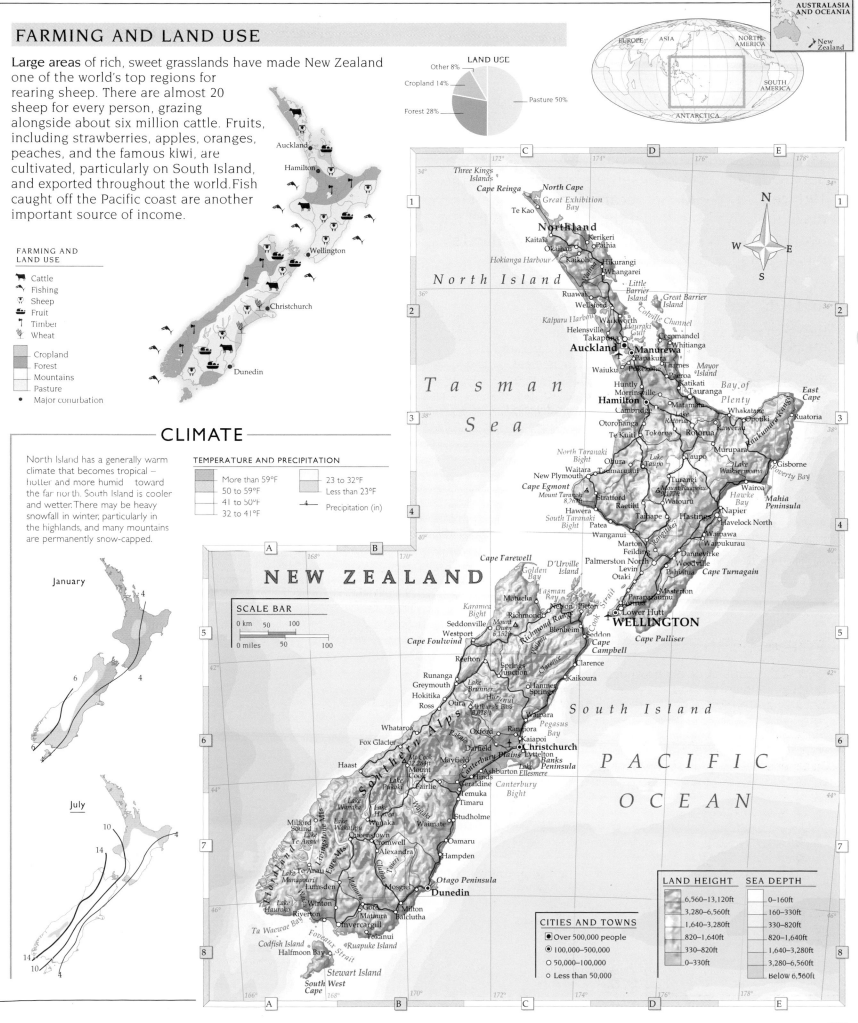

NEW ZEALAND

North Island

Three Kings Islands
Cape Reinga
North Cape
Great Exhibition Bay
Te Kao
Northland
Kaitaia
Kerikeri
Okaihau
Paihia
Kaikohe
Hikurangi
Hokianga Harbour
Wairoa
Whangarei
Little Barrier Island
Ruawai
Great Barrier Island
Wellsford
Kaipara Harbour
Coville Channel
Helensville
Warkworth
Hauraki Gulf
Coromandel
Takapuna
Whitianga
Auckland Manurewa
Papakura
Waiuku
Pukekohe
Thames
Mayor Island
Huntly
Paeroa
Katikati
Morrinsville
Tauranga
Bay of Plenty
Hamilton
Cambridge
Whakatane
Opotiki
East Cape
Matamata
Lake Rotorua
Kawerau
Ruatoria
Otorohanga
Te Kuiti
Tokoroa
Rotorua
Muruparara
North Taranaki Bight
Lake Taupo
Taupo
Ohura
Waitara
Taumarunui
Turangi
Gisborne
New Plymouth
Mount Ruapehu 9177ft
Waikaremoana
Poverty Bay
Cape Egmont
Mount Taranaki 8,261ft
Stratford
Waiouru
Wairoa
Hawke Bay
Mahia Peninsula
Hawera
Raetihi
Taihape
Hastings
Napier
South Taranaki Bight
Patea
Havelock North
Wanganui
Waipawa
Marton
Feilding
Dannevirke
Waipukurau
Palmerston North
Woodville
Cape Farewell
Levin
Pahiatua
Cape Turnagain
Cape Egmont
D'Urville Island
Otaki
Golden Bay
Paraparaumu
Masterton
Tasman Bay
Porirua
WELLINGTON
Motueka
Nelson Picton
Lower Hutt
Karamea Bight
Richmond
Cape Palliser
Seddonville
Mount Owen 6,152ft
Blenheim
Westport
Seddon
Cape Foulwind
Cape Campbell
Reefton
Clarence
Springs Junction
Runanga
Clarence
Kaikoura
Greymouth
Hanmer Springs
Hokitika
Lake Brunner
Ross
Otira
Arthur's Pass 3,018ft
South Island
Whataroa
Waipara
Oxford
Rangiora
Pegasus Bay
Fox Glacier
Darfield
Kaiapoi
Mt Cook 12,284ft
Mayfield
Christchurch
Haast
Mount Cook
Lyttelton
Banks Peninsula
Hinds
Ashburton
Canterbury Plains
Lake Ellesmere
Lake Pukaki
Fairlie
Geraldine
Canterbury Bight
Temuka
Timaru
Lake Wanaka
Studholme
Milford Sound
Lake Hawea
Waimate
Lake Te Anau
Wanaka
Oamaru
Queenstown
Cromwell
Hampden
Te Anau
Alexandra
Lake Manapouri
Lumsden
Mosgiel
Otago Peninsula
Lake Hauroko
Winton
Dunedin
Riverton
Gore
Milton
Mataura
Balclutha
Ta Waewae Bay
Invercargill
Codfish Island
Tokanui
Halfmoon Bay
Ruapuke Island
Foveaux Strait
Stewart Island
South West Cape

Tasman Sea

PACIFIC OCEAN

N W E S

LAND HEIGHT

- 6,560–13,120ft
- 3,280–6,560ft
- 1,640–3,280ft
- 820–1,640ft
- 330–820ft
- 0–330ft

SEA DEPTH

- 0–160ft
- 160–330ft
- 330–820ft
- 820–1,640ft
- 1,640–3,280ft
- 3,280–6,560ft
- Below 6,560ft

CITIES AND TOWNS

- ■ Over 500,000 people
- ◉ 100,000–500,000
- ○ 50,000–100,000
- ○ Less than 50,000

SCALE BAR

0 km 50 100
0 miles 50 100

SOUTHWEST PACIFIC

The many thousands of islands in the Pacific Ocean are scattered across an enormous area. The original inhabitants, the Polynesians, Melanesians, and Micronesians, settled the islands following the last Ice Age. In the 1700s Europeans arrived. They colonized all of the Pacific islands, introducing their culture, languages, and religion. Today many, though not all, of the islands have become independent. Their economies are simple, based largely on fishing and agriculture. Many are increasingly relying on their beautiful scenery and tropical climates to attract tourists and give a valuable boost to their economies.

LANDSCAPE

Most of the Pacific islands are extremely small, the largest landmass is the half of the island of New Guinea occupied by Papua New Guinea. The edges of the Indo-Australian and Pacific plates meet on the western edge of the area, leading to much volcanic and earthquake activity. Many of the islands are coral atolls, originally formed by volcanic activity, and some are no more than a few feet above sea level.

New Guinea (A 2)
A mountainous spine runs through the center of the island, separating the northern coast from the dense forests and mangroves found in the south.

Pacific Ocean
The Pacific Ocean is the Earth's oldest and deepest. Its name means peaceful, though it is far from being so; the highest wave ever recorded in open ocean – 112 ft – occurred during a hurricane in the Pacific.

Kavachi
Kavachi is an underwater volcano lying off the coast of New Georgia, in the Solomon Islands. It still erupts every few years.

Ring of Fire
The "Ring of Fire" is the term used to describe the string of volcanoes that surround the entire Pacific Ocean and erupt frequently because of intense stress and movement from within the Earth. The ring crosses the south Pacific, running between Vanuatu and New Caledonia, along the edge of the Solomon Islands, and between New Britain and New Guinea.

Sea trenches
Deep trenches mark the seafloor boundary where the Indo-Australian plate "dives" under the Pacific plate.

Coral atolls
Volcanic activity in the Pacific has led to the creation of many islands. These islands become fringed with a ring of coral. When the islands subside beneath the water once again, only the circle of coral is left, forming an atoll.

INDUSTRY

Today, the main industry for many of the Pacific islands is tourism. Food processing and small-scale textile industries are also common on many islands.

INDUSTRY
- 🍺 Brewing
- 🥫 Food processing
- 👕 Textiles
- 🌲 Timber processing
- ⛏ Mining
- 🏛 Tourism

- ● Major industrial center
- — Major road

FARMING AND LAND USE

Most farming that takes place on the Pacific islands is at a subsistence level, and many people keep pigs and chickens. A few crops are grown for export, especially oil palms, and coconuts, which are dried in the sun to produce copra. Many islanders make their living from the rich fishing grounds of the Pacific. The thick forests of Papua New Guinea are increasingly cut down for timber.

Lae
Port Moresby
Honiara
Port-Vila
Suva
Nouméa

LAND USE

- Fishing
- Bananas
- Cocoa
- Coconuts
- Oil palms
- Rubber
- Timber

- Cropland
- Forest
- Wetland
- Major conurbation

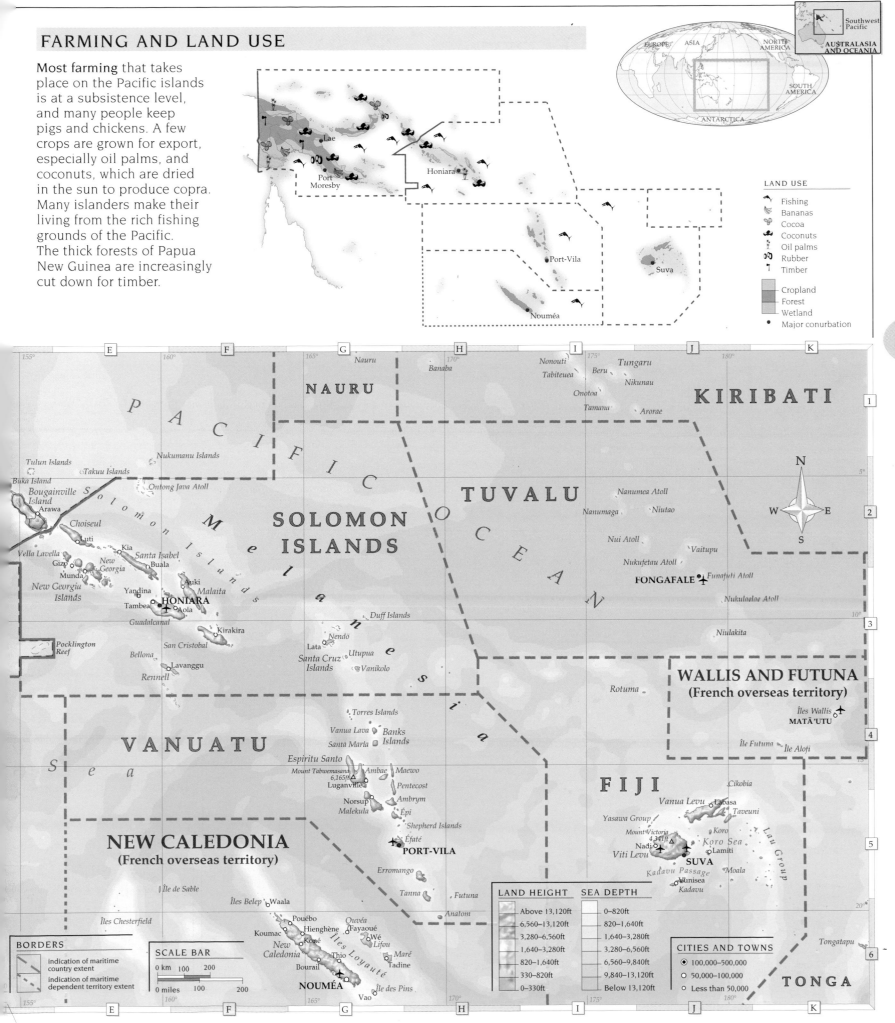

LAND HEIGHT	SEA DEPTH
Above 13,120ft	0–820ft
6,560–13,120ft	820–1,640ft
3,280–6,560ft	1,640–3,280ft
1,640–3,280ft	3,280–6,560ft
820–1,640ft	6,560–9,840ft
330–820ft	9,840–13,120ft
0–330ft	Below 13,120ft

BORDERS

- indication of maritime country extent
- indication of maritime dependent territory extent

SCALE BAR

0 km 100 200
0 miles 100 200

CITIES AND TOWNS

- ● 100,000–500,000
- ◉ 50,000–100,000
- ○ Less than 50,000

ANTARCTICA

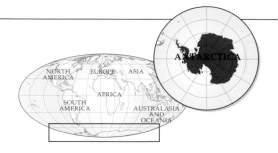

The continent of Antarctica has no permanent human population and very few animals can survive on the frozen land, although the surrounding waters teem with fish and mammals. Even in the summer, the temperature is rarely above freezing and the sea-ice only partly melts; in winter, temperatures plummet to −112°F. The only people who live in Antarctica are teams of scientists who study the wildlife and monitor the ice for changes in the Earth's atmosphere.

THE LANDSCAPE

Frozen seas
During the cold winter months, the water surrounding Antarctica freezes, almost doubling the size of the continent.

Antarctica is the world's most southerly continent. It is also the world's coldest continent and its highest, mainly due to the great ice sheet – up to 1.25 miles thick in parts – that lies over the mountains of the Antarctic Peninsula and the plateau of Greater Antarctica.

Lambert Glacier (E4)
The Lambert Glacier is the world's largest series of glaciers. It is 50 miles wide at the coast and reaches more than 180 miles inland.

Transantarctic Mountains (C5)
The Transantarctic Mountains run across the continent, splitting it into Greater and Lesser Antarctica.

Ice sheet
A massive sheet of ice, about 15,700 ft thick at its deepest point, covers almost the entire area of Antarctica. It contains most of the freshwater on Earth. The weight of the ice pushes the land down below sea level.

The Ross Ice Shelf (C5)
The Ross Sea is part of the Pacific Ocean. This deep bay is covered with a thick sheet of ice that floats on the ocean.

RESOURCES

The mountains of Antarctica have rich mineral reserves. Gold, iron, and coal are found, and there is natural gas in the surrounding water. The unique and abundant marine wildlife is Antarctica's greatest resource. Colonies of penguins breed on the ice sheet, and whales, seals, and many bird and fish species thrive in the icy waters.

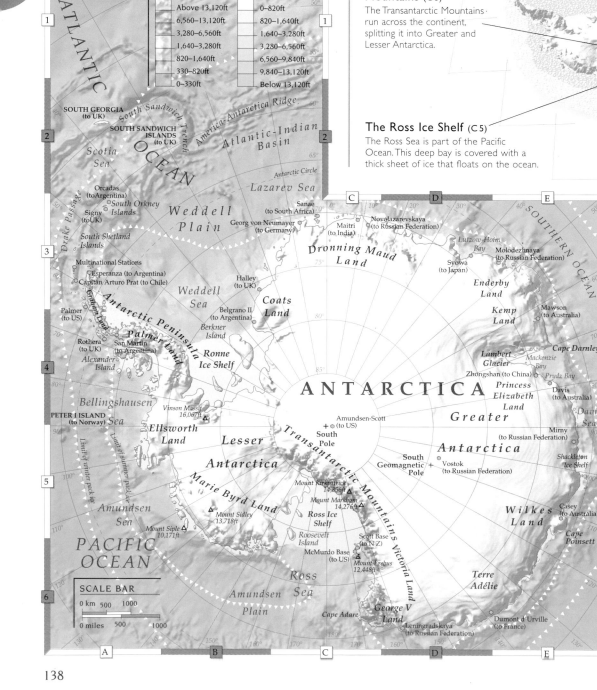

RESOURCES (including wildlife)

- Fish
- Penguins
- Seals
- Whales
- Coal
- Minerals
- Gas

THE ARCTIC

The ice-covered Arctic Ocean is encircled by the most northerly parts of Europe, North America, and Asia. Very few people live in the often-freezing conditions. Those who do, including the Sami of northern Scandinavia, the Siberian Yugyt and Nenet people, and the Canadian Inuit, were nomads who lived by hunting and herding. Some live like this today, but many have now settled in small towns.

THE LANDSCAPE

The Arctic Ocean is the smallest ocean in the world, covering a total area of 5,440,000 sq miles. The ocean is divided into two large basins, divided by three great underwater mountain ranges including the Lomonosov Ridge which is more than 9,842 ft high on average.

Lomonosov Ridge (C4)

Arctic islands (A4)
In the far north of Canada, there are many thousands of islands including Baffin Island and Victoria Island. Many of them are almost entirely surrounded by pack ice.

Pack ice
Much of the Arctic Ocean is permanently covered by pack ice. When the ice breaks up, it forms enormous floating ice masses called icebergs.

Greenland (A3)
Greenland is the world's largest island. It is covered by a huge ice sheet, more than 649,960 sq miles across. The weight of the ice has pushed most of the land below sea level.

Sastrugi
Snow, blown by strong winds, can scratch deep patterns in the snow. These patterns are known as sastrugi and line up with the direction of the wind.

RESOURCES

Coal, oil, and gas are found beneath the Arctic Ocean and in Canada, Alaska, and Russia. Fears about damage to the environment and the cost of extracting these resources have restricted the quantities removed. Overfishing has reduced fish stocks to very low levels. Quotas have been put in place to allow them to revive.

SCALE BAR
0 km 250 500
0 miles 250 500

CITIES AND TOWNS
● 100,000–500,000
○ Less than 50,000

SEA DEPTH
0–820ft
820–1,640ft
1,640–3,280ft
3,280–6,560ft
6,560–9,840ft
9,840–13,120ft
Below 13,120ft

RESOURCES
⌐ Fish
Coal
Minerals
Oil and gas
● Major town/city

GLOSSARY

This glossary defines certain geographical and technical terms used in this Atlas.

Acid rain Rain, sleet, snow or mist that has absorbed waste gases from fossil-fueled power stations and vehicle exhausts, becoming acidic and poisonous.

Alluvium Material deposited by a river, such as silt, sand, and mud

Archipelago A group, or chain, of islands.

Atoll A circular or horseshoe-shaped coral reef enclosing a shallow area of water (lagoon).

Aquifer A body of rock that can absorb water. It may be a source of water for wells or springs.

Bar, coastal An offshore strip of sand or shingle, either above or below the water.

Biodiversity The quantity of different animal or plant species in a given area.

Birthrate The number of live births per 1,000 individuals annually within a population.

Cash crop Agricultural produce grown for sale, often for foreign export, rather than to be consumed by the country or area where it was grown.

Climate The long term trends in weather conditions for an area.

Coniferous forest A type of forest containing trees or shrubs, like pines and firs, that have needles instead of leaves. They are found in temperate zones.

Continental plates The huge interlocking plates that make up the Earth's surface. A plate boundary is an area where two plates meet, and is the point at which earthquakes occur most frequently.

Conurbation A large urban area created by the merging of several towns.

Coral reef An underwater barrier created by colonies of coral polyps. The polyps secrete a protective skeleton of calcium carbonate, and reefs develop as live polyps build on the skeletons of dead generations.

Core The layers of liquid rock and solid iron at the center of the Earth.

Crust The hard, thin outer shell of the Earth. The crust floats on the mantle, which is softer, but more dense.

Deciduous forest A type of broadleaf forest found in temperate regions.

Deforestation Cutting down trees or forest for timber or farmland. It can lead to soil erosion, flooding, and landslides.

Delta A low-lying, fan-shaped area at a river mouth, formed by the deposition of successive layers of sediment. Slowing as it enters the sea, a river deposits sediment and may, as a result, split into many smaller channels called distributaries.

Deposition The laying down of material broken down by erosion or weathering and transported by the wind, water, or gravity.

Desertification The spread of desert conditions into a region that was not previously a desert.

Drainage basin The land drained by a river and its tributaries.

Drought A long period of continuously low rainfall.

Earthquake A trembling or shaking of the ground caused by the sudden movement of rocks in the Earth's crust – and sometimes deeper than the crust. Earthquakes occur most frequently along continental plate boundaries.

Economy The organization of a country's finances, exports, imports, industry, agriculture, and services.

Ecosytem A community of species dependent on each other and on the habitat in which they live.

Equator The 0° line of latitude. Equatorial climates are hot and there is plenty of rain.

Erosion The wearing down of the land surface by running water, waves, moving ice, wind, and weather.

Estuary The mouth of a river, where the saltwater from the sea meets the freshwater of the river.

Fault A crack or fracture in the Earth along which there has been movement of the rock masses relative to one another.

Fjord A coastal valley that was sculpted by glacial action.

Flood plain The broad, flat part of a river valley, next to the river itself, formed by sediment deposited during flooding.

Geyser A fountain of hot water or steam that erupts periodically as a result of underground streams coming into contact with hot rocks.

GDP Gross Domestic Product. The total value of goods and services produced by a country, excluding income from foreign countries.

GIS Geographic Information System. A computerized system for the collection, storage, and retrieval of geographic data.

Glacier A huge mass of ice made up of compacted and frozen snow, that moves slowly, eroding and depositing rock.

Glaciation The molding of the land by a glacier or ice sheet.

GNP Gross National Product. The total value of goods and services produced by a country.

Groundwater Water that has seeped into the pores, cavities, and cracks of rocks or into soil and water held in an aquifer or permeable rock.

Gully A deep, narrow chasm eroded in the landscape by a fast-flowing stream.

Heavy industry Industry that uses large amounts of energy and raw materials to produce heavy goods, such as machinery, ships, or locomotives.

Humidity The moisture content of the air.

Hurricane Violent tropical storms, also known as cyclones in the Indian Ocean and typhoons in the Pacific Ocean.

Hydroelectric power Energy produced by harnessing the rapid movement of water down steep mountain slopes to drive turbines to generate electricity.

Ice Age Periods of time in the past when much of the Earth's surface was covered by massive ice sheets. The most recent Ice Age began two million years ago and ended 10,000 years ago.

Iceberg A floating mass of ice that has broken off from a glacier or ice sheet.

Ice sheet A massive area of ice, thousands of feet thick.

Irrigation The artificial supply of water to dry areas – mainly for agricultural use. Water is carried or pumped to the area through pipes or ditches.

Lagoon A shallow stretch of coastal saltwater behind a partial barrier such as a sandbank or coral reef.

Latitude The distance north or south of the equator, measured in degrees, and shown on a globe as imaginary circles running around the Earth parallel to the equator.

Lava The molten rock, magma, that erupts onto the Earth's surface through a volcano, or through a fault or crack in the Earth's crust. Lava refers to the rock both in its liquid and its later, solidified form.

Load The material that is carried by a river or stream.

Longitude The distance, measured in degrees, east or west of the Prime Meridian.

Limestone A type of rock, formed by sediment, through which water can pass.

Magma Underground, molten rock, that is very hot and highly charged with gas. It originates in the Earth's lower crust or mantle.

Mantle The layer of the Earth's interior between the crust and the core. It is about 1,800 miles thick.

Map projection A mathematical formula that is used to show the curved surface of the Earth on a flat map.

Market gardening The intensive growing of fruit and vegetables close to large local markets.

Meander A looplike bend in a river. As a river nears the sea, it tends to wind more and more. The bigger the river and the shallower its slope, the more likely it is that meanders will form.

Mediterranean climate A temperate climate of hot, dry summers and warm, damp winters.

Meltwater Water that has melted from glaciers or ice sheets.

Mestizo A person of mixed native American and European origin.

Mineral A chemical compound that occurs naturally in the Earth.

Monsoon Winds that change direction according to the seasons. They are most common in South and East Asia, where they blow from the southwest in summer, bringing heavy rainfall, and the northeast in winter.

Moraine Sand and gravel that have been deposited by a glacier or ice sheet.

Nomads (nomadic) Wandering communities who move around in search of suitable pasture for their herds of animals.

Oasis A fertile area in a desert, usually watered by an underground aquifer.

Pack ice Ice masses more than 10 ft thick that form on the sea surface and are not attached to a landmass.

Pacific Rim The name given to the economically dynamic countries bordering the Pacific Ocean.

Peat Decomposed vegetation found in bogs. It can be dried and used as fuel.

Per capita A latin term meaning "for each person."

Plantation A large farm on which only one crop is usually grown, e.g. bananas or coffee.

Plain A flat, level region of land, often relatively low-lying.

Plateau A large area of high, flat land. When surrounded by steep slopes it is called a tableland.

Peninsula A thin strip of land surrounded on three of its sides by water. Large examples include Italy, Florida, and Korea.

Permafrost Permanently frozen ground, in which temperatures have remained below 32°F for more than two years.

Precipitation The fall of moisture from the atmosphere onto the surface of the Earth, as dew, hail, rain, sleet, or snow.

Prairie A Spanish-American term for grassy plains, with few or no trees.

Prime Meridian 0° longitude. Also known as the Greenwich Meridian because it runs through Greenwich in England.

Rain forest Dense forests in tropical zones with high rainfall, temperature and humidity.

Rain shadow An area downwind from high terrain that has little or no rainfall because it has fallen upon the high relief.

Remote-sensing A way of obtaining information about the environment by using unmanned equipment, such as a satellite, that relays the information to a point where it is collected.

Ria A flooded V-shaped river valley or estuary flooded by a rise in sea level or sinking land.

Rift valley A long, narrow depression in the Earth's crust, formed by the sinking of rocks between two faults.

Savanna Open grassland, where an annual dry season prevents the growth of most trees. They lie between the tropical rain forest and hot desert regions.

Scale The relationship between distance on a map and on the Earth's surface

Sediment Grains of rock transported and deposited by rivers, sea, ice, or wind.

Semiarid Areas between deserts and better-watered areas, where there is sufficient moisture to support a little more vegetation than in a true desert.

Service industry An industry that supplies services, such as banking, rather than producing manufactured goods.

Shanty town An area in or around a city where people live in temporary shacks, usually without basic facilities such as running water.

Silt Small particles, finer than sand, often carried by water and deposited on riverbanks, at river mouths, and harbors.

Soil A thin layer of rock particles mixed with the remains of dead organisms. Soil occurs naturally on the surface of the Earth and provides a medium for plants to grow.

Soil erosion The wearing away of soil more quickly than it is replaced by natural processes. Over-grazing and the clearing of land for farming, speeds up the process.

Sorghum A type of grass found in South America, similar to sugarcane.

Spit A narrow bank of pebbles or sand extending out from the seashore. Spits are made out of material transported along the coast by currents, wind, and waves.

Staple crop The main food crop grown in a region, for example, rice in Southeast Asia.

Steppe Large areas of dry grassland in the Northern Hemisphere – particularly found in southeast Europe and central Asia.

Subsistence farming A method of farming in which enough food is produced to feed farmers and their families but not providing any extra to generate an income.

Taiga A Russian name given to the belt of coniferous forest found in Russia, that borders tundra in the north and mixed forests and grasslands in the south.

Temperate The mild, variable climate found in areas between the tropics and cold polar regions.

Terrace Steps cut into steep slopes to create flat surfaces for cultivating crops.

Tropics An area between the equator and the Tropic of Cancer and Tropic of Capricorn that has heavy rainfall, high temperatures, and lacks any clear seasonal variation.

Tundra The land area lying in the very cold northern regions of Europe, Asia, and Canada, where winters are long and cold and the ground beneath the surface is permanently frozen.

U-shaped valley A river valley that has been deepened and widened by a glacier. They are flat-bottomed and steep-sided, and usually much deeper than river valleys.

V-shaped valley A typical valley eroded by a river in its upper course.

Volcano An opening or vent in the Earth's crust where magma erupts. Volcanos are caused by the movement of the Earth's plates. When the plates collide or spread apart, magma is forced to the surface, at or near the place where the plates meet.

Watershed The dividing line between one drainage basin and another.

INDEX

A

ARMENIA

Aachen 77 A5 W Germany
Aalen 77 C6 S Germany
Aalsmeer 68 D4 C Netherlands
Aalst 68 C6 C Belgium
Aalten 68 F4 E Netherlands
Aalter 68 B6 NW Belgium
Äänekoski 67 E4 C Finland
Aare 77 B8 ≈ W Switzerland
Aba 128 E1 NE Congo (Zaire)
Aba 124 F5 S Nigeria
Abadan 99 D3 SW Iran
Abadla 122 C2 W Algeria
Abakan 94 E5 S Russ. Fed.
Abashiri 103 G1 NE Japan
Abbeville 73 D1 N France
Abéché 124 H3 SE Chad
Abengourou 124 D5 E Ivory Coast
Aberdeen 71 D3 NE Scotland, UK
Aberdeen 47 C3 South Dakota, USA
Aberdeen 53 B2 Washington, USA
Aberystwyth 71 C7 W Wales, UK
Abha 99 B6 SW Saudi Arabia
Abidjan 124 C5 S Ivory Coast
Abilene 48 G3 Texas, USA
Åbo see Turku
Aboisso 124 D5 SE Ivory Coast
Abou-Déïa 124 H4 SE Chad
Abrantes 75 B4 C Portugal
Abruzzese, Appennino 79 D5 ⛰ C Italy
Absaroka Range 51 D3 ⛰ NW USA
Abu Dhabi 99 E4 ● C United Arab Emirates
Abu Hamed 127 C1 N Sudan
Abuja 124 F4 ● C Nigeria
Abunã, Rio 115 D5 ≈ Bolivia/Brazil
Abuye Meda 127 D3 ▲ C Ethiopia
Acalayong 124 F6 SW Equatorial Guinea
Acaponeta 57 D4 C Mexico
Acapulco 57 F6 S Mexico
Accra 124 D5 ● SE Ghana
Achacachi 117 A2 W Bolivia
Acklins Island 61 E3 Island, SE Bahamas
Aconcagua, Cerro 117 A5 ▲ W Argentina
A Coruña 75 B1 NW Spain
Acre 115 C5 ◐ State, W Brazil
Acuña 57 E2 NE Mexico
Ada 47 D8 Oklahoma, USA
Adamawa Highlands 124 G5 Plateau, NW Cameroon
Adams, Mount 53 B3 ▲ Washington, USA
'Adan see Aden
Adana 97 D5 S Turkey
Adapazarı 97 B2 NW Turkey
Adare, Cape 138 C6 Headland, Antarctica
Ad Dahna' 99 C4 Desert, E Saudi Arabia
Ad Dammam 99 D4 NE Saudi Arabia
Addis Ababa 127 D3 ● C Ethiopia
Adelaide 133 E6 S Australia
Aden 99 C7 SW Yemen
Aden, Gulf of 127 F2 Gulf, NW Arabian Sea
Adige 79 C2 ≈ N Italy
Adirondack Mountains 41 D3 ⛰ New York, USA
Adis Abeba see Addis Ababa
Adıyaman 97 E4 SE Turkey
Admiralty Islands 137 B1 Island group, N PNG
Adra 75 E6 S Spain
Adrar 122 D3 C Algeria
Adrian 44 E5 Michigan, USA
Adriatic Sea 88 F2 Sea, N Mediterranean Sea
Adycha 94 G3 ≈ NE Russ. Fed.
Aegean Sea 83 F5 Sea, NE Mediterranean Sea
Aeolian Islands 79 D7 Island group, S Italy
Afareaitu 137 A5 W French Polynesia
Afghanistan 101 D5 ◆ Islamic state, C Asia
Afmadow 127 E5 S Somalia
Africa 118 Continent
Africa, Horn of 118 Physical region, Ethiopia/Somalia
Afyon 97 B3 W Turkey
Agadez 124 F3 C Niger
Agadir 122 B2 SW Morocco
Agana 55 ○ NW Guam
Agaro 127 D4 W Ethiopia
Agat 55 W Guam
Agathónisi 83 F6 Island, Dodecanese, Greece
Agde 73 D6 S France
Agen 73 C6 SW France
Agialousa 88 D6 NE Cyprus
Ágios Nikólaos 83 F7 Crete, Greece
Agra 107 D3 N India
Ağri 97 G3 NE Turkey
Agrigento 79 C8 Sicily, Italy
Agropoli 79 D6 S Italy
Aguadilla 55 W Puerto Rico
Aguadulce 59 G7 S Panama
Aguán, Río 59 D2 ≈ N Honduras
Agua Prieta 57 C2 NW Mexico
Aguascalientes 57 E4 C Mexico
Aguilas 75 E5 SE Spain
Aguililla 57 E5 SW Mexico
Ahaggar 122 E4 High plateau region, SE Algeria
Ahmadabad 107 C4 W India
Ahmadnagar 107 D5 W India
Ahuachapan 59 B4 W El Salvador
Ahvaz 99 D3 SW Iran
Aiken 43 G4 South Carolina, USA
Ailigandí 59 I6 NE Panama
'Aïn Ben Tili 124 C1 N Mauritania
Aiquile 117 B2 C Bolivia
Aïr, Massif de l' 124 F2 ⛰ NC Niger
Aix-en-Provence 73 E6 SE France
Ajaccio 73 G6 Corsica, France
Aj Bogd Uul 105 D2 ⛰ SW Mongolia
Ajdabiya 122 G2 NE Libya
Ajmer 107 D3 N India
Ajo 48 B3 Arizona, USA
Akasha 127 C1 N Sudan
Akchâr 124 A2 Desert, W Mauritania
Akhalts'ikhe 97 G2 SW Georgia
Akhdar, Al Jabal al 122 G2 Hill range, NE Libya
Akhisar 97 A3 W Turkey
Akhmim 122 I3 C Egypt
Akhtubinsk 87 B7 SW Russ. Fed.
Akimiski Island 35 C3 Island, NW Terr., C Canada
Akita 103 F3 C Japan
Akjoujt 124 B2 W Mauritania
Akkeshi 103 H1 NE Japan
Aklavik 33 E3 NW Terr., NW Canada
Akmola 94 C5 ● N Kazakhstan
Akpatok Island 35 E1 Island, NW Terr., E Canada
Akron 44 F6 Ohio, USA
Akrotiri Sovereign Base Area 88 C6 Air base, S Cyprus
Aksai Chin 105 B3 Disputed region, China/India
Aksaray 97 D4 C Turkey
Akşehir 97 C4 W Turkey
Aksu He 105 B2 ≈ China/Kyrgyzstan
Aktau 94 A5 W Kazakhstan
Aktyubinsk 94 B4 NW Kazakhstan
Akure 124 E5 SW Nigeria
Akureyri 67 A1 N Iceland
Alabama 43 D5 ◐ State, S USA
Alabama River 43 D5 ≈ Alabama, USA
Alaca 97 D3 N Turkey
Alagoas 115 H5 ◐ State, E Brazil
Alajuela 59 E6 C Costa Rica
Alakanuk 54 D2 Alaska, USA
Al 'Amarah 99 C3 E Iraq
Alamo 51 B6 Nevada, USA
Alamogordo 48 D3 New Mexico, USA
Alamosa 51 F6 Colorado, USA
Aland Islands 67 D5 Island group, Finland
Aland Sea 67 D5 Sea waterway, Finland/Sweden
Alanya 97 C5 S Turkey
Al 'Aqabah 88 K6 SW Jordan
Alaşehir 97 A4 W Turkey
Alaska 54 D2 ◐ State, NW USA
Alaska, Gulf of 54 D3 Gulf Canada/USA
Alaska Peninsula 54 D3 Peninsula Alaska, USA
Alaska Range 51 E2 Mountain range Alaska, USA
Alazeya 94 H2 ≈ NE Russ. Fed.
Albacete 75 E4 C Spain
Al Bahah 99 B5 SW Saudi Arabia
Alba Iulia 85 B6 W Romania
Albania 83 C3 ◆ Republic, SE Europe
Albany 133 B6 W Australia
Albany 43 F5 Georgia, USA
Albany 41 E4 New York, USA
Albany 53 B3 Oregon, USA
Albany 35 C4 ≈ Ontario, S Canada
Al Bayda' 122 H2 NE Libya
Albergaria-a-Velha 75 B3 N Portugal
Albert 73 D1 N France
Alberta 33 F6 ◐ Province, SW Canada
Albert, Lake 127 B5 ◎ Congo (Zaire)/Uganda
Albert Lea 47 E4 Minnesota, USA
Albertville see Kalemie
Albi 73 D6 S France
Ålborg 67 B6 N Denmark
Albuquerque 48 D2 New Mexico, USA
Albury 133 G6 NSW, SE Australia
Alcácer do Sal 75 B4 W Portugal
Alcalá de Henares 75 D3 C Spain
Alcamo 79 C8 Sicily, Italy
Alcañiz 75 F3 NE Spain
Alcántara, Embalse de 75 B4 ▣ W Spain
Alcoy 75 F4 E Spain
Aldabra Group 128 G3 Island group, SW Seychelles
Aldan 94 G3 ≈ NE Russ. Fed.
Alderney 71 D9 Island, Channel Islands
Aleg 124 B3 SW Mauritania
Aleksin 87 A5 W Russ. Fed.
Alençon 73 C3 N France
Alenuihaha Channel 55 D2 Channel Hawaii, USA
Aleppo 99 B1 NW Syria
Alert 33 H1 Ellesmere Island, NW Terr., N Canada
Alès 73 D6 S France
Alessandria 79 B2 N Italy
Ålesund 67 A4 S Norway
Aleutian Basin 15 Undersea feature, S Bering Sea
Aleutian Islands 54 B2 Island group, Alaska, USA
Aleutian Trench 15 Undersea feature, S Bering Sea
Alexander Archipelago 54 E4 Island group, Alaska, USA
Alexander City 43 E5 Alabama, USA
Alexander Island 138 A4 Island, Antarctica
Alexandra 135 B7 South Island, NZ
Alexandria 122 I2 N Egypt
Alexandria 43 B5 Louisiana, USA
Alexandria 47 D3 Minnesota, USA
Alexandroúpoli 83 F4 NE Greece
Alfeiós 83 D6 ≈ S Greece
Alga 94 B4 NW Kazakhstan
Algarve 75 B5 Cultural region, S Portugal
Algeciras 75 C6 SW Spain
Algemesí 75 F4 E Spain
Algeria 122 C3 ◆ Republic, N Africa
Al Ghabah 99 F5 C Oman
Alghero 79 A5 Sardinia, Italy
Algiers 122 E1 ● N Algeria
Algona 47 E4 Iowa, USA
Al Hajar al Gharbi 99 E4 ⛰ N Oman
Al Hasakah 99 B1 NE Syria
Al Hillah 99 C2 C Iraq
Al Hufuf 99 D4 NE Saudi Arabia
Aliákmonas 83 E4 ≈ N Greece
Alíartos 83 E5 C Greece
Ali-Bayramli 97 J2 SE Azerbaijan
Alicante 75 F5 SE Spain
Alice 48 G5 Texas, USA
Alice Springs 133 E3 Northern Territory, C Australia
Alindao 124 H5 S CAR
Aliquippa 41 B5 Pennsylvania, USA
Al Jaghbub 122 H3 NE Libya
Al Jawf 99 B3 NW Saudi Arabia
Al Jazirah 99 B2 Physical region, Iraq/Syria
Al Khufrah 122 H4 SE Libya
Al Khums 122 F2 NW Libya
Alkmaar 68 C3 NW Netherlands
Al Kut 99 C2 E Iraq
Al Ladhiqiyah 99 A2 W Syria
Allahabad 107 E3 N India
Allegheny Mountains 43 G2 ⛰ NE USA
Allegheny Plateau 41 C4 ⛰ NE USA
Allentown 41 D5 Pennsylvania, USA
Alleppey 107 D7 SW India
Alliance 47 A4 Nebraska, USA
Alma-Ata 94 C6 SE Kazakhstan
Almada 75 A4 W Portugal
Al Mahrah 99 D6 ⛰ E Yemen
Al Majma'ah 99 C4 C Saudi Arabia
Almansa 75 F4 C Spain
Almaty see Alma-Ata
Almelo 68 F3 E Netherlands
Almendra, Embalse de 75 C3 Reservoir, NW Spain
Almendralejo 75 C4 W Spain
Almere 68 D3 C Netherlands
Almería 75 E6 S Spain
Al'met'yevsk 87 D6 W Russ. Fed.
Almirante 59 F6 NW Panama
Al Mukalla 99 D7 SE Yemen
Alofi, Île 137 K4 Island, S Wallis and Futuna
Alónnisos 83 E5 Island, Vóreioi Sporádes, Greece
Álora 75 D6 S Spain
Alor, Kepulauan 109 F8 Island group, E Indonesia
Alotau 137 C3 SE PNG
Alpena 44 E3 Michigan, USA
Alpha Cordillera 139 B4 Undersea feature, Arctic Ocean
Alphen aan den Rijn 68 C4 C Netherlands
Alpine 48 E4 Texas, USA
Alps 62 ⛰ C Europe
Al Qamishli 99 B1 NE Syria
Al Qunaytirah 99 H5 SW Syria
Alsace 73 F2 Cultural region, NE France
Alsdorf 77 A5 W Germany
Alta 67 D1 N Norway
Altai Mountains 105 C2 ⛰ Asia/Europe
Altamaha River 43 F5 ≈ Georgia, USA
Altamira 115 F4 NE Brazil
Altamura 79 E6 SE Italy
Altar, Desierto de 57 A1 Desert, Mexico/USA
Altay 105 C2 NW China
Altay 105 D2 W Mongolia
Alton 44 B7 Illinois, USA
Altoona 41 C5 Pennsylvania, USA
Altun Shan 105 C3 ⛰ NW China
Alturas 53 C5 California, USA
Altus 47 C8 Oklahoma, USA
Al 'Uwaynat 122 F4 SW Libya
Alva 47 C7 Oklahoma, USA
Alvarado 57 G5 E Mexico
Alvin 48 H4 Texas, USA
Al Wajh 99 A4 NW Saudi Arabia
Alwar 107 D3 N India
Al Wari'ah 99 C3 N Saudi Arabia
Alytus 67 E7 S Lithuania
Alzette 68 E9 ≈ S Luxembourg
Amadeus, Lake 133 D4 Seasonal lake, Northern Territory, C Australia
Amadi 127 C4 SW Sudan
Amadjuak Lake 33 I3 ◎ Baffin Island, NW Terr., N Canada
Amakusa-nada 103 C8 Gulf, SW Japan
Åmål 67 C5 S Sweden
Amami-gunto 103 A7 Island group, SW Japan
Amami-o-shima 103 A7 Island, S Japan
Amantea 79 E7 SW Italy
Amapá 115 F3 ◐ State, NE Brazil
Amarapura 109 A2 C Myanmar
Amarillo 48 F2 Texas, USA
Amay 68 D7 E Belgium
Amazon 115 F3 ≈ Brazil/Peru
Amazonas 115 C4 ◐ State, N Brazil
Amazon Basin 115 E4 Basin, N South America
Amazon, Mouths of the 115 G3 Delta, NE Brazil
Ambae 137 G4 Island, C Vanuatu
Ambam 124 F6 S Cameroon
Ambanja 128 G4 N Madagascar
Ambarchik 94 H2 NE Russ. Fed.
Ambérieu-en-Bugey 73 E5 E France
Amboasary 128 G6 S Madagascar
Ambon 109 G7 E Indonesia
Ambositra 128 G5 SE Madagascar
Amboy 53 D8 California, USA
Ambriz 128 B3 NW Angola
Ambrym 137 G5 Island, C Vanuatu
Amchitka Island 54 A2 Island Aleutian Islands, Alaska, USA
Amdo 105 C4 W China
Ameland 68 D1 Island, Waddeneilanden, N Netherlands
America-Antarctica Ridge 138 B2 Undersea feature, S Atlantic Ocean
American Falls Reservoir 51 C4 ▣ Idaho, USA
American Samoa 55 US ◇ W Polynesia
Amersfoort 68 D4 C Netherlands
Ames 47 E5 Iowa, USA
Amga 94 G4 ≈ NE Russ. Fed.
Amherst 35 F5 Nova Scotia, SE Canada
Amiens 73 D1 N France
Amindivi Islands 107 C7 Island group, Laccadive Islands, India
Amistad Reservoir 48 F4 ▣ Mexico/USA
Amman 99 A2 ● NW Jordan
Ammassalik 139 A6 S Greenland
Ammochostos see Famagusta
Amol 99 D1 N Iran
Amorgós 83 F6 Island, Cyclades, Greece
Amos 35 D4 Québec, SE Canada
Amourj 124 C3 SE Mauritania
Ampato, Nevado 115 B6 ▲ S Peru
Amposta 75 F3 NE Spain
Amravati 107 D4 C India
Amritsar 107 D2 N India
Amstelveen 68 D4 C Netherlands
Amsterdam 68 C4 ● C Netherlands
Am Timan 124 H4 SE Chad
Amu Darya 101 D3 ≈ C Asia
Amu-Dar'ya 101 E4 NE Turkmenistan
Amund Ringnes Island 33 H2 Island, Sverdrup Islands, NW Terr., N Canada
Amundsen Gulf 33 F3 Gulf, NW Terr., N Canada
Amundsen Plain 138 B6 Undersea feature, S Pacific Ocean
Amundsen-Scott 138 C4 US research station, Antarctica
Amundsen Sea 138 A5 Sea, S Pacific Ocean
Amuntai 109 E7 C Indonesia
Amur 94 H5 ≈ China/Russ. Fed.
Anabar 94 F3 ≈ NE Russ. Fed.
Anaconda 51 C2 Montana, USA
Anacortes 53 B1 Washington, USA
Anadyr' 94 H2 ≈ NE Russ. Fed.
Anadyr, Gulf of 94 I1 Gulf, NE Russ. Fed.
Anáfi 83 F6 Island, Cyclades, Greece
Analalava 128 G4 NW Madagascar
Anamur 97 C5 S Turkey
Anantapur 107 D6 S India
Anápolis 115 G6 C Brazil
Anar 99 E3 C Iran
Anar Darreh 101 D5 W Afghanistan
Anatolia 97 C4 Plateau, C Turkey
Anatom 137 H6 Island, S Vanuatu
Añatuya 117 B4 N Argentina
Anchorage 54 E3 Alaska, USA
Ancona 79 D4 C Italy
Ancud 117 A7 S Chile
Åndalsnes 67 B4 S Norway
Andalucía see Andalusia
Andalusia 43 E6 Alabama, USA
Andalusia 75 D5 Cultural region, S Spain
Andaman Islands 107 H4 Island group, India, NE Indian Ocean
Andaman Sea 107 H5 Sea, NE Indian Ocean
Andenne 68 D7 SE Belgium
Anderlues 68 C7 S Belgium
Andersen Air Force Base 55 Air base, NE Guam
Anderson 44 D6 Indiana, USA
Andhra Pradesh 107 E6 Cultural region, E India
Andijon 101 G3 E Uzbekistan
Andkhvoy 101 E4 N Afghanistan
Andong 103 C6 E South Korea
Andorra 73 C7 ◆ Monarchy, SW Europe
Andorra la Vella 73 B7 ● C Andorra
Andover 71 E8 S England, UK
Andøya 67 C2 Island, C Norway
Andreanof Islands 54 A2 Island group, Aleutian Islands, Alaska, USA
Andrews 48 F3 Texas, USA
Andria 79 E6 SE Italy
Ándros 83 F5 Island, Cyclades, Greece
Andros Island 61 C2 Island, NW Bahamas
Andros Town 61 D2 NW Bahamas
Anepmete 137 C2 E PNG
Angara 94 E4 ≈ C Russ. Fed.
Angarsk 94 F5 S Russ. Fed.
Ånge 67 C4 C Sweden
Ángel de la Guarda, Isla 57 B2 Island, NW Mexico
Angeles 109 F3 N Philippines
Angel Falls 115 D2 Waterfall, E Venezuela
Ångermanälven 67 D3 ≈ N Sweden
Angermünde 77 E3 NE Germany
Angers 73 C3 NW France
Anglesey 71 C6 Island, NW Wales, UK
Anglet 73 B6 SW France
Angleton 48 H5 Texas, USA
Ang Nam Ngum 109 B3 ◎ C Laos
Angola 128 B3 ◆ Republic, SW Africa
Angola Basin 15 Undersea feature, E Atlantic Ocean
Angoram 137 B1 NW PNG
Angostura, Presa de la 57 H6 ▣ SE Mexico
Angoulême 73 C5 W France
Angoumois 73 C5 Cultural region, W France
Angren 101 G3 E Uzbekistan
Anguilla 61 J4 UK ◇ E West Indies
Anguilla Cays 61 C2 Islets, SW Bahamas
Animas 40 C3 New Mexico, USA
Anjou 73 C3 Cultural region, NW France
Anjouan 128 G4 Island, SE Comoros
Anju 103 A5 W North Korea
Ankara 97 C3 ● C Turkey
Ankeny 47 E5 Iowa, USA
Anklam 77 D2 NE Germany
Annaba 122 E1 NE Algeria
An Nafud 99 B3 Desert, NW Saudi Arabia
An Najaf 99 C3 S Iraq
Annapolis 43 H1 Maryland, USA
Annapurna 107 F2 ▲ C Nepal
Ann Arbor 44 E5 Michigan, USA
An Nasiriyah 99 C3 SE Iraq
Annecy 73 E5 E France
Anniston 43 E4 Alabama, USA
Anqing 105 G4 E China
Anshun 105 E5 S China
Anson 48 G3 Texas, USA
Ansongo 124 D3 E Mali
Antakya 97 E5 S Turkey
Antalaha 128 H4 NE Madagascar
Antalya 97 B5 SW Turkey
Antalya, Gulf of 97 B5 Gulf, SW Turkey
Antananarivo 128 G5 ● C Madagascar
Antarctica 138 C4 Continent
Antarctic Peninsula 138 A4 Peninsula, Antarctica
Antequera 75 D5 S Spain
Antibes 73 F6 SE France
Anticosti, Île d' 35 F4 Island, Québec, E Canada
Antigua 61 J5 Island, S Antigua and Barbuda, Leeward Islands
Antigua and Barbuda 61 J4 ◆ Commonwealth Republic, E West Indies
Antikythira 83 E7 Island, S Greece
Antofagasta 117 A3 N Chile
Antony 73 D2 N France
Antsirañana 128 G4 N Madagascar
Antsohihy 128 G4 NW Madagascar
Antwerp 68 C6 N Belgium
Antwerpen see Antwerp
Anuradhapura 107 E7 C Sri Lanka
Anyang 105 F3 C China
A'nyêmaqên Shan 105 D4 ⛰ C China
Anzio 79 C5 C Italy
Aola 137 C3 C Solomon Islands
Aomori 103 G3 C Japan
Aosta 79 A2 NW Italy
Aoukâr 124 B2 Plateau, C Mauritania
Aouk, Bahr 124 H4 ≈ CAR/Chad
Aozou 124 G2 N Chad
Apalachee Bay 43 E6 Bay, SE USA
Apalachicola River 43 E6 ≈ SE USA
Apaporis, Río 115 C3 ≈ Brazil/Colombia
Apatity 87 B2 NW Russ. Fed.
Apeldoorn 68 E4 E Netherlands
Apennines 79 C3 ⛰ Italy
Apia 137 B5 ● SE Samoa
Apolima Strait 137 A5 Strait, C Pacific Ocean
Apostle Islands 44 B2 Island group, Wisconsin, USA
Appalachian Mountains 43 F3 ⛰ E USA
Appingedam 68 F2 NE Netherlands
Appleton 44 C4 Wisconsin, USA
Apra Heights 55 W Guam
Apulia 79 F6 Cultural region, SE Italy
Apuseni, Munţii 85 A6 ⛰ W Romania
Aqaba, Gulf of 99 A3 Gulf, NE Red Sea
Aqchah 101 F4 N Afghanistan
Aquitaine 73 B6 Cultural region, SW France
'Arabah, Wadi al 99 H7 Dry watercourse, Israel/Jordan
Arabian Basin 15 Undersea feature, N Arabian Sea
Arabian Peninsula 99 C4 Peninsula, SW Asia
Arabian Sea 90 Sea, NW Indian Ocean
Aracaju 115 I5 E Brazil
'Arad 99 H6 S Israel
Arad 85 A6 W Romania
Arafura Sea 109 H8 Sea, W Pacific Ocean
Aragón 75 E3 Autonomous community, E Spain
Araguaia, Río 115 F5 ≈ C Brazil
Araguari 115 G7 SE Brazil
Arak 99 D2 W Iran
Arakan Yoma 109 A2 ⛰ W Myanmar
Aral Sea 101 D1 Inland sea, Kazakhstan/Uzbekistan
Aral'sk 94 B5 SW Kazakhstan
Aranda de Duero 75 D2 N Spain
Aranjuez 75 D3 C Spain
Araouane 124 D2 N Mali
'Ar'ar 99 B3 NW Saudi Arabia
Ararat, Mount 97 G3 ▲ E Turkey
Aras 97 I3 ≈ SW Asia
Arawa 137 D2 Bougainville Island, NE PNG
Arbil 99 C2 N Iraq
Arbroath 71 D4 E Scotland, UK
Arcachon 73 B5 SW France
Arcata 53 A5 California, USA
Archangel 87 C3 NW Russ. Fed.
Archidona 75 D5 S Spain
Arco 79 C2 N Italy
Arco 51 C3 Idaho, USA
Arctic Ocean 139 C3 Ocean
Arda 83 F3 ≈ Bulgaria/Greece
Ardabil 99 D1 NW Iran
Ardas 83 F3 ≈ Bulgaria/Greece
Ardèche 73 D6 Cultural region, E France
Ardennes 68 D8 Physical region, Belgium/France
Ardmore 47 D8 Oklahoma, USA
Arecibo 55 C Puerto Rico
Arenal, Volcán 59 E6 🌋 NW Costa Rica
Arendal 67 B6 S Norway
Arenys de Mar 75 G2 NE Spain
Areópoli 83 E6 S Greece
Arequipa 115 C6 SE Peru
Arezzo 79 C4 C Italy
Argenteuil 73 D2 N France
Argentina 117 A6 ◆ Republic, S South America
Argentine Basin 14 Undersea basin, SW Atlantic Ocean
Arghandab, Darya-ye 101 E5 ≈ SE Afghanistan
Argo 127 C1 N Sudan
Argun 105 F1 ≈ China/Russ. Fed.
Argyle, Lake 133 D2 Salt lake, W Australia
Århus 67 B7 C Denmark
Arica 117 A2 N Chile
Arizona 48 A2 ◐ State, SW USA
Arkansas 43 B3 ◐ State, S USA
Arkansas City 47 D7 Kansas, USA
Arkansas River 43 B4 ≈ C USA
Arkhangel'sk see Archangel
Arles 73 E6 SE France
Arlington 48 H3 Texas, USA
Arlington 43 H1 Virginia, USA
Arlon 68 E9 SE Belgium
Armagh 71 B5 S Northern Ireland, UK
Armagnac 73 C6 Cultural region, S France
Armenia 115 B2 W Colombia

◐ Administrative region ◆ Country ● Country capital ◇ Dependent territory ○ Dependent territory capital ⛰ Mountain range ▲ Mountain 🌋 Volcano ≈ River ◎ Lake ▣ Reservoir

141

◆ Administrative region   ◆ Country   ● Country capital   ◊ Dependent territory   ○ Dependent territory capital   ▲ Mountain range   ▲ Mountain   ☈ Volcano   ☞ River   ☉ Lake   ▣ Reservoir

◈ Administrative region   ◆ Country   ● Country capital   ◇ Dependent territory   ○ Dependent territory capital   ▲ Mountain range   ▲ Mountain   ℞ Volcano   ↭ River   ⊙ Lake   ⊡ Reservoir

E

EAST GRAND FORKS

East Grand Forks 47 D2 Minnesota, USA
East Kilbride 71 D4 S Scotland, UK
East Korea Bay 103 B5 *Bay,* E North Korea
Eastleigh 71 E8 S England, UK
East Liverpool 44 F6 Ohio, USA
East London 128 D7 S South Africa
Eastmain 35 D4 ≈ Québec, C Canada
East Novaya Zemlya Trough 139 E5 *Undersea feature,* W Kara Sea
East Pacific Rise 14 *Undersea feature,* E Pacific Ocean
East Saint Louis 44 A7 Illinois, USA
East Siberian Sea 139 C2 *Sea,* Arctic Ocean
Eau Claire 44 A3 Wisconsin, USA
Ebensee 77 E7 N Austria
Eberswalde-Finow 77 D3 E Germany
Ebetsu 103 F2 NE Japan
Ebolowa 124 F6 S Cameroon
Ebro 75 E2 ≈ NE Spain
Echo Bay 33 G4 NW Terr., NW Canada
Echt 68 E6 SE Netherlands
Ecija 75 C5 SW Spain
Ecuador 115 B3 ◆ *Republic,* NW South America
Ed Da'ein 127 B3 W Sudan
Ed Damazin 127 C3 E Sudan
Ed Damer 127 C2 NE Sudan
Ed Debba 127 C2 N Sudan
Ede 68 E4 C Netherlands
Ede 124 E5 SW Nigeria
Eden 48 G4 Texas, USA
Edgeley 47 C2 North Dakota, USA
Edinburg 48 G6 Texas, USA
Edinburgh 71 D4 *National region capital,* S Scotland, UK
Edirne 97 A2 NW Turkey
Edison 41 E5 New Jersey, USA
Edmonds 53 B2 Washington, USA
Edmonton 33 G6 Alberta, SW Canada
Edmundston 35 F5 New Brunswick, SE Canada
Edolo 79 C2 N Italy
Edremit 97 A3 NW Turkey
Edward, Lake 128 D2 ◎ Congo (Zaire)/Uganda
Edwards Plateau 48 F4 *Plain,* Texas, USA
Eeklo 68 D6 NW Belgium
Eemshaven 68 F1 NE Netherlands
Eersel 68 D5 S Netherlands
Éfaté 137 H5 *Island,* C Vanuatu
Effingham 44 C7 Illinois, USA
Efstratios, Agios 83 F5 *Island,* Vóreion Aigaíon, E Greece
Egadi Island 79 B8 *Island group,* S Italy
Eger 81 E7 NE Hungary
Éghezèe 68 D7 C Belgium
Egmont, Cape 135 C4 *Headland,* North Island, NZ
Egypt 122 I4 ◆ *Republic,* NE Africa
Eibar 75 E1 N Spain
Eibergen 68 F4 E Netherlands
Eidfjord 67 A5 S Norway
Eifel 77 A5 *Plateau,* W Germany
Eiger 77 B8 ▲ C Switzerland
Eigg 71 C4 *Island,* W Scotland, UK
Eight Degree Channel 107 C8 *Channel,* India/Maldives
Eighty Mile Beach 133 B3 *Beach,* W Australia
Eijsden 68 E7 SE Netherlands
Eindhoven 68 D5 S Netherlands
Eisenhüttenstadt 77 E4 E Germany
Eisenstadt 77 F7 E Austria
Eisleben 77 C4 C Germany
Eivissa *see* Ibiza
Ejea de los Caballeros 75 E2 NE Spain
Ejin Qi 105 E3 N China
El 'Alamein 122 I2 N Egypt
Elat 99 G7 S Israel
El'Atrun 127 B2 NW Sudan
Elâzığ 97 F3 E Turkey
Elba 79 B4 *Island,* Archipelago Toscano, C Italy
Elbe 77 C3 ≈ Czech Republic/Germany
Elbert, Mount 51 E5 ▲ Colorado, USA
Elbląg 81 E2 N Poland
El'brus 87 A8 ▲ SW Russ. Fed.
El Burgo de Osma 75 E2 C Spain
Elburz Mountains 99 D2 ⛰ N Iran
El Cajon 53 D9 California, USA
El Calafate 117 A8 S Argentina
El Campo 48 H5 Texas, USA
El Centro 53 D9 California, USA
Elche 75 F5 E Spain
El Chichónal, Volcán 57 G5 ✵ SE Mexico
Elda 75 F4 E Spain
Eldorado 117 D4 NE Argentina
El Dorado 57 C4 C Mexico
El Dorado 43 B4 Arkansas, USA
El Dorado 47 D7 Kansas, USA
Eldoret 127 D5 W Kenya
Elektrostal' 87 B5 W Russ. Fed.
Elemi Triangle 127 C4 *Disputed region,* Kenya/Sudan
Elephant Butte Reservoir 48 D3 ▣ New Mexico, USA
Eleuthera Island 61 D1 *Island,* N Bahamas
El Fasher 127 B3 W Sudan
El Geneina 127 A3 W Sudan
Elgin 71 D3 NE Scotland, UK
Elgin 44 C5 Illinois, USA
El Giza 122 I2 N Egypt
El Goléa 122 D2 C Algeria
El Hank 124 C1 *Cliff,* N Mauritania
Elida 48 E3 New Mexico, USA
Elista 87 B8 SW Russ. Fed.
Elizabeth 133 E6 S Australia
Elizabeth City 43 I3 North Carolina, USA
Elizabethtown 43 E2 Kentucky, USA
Ełk 81 F2 NE Poland
Elk City 47 C8 Oklahoma, USA
El Kharga 122 I3 C Egypt
Elkhart 44 D5 Indiana, USA
Elk River 47 E3 Minnesota, USA
Ellef Ringnes Island 33 G2 *Island,* NW Terr., N Canada
Ellensburg 53 C2 Washington, USA
Ellesmere Island 33 H1 *Island,* Queen Elizabeth Islands, NW Terr., N Canada
Ellesmere, Lake 135 C6 ◎ South Island, NZ
Elliston 133 E5 S Australia
Ellsworth 41 G2 Maine, USA
Ellsworth Land 138 A5 *Physical region,* Antarctica
El Mahbas 122 B3 SW Western Sahara
El Minya 122 I3 C Egypt
Elmira 41 C4 New York, USA
El Mreyyé 124 C2 *Desert,* E Mauritania
Elmshorn 77 C2 N Germany
El Muglad 127 B3 C Sudan
El Obeid 127 C3 C Sudan
El Oued 122 E2 NE Algeria
Eloy 48 B3 Arizona, USA
El Paso 48 D4 Texas, USA
El Porvenir 59 H6 N Panama
El Progreso 59 C3 NW Honduras
El Puerto de Santa María 75 C6 S Spain
El Rama 59 E4 SE Nicaragua
El Real 59 I6 SE Panama
El Reno 47 C8 Oklahoma, USA
El Salvador 59 B4 ◆ *Republic,* Central America
El Sáuz 57 C2 N Mexico
Elst 68 E4 E Netherlands
El Sueco 57 C2 N Mexico
El Tigre 115 D2 W Colombia
Elvas 75 B4 C Portugal
El Vendrell 75 G3 NE Spain
Elwell, Lake 51 D1 ▣ Montana, USA
Ely 51 C5 Nevada, USA
El Yunque 55 ▲ E Puerto Rico
Emba 94 B5 W Kazakhstan
Emden 77 B3 NW Germany
Emerald 133 G4 Queensland, E Australia
Emeti 137 A2 SW PNG
Emi Koussi 124 H2 ▲ N Chad
Emmeloord 68 E3 N Netherlands
Emmen 68 F3 NE Netherlands
Emmendingen 77 B7 SW Germany
Emory Peak 48 E5 ▲ Texas, USA
Empalme 57 B3 NW Mexico
Emperor Seamounts 15 *Undersea feature,* NW Pacific Ocean
Emporia 47 D6 Kansas, USA
Ems 77 B3 ≈ NW Germany
Encarnación 117 C4 S Paraguay
Encinitas 53 D9 California, USA
Encs 81 F6 NE Hungary
Endeavour Strait 133 F1 *Strait,* Queensland, NE Australia
Enderby Land 138 D3 *Physical region,* Antarctica
Enghien 68 C7 SW Belgium
England 71 D6 *National region,* UK
English Channel 71 E8 *Channel,* NW Europe
Enguri 97 G1 ≈ NW Georgia
Enid 47 C7 Oklahoma, USA
Ennedi 124 H2 *Plateau,* E Chad
Ennis 71 A6 W Ireland
Ennis 48 H3 Texas, USA
Enniskillen 71 B5 SW Northern Ireland, UK
Enns 77 E7 ≈ C Austria
Enschede 68 F4 E Netherlands
Ensenada 57 A1 NW Mexico
Entebbe 127 C5 S Uganda
Entroncamento 75 B4 C Portugal
Enugu 124 F5 S Nigeria
Epéna 128 B1 NE Congo
Ephrata 41 D5 Pennsylvania, USA
Épi 137 H5 *Island,* C Vanuatu
Épinal 73 F3 NE France
Equatorial Guinea 124 F6 ◆ *Republic,* C Africa
Erciş 97 G3 E Turkey
Erdenet 105 E2 N Mongolia
Erdi 124 H2 *Plateau,* NE Chad
Erebus, Mount 138 C6 ✵ Ross Island, Antarctica
Ereğli 97 D4 S Turkey
Erenhot 105 F2 NE China
Erfurt 77 C5 C Germany
Ergene Nehri 97 A2 ≈ NW Turkey
Ergun He *see* Argun
Erie 41 B4 Pennsylvania, USA
Erie, Lake 44 F5 ◎ Canada/USA
Eritrea 127 D2 ◆ *Transitional government,* E Africa
Erlangen 77 C6 S Germany
Ermelo 68 E3 C Netherlands
Ermióni 83 E6 S Greece
Ernakulam 107 D7 SW India
Erode 107 D7 SE India
Erquelinnes 68 C7 S Belgium
Er-Rachidia 122 C2 E Morocco
Er Rahad 127 C3 C Sudan
Erromango 137 G5 *Island,* S Vanuatu
Erzgebirge *see* Ore Mountains
Erzincan 97 F3 E Turkey
Erzurum 97 G3 NE Turkey
Esbjerg 67 A7 W Denmark
Escanaba 44 C3 Michigan, USA
Esch-sur-Alzette 68 E9 S Luxembourg
Escondido 53 D9 California, USA
Escudilla Mountain 48 C3 ▲ Arizona, USA
Escuinapa 57 D4 C Mexico
Escuintla 59 A3 S Guatemala
Escuintla 57 H6 SE Mexico
Eshkamesh 101 F4 NE Afghanistan
Eskişehir 97 B3 W Turkey
Esmeraldas 115 B3 N Ecuador
Espanola 48 D2 New Mexico, USA
Esperance 133 C5 W Australia
Esperanza 57 C3 NW Mexico
Esperanza 138 A3 *Argentinian research station,* Antarctica
Espírito Santo 115 G7 ◐ *State,* E Brazil
Espiritu Santo 137 G4 *Island,* W Vanuatu
Espoo 67 E5 S Finland
Esquel 117 A7 SW Argentina
Essaouira 122 B2 W Morocco
Essen 68 C5 N Belgium
Essen 77 A4 W Germany
Estacado, Llano 48 F3 *Plain,* SW USA
Estados, Isla de los 117 B9 *Island,* S Argentina
Estância 115 I5 E Brazil
Estelí 59 D4 NW Nicaragua
Estella 75 E2 N Spain
Estepona 75 C6 S Spain
Estevan 33 H7 Saskatchewan, S Canada
Estonia 67 F6 ◆ *Republic,* NE Europe
Estrela, Serra da 75 B3 ⛰ C Portugal
Estremoz 75 B4 S Portugal
Esztergom 81 D7 N Hungary
Étalle 68 D9 SE Belgium
Etawah 107 E3 N India
Ethiopia 127 D4 ◆ *Republic,* E Africa
Ethiopian Highlands 127 D4 *Plateau,* N Ethiopia
Etna, Monte 79 D8 ✵ Sicily, Italy
Etosha Pan 128 B5 *Salt lake,* N Namibia
Ettelbrück 68 E8 C Luxembourg
Euboea 83 E5 *Island,* C Greece
Eucla 133 D5 W Australia
Euclid 44 F5 Ohio, USA
Eufaula Lake 47 E8 ▣ Oklahoma, USA
Eugene 53 B4 Oregon, USA
Eupen 68 E7 E Belgium
Euphrates 99 C3 ≈ SW Asia
Eureka 53 A5 California, USA
Eureka 51 C1 Montana, USA
Eureka 51 B5 Nevada, USA
Europe 62 *Continent*
Eutin 77 C2 N Germany
Evansdale 47 F4 Iowa, USA
Evanston 44 C5 Illinois, USA
Evanston 51 D4 Wyoming, USA
Evansville 44 C8 Indiana, USA
Eveleth 47 E2 Minnesota, USA
Everard, Lake 133 D5 *Salt lake,* S Australia
Everest, Mount 105 B5 ▲ China/Nepal
Everett 53 B2 Washington, USA
Everglades City 43 G8 Florida, USA
Everglades, The 43 G8 *Wetland,* SE USA
Evje 67 B6 S Norway
Évora 75 B4 C Portugal
Évreux 73 D2 N France
Évros 83 F4 ≈ SE Europe
Evvoia *see* Euboea
Ewa Beach 55 B1 Oahu, Hawaii, USA
Excelsior Springs 47 E6 Missouri, USA
Exe 71 D8 ≈ SW England, UK
Exeter 71 D8 SW England, UK
Exmouth 133 A3 W Australia
Exmouth 71 D8 SW England, UK
Exmouth Gulf 133 A3 *Gulf,* W Australia
Extremadura 75 C4 *Cultural region,* W Spain
Exuma Cays 61 D2 *Islets,* C Bahamas
Exuma Sound 61 D2 *Sound,* C Bahamas
Eyre Basin, Lake 133 E4 *Salt lake,* S Australia
Eyre Mountains 135 B7 ⛰ South Island, NZ
Eyre North, Lake 133 E4 *Salt lake,* S Australia
Eyre Peninsula 133 E5 *Peninsula,* S Australia
Eyre South, Lake 133 E5 *Salt lake,* S Australia

F

Faaa 137 A6 W French Polynesia
Fabens 48 D4 Texas, USA
Fada 124 H2 E Chad
Fada-Ngourma 124 D4 E Burkina
Faenza 79 C3 N Italy
Fagamalo 137 A4 N Samoa
Fagne 68 C8 *Hill range,* S Belgium
Faguibine, Lac 124 C3 ◎ NW Mali
Fairbanks 54 E2 Alaska, USA
Fairfield 53 B6 California, USA
Fair Isle 71 E2 *Island,* NE Scotland, UK
Fairlie 135 B6 South Island, NZ
Fairmont 47 E4 Minnesota, USA
Faisalabad 107 D2 NE Pakistan
Faizabad 107 E3 N India
Fakfak 109 H7 E Indonesia
Falam 109 A2 W Myanmar
Falconara Marittima 79 D4 C Italy
Falcon Reservoir 48 G6 ▣ Mexico/USA
Falealupo 137 A4 NW Samoa
Falkland Islands 117 C8 *UK* ◇ SW Atlantic Ocean
Fallbrook 53 D9 California, USA
Falmouth 71 C8 SW England, UK
Falster 67 B7 *Island,* SE Denmark
Falun 67 C5 C Sweden
Famagusta 88 D6 E Cyprus
Famagusta Bay 88 D6 *Bay,* E Cyprus
Famenne 68 D8 *Physical region,* SE Belgium
Fano 79 D3 C Italy
Farafangana 128 G6 SE Madagascar
Farah 101 D5 W Afghanistan
Farah Rud 101 D5 ≈ W Afghanistan
Faranah 124 B4 S Guinea
Farasan, Jaza'ir 99 B6 *Island group,* SW Saudi Arabia
Farewell, Cape 135 C4 *Headland,* South Island, NZ
Farghona 101 G3 E Uzbekistan
Fargo 47 D2 North Dakota, USA
Faribault 47 E3 Minnesota, USA
Faridabad 107 D3 N India Asia
Farkhor 101 F4 SW Tajikistan
Farmington 47 G7 Missouri, USA
Farmington 48 C1 New Mexico, USA
Faro 75 B5 S Portugal
Farquhar Group 128 H3 *Island group,* S Seychelles
Fastiv 85 D4 NW Ukraine
Fauske 67 C2 C Norway
Faxaflói 67 A1 *Bay,* W Iceland
Faya 124 H2 N Chad
Fayaoué 137 G6 C New Caledonia
Fayetteville 43 A3 Arkansas, USA
Fayetteville 43 H3 North Carolina, USA
Fdérik 124 B1 NW Mauritania
Fear, Cape 43 H4 *Headland,* Bald Head Island, North Carolina, USA
Fécamp 73 C1 N France
Fehérgyarmat 81 G7 E Hungary
Fehmarn 77 C2 *Island,* N Germany
Fehmarn Belt 77 C2 *Strait,* Denmark/Germany
Feijó 115 C5 W Brazil
Feilding 135 D4 North Island, NZ
Feira de Santana 115 H5 E Brazil
Felanitx 75 H4 Majorca, Spain
Felipe Carrillo Puerto 57 I4 SE Mexico
Felixstowe 71 F7 E England, UK
Femunden 67 B4 ◎ S Norway
Fenoarivo 128 G5 E Madagascar
Feodosiya 85 F6 S Ukraine
Fergana Valley 101 G3 *Basin,* Tajikistan/Uzbekistan
Fergus Falls 47 D2 Minnesota, USA
Ferkessédougou 124 C4 N Ivory Coast
Fermo 79 D4 C Italy
Ferrara 79 C3 N Italy
Ferrol 75 B1 NW Spain
Ferwerd 68 E2 N Netherlands
Fethiye 97 B5 SW Turkey
Fetlar 71 E1 *Island,* NE Scotland, UK
Feyzabad 101 G4 NE Afghanistan
Fez 122 C1 N Morocco
Fianarantsoa 128 G5 C Madagascar
Fianga 124 G4 SW Chad
Fier 83 D4 SW Albania
Figeac 73 D5 S France
Figueira da Foz 75 A3 W Portugal
Figueres 75 H2 E Spain
Figuig 122 D2 E Morocco
Fiji 137 I5 ◆ *Republic,* SW Pacific Ocean
Filadelfia 59 D6 W Costa Rica
Filipstad 67 C5 C Sweden
Finale Ligure 79 B3 NW Italy
Findlay 44 E6 Ohio, USA
Finger Lakes 41 C4 *Lakes,* New York, USA
Finike 97 B5 SW Turkey
Finland 67 E4 ◆ *Republic,* N Europe
Finland, Gulf of 67 E5 *Gulf,* E Baltic Sea
Finnmarksvidda 67 D1 *Physical region,* N Norway
Finschhafen 137 C2 C PNG
Finsterwalde 77 D4 E Germany
Fiordland 135 A7 *Physical region,* South Island, NZ
Firenze *see* Florence
Fischbacher Alpen 77 F7 ⛰ E Austria
Fish 128 C6 ≈ S Namibia
Fishguard 71 C7 SW Wales, UK
Fisterra, Cabo 75 A1 *Headland,* NW Spain
Fito 137 B5 ▲ C Samoa
Fitzroy Crossing 133 C2 W Australia
Fitzroy River 133 C2 ≈ W Australia
Flagstaff 48 B2 Arizona, USA
Fläming 81 A3 *Hill range,* NE Germany
Flanders 68 A6 *Cultural region,* Belgium/France
Flathead Lake 51 C2 ◎ Montana, USA
Flattery, Cape 53 A1 *Headland,* Washington, USA
Flensburg 77 C2 N Germany
Flinders Island 133 G7 *Island,* Tasmania, SE Australia
Flinders Ranges 133 F5 ⛰ S Australia
Flinders River 133 F3 ≈ Queensland, N Australia
Flin Flon 33 H6 Manitoba, C Canada
Flint 44 E4 Michigan, USA
Flint Island 131 *Island,* Line Islands, E Kiribati
Florence 79 D3 C Italy
Florence 43 D4 Alabama, USA
Florence 43 G4 South Carolina, USA
Florencia 115 B3 S Colombia
Flores 59 B2 N Guatemala
Flores 109 F8 *Island,* Nusa Tenggara, C Indonesia
Flores Sea 109 E8 *Sea,* C Indonesia
Floriano 115 H4 E Brazil
Florianópolis 115 G8 S Brazil
Florida 117 C5 S Uruguay
Florida 43 F6 ◐ *State,* SE USA
Florida Keys 43 G9 *Island group,* SE USA
Florida, Straits of 43 H9 *Strait,* Atlantic Ocean/Gulf of Mexico
Florissant 47 G6 Missouri, USA
Fly 137 A2 ≈ Indonesia/PNG
Foča 83 C2 SE Bosnia and Herzegovina
Focşani 85 C6 E Romania
Foggia 79 E5 SE Italy
Foix 73 C7 S France
Foleyet 35 C5 Ontario, S Canada
Foligno 79 D4 C Italy
Folkestone 71 F7 SE England, UK
Fond du Lac 44 C4 Wisconsin, USA
Fongafale 137 J3 ● Funafuti Atoll, SE Tuvalu
Fonseca, Gulf of 59 C4 *Gulf,* C Central America
Fontainebleau 73 D3 N France
Fontenay-le-Comte 73 C4 NW France
Fonyód 81 D8 W Hungary
Forchheim 77 C6 SE Germany
Forfar 71 D4 E Scotland, UK
Forlì 79 C3 N Italy
Formentera 75 G4 *Island,* Balearic Islands, Spain
Formosa 117 C4 NE Argentina
Formosa, Serra 115 F5 ⛰ C Brazil
Forrest City 43 C3 Arkansas, USA
Fort Albany 35 C4 Ontario, C Canada
Fortaleza 117 B1 N Bolivia
Fortaleza 115 H4 NE Brazil
Fort Collins 51 F5 Colorado, USA
Fort Davis 48 E4 Texas, USA
Fort-de-France 61 K5 ○ W Martinique
Fort Dodge 47 E4 Iowa, USA
Fortescue River 133 B3 ≈ W Australia
Fort Frances 35 A4 Ontario, S Canada
Fort Good Hope 33 F4 NW Terr., NW Canada
Forth 71 C4 ≈ C Scotland, UK
Forth, Firth of 71 D4 *Estuary,* E Scotland, UK
Fort Lauderdale 43 G8 Florida, USA
Fort Liard 33 F5 NW Terr., W Canada
Fort Madison 47 F5 Iowa, USA
Fort McMurray 33 G6 Alberta, C Canada
Fort McPherson 33 E4 NW Terr., NW Canada
Fort Morgan 51 F5 Colorado, USA
Fort Myers 43 G8 Florida, USA
Fort Nelson 33 F5 British Columbia, W Canada
Fort Peck Lake 51 E2 ▣ Montana, USA
Fort Pierce 43 G8 Florida, USA
Fort Providence 33 F5 NW Terr., W Canada
Fort St.John 33 F6 British Columbia, W Canada
Fort Scott 47 E7 Kansas, USA
Fort Severn 35 B2 Ontario, C Canada
Fort-Shevchenko 94 A5 W Kazakhstan
Fort Simpson 33 F5 NW Terr., W Canada
Fort Smith 33 G5 NW Terr., W Canada
Fort Smith 43 A3 Arkansas, USA
Fort Stockton 48 E4 Texas, USA
Fort Vermilion 33 F6 Alberta, W Canada
Fort Walton Beach 43 D6 Florida, USA
Fort Wayne 44 D6 Indiana, USA
Fort William 71 C4 N Scotland, UK
Fort Worth 48 H3 Texas, USA
Fort Yukon 54 F2 Alaska, USA
Fougères 73 C2 NW France
Foulwind, Cape 135 B5 *Headland,* South Island, NZ
Foumban 124 F5 NW Cameroon
Foveaux Strait 135 A8 *Strait,* S NZ
Foxe Basin 33 I3 *Sea,* NW Terr., N Canada
Fox Glacier 135 B6 South Island, NZ
Fox Mine 33 H6 Manitoba, C Canada
Fraga 75 F2 NE Spain
Fram Basin 139 C4 *Undersea feature,* Arctic Ocean
France 73 C4 ◆ *Republic,* W Europe
Franceville 128 B2 E Gabon
Franche-Comté 73 E4 *Cultural region,* E France
Francis Case, Lake 47 C4 ▣ South Dakota, USA
Francisco Escárcega 57 H5 SE Mexico
Francistown 128 D5 North East, NE Botswana
Frankfort 43 E2 Kentucky, USA
Frankfurt am Main 77 B5 SW Germany
Frankfurt an der Oder 77 E4 E Germany
Fränkische Alb 77 C6 ⛰ S Germany
Franklin 43 D3 Tennessee, USA
Franklin D. Roosevelt Lake 53 C2 ▣ Washington, USA
Franz Josef Land 94 D1 *Island group,* N Russ. Fed.
Fraserburgh 71 D3 NE Scotland, UK
Fraser Island 133 H4 *Island,* Queensland, E Australia
Fray Bentos 117 C5 W Uruguay
Fredericksburg 43 H2 Virginia, USA
Fredericton 35 F5 New Brunswick, SE Canada
Frederiksted 55 S Virgin Islands (US)
Fredonia 48 B1 Arizona, USA
Fredrikstad 67 B5 S Norway
Freeport 61 D1 N Bahamas
Freeport 44 B5 Illinois, USA
Freeport 48 H5 Texas, USA
Freetown 124 B4 ● W Sierra Leone
Freiburg im Breisgau 77 B7 SW Germany
Fremantle 133 B5 W Australia
Fremont 47 D5 Nebraska, USA
Fremont 44 E6 Ohio, USA
French Guiana 115 F2 *French* ◇ N South America
French Polynesia 131 *French* ◇, S Pacific Ocean
Fresnillo 57 E4 C Mexico
Fresno 53 C7 California, USA
Frías 117 B4 N Argentina
Friedrichshafen 77 B7 S Germany
Frohavet 67 B4 *Sound,* C Norway
Frome, Lake 133 F5 *Salt lake,* S Australia
Frontera 57 H5 SE Mexico
Frontignan 73 D6 S France
Frøya 67 B4 *Island,* W Norway
Frýdek-Místek 81 D6 SE Czech Republic
Fuengirola 75 D6 S Spain
Fuerte Olimpo 117 C3 NE Paraguay
Fuji, Mount 103 F6 ▲ Honshu, SE Japan
Fukui 103 F6 SW Japan
Fukuoka 103 D7 SW Japan
Fukushima 103 G4 C Japan
Fulda 77 C5 C Germany
Funafuti Atoll 137 J3 *Atoll,* C Tuvalu
Fundy, Bay of 35 F5 *Bay,* Canada/USA
Fürth 77 C6 S Germany
Furukawa 103 G4 C Japan
Fushun 105 G2 NE China
Füssen 77 C7 S Germany
Futuna 137 H5 *Island,* S Vanuatu
Futuna, Île 137 J4 *Island,* S Wallis and Futuna
Fuxin 105 G2 NE China
Fuzhou 105 G5 SE China
Fyn 67 B7 *Island,* C Denmark

G

Gaalkacyo 127 F4 C Somalia
Gabela 128 B3 W Angola
Gabès 122 F2 E Tunisia
Gabès, Golfe de 122 F2 *Gulf,* E Tunisia
Gabon 128 A1 ◆ *Republic,* C Africa
Gaborone 128 D6 ● SE Botswana
Gabrovo 83 F3 C Bulgaria
Gadag 107 D6 W India
Gadsden 43 E4 Alabama, USA
Gaeta 79 D5 C Italy
Gaeta, Gulf of 79 C5 *Gulf,* C Italy
Gafsa 122 E2 W Tunisia
Gagnoa 124 C5 C Ivory Coast
Gagra 97 F1 NW Georgia
Gaillac 73 C6 S France
Gainesville 43 F6 Florida, USA
Gainesville 43 F4 Georgia, USA
Gainesville 48 H3 Texas, USA
Gairdner, Lake 133 E5 *Salt lake,* S Australia
Galán, Cerro 117 A4 ▲ NW Argentina
Galanta 81 D7 SW Slovakia
Galapagos Islands 115 A7 *Island group,* Ecuador
Galashiels 71 D5 SE Scotland, UK
Galaţi 85 D7 E Romania
Galesburg 44 B6 Illinois, USA
Galicia 75 B1 *Cultural region,* NW Spain
Galle 107 E8 SW Sri Lanka
Gallipoli 79 F6 SE Italy
Gällivare 67 D2 N Sweden
Gallup 48 C2 New Mexico, USA

146

◐ Administrative region ◆ Country ● Country capital ◇ Dependent territory ○ Dependent territory capital ⛰ Mountain range ▲ Mountain ✵ Volcano ≈ River ◎ Lake ▣ Reservoir

◆ Administrative region ◆ Country ● Country capital ◇ Dependent territory ○ Dependent territory capital ▲ Mountain range ▲ Mountain ☆ Volcano ≈ River ● Lake ⊡ Reservoir

◈ Administrative region ◆ Country ● Country capital ◇ Dependent territory ◎ Dependent territory capital ▲ Mountain range ▲ Mountain ⚑ Volcano ⚡ River ● Lake ▨ Reservoir

N

CAR Central African Republic   **FYR** Former Yugoslavian Republic   **NSW** New South Wales   **NZ** New Zealand   **PNG** Papua New Guinea   **Russ. Fed.** Russian Federation   **UAE** United Arab Emirates   **UK** United Kingdom   **USA** United States of America

153

CAR Central African Republic FYR Former Yugoslavian Republic NSW New South Wales NZ New Zealand PNG Papua New Guinea Russ. Fed. Russian Federation UAE United Arab Emirates UK United Kingdom USA United States of America

155

SABLE, ILE DE

Sable, Île de 137 E5 Island, NW New Caledonia
Sable Island 35 G5 Island, Nova Scotia, SE Canada
Sabzevar 99 E1 NE Iran
Sachsen see Saxony
Sachs Harbour 33 F3 Banks Island, NW Terr., N Canada
Sacramento 53 B6 California, USA
Sacramento Mountains 48 D3 ⛰ New Mexico, USA
Sacramento River 53 B6 ≈ California, USA
Sacramento Valley 53 B6 Valley, California, USA
Sa'dah 99 C6 NW Yemen
Sado 103 F4 Island, C Japan
Säffle 67 C5 C Sweden
Safford 48 C3 Arizona, USA
Safi 122 B2 W Morocco
Safid Kuh, Selseleh-ye 101 D5 ⛰ W Afghanistan
Saga 103 D7 Kyushu, SW Japan
Sagaing 109 A2 C Myanmar
Sagami-nada 103 G6 Inlet, SW Japan
Saganaga Lake 47 F1 ◎ Minnesota, USA
Sagar 107 E4 C India
Saginaw 44 E4 Michigan, USA
Saginaw Bay 44 E4 Lake bay, Michigan, USA
Sagua la Grande 61 C2 C Cuba
Sagunto 75 F4 E Spain
Sahara 124 D2 Desert, N Africa
Saharan Atlas 122 D2 ⛰ Algeria/Morocco
Sahel 124 E3 Physical region, C Africa
Sahiwal 107 D2 E Pakistan
Saidpur 107 F3 NW Bangladesh
Saimaa 67 F4 ◎ SE Finland
St Albans 71 E7 E England, UK
Saint Albans 43 F2 West Virginia, USA
St Andrews 71 D4 E Scotland, UK
St.Anthony 35 G3 Newfoundland, Newfoundland and Labrador, SE Canada
Saint Augustine 43 G6 Florida, USA
St Austell 71 C8 SW England, UK
St-Barthélemy 61 J4 Island, N Guadeloupe
St-Brieuc 73 B2 NW France
St. Catherines 35 D6 Ontario, S Canada
St-Chamond 73 E5 E France
Saint Clair, Lake 41 A4 ◎ Canada/USA
St-Claude 73 E4 E France
Saint Cloud 47 E3 Minnesota, USA
St. Croix Island 55 Island, S Virgin Islands (US)
Saint Croix River 44 A3 ≈ N USA
St-Dié 73 F3 NE France
St-Egrève 73 E5 E France
Saintes 73 B4 W France
St-Étienne 73 E5 E France
St-Flour 73 D5 C France
St-Gaudens 73 C6 S France
Saint George 133 G4 Queensland, E Australia
Saint George 51 C6 Utah, USA
St-Georges 35 E5 Québec, SE Canada
St George's 61 K7 ● SW Grenada
St George's Channel 71 C7 Channel, Ireland/Wales, UK
Saint Helena 26 UK ◇, S Atlantic Ocean
St.Helena Bay 128 B7 Bay, SW South Africa
St.Helens, Mount 53 B2 ♨ Washington, USA
St Helier 71 D9 ○ S Jersey, Channel Islands
Saint Ignace 44 D3 Michigan, USA
St-Jean, Lac 35 E4 ◎ Québec, SE Canada
St.John 35 F5 New Brunswick, SE Canada
Saint John 41 G1 ≈ Canada/USA
St. John Island 55 Island, Virgin Islands (US)
St John's 61 J4 ● Antigua, Antigua and Barbuda
St John's 35 H4 Newfoundland, Newfoundland and Labrador, E Canada
Saint Johns 48 C2 Arizona, USA
Saint Joseph 47 E6 Missouri, USA
St Julian's 88 B6 N Malta
St Kilda 71 B3 Island, NW Scotland, UK
St. Lawrence, Gulf of 35 F4 Gulf, NW Atlantic Ocean
Saint Lawrence Island 54 C1 Island Alaska, USA
Saint Lawrence River 41 D2 ≈ Canada/USA
St-Lô 73 C2 N France
St-Louis 73 F3 NE France
Saint Louis 124 A3 NW Senegal
Saint Louis 47 G6 Missouri, USA
St Lucia 61 J6 ◆ Commonwealth Republic, SE West Indies
St Lucia Channel 61 K6 Channel, Martinique/Saint Lucia
St-Malo 73 B2 NW France
St-Malo, Golfe de 73 B2 Gulf, NW France
St-Martin 61 J4 Island, N Guadeloupe
St.Matthias Group 137 C1 Island group, NE PNG
St.Moritz 77 C8 SE Switzerland
St-Nazaire 73 B3 NW France
St-Omer 73 D1 N France
Saint Paul 47 E3 Minnesota, USA
St Peter Port 71 D9 ○ C Guernsey, Channel Islands
Saint Petersburg 87 A4 NW Russ. Fed.
Saint Petersburg 43 F7 Florida, USA
St Pierre and Miquelon 35 G4 French ◇ NE North America
St-Quentin 73 D2 N France
St. Thomas Island 55 Island, Virgin Islands (US)
Saint Vincent 61 J6 Island, N Saint Vincent and the Grenadines
Saint Vincent and the Grenadines 61 J6 ◆ Commonwealth Republic, SE West Indies
Saint Vincent Passage 61 K6 Passage, Saint Lucia/Saint Vincent and the Grenadines
Sajama, Nevado 117 A2 ▲ W Bolivia
Sajószentpéter 81 F7 NE Hungary
Sakakawea, Lake 47 B2 ⊡ North Dakota, USA
Sakata 103 F4 Honshu, C Japan
Sakhalin 94 I4 Island, SE Russ. Fed.
Saki 97 I2 NW Azerbaijan
Sakishima-shoto 103 A8 Island group, SW Japan
Sala 67 C5 C Sweden
Sala Consilina 79 E6 S Italy
Salado, Río 117 B4 ≈ E Argentina
Salado, Río 117 B5 ≈ C Argentina
Salalah 99 E6 SW Oman
Salamá 59 B3 C Guatemala
Salamanca 117 A5 C Chile
Salamanca 75 C3 NW Spain
Salang Tunnel 101 F4 Tunnel, C Afghanistan
Salantai 67 E7 NW Lithuania
Salavat 87 D6 W Russ. Fed.
Šalčininkai 67 F7 SE Lithuania
Sale 133 E8 Victoria, SE Australia
Salé 122 C1 NW Morocco
Salekhard 94 D3 N Russ. Fed.
Salelologa 137 A5 C Samoa
Salem 107 D7 SE India
Salem 53 B3 Oregon, USA
Salerno 79 D6 S Italy
Salerno, Gulf of 79 D6 Gulf, S Italy
Salihorsk 85 C3 S Belarus
Salina 47 D6 Kansas, USA
Salina 51 D6 Utah, USA
Salina Cruz 57 G6 SE Mexico
Salinas 53 B7 California, USA
Salisbury 71 E8 S England, UK
Salmon 51 C3 Idaho, USA
Salmon River 51 B3 ≈ Idaho, USA
Salmon River Mountains 51 B3 ⛰ Idaho, USA
Salo 67 E5 SW Finland
Salon-de-Provence 73 E6 SE France
Salonica 83 E4 N Greece
Sal'sk 87 A8 SW Russ. Fed.
Salta 117 B4 NW Argentina
Saltash 71 D8 SW England, UK
Saltillo 57 E3 NE Mexico
Salt Lake City 51 D5 Utah, USA
Salto 117 C5 N Uruguay
Salton Sea 53 D9 ◎ California, USA
Salvador 115 H6 E Brazil
Salween 109 B2 ≈ SE Asia
Salyan 107 E3 W Nepal
Salzburg 77 D7 N Austria
Salzgitter 77 C4 C Germany
Salzwedel 77 C3 N Germany
Samalayuca 57 C2 N Mexico
Samar 109 F4 Island, C Philippines
Samara 87 C6 W Russ. Fed.
Samarinda 109 E6 C Indonesia
Samarqand 101 F3 C Uzbekistan
Samaxi 97 I2 C Azerbaijan
Sambalpur 107 F4 E India
Sambava 128 H4 NE Madagascar
Sambir 85 B4 NW Ukraine
Sambre 73 E1 ≈ Belgium/France
Samfya 128 D3 N Zambia
Samoa 137 B4 ◆ Monarchy, W Polynesia
Sámos 83 F5 Island, Dodecanese, Greece
Samothráki 83 F4 Island, NE Greece
Sampit 109 D7 C Indonesia
Sam Rayburn Reservoir 48 I4 ⊡ Texas, USA
Samsun 97 E2 N Turkey
Samtredia 97 G1 W Georgia
Samui, Ko 109 B5 Island, SW Thailand
San 124 C3 C Mali
San 81 G5 ≈ SE Poland
Sana 83 B2 ≈ NW Bosnia and Herzegovina
Sana 99 C6 ● W Yemen
San'a' see Sana
Sanae 138 B3 South African research station, Antarctica
Sanaga 124 G5 ≈ C Cameroon
Sanandaj 99 C2 W Iran
San Andrés, Isla de 59 F4 Island, NW Colombia
San Andrés Tuxtla 57 G5 E Mexico
San Angelo 48 F1 Texas, USA
San Antonio 59 B2 S Belize
San Antonio 117 A5 C Chile
San Antonio 48 G5 Texas, USA
San Antonio Oeste 117 B7 E Argentina
Sanaw 99 D6 NE Yemen
San Benedicto, Isla 57 B5 Island, W Mexico
San Benito 59 B2 N Guatemala
San Bernardino 53 D8 California, USA
San Blas 57 C3 C Mexico
San Blas, Cape 43 D7 Headland, SE USA
San Blas, Cordillera de 59 H6 ⛰ NE Panama
San Carlos 59 E5 S Nicaragua
San Carlos 48 C3 Arizona, USA
San Carlos de Bariloche 117 A7 SW Argentina
San Clemente Island 53 C9 Island, Channel Islands, California, USA
San Cristobal 137 F3 Island, SE Solomon Islands
San Cristóbal 115 C2 W Venezuela
San Cristóbal de Las Casas 57 H5 SE Mexico
San Cristóbal, Isla 115 B7 Island, Galapagos Islands, Ecuador
Sancti Spíritus 61 C3 C Cuba
Sancy, Puy de 73 D5 ▲ C France
Sandakan 109 E5 East Malaysia
Sandanski 83 E3 SW Bulgaria
Sanday 71 D2 Island, NE Scotland, UK
Sanders 48 C2 Arizona, USA
Sand Hills 47 B4 ⛰ Nebraska, USA
San Diego 53 D9 California, USA
Sandnes 67 A5 S Norway
Sandomierz 81 F5 SE Poland
Sandoway 109 A3 W Myanmar
Sandpoint 51 B1 Idaho, USA
Sand Springs 47 D7 Oklahoma, USA
Sandusky 44 E5 Ohio, USA
Sandvika 67 B5 S Norway
Sandviken 67 D5 C Sweden
Sandy City 51 D5 Utah, USA
Sandy Lake 35 A3 ◎ Ontario, C Canada
San Esteban 59 D3 C Honduras
San Fernando 75 C6 S Spain
San Fernando 61 K7 Trinidad, Trinidad and Tobago
San Fernando del Valle de Catamarca 117 B4 NW Argentina
San Francisco 53 B7 California, USA
San Francisco del Oro 57 D3 N Mexico
San Francisco de Macorís 61 G4 C Dominican Republic
Sangan, Kuh-e 101 E5 ⛰ C Afghanistan
Sangir, Kepulauan 109 F6 Island group, N Indonesia
Sangli 107 D5 W India
Sangmélima 124 G6 S Cameroon
Sangre de Cristo Mountains 48 E1 ⛰ C USA
San Ignacio 59 B2 W Belize
San Ignacio 117 B2 N Bolivia
San Ignacio 57 B3 W Mexico
San Joaquin Valley 53 C7 Valley, California, USA
San Jorge, Golfo 117 B8 Gulf, S Argentina
San José 117 C2 E Bolivia
San José 59 E6 ● C Costa Rica
San José 59 A4 S Guatemala
San Jose 53 B7 California, USA
San José del Guaviare 115 C3 S Colombia
San Juan 117 A5 W Argentina
San Juan 55 ○ NE Puerto Rico
San Juan Bautista 117 C4 S Paraguay
San Juan de Alicante 75 F5 E Spain
San Juan del Norte 59 E5 SE Nicaragua
San Juanito, Isla 57 C4 Island, C Mexico
San Juan Mountains 51 E6 ⛰ Colorado, USA
San Juan, Río 59 E5 ≈, S Nicaragua
San Juan River 51 E6 ≈ W USA
Sankt-Peterburg see Saint Petersburg
Sankt Gallen 77 B7 NE Switzerland
Sankt Pölten 77 E7 N Austria
Sankuru 128 C2 ≈ C Congo (Zaire)
Şanlıurfa 97 F4 S Turkey
San Lorenzo 117 B3 S Bolivia
Sanlúcar de Barrameda 75 C6 S Spain
San Lucas Cape 57 C4 Headland, W Mexico
San Luis 117 B5 C Argentina
San Luis 59 B2 NE Guatemala
San Luis 57 A1 NW Mexico
San Luis Obispo 53 B8 California, USA
San Luis Potosí 57 E4 C Mexico
San Marcos 59 A3 W Guatemala
San Marcos 48 G4 Texas, USA
San Marino 79 D3 ● C San Marino
San Marino 79 D3 ◆ Republic, S Europe
San Martín 138 A4 C Argentina
San Matías 117 C2 E Bolivia
San Matías, Gulf of 117 B7 Gulf, E Argentina
Sanmenxia 105 F4 C China
San Miguel 59 B4 SE El Salvador
San Miguel 57 D2 N Mexico
San Miguel de Tucumán 117 B4 N Argentina
San Miguelito 59 E5 S Nicaragua
San Miguelito 59 H6 C Panama
San Miguel, Río 117 B2 ≈ E Bolivia
Sanok 81 F6 SE Poland
San Pablo 117 B3 S Bolivia
San Pedro 59 C1 NE Belize
San-Pédro 124 C5 S Ivory Coast
San Pedro 57 D3 NE Mexico
San Pedro de la Cueva 57 C2 NW Mexico
San Pedro Mártir, Sierra 57 A2 ⛰ NW Mexico
San Pedro Sula 59 C3 NW Honduras
San Rafael 117 A5 W Argentina
San Rafael Mountains 53 C8 ⛰ California, USA
San Ramón de la Nueva Orán 117 B3 N Argentina
San Remo 79 A3 NW Italy
San Salvador 59 B4 ● SW El Salvador
San Salvador 61 E2 Island, E Bahamas
San Salvador de Jujuy 117 B3 N Argentina
Sansanné-Mango 124 D4 N Togo
Sansepolcro 79 C4 C Italy
San Severo 79 E5 SE Italy
Santa Ana 117 B2 N Bolivia
Santa Ana 59 B4 NW El Salvador
Santa Ana 53 D9 California, USA
Santa Barbara 57 D3 N Mexico
Santa Barbara 53 C8 California, USA
Santa Catalina 59 G6 W Panama
Santa Catalina Island 53 C9 Island, Channel Islands, California, USA
Santa Catarina 115 F8 ◐ State, S Brazil
Santa Clara 61 C3 C Cuba
Santa Comba 75 B1 NW Spain
Santa Cruz 117 B2 C Bolivia
Santa Cruz 53 B7 California, USA
Santa Cruz del Quiché 59 A3 W Guatemala
Santa Cruz, Isla 115 B7 Island, Galapagos Islands, Ecuador
Santa Cruz Islands 137 G3 Island group, E Solomon Islands
Santa Cruz, Río 117 A8 ≈ S Argentina
Santa Elena 59 B2 W Belize
Santa Fe 117 C5 C Argentina
Santa Fe 48 D2 New Mexico, USA
Santa Genoveva 57 B4 ▲ W Mexico
Santa Isabel 137 E2 Island, N Solomon Islands
Santa Lucia Range 53 B8 ⛰ California, USA
Santa Margarita, Isla 57 B4 Island, W Mexico
Santa Maria 115 F8 S Brazil
Santa Maria 53 C8 California, USA
Santa Maria 137 G4 Island, Banks Islands, N Vanuatu
Santa María, Isla 115 A7 Island, Galapagos Islands, Ecuador
Santa Marta 115 B1 N Colombia
Santander 75 D1 N Spain
Santarém 115 F4 N Brazil
Santarém 75 A4 W Portugal
Santa Rosa 117 B6 C Argentina
Santa Rosa 53 B6 California, USA
Santa Rosa 48 E2 New Mexico, USA
Santa Rosa de Copán 59 B3 W Honduras
Santa Rosa Island 53 B9 Island, California, USA
Sant Carles de la Ràpita 75 F3 NE Spain
Santiago 117 A5 ● C Chile
Santiago 61 G4 N Dominican Republic
Santiago 59 G7 S Panama
Santiago 75 B1 NW Spain
Santiago de Cuba 61 E4 E Cuba
Santiago del Estero 117 B4 C Argentina
Santo Domingo 61 G4 ● SE Dominican Republic
Santos 115 G7 S Brazil
Santo Tomé 117 C4 NE Argentina
San Valentín, Cerro 117 A8 ▲ S Chile
San Vicente 59 C4 C El Salvador
São Francisco, Rio 115 G6 ≈ E Brazil
São Hill 127 D7 S Tanzania
São João da Madeira 75 B3 N Portugal
São Luís 115 G4 NE Brazil
São Manuel, Rio 115 E5 ≈ C Brazil
Saona, Isla 61 G4 Island, SE Dominican Republic
Saône 73 E5 ≈ E France
São Paulo 115 G7 S Brazil
São Paulo 115 F7 ◐ State, S Brazil
São Roque, Cabo de 115 I4 Headland, E Brazil
São Tomé 124 E6 ● S Sao Tome and Principe
São Tomé 124 F6 Island, S Sao Tome and Principe
Sao Tome and Principe 124 E6 ◆ Republic, E Atlantic Ocean
São Vicente, Cabo de 75 A5 Headland, S Portugal
Sapele 124 E5 S Nigeria
Sa Pobla 75 H4 Majorca, Spain
Sappir 99 H7 S Israel
Sapporo 103 F2 NE Japan
Sapri 79 E6 S Italy
Sapulpa 47 D8 Oklahoma, USA
Saqqez 99 C2 NW Iran
Sarajevo 83 C2 ● SE Bosnia and Herzegovina
Saraktash 87 D7 W Russ. Fed.
Saran' 94 C5 C Kazakhstan
Sarandë 83 D4 S Albania
Saransk 87 B6 W Russ. Fed.
Sarasota 43 F8 Florida, USA
Saratoga Springs 41 E3 New York, USA
Saratov 87 B7 W Russ. Fed.
Sarawak 109 D6 Cultural region, S Malaysia
Sardegna see Sardinia
Sardinia 79 B6 Island, Italy
Sargodha 107 C2 NE Pakistan
Sarh 124 H4 S Chad
Sari 99 D1 N Iran
Saría 83 G7 Island, SE Greece
Sarıkamış 97 G2 NE Turkey
Sarikol Range 101 H3 ⛰ China/Tajikistan
Sariwon 103 A5 SW North Korea
Sark 71 E9 Island, Channel Islands
Şarkışla 97 E3 C Turkey
Sarmiento 117 B7 S Argentina
Sarnia 35 C6 Ontario, S Canada
Sarny 85 C4 NW Ukraine
Sarpsborg 67 B5 S Norway
Sartène 73 G6 Corsica, France
Sarthe 73 C3 Cultural region, N France
Sárti 83 E4 N Greece
Sarykamyshkoye Ozero 101 C2 Salt lake, Kazakhstan/Uzbekistan
Sary-Tash 101 G3 SW Kyrgyzstan
Sasalaguan, Mount 55 ▲ S Guam
Sasebo 103 C7 SW Japan
Saskatchewan 33 G5 ◐ Province, SW Canada
Saskatchewan 33 H6 ≈ Manitoba/Saskatchewan, C Canada
Saskatoon 33 G7 Saskatchewan, S Canada
Sasovo 87 B6 W Russ. Fed.
Sassandra 124 C5 S Ivory Coast
Sassandra 124 C5 ≈ S Ivory Coast
Sassari 79 A5 Sardinia, Italy
Sassenheim 68 C4 W Netherlands
Sassnitz 77 D2 NE Germany
Sátoraljaújhely 81 F7 NE Hungary
Satpura Range 107 D4 ⛰ C India
Satsunan-shoto 103 A7 Island group, Nansei-shoto, SW Japan
Sattanen 67 E2 NE Finland
Satu Mare 85 B5 NW Romania
Saudi Arabia 99 C5 ◆ Monarchy, SW Asia
Saulkrasti 67 E6 C Latvia
Sault Ste.Marie 35 C5 Ontario, S Canada
Sault Sainte Marie 44 D2 Michigan, USA
Saumur 73 C3 NW France
Saurimo 128 C3 NE Angola
Savá 59 D2 N Honduras
Sava 83 D2 ≈ SE Europe
Savai'i 137 A4 Island, NW Samoa
Savannah 43 G5 Georgia, USA
Savannah River 43 G5 ≈ SE USA
Save, Rio 128 E5 ≈ Mozambique/Zimbabwe
Saverne 73 F3 NE France
Savigliano 79 A2 NW Italy
Savinskiy 87 C4 NW Russ. Fed.
Savissivik 139 A4 N Greenland
Savoie 73 E5 Cultural region, E France
Savona 79 B3 NW Italy
Savu Sea 109 F8 Sea, S Indonesia
Sawqirah 99 E6 S Oman
Saxony 77 D4 Cultural region, E Germany
Sayat 101 E3 E Turkmenistan
Sayaxché 59 B2 N Guatemala
Sayhut 99 D6 E Yemen
Saynshand 105 F2 SE Mongolia
Sayre 41 D4 Pennsylvania, USA
Say'un 99 D6 C Yemen
Scafell Pike 71 C5 ▲ NW England, UK
Scandinivia 62 Geophysical region, NW Europe
Scarborough 61 K7 Trinidad and Tobago
Scarborough 71 E5 N England, UK
Schaerbeek 68 C6 C Belgium
Schaffhausen 77 B7 N Switzerland
Schagen 68 C3 NW Netherlands
Scheessel 77 C3 NW Germany
Schefferville 35 E3 Québec, E Canada
Scheldt 68 C6 ≈ W Europe
Schell Creek Range 51 C5 ⛰ Nevada, USA
Schenectady 41 E4 New York, USA
Schertz 48 G5 Texas, USA
Schiermonnikoog 68 E1 Island, Waddeneilanden, N Netherlands
Schijndel 68 D5 S Netherlands
Schiltigheim 73 F3 NE France
Schleswig 77 C2 N Germany
Schleswig-Holstein 77 C2 Cultural region, N Germany
Schönebeck 77 D4 C Germany
Schoten 68 C6 N Belgium
Schouwen 68 B5 Island, SW Netherlands
Schwäbische Alb 77 B7 ⛰ S Germany
Schwandorf 77 D6 SE Germany
Schwarzwald see Black Forest
Schwaz 77 D7 W Austria
Schweinfurt 77 C5 SE Germany
Schwerin 77 C3 N Germany
Schwyz 77 B8 C Switzerland
Scilly, Isles of 71 C9 Island group, SW England, UK
Scioto River 44 E7 ≈ Ohio, USA
Scotia Sea 138 A2 Sea, SW Atlantic Ocean
Scotland 71 C4 National region, UK
Scott Base 138 C6 NZ research station, Antarctica
Scottsbluff 47 A5 Nebraska, USA
Scottsboro 43 E4 Alabama, USA
Scottsdale 48 B3 Arizona, USA
Scranton 41 D4 Pennsylvania, USA
Scutari, Lake 83 C3 ◎ Albania/Yugoslavia
Searcy 43 B3 Arkansas, USA
Seattle 53 B2 Washington, USA
Sébaco 59 D4 W Nicaragua
Sebastián Vizcaín, Bahía 57 A2 Bay, NW Mexico
Secunderabad 107 E5 C India
Sedan 73 E2 N France
Seddon 135 D5 South Island, NZ
Seddonville 135 C5 South Island, NZ
Sédhiou 124 A4 SW Senegal
Sedona 48 B2 Arizona, USA
Seesen 77 C4 C Germany
Segezha 87 B3 NW Russ. Fed.
Ségou 124 C3 C Mali
Segovia 75 D3 C Spain
Séguédine 124 G2 NE Niger
Seguin 48 G5 Texas, USA
Segura 75 E5 ≈ S Spain
Seinäjoki 67 E4 W Finland
Seine 73 D2 ≈ N France
Seine, Baie de la 73 C2 Bay, N France
Sekondi-Takoradi 124 D5 S Ghana
Selenga 105 E2 ≈ Mongolia/Russ. Fed.
Sélestat 73 F3 NE France
Selfoss 67 A1 SW Iceland
Sélibabi 124 B3 S Mauritania
Selma 53 C7 California, USA
Semarang 109 D8 Java, C Indonesia
Sembé 128 B1 NW Congo
Seminole 48 E3 Texas, USA
Seminole, Lake 43 E6 ⊡ SE USA
Semipalatinsk 94 D5 E Kazakhstan
Semnān 99 E2 N Iran
Semois 68 D8 ≈ SE Belgium
Senachwine Lake 44 B6 ◎ Illinois, USA
Sendai 103 G4 C Japan
Sendai 103 D8 SW Japan
Sendai-wan 103 G4 Bay, E Japan
Senec 81 D7 W Slovakia
Senegal 124 A3 ◆ Republic, W Africa
Senegal 124 A3 ≈ W Africa
Seney Marsh 44 D2 Wetland, Michigan, USA
Senftenberg 77 E4 E Germany
Sênggê Zangbo 105 B4 ≈ W China
Senica 81 D6 W Slovakia
Senja 67 C1 Island, N Norway
Senkaku-shoto 103 A8 Island group, SW Japan
Senlis 73 D2 N France
Sennar 127 C3 C Sudan
Sens 73 D3 C France
Seoul 103 B6 ● NW South Korea
Sepik 137 A2 ≈ Indonesia/PNG
Sept-Îles 35 F4 Québec, SE Canada
Seraing 68 D7 E Belgium
Serakhs 101 D4 S Turkmenistan
Seram, Pulau 109 G7 Island, Maluku, E Indonesia
Serang 109 C7 Java, C Indonesia
Serasan, Selat 109 D6 Strait, Indonesia/Malaysia
Serbia 83 D2 ◐ Republic, Yugoslavia
Seremban 109 B6 Peninsular Malaysia
Serengeti Plain 127 C6 Plain, N Tanzania
Serenje 128 D4 E Zambia
Sérifos 83 E6 Island, Cyclades, Greece
Serov 94 C4 C Russ. Fed.
Serowe 128 D5 SE Botswana
Serpukhov 87 A5 W Russ. Fed.
Sesto San Giovanni 79 B2 N Italy
Sète 73 D6 S France
Setesdal 67 B5 Valley, S Norway
Sétif 122 E1 N Algeria
Setté Cama 128 A2 SW Gabon
Setúbal 75 A4 W Portugal
Setúbal, Baía de 75 A5 Bay, W Portugal
Seul, Lac 35 A4 ◎ Ontario, S Canada
Sevan 97 H2 C Armenia
Sevan, Lake 97 H2 ◎ E Armenia
Sevastopol' 85 F7 S Ukraine
Severn 35 B3 ≈ Ontario, S Canada
Severn 71 D7 ≈ England/Wales, UK
Severnaya Zemlya 94 E2 Island group, N Russ. Fed.
Severnyy 87 E3 NW Russ. Fed.
Severodvinsk 87 C3 NW Russ. Fed.
Severomorsk 87 C2 NW Russ. Fed.
Sevier Lake 51 C6 ◎ Utah, USA
Sevilla see Seville
Seville 75 B5 S Spain
Seychelles 118 ◆ Republic, W Indian Ocean
Seydhisfjördhur 67 B1 E Iceland
Seydi 101 E3 E Turkmenistan
Seymour 48 C3 Texas, USA
Sfântu Gheorghe 85 C6 C Romania

156

◐ Administrative region ◆ Country ● Country capital ◇ Dependent territory ○ Dependent territory capital ⛰ Mountain range ▲ Mountain ♨ Volcano ≈ River ◎ Lake ⊡ Reservoir

◆ Administrative region   ◆ Country   ● Country capital   ◇ Dependent territory   O Dependent territory capital   ▲ Mountain range   ▲ Mountain   ⊼ Volcano   ⋞ River   ⊚ Lake

WESTERLAND

Tutuila 55 *Island* W American Samoa
Tuvalu 137 H2 ◆ *Commonwealth Republic*, SW Pacific Ocean
Tuwayq, Jabal 99 C5 ▲ C Saudi Arabia
Tuxpan 57 E5 C Mexico
Tuxpan 57 D4 C Mexico
Tuxpán 57 F4 E Mexico
Tuxtepec 57 G5 S Mexico
Tuxtla 57 H5 SE Mexico
Tuy Hoa 109 D4 S Vietnam
Tuzla 83 C2 NE Bosnia and Herzegovina
Tuz, Lake 97 C3 ◎ C Turkey
Tver' 87 A5 W Russ. Fed.
Twin Falls 51 C4 Idaho, USA
Tychy 81 E5 S Poland
Tyler 48 H3 Texas, USA
Tympáki 83 F7 Crete, Greece
Tynda 94 G5 SE Russ. Fed.
Tyne 71 D5 ∽ N England, UK
Tyrrhenian Sea 79 B6 *Sea*, N Mediterranean Sea
Tyumen' 94 C4 C Russ. Fed.
Tyup 101 I2 NE Kyrgyzstan
Tywyn 71 D7 W Wales, UK
Tuong Duong 109 C3 N Vietnam

U

Ubangi 124 H5 ∽ C Africa
Ube 103 D7 SW Japan
Ubeda 75 D5 S Spain
Uberaba 115 G7 SE Brazil
Uberlândia 115 F7 SE Brazil
Ubon Ratchathani 109 C3 E Thailand
Ubrique 75 C6 S Spain
Ucayali, Río 115 B4 ∽ C Peru
Uchiura-wan 103 F2 *Bay*, NW Pacific Ocean
Uchquduq 101 E2 N Uzbekistan
Uchtagan, Peski 101 C2 *Desert*, NW Turkmenistan
Udaipur 107 D3 N India
Uddevalla 67 B6 S Sweden
Udine 79 D2 NE Italy
Udon Thani 109 B3 N Thailand
Udupi 107 D6 SW India
Uele 128 C1 ∽ NE Congo (Zaire)
Uelzen 77 C3 N Germany
Ufa 87 D6 W Russ. Fed.
Uganda 127 C5 ◆ *Republic*, E Africa
Uglovka 87 A4 W Russ. Fed.
Uíge 128 B3 NW Angola
Uinta Mountains 51 D5 ▲ Utah, USA
Uitenhage 128 D7 S South Africa
Uithoorn 68 D4 C Netherlands
Ujungpandang 109 E7 Celebes, C Indonesia
Ukhta 87 D4 NW Russ. Fed.
Ukiah 53 B6 California, USA
Ukmergė 67 E7 C Lithuania
Ukraine 85 C4 ◆ *Republic*, SE Europe
Ulaanbaatar *see* Ulan Bator
Ulaangom 105 D1 NW Mongolia
Ulan Bator 105 E2 ● C Mongolia
Ulanhot 105 G2 N China
Ulan-Ude 94 F5 S Russ. Fed.
Ulft 68 E4 E Netherlands
Ullapool 71 C3 N Scotland, UK
Ulm 77 C7 S Germany
Ulsan 103 C6 SE South Korea
Ulster 71 B5 *Cultural region*, Ireland/Northern Ireland, UK
Ulungur Hu 105 C2 ◎ NW China
Uluru 133 D4 *Rocky outcrop*, Northern Territory, C Australia
Ul'yanovsk 87 C6 W Russ. Fed.
Umán 57 H4 SE Mexico
Uman' 85 D5 C Ukraine
Umbro-Marchigiano, Appennino 79 D4 ▲ C Italy
Umeå 67 D4 N Sweden
Umeälven 67 D3 ∽ N Sweden
Umiat 54 E1 Alaska, USA
Umm Buru 127 A2 W Sudan
Umm Ruwaba 127 C3 C Sudan
Umnak Island 54 B2 *Island* Aleutian Islands, Alaska, USA
Umtata 128 D7 SE South Africa
Una 83 B1 ∽ Bosnia and Herzegovina/Croatia
Unac 83 B2 ∽ W Bosnia and Herzegovina
Unalaska Island 54 B3 *Island* Aleutian Islands, Alaska, USA
Uncía 117 B2 C Bolivia
Uncompahgre Peak 51 E6 ▲ Colorado, USA
Ungava Bay 35 E2 *Bay*, Québec, E Canada
Ungava, Péninsule d' 35 D1 *Peninsula*, Québec, SE Canada
Unimak Island 54 B3 *Island*, Aleutian Islands, Alaska, USA
Union City 43 D3 Tennessee, USA
Uniontown 41 B5 Pennsylvania, USA
United Arab Emirates 99 E4 ◆ *Federation*, SW Asia
United Kingdom 71 C5 ◆ *Monarchy*, NW Europe
United States of America 38 ◆ *Federal Republic*, North America
Unst 71 E1 *Island*, NE Scotland, UK
Ünye 97 E2 W Turkey
Upala 59 E5 NW Costa Rica
Upemba, Lac 128 D3 ◎ SE Congo (Zaire)
Upolu 137 B5 *Island*, SE Samoa
Upper Darby 41 D5 Pennsylvania, USA
Upper Klamath Lake 53 B4 ◎ Oregon, USA
Upper Lough Erne 71 B6 ◎ SW Northern Ireland, UK
Upper Red Lake 47 E2 ◎ Minnesota, USA
Uppsala 67 D5 C Sweden
Ural 94 B4 ∽ Kazakhstan/Russ. Fed.
Ural Mountains 94 C3 ▲ Kazakhstan/Russ. Fed.
Ural'sk 94 B4 NW Kazakhstan
Ural'skiye Gory *see* Ural Mountains
Urbandale 47 E5 Iowa, USA
Uren' 87 C5 W Russ. Fed.
Urganch 101 D2 W Uzbekistan
Urgut 101 F3 C Uzbekistan
Urmia, Lake 99 C1 ◎ NW Iran
Uroteppa 101 F3 NW Tajikistan
Uruapan 57 E5 SW Mexico
Uruguay 117 C5 ◆ *Republic*, E South America
Uruguay 117 C5 ∽ E South America
Ürümqi 105 C2 NW China
Urup, Ostrov 94 I4 *Island*, Kurile Islands, SE Russ. Fed.
Uruzgan 101 F5 C Afghanistan
Usa 87 E3 ∽ NW Russ. Fed.
Uşak 97 B3 W Turkey
Ushuaia 117 B9 S Argentina
Usinsk 87 D3 NW Russ. Fed.
Usol'ye-Sibirskoye 94 F5 C Russ. Fed.
Ussel 73 D5 C France
Ussuriysk 94 H6 SE Russ. Fed.
Ustica 79 C7 Sicily, SW Italy
Ust'-Ilimsk 94 F4 C Russ. Fed.
Ústí nad Labem 81 B5 N Czech Republic
Ustka 81 C1 NW Poland
Ust'-Kamchatsk 94 I3 E Russ. Fed.
Ust'-Kamenogorsk 94 D5 E Kazakhstan
Ust'-Kut 94 F5 C Russ. Fed.
Ust'-Olenek 94 F3 NE Russ. Fed.
Ustyurt Plateau 101 C1 *Plateau*, Kazakhstan/Uzbekistan
Usulután 59 C4 SE El Salvador
Usumacinta, Río 59 A2 ∽ Guatemala/Mexico
Utah 51 C5 ◆ *State*, W USA
Utah Lake 51 C5 ◎ Utah, USA
Utica 41 D3 New York, USA
Utrecht 68 D4 C Netherlands
Utsunomiya 103 G5 S Japan
Uttar Pradesh 107 E3 *Cultural region*, N India
Utupua 137 G3 *Island*, Santa Cruz Islands, E Soloman Islands
Uulu 67 E6 SW Estonia
Uvalde 48 G5 Texas, USA
Uvs Nuur 105 D1 ◎ Mongolia/Russ. Fed.
'Uwaynat, Jabal al 127 B1 ▲ Libya/Sudan
Uyo 124 F5 S Nigeria
Uyuni 117 B3 W Bolivia
Uzbekistan 101 D2 ◆ *Republic*, C Asia
Uzhhorod 85 B5 W Ukraine

V

Vaal 128 D6 ∽ C South Africa
Vaals 68 E7 SE Netherlands
Vaasa 67 D4 W Finland
Vaassen 68 E4 E Netherlands
Vác 81 E7 N Hungary
Vadodara 107 C4 W India
Vaduz 77 C8 ● W Liechtenstein
Váh 81 D6 ∽ W Slovakia
Vaitupu 137 J2 *Atoll*, C Tuvalu
Valdai Hills 87 A5 *Hill range*, Russ. Fed.
Valday 87 A4 W Russ. Fed.
Valdecañas, Embalse de 75 C4 ⊡ W Spain
Valdepeñas 75 D4 C Spain
Valdés, Península 117 B7 *Peninsula*, SE Argentina
Valdez 54 E3 Alaska, USA
Valdivia 117 A6 C Chile
Val-d'Or 35 D5 Québec, SE Canada
Valdosta 43 F6 Georgia, USA
Valence 73 E5 E France
Valencia 75 F4 E Spain
Valencia 115 D1 N Venezuela
Valencia, Gulf of 75 F4 *Gulf*, Spain
Valenciennes 73 E1 N France
Valentine 47 B4 Nebraska, USA
Valjevo 83 D2 W Yugoslavia
Valjok 67 E1 N Norway
Valkenswaard 68 D5 S Netherlands
Valladolid 57 I4 SE Mexico
Valladolid 75 D2 NW Spain
Vall d'Uxó 75 F4 E Spain
Vallejo 53 B6 California, USA
Vallenar 117 A4 N Chile
Valletta 88 B6 ● E Malta
Valley City 47 C2 North Dakota, USA
Valls 75 G3 NE Spain
Valparaíso 117 A5 C Chile
Valparaiso 44 C5 Indiana, USA
Valverde del Camino 75 C5 S Spain
Van 97 G3 E Turkey
Vanadzor 97 H2 N Armenia
Van Buren 41 G1 Maine, USA
Vanceboro 41 H2 Maine, USA
Vancouver 33 F7 British Columbia, SW Canada
Vancouver 53 B3 Washington, USA
Vancouver Island 33 E7 *Island*, British Columbia, SW Canada
Van Diemen Gulf 133 D1 *Gulf*, Northern Territory, N Australia
Vänern 67 C6 ◎ S Sweden
Vangaindrano 128 G6 SE Madagascar
Van Gölü *see* Van, Lake
Van Horn 48 E4 Texas, USA
Vanikolo 137 G3 *Island*, Santa Cruz Islands, E Solomon Islands
Vanimo 137 A1 NW PNG
Van, Lake 97 G4 *Salt lake*, E Turkey
Vannes 73 B3 NW France
Vantaa 67 E5 S Finland
Vanua Lava 137 G4 *Island*, Banks Islands, N Vanuatu
Vanua Levu 137 J5 *Island*, N Fiji
Vanuatu 137 E4 ◆ *Republic*, SW Pacific Ocean
Van Wert 44 D6 Ohio, USA
Vao 137 G6 S New Caledonia
Varanasi 107 F3 N India
Varangerfjorden 67 F1 *Fjord*, N Norway
Varangerhalvoya 67 E1 *Peninsula*, N Norway
Varaždin 83 B1 N Croatia
Varberg 67 B6 S Sweden
Vardar 83 E4 ∽ FYR Macedonia/Greece
Varde 67 B7 W Denmark
Varese 79 B2 N Italy
Vârful Moldoveanu 85 B6 ▲ C Romania
Varkaus 67 F4 C Finland
Varna 83 G2 NE Bulgaria
Varnenski Zaliv 97 A1 *Bay*, E Bulgaria
Vasa *see* Vaasa
Vasilikí 83 D5 Lefkáda, Ionian Islands, Greece
Vaslui 85 D6 C Romania
Västerås 67 C5 C Sweden
Vatican City 79 C5 ◆ *Papal state*, S Europe
Vatnajökull 67 A1 *Glacier*, SE Iceland
Vättern 67 C6 ◎ S Sweden
Vaughn 48 D2 New Mexico, USA
Vaupés, Río 115 C3 ∽ Brazil/Colombia
Vavuniya 107 E7 N Sri Lanka
Vawkavysk 85 B3 W Belarus
Växjö 67 C6 S Sweden
Vaygach, Ostrov 87 E2 *Island*, NW Russ. Fed.
Veendam 68 F2 NE Netherlands
Veenendaal 68 D4 C Netherlands
Vega 67 C3 *Island*, C Norway
Veisiejai 67 E7 S Lithuania
Vejer de la Frontera 75 C6 S Spain
Veldhoven 68 D5 S Netherlands
Velebit 83 B2 ▲ C Croatia
Velenje 77 E8 N Slovenia
Velika Morava 83 D2 ∽ C Yugoslavia
Velikiye Luki 87 A5 W Russ. Fed.
Veliko Turnovo 83 F3 N Bulgaria
Vel'ký Krtíš 81 E7 S Slovakia
Vella Lavella 137 D2 *Island*, New Georgia Islands, NW Solomon Islands
Vellore 107 E6 SE India
Velsen-Noord 68 C3 W Netherlands
Vel'sk 87 C4 NW Russ. Fed.
Vendôme 73 C3 C France
Venezia *see* Venice
Venezuela 115 C2 ◆ *Republic*, N South America
Venezuela, Gulf of 115 C1 *Gulf*, NW Venezuela
Venice 79 D2 NE Italy
Venice 43 C7 Louisiana, USA
Venice, Gulf of 79 D3 *Gulf*, N Adriatic Sea
Venlo 68 E5 SE Netherlands
Venta 67 E6 ∽ Latvia/Lithuania
Vent, Îles du 137 A6 *Island group*, Archipel de la Société, W French Polynesia
Ventimiglia 79 A3 NW Italy
Ventspils 67 E6 NW Latvia
Vera 117 C4 C Argentina
Veracruz 57 F5 E Mexico
Vercelli 79 B2 NW Italy
Verdalsøra 67 C4 C Norway
Verde, Costa 75 D1 *Coastal region*, N Spain
Verden 77 B3 NW Germany
Verkhoyanskiy Khrebet 94 G3 ▲ NE Russ. Fed.
Vermillion 47 D4 South Dakota, USA
Vermont 41 E3 ◆ *State*, NE USA
Vernal 51 D5 Utah, USA
Vernon 48 G2 Texas, USA
Verona 79 C2 NE Italy
Versailles 73 D2 N France
Verviers 68 E7 E Belgium
Vesdre 68 F7 ∽ E Belgium
Vesoul 73 F3 E France
Vesterålen 67 C2 *Island*, NW Norway
Vestfjorden 67 C2 *Fjord*, C Norway
Vestmannaeyjar 67 A2 S Iceland
Vesuvio 79 D6 ▲ S Italy
Veszprém 81 D8 W Hungary
Veurne 68 A6 W Belgium
Viacha 117 A2 W Bolivia
Viana do Castelo 75 B2 NW Portugal
Vianen 68 D4 C Netherlands
Viareggio 79 B3 C Italy
Viborg 67 B6 NW Denmark
Vic 75 G2 NE Spain
Vicenza 79 C2 NE Italy
Vichy 73 D4 C France
Vicksburg 43 C5 Mississippi, USA
Victoria 33 E7 Vancouver Island, British Columbia, SW Canada
Victoria 88 A6 NW Malta
Victoria 119 ● SW Seychelles
Victoria 48 H5 Texas, USA
Victoria 133 F6 ◆ *State*, SE Australia
Victoria Falls 128 C5 *Waterfall*, Zambia/Zimbabwe
Victoria Island 33 G3 *Island*, NW Terr., NW Canada
Victoria, Lake 127 C5 ◎ E Africa
Victoria Land 138 D6 *Physical region*, Antarctica
Victoria, Mount 137 I5 ▲ Viti Levu, W Fiji
Victoria River 133 D2 ∽ W Australia
Victorville 53 D8 California, USA
Vidalia 43 F5 Georgia, USA
Vidin 83 E2 NW Bulgaria
Viedma 117 B7 E Argentina
Vienna 77 F7 ● NE Austria
Vienne 73 E5 E France
Vienne 73 C4 ∽ W France
Vientiane 109 B3 ● C Laos
Vieques 55 E Puerto Rico
Vieques, Isla de 55 *Island*, E Puerto Rico
Vierzon 73 D3 C France
Vietnam 109 C4 ◆ *Republic*, SE Asia
Vieux Fort 61 K6 S Saint Lucia
Vigo 75 B2 NW Spain
Vijayawada 107 E5 SE India
Vila do Conde 75 B2 NW Portugal
Vilafranca del Penedès 75 G2 NE Spain
Viljaka 67 F6 NE Latvia
Vilalba 75 B1 NW Spain
Vila Nova de Gaia 75 B3 NW Portugal
Vila Real 75 B3 N Portugal
Vilhelmina 67 C3 N Sweden
Viliya 85 C2 ∽ W Belarus
Villa Bella 117 B1 N Bolivia
Villacarrillo 75 E5 S Spain
Villach 77 E8 S Austria
Villacidro 79 A6 Sardinia, Italy
Villafranca de los Barros 75 C4 W Spain
Villahermosa 57 H5 SE Mexico
Villajoyosa 75 F4 E Spain
Villa María 117 B5 C Argentina
Villa Martín 117 A3 SW Bolivia
Villanueva 57 E4 C Mexico
Villanueva de la Serena 75 C4 W Spain
Villanueva de los Infantes 75 E4 C Spain
Villarrica 117 C4 SE Paraguay
Villavicencio 115 C2 C Colombia
Villaviciosa 75 C1 N Spain
Villazon 117 B3 S Bolivia
Villena 75 F4 E Spain
Villeurbanne 73 E5 E France
Villingen-Schwenningen 77 B7 S Germany
Vilnius 67 F7 ● SE Lithuania
Vilvoorde 68 C6 C Belgium
Vilyuy 94 G4 ∽ NE Russ. Fed.
Viña del Mar 117 A5 C Chile
Vinaròs 75 F3 E Spain
Vincennes 44 C7 Indiana, USA
Vindhya Range 107 D4 ▲ N India
Vineland 41 D6 New Jersey, USA
Vinh 109 C3 N Vietnam
Vinita 47 E7 Oklahoma, USA
Vinnytsya 85 D5 C Ukraine
Vinson Massif 138 A4 ▲ Antarctica
Viranşehir 97 F4 SE Turkey
Virginia 47 E2 Minnesota, USA
Virginia 43 H2 ◆ *State*, NE USA
Virginia Beach 43 I2 Virginia, USA
Virgin Islands (US) 55 *US* ◇ E West Indies
Virgin Passage 55 *Passage* Puerto Rico/Virgin Islands (US)
Virovitica 83 C1 NE Croatia
Virton 68 D9 SE Belgium
Vis 83 B3 *Island*, S Croatia
Visakhapatnam 107 F5 SE India
Visalia 53 C7 California, USA
Visby 67 D6 Gotland, SE Sweden
Viscount Melville Sound 33 G2 *Sound*, NW Terr., N Canada
Visé 68 E7 E Belgium
Viseu 75 B3 N Portugal
Vistula 81 E2 ∽ C Poland
Vistula Lagoon 81 E1 *Lagoon*, Poland/Russ. Fed.
Viterbo 79 C4 C Italy
Vitiaz Strait 137 B2 *Strait*, NE PNG
Viti Levu 137 I5 *Island*, W Fiji
Vitim 94 G5 ∽ C Russ. Fed.
Vitória 115 H7 SE Brazil
Vitória da Conquista 115 H6 E Brazil
Vitoria-Gasteiz 75 E2 N Spain
Vitré 73 B3 NW France
Vitsyebsk 85 D2 NE Belarus
Vittoria 79 D8 Sicily, Italy
Vizianagaram 107 F5 E India
Vlaardingen 68 C4 SW Netherlands
Vladikavkaz 87 B9 SW Russ. Fed.
Vladimir 87 B5 W Russ. Fed.
Vladivostok 94 H6 SE Russ. Fed.
Vlagtwedde 68 F2 NE Netherlands
Vlieland 68 C2 *Island*, Waddeneilanden, N Netherlands
Vlijmen 68 D5 S Netherlands
Vlissingen 68 B5 SW Netherlands
Vlorë 83 C4 SW Albania
Vöcklabruck 77 E7 NW Austria
Vohimena, Tanjona 128 F6 *Headland*, S Madagascar
Voiron 73 E5 E France
Vojvodina 83 D1 *Cultural region*, N Yugoslavia
Volga 87 B7 ∽ NW Russ. Fed.
Volga Uplands 87 B6 ▲ W Russ. Fed.
Volgodonsk 87 A7 SW Russ. Fed.
Volgograd 87 B7 SW Russ. Fed.
Volkhov 87 A4 NW Russ. Fed.
Volnovakha 85 G5 SE Ukraine
Volodymyr-Volyns'kyy 85 B4 NW Ukraine
Vologda 87 B4 W Russ. Fed.
Vólos 83 E5 C Greece
Vol'sk 87 C6 W Russ. Fed.
Volta 124 D5 ∽ SE Ghana
Volta, Lake 124 D5 ⊡ SE Ghana
Volturno 79 D5 ∽ S Italy
Volzhskiy 87 B7 SW Russ. Fed.
Voorst 68 E4 E Netherlands
Vorderrhein 77 B8 ∽ SE Switzerland
Vorkuta 87 E3 NW Russ. Fed.
Voronezh 87 A6 W Russ. Fed.
Võrtsjärv 67 E6 ◎ SE Estonia
Võru 67 F6 SE Estonia
Vosges 73 F3 ▲ NE France
Vostok 138 D5 *Russian research station*, Antarctica
Vranov nad Topl'ou 81 F6 E Slovakia
Vratsa 83 E3 NW Bulgaria
Vrbas 83 C2 ∽ N Bosnia and Herzegovina
Vrbas 83 C1 NW Yugoslavia
Vršac 83 D1 NE Yugoslavia
Vsetín 81 D6 E Czech Republic
Vukovar 83 C1 E Croatia
Vulcano 79 D7 *Island*, Aeolian Islands, S Italy
Vung Tau 109 C4 S Vietnam
Vunisea 137 J5 SE Fiji
Vyatka 87 C5 ∽ NW Russ. Fed.
Vyborg 87 A4 NW Russ. Fed.

W

Wa 124 D4 NW Ghana
Waal 68 D4 ∽ S Netherlands
Waala 137 F6 W New Caledonia
Wabash 44 D6 Indiana, USA
Wabash River 44 D6 ∽ N USA
Waco 48 H4 Texas, USA
Waddan 122 G3 NW Libya
Waddeneilanden *see* West Frisian Islands
Waddenzee 68 D2 *Sea*, SE North Sea
Waddington, Mount 33 E7 ▲ British Columbia, SW Canada
Wadi Halfa 127 C1 N Sudan
Wad Medani 127 C2 C Sudan
Waflia 109 G7 E Indonesia
Wagga Wagga 133 G6 NSW, SE Australia
Wagin 133 B5 W Australia
Wah 107 C1 NE Pakistan
Wahai 109 G7 E Indonesia
Wahiawa 55 B1 Oahu, Hawaii, USA
Wahibah Sands 99 E5 *Desert*, N Oman
Wahpeton 47 D2 North Dakota, USA
Waiau 135 A8 ∽ South Island, NZ
Waigeo, Pulau 109 G6 *Island*, Maluku, E Indonesia
Waikaremoana, Lake 135 E3 ◎ North Island, NZ
Wailuku 55 C2 Maui, Hawaii, USA
Waimate 135 B7 South Island, NZ
Waimea 55 D2 Hawaii, USA
Waiouru 135 D4 North Island, NZ
Waipara 135 C6 South Island, NZ
Waipawa 135 D4 North Island, NZ
Waipukurau 135 D4 North Island, NZ
Wairau 135 C5 ∽ South Island, NZ
Wairoa 135 D4 North Island, NZ
Wairoa 135 D2 ∽ North Island, NZ
Waitaki 135 B7 ∽ South Island, NZ
Waitara 135 C4 North Island, NZ
Waiuku 135 D3 North Island, NZ
Wakasa-wan 103 E6 *Bay*, C Japan
Wakatipu, Lake 135 B7 ◎ South Island, NZ
Wakayama 103 E6 SW Japan
Wakkanai 103 F1 NE Japan
Wałbrzych 81 C5 SW Poland
Walcourt 68 C8 S Belgium
Wałcz 81 C2 NW Poland
Wales 71 D7 *National region*, Wales, UK
Wales 54 D1 Alaska, USA
Walgett 133 G5 NSW, SE Australia
Walker Lake 51 A6 ◎ Nevada, USA
Wallace 51 B2 Idaho, USA
Wallachia 85 B7 *Cultural region*, S Romania
Walla Walla 53 C3 Washington, USA
Wallis and Futuna 137 I4 *French* ◇ C Pacific Ocean
Wallis, Îles 137 K4 *Island group*, N Wallis and Futuna
Walnut Ridge 43 C3 Arkansas, USA
Walvis Bay 128 B5 NW Namibia
Wanaka 135 B7 South Island, NZ
Wanaka, Lake 135 A7 ◎ South Island, NZ
Wandel Sea 139 C5 *Sea*, Arctic Ocean
Wanganui 135 D4 North Island, NZ
Wangaratta 133 G6 Victoria, SE Australia
Wanlaweyn 127 F5 SW Somalia
Wanxian 105 F4 C China
Warangal 107 E5 C India
Warburg 77 B4 W Germany
Ware 33 E6 British Columbia, W Canada
Waremme 68 D7 E Belgium
Waren 77 D3 NE Germany
Warkworth 135 D2 North Island, NZ
Warm Springs 51 B6 Nevada, USA
Warnemünde 77 D2 NE Germany
Warner 47 E8 Oklahoma, USA
Warnes 117 B2 C Bolivia
Warrego River 133 G5 *Seasonal river*, NSW/Queensland, E Australia
Warren 44 E5 Michigan, USA
Warren 44 F6 Ohio, USA
Warren 41 B4 Pennsylvania, USA
Warri 124 E5 S Nigeria
Warrnambool 133 F6 Victoria, SE Australia
Warsaw 81 F3 ● C Poland
Warszawa *see* Warsaw
Warta 81 D4 ∽ W Poland
Warwick 133 H5 Queensland, E Australia
Warwick 41 F4 Rhode Island, USA
Washington 44 C7 Indiana, USA
Washington 53 B3 ◆ *State*, NW USA
Washington DC 43 H1 ● District of Columbia, NE USA
Washington, Mount 41 F3 ▲ New Hampshire, USA
Wash, The 71 E6 *Inlet*, E England, UK
Waspam 59 E3 NE Nicaragua
Waterbury 41 E4 Connecticut, USA
Waterford 71 B7 S Ireland
Waterloo 47 F4 Iowa, USA
Watersmeet 44 B2 Michigan, USA
Watertown 41 D3 New York, USA
Watertown 47 D3 South Dakota, USA
Waterville 41 G2 Maine, USA
Watford 71 E7 E England, UK
Watford City 47 A2 North Dakota, USA
Watrous 48 E2 New Mexico, USA
Watsa 128 D1 NE Congo (Zaire)
Watts Bar Lake 43 E3 ⊡ Tennessee, USA
Wau 127 B4 S Sudan
Waukegan 44 C5 Illinois, USA
Waukesha 44 C4 Wisconsin, USA
Wausau 44 B3 Wisconsin, USA
Waverly 47 F4 Iowa, USA
Wavre 68 C7 C Belgium
Wawa 35 C5 Ontario, S Canada
Wawa, Río 59 E3 ∽ NE Nicaragua
Waycross 43 F6 Georgia, USA
Wé 137 G6 E New Caledonia
Weam 137 A3 SW PNG
Webster City 47 E4 Iowa, USA
Weddell Plain 138 B3 *Undersea feature*, SW Atlantic Ocean
Weddell Sea 138 B3 *Sea*, SW Atlantic Ocean
Weed 53 B5 California, USA
Weener 77 B3 NW Germany
Weert 68 E6 SE Netherlands
Weesp 68 D4 C Netherlands
Węgorzewo 81 F2 NE Poland
Weimar 77 C5 C Germany
Weiser 51 B3 Idaho, USA
Weissenburg 77 C6 SE Germany
Weiswampach 68 E8 N Luxembourg
Wejherowo 81 D1 NW Poland
Weldiya 127 E3 N Ethiopia
Welkom 128 D6 C South Africa
Wellesley Islands 133 F2 *Island group*, Queensland, N Australia
Wellington 135 D5 ● North Island, NZ
Wellington 47 D7 Kansas, USA
Wellington 48 F2 Texas, USA
Wellington, Isla 117 A8 *Island*, S Chile
Wells 51 C5 Nevada, USA
Wellsford 135 D2 North Island, NZ
Wells, Lake 133 C4 ◎ W Australia
Wels 77 E7 N Austria
Wemmel 68 C6 C Belgium
Wenatchee 53 C2 Washington, USA
Wenchi 124 D5 W Ghana
Wenquan 105 C4 C China
Wenzhou 105 G5 SE China
Werkendam 68 D5 S Netherlands
Weser 77 B3 ∽ NW Germany
Wessel Islands 133 E1 *Island group*, Northern Territory, N Australia
West Bank 99 H6 *Disputed region*, SW Asia
West Bend 44 C4 Wisconsin, USA
West Bengal 107 F4 *State*, NE India
West Des Moines 47 E5 Iowa, USA
Westerland 77 B2 N Germany

CAR Central African Republic FYR Former Yugoslavian Rebublic NSW New South Wales NZ New Zealand PNG Papua New Guinea Russ. Fed. Russian Federation UAE United Arab Emirates UK United Kingdom USA United States of America 159

◆ Administrative region ◆ Country ● Country capital ◊ Dependent territory ○ Dependent territory capital ▲ Mountain range ▲ Mountain ☀ Volcano ≈ River ○ Lake ▣ Reservoir

NORTH AMERICA

CANADA

UNITED STATES OF AMERICA

MEXICO

BELIZE

COSTA RICA

EL SALVADOR

GUATEMALA

HONDURAS

SOUTH AMERICA

GRENADA

HAITI

JAMAICA

ST KITTS & NEVIS

ST LUCIA

ST VINCENT & THE GRENADINES

TRINIDAD & TOBAGO

COLOMBIA

AFRICA

URUGUAY

CHILE

PARAGUAY

ALGERIA

EGYPT

LIBYA

MOROCCO

TUNISIA

LIBERIA

MALI

MAURITANIA

NIGER

NIGERIA

SENEGAL

SIERRA LEONE

TOGO

BURUNDI

DJIBOUTI

ERITREA

ETHIOPIA

KENYA

RWANDA

SOMALIA

SUDAN

EUROPE

SOUTH AFRICA

SWAZILAND

ZAMBIA

ZIMBABWE

DENMARK

FINLAND

ICELAND

NORWAY

MONACO

ANDORRA

PORTUGAL

SPAIN

ITALY

SAN MARINO

VATICAN CITY

AUSTRIA

BOSNIA & HERZEGOVINA

CROATIA

MACEDONIA

YUGOSLAVIA
(SERBIA & MONTENEGRO)

BULGARIA

GREECE

MOLDOVA

ROMANIA

ASIA

ARMENIA

AZERBAIJAN

GEORGIA

TURKEY

IRAQ

ISRAEL

JORDAN

LEBANON

IRAN

KAZAKHSTAN

KYRGYZSTAN

TAJIKISTAN

TURKMENISTAN

UZBEKISTAN

AFGHANISTAN

PAKISTAN

SOUTH KOREA

TAIWAN

JAPAN

BRUNEI

INDONESIA

MALAYSIA

SINGAPORE

MYANMAR

AUSTRALASIA & OCEANIA

MAURITIUS

SEYCHELLES

AUSTRALIA

NEW ZEALAND

PAPUA NEW GUINEA

SOLOMON ISLANDS

MARSHALL ISLANDS

MICRONESIA